Growing Up Poor

1. An improvised street swing.

Growing Up Poor

Home, School and Street in London 1870–1914

Anna Davin

Rivers Oram Press
London

First published in 1996 by
Rivers Oram Press
144 Hemingford Road, London N1 1DE

Published in the USA by
Paul and Company
Post Office Box 442, Concord, MA 01742

Set in 10/12 pt Baskerville by
N-J Design Associates
and printed in
Great Britain by T.J. Press (Padstow) Ltd, Padstow, Cornwall

British Library Cataloguing in Publication Data
A catalogue record for this book is available from the British
Library

ISBN 1–85489–062–X
ISBN 1–85489–063–8 (pbk)

Cover illustrations

From a set of London photographs by Horace Warner (1871–1939),
bought in 1912 by the Bedford Institute, Spitalfields (*Courtesy of the Library
of the Society of Friends, London*).

To the memory of my mother and father,
Winnie and Dan Davin

Contents

———◆———

List of Illustrations

———◆———

1. *Frontispiece:*
   An improvised street swing. (*Mrs H.M. Stanley [Dorothy Tennant],* London Street Arabs, *1890*)

2. Whitechapel children around 1900. (*Tower Hamlets Local History Library, courtesy of the Whitechapel Mission*)

3. Unknown interior *c.*1900. (*Sunday School Union lantern slide, courtesy of the Library of the Society of Friends, London*)

4. Inhabitants of Providence Place, Finsbury. (*Francis Warner photograph, in George Newman,* Some Notes on the Housing Question in Finsbury, *1901. Courtesy of the Library of the Society of Friends*)

5. An idealized view of the transition from slum to 'model' dwelling. (*George R. Sims,* Living London *vol.1, 1901–2*)

6. East End boys enjoying a battered 'horse' tricycle. (*Courtesy of Springboard Educational Trust*)

7. Orange Street school, Southwark. (*R. Robson,* School Architecture, *1874, Leicester 1972. Courtesy of the Bartlett School of Architecture and Design, University College, London*)

8. Kindergarten provision at the Hoxton Mission crèche, 1900. (*Courtesy of Hackney Archives Department*)

9. An early twentieth-century 'little mother'. (*From London photographs by Horace Warner (1871–1939) bought in 1912 by the Bedford Institute, Spitalfields. Courtesy of the Library of the Society of Friends*)

10. Teacher and class in the Isle of Dogs, 1897–8. (*Courtesy of Island History Trust, London*)

11. Training for a domestic future. (*Courtesy of Greater London Record Office*)

12. Outdoor washing. (*From London photographs by Horace Warner (1871–1939) bought in 1912 by the Bedford Institute, Spitalfields. Courtesy of the Library of the Society of Friends*)

13. Children chopping wood and with a home-made barrow. (*From London photographs by Horace Warner (1871–1939) bought in 1912 by the Bedford Institute, Spitalfields. Courtesy of the Library of the Society of Friends*)

14. Making matchboxes: a domestic production line. (*Tower Hamlets Local History Library, courtesy of the Salvation Army*)

15. Union Jacks at school. (*Courtesy of Island History Trust*)

List of Tables

———◆———

Common Abbreviations

BMJ   *British Medical Journal*
COS   Charity Organization Society
HMI   Her/His Majesty's Inspector
LCC   London County Council
LGB   Local Government Board
MOH   Medical Officer of Health
OED   Oxford English Dictionary
PP   Parliamentary Papers
RC   Royal Commission
SC   Select Commission
SBL   School Board of London
WIC   Women's Industrial Council

Acknowledgments

———◆———

M ORE PEOPLE have supported and encouraged this work over the years than I can possibly list. Members of study groups (especially the London Feminist History Group), fellow students, participants in History Workshops and the many seminars which I have addressed or attended, and my students have all at various times helped to shape my ideas, suggested new questions and sources, and criticized successive formulations of my findings.

Accompanying (if sometimes delaying) my work since 1976 has been editorial work on *History Workshop Journal*. From my fellow editors I have received constant stimulus and support. With those whose work was closest to my own, notably Raphael Samuel, discussion and the sharing of material and ideas has been especially fruitful.

Besides all those from whom I have learned in informal situations, I must thank those who were my teachers. At Warwick in my undergraduate days, it was Edward Thompson who nurtured the historical passion which his *Making of the English Working Class* had already wakened in me, and Fred Reid whose sharp questioning helped me to discipline it and who led me into the nineteenth century. Eric Hobsbawm presided over my long graduate years: I first presented my work at his seminar; and learnt much from him and his work.

My thanks too to the many librarians and archivists who made possible my exploration of books and records, especially in the British Library and the Greater London Record Office; and to the Master and Fellows of Trinity College, Cambridge, for use of the papers of A.J. Munby. Sylvia Carlyle (Library of the Society of Friends) and Eve Hostettler (Island History Trust) were particularly helpful in my search for illustrations.

To name all the friends to whom I owe gratitude would be impossible; to name none is out of the question. My thanks to friends in Binghamton, New York, over my years as visiting teacher there, for comments, discussions and hospitality: among others, to Elsa Barkley Brown, Ken Barr, Deborah Britzman, Darrell Colombo, Donna De Voist, Sarah Elbert, Phil Kraft, Laura Lamash, Mid Semple and Dick Trexler; and to other friends in North America for encouragement and comments on chapters, amongst them: Hal Benenson, Ann Elsdon, Mary Fillmore, Keitha Fine, John Gillis,

Linda Gordon, Alice Kessler Harris, Seth Koven, Jan Lambertz, Joy Parr, Alison Prentice, Ellen Ross, Mick Taussig, Martha Vicinus, Judith Walkowitz, Daniel Walkowitz, Al Young and Marilyn Young.

My thanks to friends in Australia and New Zealand (and to the Humanities Faculty of Australian National University, for a three-month fellowship in 1984): Jill Matthews especially, and among others, Judith Allen, Barbara Brookes, Ian Davey, Jim Hammerton, Charlotte Macdonald, Susan Magarey, and Sue Sheridan.

My thanks nearer home to Sally Alexander, Timothy Ashplant, Logie Barrow, Guy Boanas, Katherine Bright-Holmes, Mary Chamberlain, Norma Clark, Leonore Davidoff, Carol Dyhouse, Liz Fidlon, Catherine Hall, Richard Handyside, Luke Hodgkin, Alun Howkins, Angela John, Richard Johnson, the late Jane Kenrick, Mary Kennedy, Marion Kozak, Jane Lewis, Selma Leydesdorff, Jill Liddington, the late Tim Mason, Frances Migniuolo, Juliet Mitchell, Lyndal Roper, Jo Stanley, Nick Stargardt, Gareth Stedman Jones, Anne Summers, Barbara Taylor, Edward and Dorothy Thompson, John Tosh, Bruno Vitale, Jeffrey Weeks, Jerry White, Michael Wolfers, and Eileen Yeo.

Thanks, finally, to my nearest and dearest: the cliché 'without whom' etc. is inescapable because true. Here too the list could be long. My mother and father (and their friends: especially, for me, Joyce Cary and John and Anne Willett) provided my sisters and me as children and all our lives with an exceptionally auspicious environment of love, intellectual and cultural stimulus and support. My sisters' interest and support for me and my work has never wavered and is beyond thanks. My children, Dom, Kate and Mick Hodgkin, and Sally Davin, have grown up with this work. They have also contributed to it, through the stimulus to my thinking about childhood supplied by the practice of parenthood, through their long years of help and understanding on the domestic front, and in fruitful discussions about my work. With Diane Gold, Geraldine Holden and Abbas Vali they have also produced a new generation—Sam, Jo, Rosa, Eva and Vian— whose childhood affords me continual interest and delight. Finally, the loving and practical support of Henry Tillotson enabled me to release my hold on a project long 'almost-finished', and to make time for bicycle, tent, boat and allotment, besides kitchen and study.

Introduction:
Patterns of Childhood

———————◄◆►———————

THIS BOOK is an exploration of childhood in the London working class in the last decades of the nineteenth century and at the beginning of the twentieth century and of how it was changing over these decades. The primary focus is on female children, partly because previous work has tended to focus on boys, but rather more in order to keep in the foreground the different roles, expectations and experience of girls and of boys, of women and of men, since a grasp of how sexual divisions have operated and changed is necessary for analysis both of the past and of the present.[1]

In concentrating on childhood, I keep in mind its relation to the adult world and the variable and uncertain nature of the no-man's-land between them. Similarly, it is impossible to ignore boys' experience even when focussing on the childhood of girls; and any study of the poor must take account of the rich, and of differences and connections between one class and another. One major concern in this book is with class difference around childhood: with the gulf between the definitions and experiences of childhood which prevailed on the one hand in the working class, and on the other in the middle (and, to some extent, the upper) class, and with whether, how, and how far, this gulf was bridged during these decades.

My original intention was to study the working lives of women in late nineteenth-century London, from infancy to old age. I wanted to find out about their total life experience, and what influenced it. I wanted to know about their upbringing, their work, their families (those they were born in and those they made), their husbands and friends, their difficulties and pleasures, their health, and about how growing older affected all these.

I decided to concentrate first on their childhood, since knowing about that experience, and about socializing forces such as home, school or work, would help me to understand their adult lives. For of course where, when and how they were brought up would influence not only their economic and social choices as they became adults, but also their sense of their own identity and their relation to society as a whole. As it turned out, childhood itself displaced my initial theme, but I did not entirely lose the original perspective: throughout the years of this study I retained the sense of childhood as part of a continuum.

1

I have tried both to uncover something of the children's experience, and to understand the place of their childhood at various levels—economic and demographic, in socialization, and in relation to the sexual division of labour and the reproduction of the labour force. The period 1870 to 1914 is a significant one in all these respects. It was a time of swift if uneven transition, when together economic change, state intervention and shifts in ideology (working-class and ruling-class interacting) brought about considerable changes in childhood in the British working class.

Children and Adults

We all know that children differ from adults. We learn from history that how much they differ, and how, varies with time and place. Childhood, like the family, or marriage, or adolescence or old age, is lived in a cultural and economic context; its character and ideology cannot be assumed. Even the pace of physical and psychological development differs between societies or social groups.

In any culture or society, nevertheless, childhood is ultimately defined in relation to adulthood. Adults approach or reach adult status by leaving childhood; and frequently their adult authority is confirmed through their control or support of children (or both). 'Grown-ups' remind themselves that they are adult by reviewing the past they have grown out of. Children are always those who are not yet adult. Moreover, children's relative helplessness, especially in their early years, usually makes them both dependent on and subordinate to their elders. Their survival depends entirely or partly on adults; adults in return exact obedience and determine how they spend their time.

The duration of that period of dependence and subordination, however, is not fixed (not even by the biological benchmarks of puberty or mature growth), and nor is its content. What is seen as appropriate, at what age, for which children, varies between societies and also within them and over time. Conventions based on gender difference intersect with assumptions about age, and both operate within social and economic structures, so that much also depends on the specific situation of child and adult.

Where adult life is hard, hands are few and labour is intensive, children are soon called upon to work. This does not necessarily mean they 'grow up' faster: if their labour is a significant resource, adults will retain control of it as long as they can. Indeed, where young people feel an obligation to help parents and family, as for instance when their labour or earnings contribute significantly to a shared domestic economy, they may be stuck for years in the contributory and subordinate position of a child though physically and even subjectively adult. Being female can have the same effect. So can expectation of inheritance, whether of land, a business, of an occupational role or a post. Forms of employment where the relationship is supposedly familial, like apprenticeship and domestic service, may likewise hold young workers back from adult independence.

In the world of wages, low status and lack of power expose the unprotected young to particularly intense exploitation, as child and juvenile labour. Overwork in bad conditions means some never reach adulthood; coercion may keep even young adults subservient. Early industrialization in Britain, the United States and Japan provided obvious instances of such patterns, and there are new variants in parts of the third world today.

Exemption from work is not a defining characteristic of childhood where children's labour is useful and needed. It may become so where adult labour is plentiful and not under pressure, especially if children are relatively few in the demographic equation. Then, as more resources are available for childcare and the need for youthful labour is less, childhood may be prolonged and sheltered, and this comes to be seen as defining it.

In England the transition to a prolonged and sheltered childhood happened, unevenly, between the eighteenth and the twentieth centuries, along with other long-term economic, political and social transformations. Changes in the nature and organization of work produced a growing separation between paid and unpaid labour and more social differentiation, whether by class, employment and social group, by gender or by age; and at the same time concentrated more people into towns. In the first decades of industrialization with labour needs acute, adult male workers often reluctant to enter the factory, and employers keen to reduce labour costs (and potential conflict), children were extensively employed in the new textile mills. In the course of the nineteenth century employers' mutating requirements for profitable output reduced the usefulness of child labour in large-scale production; state intervention placed increasing restraints on its use; and rising real wages made children's earnings less necessary to the domestic economy. Greater public value came to be set on human life and health (at least if it was white and of the right 'racial stock'), and thus fuelled state concern with the conditions of childhood, since children's welfare was now seen as relevant to the country's productive and military potential. This political concern also met with ready acceptance because of a popular cult of childhood in the later nineteenth century, itself sustained and served by the commercial use of images of rosy-cheeked children at play or of wan, pathetic 'orphans of the storm'. Meanwhile, proliferating experts in medicine, social work and education (new professionals as well as voluntary workers) pontificated about 'proper' practice in child-rearing.

The introduction of compulsory school from the 1870s was fuelled by visions of childhood as a period of carefree dependence. For poor families, however, it often made the struggle for daily living still more difficult, since it limited children's ability to help. Towards the end of the century, as confidence grew in the instrumental benefits and general usefulness of schooling and as more people's living standards rose, conflict over the priorities for school-age children diminished, or survived mainly in more diffuse form, as with the absence of girls when 'needed at home'. (Children's participation in unpaid, domestic labour was not generally seen as a problem.)

Nineteenth-century London children worked in a range of contexts, and with varying fortunes moved between them. The working child might have the freedom of the street arab or the responsibility of the substitute 'little mother'; might furnish indispensable labour or earnings to a family economy; or, wholly dependent, might 'help' with chores and errands, possibly receiving pocket money in recognition. Between the mid-nineteenth century and the early twentieth century that range was contracting and 'help' was usually what was expected.

As now, 'child' was a relative term used in two main ways. It specified both 'child-of-parent', and 'child-not-yet-adult'. In the general understanding, children formed a wide age cohort linked to biological development: roughly under fifteen or before puberty.[2] But the upper limit of childhood varied with context, and rose unevenly in the second half of the century. Protective labour legislation gradually raised the permitted age for first employment (in 1874 it was made ten in textile factories, extended in 1878 to workshops and non-textile factories; in 1891 it went up to eleven; in 1901 to twelve); and regulated employment of 'young persons' of thirteen to eighteen. Criminal responsibility could be attributed from as young as seven, though sanctions were increasingly differentiated for those under sixteen.[3] For legal rights to inherit, take legal action or vote, infancy lasted till twenty-one. The Poor Law counted those over fifteen as adult. A mid-century Catholic mission to East End was intended not 'only for children who were going to school, or those under fourteen...but also, and indeed principally, for big boys and girls who were at work, up to the age of seventeen and eighteen'.[4] The 1876 Elementary Education Act defined a child as between five and fourteen years of age, but even in 1900 some rural school boards let children leave at ten. In the 1908 Children Act 'child' meant under fourteen, 'young person' fourteen to sixteen; it's provisions used sometimes fourteen and sometimes sixteen as upper limits.

Sex made a difference: girls were held to need protection for longer. For the Prevention of Cruelty Act (1889) and the LCC's Public Control Committee in 1900, a child was a boy under fourteen or a girl under sixteen. The age of consent (which affected girls only) was raised from twelve to thirteen in 1875, then to sixteen in 1885, though some social purity campaigners argued that eighteen or even twenty-one should be the 'age of female responsibility'.[5]

Over these decades the definition of childhood centred increasingly on the question of dependence. The relation of child to adult always involved subordination and dependence; but to varying degrees and with varying age boundaries. From the mid-nineteenth century, with dependent and sheltered childhood firmly established for the middle class, reformers extended similar standards to working-class children. Autonomy, both economic and social, was now an adult prerogative. Children's right was to a 'natural' childhood state of innocence and irresponsibility; any whose knowledge and responsibility were 'adult' needed rescue.

Orphanage work, 'ragged schools',[6] campaigns against child labour and neglect, penal reform, and (especially) expansion of education, all helped to reduce childhood autonomy and eliminate the independent child. Street arab and substitute mother were rescued; school replaced full-time employment; national and local laws restricted other forms of child employment. At the same time, the working-class family economy was being transformed by rising living standards and ideological shifts; children's earnings grew less important, and they could be dependent for longer, though their unpaid work remained important in the domestic economy.

Twentieth-century demographic change produced a lower ratio of children to adults. This, with the safety net of state benefits developed after the Second World War, further reduced the need for early wage-earning, and in turn reinforced feeling against it. Organized labour also tried to limit the use of young workers, so as to protect wage standards based on skill and experience. Youthful dependence has now been further lengthened by contracting labour needs in production, high levels of unemployment among school leavers and increased emphasis on training. On the other hand, the demand for low-paid shift employment in the service sector combines both with family need and with the pressures of consumer culture to push teenagers into Saturday and other part-time work if they can find it.

So the relationship between children and work has changed in all aspects connected with employment—the age at which paid work may begin, the character of work, its hours and conditions, who makes the decision about starting it, what wages are paid, and who spends them on what.

As regards unpaid work, there has also been much change. Many of the needs which once required hours of work from household members are now met through purchase of goods or of services. Water is on tap, it does not have to be drawn from pump or well and carried in. Light and heat require no effort and create no mess. The range of domestic livestock needing care has shrunk down to cat or dog, pet rodent, bird or the occasional rabbit. Eggs are not collected; milk is delivered or, more often now, fetched in bottles and cartons; fruit and greens come from market or shop. Bought tins, jars, packets and frozen food have replaced the stocks which rural women, helped by children, once preserved, pickled, salted or smoked against the winter. Socks and stockings are bought, not knitted and seldom darned. Sewing is a hobby not an essential skill; and clothes and household linen are largely bought. When, exceptionally, clothes are 'home-made', this refers only to the cutting out and sewing of bought cloth, not to the full process of domestic production—carding, spinning, dyeing, and weaving, as well. Whereas late nineteenth-century town children were constantly sent to the corner shop for pennyworths of this and that (or for tobacco or beer), today better storage provision and changed retail practices mean that shopping is more likely done in bulk, by at least one adult, possibly with a car. Provisioning the household is too big a task to be done by children, though they may run the odd errand still.

Responsibility for care of the elderly and invalid no longer rests mainly with family and neighbours; and visits from children to bring them comforts or run their errands or do their chores are less likely than visits from district nurse, home help and social worker, or no visits. Nor is child care any longer the province of older children: they are supposed to be in school and families are generally smaller. Still more important, the pressures of child-rearing theory and of professional advice or even supervision have increased the load of responsibility and designated it as a wholly adult charge. The eight-year-old full-time little mother has given way to the teenager who sometimes babysits of an evening.

Across British cultures, it is widely held that children 'naturally'prefer fun over responsibility and that this should be indulged if possible. Such phrases as 'you're only young once' imply that work and responsibility are wholly undesirable and that it is to be expected and understood that children will not want to help. Their dependence on adults is thus intensified. It is also heightened by the ever-growing range of expensive consumer items promoted and accepted as indispensable for the young (including teenagers). And the emphasis for parents is on buying children 'the best', or indulging their desire for the latest design or fad being promoted. So the old economy (based largely on women's skills and labour, though men sometimes made toys and mended shoes) of making and repairing and of hand-me-downs, is in disfavour, while the costs of parenting increase.

Yet these changes are more complete for some than for others. Second-hand purchases seem to be back in favour, with the spread of charity shops and boot sales. Not all children have multiple outfits and shoes, or the latest toys, though most know from television what they 'should' have. Teenagers in some households will only get the 'right' clothes and shoes if they earn money towards their cost, or resort to stealing or dealing.

And of course, towards the end of the spectrum where resources are scarcest, households still exist today where children's labour, or children's greater independence, still helps to bridge the economic gap. Older children of working (especially single) parents start sooner to fend for themselves after school. The poorer the household the more they do. Like their late nineteenth-century counterparts, they get younger siblings off to school and collect and care for them afterwards. They take loads of washing to the laundrette, help with heavy bags of shopping from the supermarket, do household chores and perhaps find paid part-time work. Like poor children a hundred years ago, they may be irregular in attendance at school, tired and hungry in class, behind with school work, and liable to resist discipline. As a result, they are often seen in terms of social problems. Compulsory school now, as when it was introduced, amplifies any dissonance between the needs of the family and the demands of society, between an ideal of sheltered, dependent childhood and a reality of poverty and stress where children's help is indispensable. The label 'latchkey children', like fears that children watch 'too much' television (often meaning the wrong, adult, programmes), distils the anxiety of adults who want children to be more childlike, to have less responsibility and autonomy, to conform with expectations of childhood which are now dominant in Britain and which cut across differences of class and cultural background. At the same time, adults who do put domestic need before school requirements and child leisure are more likely to feel guilty, and their children more resentful of demands which are no longer 'normal'. Such tensions increase the probability that violence, threatened or actual, may be used to enforce obedience, and this again invites stigma and state intervention.

Looking Back

Within the larger context outlined above, the focus in this work is on how childhood was changing in the London working class in the last decades of the nineteenth century and the early twentieth century. This has not always been easy to gauge. One complication is that the evidence varies in availability and in quality. On some aspects of childhood there is plenty of official documentation (on education, employment or health, for example) though it is always, of course, selected and presented from the official point of view. It is harder to find information about aspects which did not interest reformers or the authorities, or which is not biassed by their preconceptions and the effects of their enquiries. The inner life of the family and its relationships, the extent and meaning of family violence (including sexual abuse), and the children's own views on their lives, on work and school or on childhood itself, are not easy to discover or to generalize about, especially for the earlier part of my period, when there is nothing to match the rich oral material of the 1900s.

So my conclusions are also uneven: some I make confidently, others are tentative or speculative. For example, scattered and various material suggests that gender divisions tended to become sharper as the standard of living improved, both as an overall pattern across the period, and within the life cycle of particular families, but I can present this only as my impression. Again, some children who 'did not fit' with the prevailing expectations of their neighbourhood and school (because of religion, accent, dress, colour, place of origin or whatever) suffered prejudice, but the extent and detail of its effects is hard to determine. (See Chapter 11.)

I have tried to show something of the changes both in ideology— assumptions about what should constitute childhood—and in children's actual experience. This is complicated, of course, by the fact that ideology and practice interact (and, in interacting, change), as well as by the wide variations perceptible in each. Ideology, especially dominant ideology, is easier to chart than experience. Small effort is needed to discover the concerns of those who led public discussion, whether at meetings of societies and associations, in drawing-rooms and at dinner tables, in the Houses of Parliament, committee rooms, and ministerial offices, or in departmental correspondence, parliamentary papers, and printed discussion in books and the press. The records of government and reform (and of their larger political context) allow us also to see how those who identified and formulated social 'problems' and their solutions did so always in relation to their perception of how society ought to function. One of my interests here has been to explore how assumptions about childhood, gender roles and the family affected those who were the subjects—or objects—of government and reform. But clearly there was a gulf between the assumptions and practice prevalent on the one hand amongst those whose views influenced the exercise of political power, and, on the other, in the rest of society, especially amongst the far more numerous poor. So this interest also led me to investigate how the children of the London poor, at the opposite end of the social and economic range, actually lived their childhoods. A major part of this book is therefore descriptive, aiming to convey the daily detail of poor children's lives in late nineteenth-century London.

Problems also arise from the fact that today's assumptions inevitably influence our reading of the past. It is hard to know, for instance, how to present hardships which to us seem extreme but which many children then took for granted. To dwell on them might leave the reader with an overwhelmingly vivid impression of misery, of children as victims—cold, hungry, overworked and perhaps beaten. Those aspects of poverty cannot be ignored, but they need to be given historical context, too.

As an example, take warmth. Expectations of domestic warmth were universally lower than today, and upper and middle-class memoirs include accounts of bitterly cold homes. Probably there was a generally higher tolerance of cold. But the children of the well-to-do would have food in their stomachs and warm clothes against rain, wind and snow, including boots, coats, hats, scarves, and gloves or muffs; they could change after getting wet; fires could be lit when needed; and though bedrooms were unheated they had enough bedclothes. The damp and cold endured by the children of the poor, on the other hand, perhaps stoically accepted as part of their daily lot, had no such alleviation and lowered resistance to colds and flu, to endemic disease like tuberculosis, and to the epidemic childhood diseases.

Beatings and harsh discipline, to take another example, were experienced by some children of all classes, just as there were also in all classes children whose experience of domestic discipline never included physical punishment. For the particular child, the significance of being beaten probably varied with the context. For some it was a recurrent terror, inflicted by a violent adult regularly on any pretext (bed-wetting; insufficient earning; lateness for school or work or at home; disobedience or impertinence, or even lisping or stammering),[7] or less regularly during or after drinking bouts. For others it was occasional, more a ritual assertion of continuing adult authority. Although no doubt it always hurt, it might be suffered with resignation as inescapable or even merited; or it might be bitterly resented. Much would depend on the relationship between adult and child, the spirit in which the beating was given (which probably also determined its severity), and whether the child accepted it as deserved. The attitude of peers might also have a bearing: amongst boys, especially at school, stoic acceptance of physical pain, in punishment as in fights, was highly desirable as it proved their manly strength. To understand what corporal punishment meant in a particular historical context we may have to hold back our late twentieth-century indignation and rejection of it.

Hunger and access to food, again, while of prime significance, in specific contexts have overtones to which historians should be alert. The hunger of a normally well-fed child sent to bed without supper in punishment for some small offence was not the same as the hunger of a child who had failed to earn enough coppers to buy food, or who went without a meal because there was nothing in the cupboard and no money, and who anyway never had enough to eat. Different again was the hunger of breakfasted children trapped in the classroom, waiting for the release of the bell and the rush to dinner, or of a mother, pretending to have eaten while she fed husband and children and drinking stewed tea to dull the pangs.

One of the difficulties in this work, then, has been to find a balanced way of countering the bias which stems from late-twentieth-century assumptions about childhood. To understand the specificities of children's work in London in the last decades of the nineteenth century, for instance, we have to get past stereotypes of child labour with which all of us in Britain have grown up. The term 'child labour' is an abstraction from children's work in many forms and many contexts; like female labour, even though it has usually been underpaid and exploitative, it is not so by definition. But in current use the phrase carries a heavy negative load. Because of our expectations about 'proper' childhood experience and our knowledge of how children suffered and were exploited in early industrialization (or in Californian agriculture or in third-world situations today), the idea of child labour rouses immediate moral indignation. This obstructs historical understanding, so I have preferred to use the less loaded term 'children's work'.

I recognize the danger that in trying to reduce the impact of twentieth-century ideas about childhood, in rejecting the emotional overtones of child labour, and in insisting that a working child was not simply a victim, I run the risk of presenting too rosy a view. The peril is the greater because of the common urge to take sides, which history in more or less narrative form also reinforces: of course any good story has its goodies and baddies.

Transitions

The overall pattern of change in these decades is clear. Ideologically, the view of childhood as a period of dependence and subordination gained ground across the classes, though its expected duration was still longest among the rich and shortest among the poor.[8] In practice, too, its duration was being lengthened, through state intervention (protective legislation regulating employment below specified ages, and compulsory school), through changing parental ideas (acceptance of the value of schooling and greater reluctance to set children to paid work), and through rising living standards which reduced the need for children's earnings. From the late 1880s school became the almost universal experience of British children between the ages of five and ten, and in London for longer: often from three until fourteen. Formal employment was increasingly deferred till the end of schooling, except in textile towns, where employment and school were combined under the half-time system until 1918.

Higher male wages and rising living standards permitted more specialization in the domestic economy of the working class. Domestic labour began to be not only the primary responsibility of the woman, with help from her children, but often her only responsibility, so long as misfortune did not halt the male breadwinner's wage-earning, and so long as he was prepared to turn over his wage in return for her work in the home. School leavers, as they reached their fourteenth birthday, were also expected to find work and hand over their wages, unless their contribution in domestic labour was of greater value. Boys, who commanded higher wage rates, were more likely to be sent to work even if the mother's health was poor or there were numerous small children. Girls' potential earnings, being lower, were often outweighed by their domestic usefulness. Some parents, too, might feel that girls should not go out into the world of full-time employment as soon as boys; or that a particular girl was not ready.

Within this larger pattern the changes were not uniform everywhere or in all sectors of the working class, in progress or in character; any more than they were identical for girls and for boys. How early children started some form of paid work, and what it was, depended on local and familial circumstances, and on their gender. Significant differences in the experience of boys and girls developed and were reinforced through a contradiction in the dominant ideology. For although work and childhood were seen as incompatible, work was officially defined in terms of employment and wage. Since domestic labour in the working-class family was performed by the mother and children without payment, the protective legislation designed to limit children's work in fact only limited their paid employment. Domestic work remained a major burden for many working-class children, especially girls.

So the prevailing division of labour meant that girls derived less benefit than boys from the new protective measures. Girls' domestic labour, unlike paper-selling or other forms of work done by boys, was perceived not as work but as training appropriate to their future. This was a widely-held view. As we shall see, it underlay the double standard in the enforcement of school attendance by the authorities and distorted the data collected about children's employment. It meant that mothers were more likely to call on a daughter when help was needed than on a son, and this affected both school attendance and time out of school. Mothers imparted skills which would make the girls more useful in the present, which ensured a back-up if the mother was out of action for any reason, and which were essential for the girls' expected future. Such training could be taken very seriously. A twelve-year-old girl from a large Finsbury family in 1908, for instance, had a double dose of it. Her own mother 'brought us up to know how to do housework'; and when she went back with a Jewish friend after school to help with cleaning (for which she received sixpence), her friend's mother supervised and instructed the two girls.

> she would stand over us. She would say, 'plenty of water first, and [scrub] the way of the boards, plenty of water after to rinse, then slowly dry.' And that was her tuition.[9]

There was no question of boys receiving such training, even where they shared some chores.

Conclusion

The history of children in society requires and permits exploration of the whole social structure. The overall economy, the local economy and the domestic economy, interconnecting with overall, local and domestic demography, underpin the experience of childhood. Children's lives are affected by the prevailing (or changing) divisions of labour, in both paid and unpaid work, and by how such division intersects with class, gender, age and other categories by which their society is organized and divided. Ideology, too, is affected by these various factors and in turn also has its impact, while the extent and nature of government and the state can be seen to affect both ideology and experience.

Within this complex set of interactions, and within the larger pattern of long-term change, I hope to show that the children growing up poor in late nineteenth-century London, girls and boys, had their own feelings, attitudes and stories, however distant their voices and fragmented the evidence of their stories. History has to comprise the particular as well as the general. The historian needs both zoom and wide-angle lens to show street and neighbourhood as well as city, country and world system; the individual as well as the class, age cohort, sex or race; weekly round and life cycle as well as century and *longue durée*. The challenge is to capture as well the shifting relationships between particular and general over time, both within the past that we study and between that past and our present.

2. Whitechapel children around 1900.

PART 1

---◆---

Children and Everyday Life

3. *Amenities were limited in most one and two-room homes, but a fire, a rug and a comfortable lap might compensate. Unknown interior, c.1900.*

1
Indulgence and Insecurity

———————◆———————

CHILDREN IN the urban working class in the last decades of the nineteenth century and the early years of the twentieth were both numerous and noticeable. Unlike their 'betters' they spent much time out in the street. 'Teeming' children figured in almost every depiction of a poor neighbourhood, and the crowd of children in a cramped court was a common photographic subject. 'Ragged urchins' were as clichéd an index of squalor as were blocked gutters, broken windows or washing across the street. They were often described in terms which evoked untamed animals—wild, swarming, prowling, roaming.[1] Disapproval of their alleged idleness or precocious responsibility was also common. Even pity for them was likely to be accompanied by fear and censure, as in George Gissing's novel *The Nether World* (1889). When Jane Snowden visits the poverty-stricken Clerkenwell streets where she grew up she enters:

> a disagreeable quarter, a street of squalid houses, swarming with yet more squalid children. On all the doorsteps sat little girls, themselves only just out of infancy, nursing or neglecting bald, red-eyed, doughy-limbed abortions in every stage of babyhood, hapless spawns of humanity born to embitter and brutalize yet further the lot of those who unwillingly gave them life.[2]

Old and Young

The late nineteenth-century population was altogether younger than today's. Successive generations—each larger than the last—had produced more and more children all through the century, and those who survived to adulthood died earlier than today, so the balance was weighted towards the young. In the late twentieth century the progressive effects of declining birth rates and the lengthening of life have produced a quite different age structure, with a narrower childhood base and many more older people. Between 1851 and 1891 the proportion of children in the total population of England and Wales was around 36 per cent, or more than a third; it

15

declined between 1931 and 1961 to 23 per cent, or just under a quarter, and in the 1980s to about a fifth.

Families were generally larger than today. Of couples married around 1860, a third had eight children or more, just under a third had six or seven, and the rest had four or fewer. The proportion of children was highest in the working class. Although birth rate and family size did start to decline towards the end of the century, especially from the 1890s, there was 'an inverse relationship between fertility and prosperity'.[3] So families tended to be smallest in the middle and upper classes, and largest amongst the unskilled and poor, while skilled workers and artisans (along with Lancashire textile workers) occupied an intermediate position.

Although many working-class children in the last decades of the century grew up in families of more than four, a child was not always one of a swarm, even in a big family: six or seven children could easily be spread over twenty years. Such spacing might result from efforts to prevent or end pregnancy, from unintended miscarriage or from early death.[4] As parental fertility declined with age, intervals between children also lengthened towards the end of a family. So the youngest child did not always grow up with, or even know, the older ones. Jane W., for example, born in Limehouse in 1896, was the last of her mother's seventeen children, and because of deaths and long gaps knew only four of the others.[5] In other cases contact was lost after older siblings emigrated, or through family quarrels.[6]

Position in the family affected children's experience. Most obviously, the eldest had the hardest time. Their childhood coincided with the period of maximum stress in the family life-cycle and more responsibility fell to them: 'course we had to do all the donkey work...the eldest got the blame for everything', one woman recalled; and another: 'I had babies from the time I was eight—I didn't actually lay them—but I did everything else'.[7] Conversely, the youngest might hope to be 'comparatively shielded from the many privations and hardships' endured by the rest.[8] An easier financial situation as the youngest grew up might also produce a more relaxed domestic atmosphere, where conflicts between child and parents were less likely. The youngest girl and her father often had a close relationship, making Sunday expeditions together perhaps, while an eldest, through sharing work and responsibility, was more likely to identify with her mother. Sometimes the youngest was lonely, especially if born after a long gap. In other cases younger ones could enjoy their position ('my eldest sister always seemed to be helping Mum, but the rest of us had plenty of fun'),[9] or indeed could take advantage of it. One younger sister learnt to use tears so as not to be left out: 'she only had to turn the tap on and we got a backhander [slap] so—we had to tolerate her'.[10]

Children in the middle class often had fewer siblings, especially in later decades. They too might experience the death of a brother or sister in infancy or beyond, but better living standards and falling family size in their class gave them a better chance of survival. Statistics on infant mortality suggest the difference.[11]

In the 1880s, 152 children out of every 1,000 born in London died before the age of one; in the 1890s this proportion rose to 160.[12] But the rates for poor districts were much higher than those for comfortable suburbs.[13] In 1897, for example, the medical statistician Arthur Newsholme noted:

> the infant mortality per 1,000 births ranged in London from 116 in Plumstead or 127 in Hampstead, to 157 in St Saviour's [Southwark] and 197 in St George's in the East [East End].[14]

A local analysis made in 1905 by George Newman, medical officer of health for Finsbury, linked infant mortality to poverty by using overcrowding as an index. It showed that babies born in one-room tenements died at the rate of 219 per 1,000, in two rooms 157, in three rooms 141, and only 99 in four rooms or more.[15] While overcrowding often compounded other effects of poverty, however, it was not inevitably linked with infant mortality. Shirley Murphy, London Medical Officer of Health, observed with surprise the low death rates among Jews in the very poor district of Whitechapel, who were 'living in close courts and crowded alleys under conditions which I was accustomed to find associated with high death rates wherever I had looked in London'. Rates were similarly lower among the Irish and the Italians: in all three cases the explanation usually proposed was that mothers suckled their children longer.[16]

Many poor children who survived infancy still did not reach adulthood, for virulent diphtheria, measles, scarlet fever and even smallpox made regular visitations, and as infectious diseases take a heavier toll when nutritional standards are low, the children who caught them often died. Measles, according to a medical officer of health in 1895, was 'only fatal to the children of the working and labouring classes'.[17] School logbooks noting increased rates of absence recorded the remorseless persistence of these diseases, and the strain they put upon domestic resources as well as education. Entries between October 1875 and January 1878 for Gainsborough Road School (at Hackney Wick, a poor and rough neighbourhood on the edge of the Lea Valley) mentioned 'measles and fever'; 'sickness'; 'scarlet fever, measles, colds'; 'scarlet fever'; 'smallpox and scarlet fever'; 'smallpox and scarlet fever raging'; 'smallpox still'; 'smallpox, fever and measles'; and 'measles, ringworm, severe colds'. In the course of 1892 there was measles 'almost without exception' in two streets; and children from the school had scarlet fever, diphtheria, pneumonia, whooping cough, blight; 'sore heads' (with infected sores following the attacks of headlice); mumps, scarlet fever, and even typhus.[18]

Poor women sometimes tried to avert or end pregnancies when health or family circumstances made them inopportune;[19] and some mothers let their children know they had been unintended and were regretted.

(Kathleen Woodward, born in Peckham in 1896, was a youngest child whose mother used to say 'that if she had known as much when her first child was born as she learned by the time she bore her sixth, a second child would never have been'.)[20] Elder children, too, fearing further strain on budget and energy, might resent the arrival of yet another infant. 'I 'ates 'em, I 'ates 'em. It's babies, babies, babies, and it's me that 'as to mind the bloody little bastards', one nine-year-old girl, eldest of six, reportedly sobbed hysterically on hearing of the latest arrival.[21] Some exhausted and unwilling mothers were no doubt resentful and bad-tempered or even cruel with their children.

Nevertheless the general assumption was that children were desirable; and even unwanted children were often welcomed once born. 'My mum and dad were passionately fond of children, though they had thirteen of them. They loved every one of them', recalled a woman who grew up in Lambeth in the 1900s.[22] Those born out of wedlock, according to the sociologist Charles Booth, were 'almost equally accepted as sent by Heaven'.[23] Among 'the very poorest of the people', wrote an East End doctor in 1891,

> I can certify to a general tender regard for the welfare of their children which certainly fully equals that which obtains among the shopkeeping and lower middle class, to say nothing of the higher grades.[24]

Boys and girls (of whatever class) were dressed alike for their first years, in skirts gradually shortened. The boys were then 'breeched', their petticoat and dress replaced by knickerbockers, and their hair cut.[25] This occurred between three and six, and was often quite an occasion, with visitors and cake. For girls, however, there was no parallel ceremony or rite of passage: they remained girls while their brothers became boys.

Infants were petted, cuddled and indulged. They were breast-fed while the mother's milk lasted or until her employment made it too difficult. Prams and cots were rare so they were continually held. C.H. Rolph (born in 1901) called the difference between infants transported in go-carts or prams and 'those, like me, who had to be carried everywhere till they could walk', the 'earliest of all the great class distinctions'.[26] Even asleep they might still be held: 'a child nurse is always unwilling to part with a sleeping baby' after having triumphantly '"got it to sleep her own self"'.[27] They went with parents or siblings on visits to other households or to music hall or pub.[28] At night they rarely slept alone: cots were next the parental bed and babies often ended up with the mother, especially before weaning, while small children shared beds with older ones. Lamps were sometimes left burning overnight, presumably against fear of the dark.[29] When little children cried there was no nursery door to shut off the noise, and they were fed and comforted, soothed with cuddles and a sugar-dipped rag to suck, or (by the end of the century) a rubber dummy, also sweetened. Lodgers and visitors—and parents, when funds allowed—bought them little treats, usually sweets or cheap toys or fruit, or gave them farthings and half-pennies to spend for themselves.[30]

All these indulgent practices met with disapproval from above, on grounds both of safety and health and of moral training. Deaths of sleeping babies, some no doubt due to what we now call cot-death syndrome, were indicted as 'overlaying' and blamed on alleged negligence or drunkenness. The importance of separate cots for infants was emphasized in mothercraft instruction in the 1900s, and advice given on how to convert a twopenny banana-box.[31] (Much ingenuity in fact already went into the contriving of cots: one amused account in 1869 reported the use of a variety of receptacles including a raisin-box, an egg-box, and a gooseberry sieve.)[32] Having a baby in the parental bed was seen entirely in negative terms: no cot meant either ignorance of its importance or wrong priorities in spending; not returning baby to cot meant laziness. Alternative explanations—it was the best way to keep the baby warm when heating and covers were inadequate, there was no space for a cot, a fractious child had to be soothed so that others did not wake—were rarely taken into account. Similarly, the 'noxious habit of giving infants india-rubber nipples to suck' was 'most strongly deprecated';[33] and demand feeding was criticized as 'maternal ignorance', and wonder expressed because 'to these people it seems wrong to disturb a child out of its sleep'.[34] The criticisms generally reveal both ignorance of the material constraints of poverty, and incomprehension and intolerance of a different set of child-rearing practices.[35]

Some critics held that poor parents were unfit for the task of training up good citizens. In the words of Mary Scharlieb, a doctor active in the Eugenics Society:

> the child whose parents have little sense of duty, and are deficient
> in self-control, is badly handicapped in the race of life....The
> father or mother who yields to a child's cries or importunities does
> not deserve to have the care of a moral being...[36]

Their training was criticized for being concerned only with externals and behaviour, not with character: they were told only 'to do this, never to be this'.[37]

Poor children's 'life of liberty from infancy' was deplored by the superintendent of a Southwark boys' home in the 1880s: he thought that 'London children of both sexes should be rescued at as an early an age as four and six'. (The Sister Superintendent of a nearby girls' home agreed that institutional care was desirable for children from five or six, but she also recommended crèches.)[38] Twenty years later, a doctor giving evidence to the parliamentary committee on physical deterioration was still more despairing. For him, too, the central problem was one of proper training. Working-class children were not taught self-restraint: 'from their earliest years' they were 'a great deal more spoiled than the children of the better class'; they were 'given things to play with which they ought not to have';

and they got halfpence and farthings at an early age 'to buy all sorts of sweets and unwholesome things'. They were already 'most unruly and intractable by the time they reached school'. His rather desperate solution was 'to take every child as soon as it was born and put it away in a Government home of some kind'.[39]

Charles Booth, though he and his collaborators noted 'spoiling', was less censorious. Among the poor, he thought, 'there are no doubt terrible cases of neglect and cruelty, but on the whole kindness and affection reign, though it may be careless kindness and ill-regulated affection', with 'little parental control'.[40] In better-off sections of the working class, he suggested, the young ('provided they have decent parents') might have 'less chance of surviving' than in rich families, but their lives were certainly happier, 'free from the paraphernalia of servants, nurses and governesses'.

> They are more likely to suffer from spoiling than harshness, for they are made much of, being commonly the pride of their mother, who will sacrifice much to see them prettily dressed, and the delight of their father's heart.[41]

'Spoiling' did not in fact last long. As children grew older they soon had to learn to put the needs of the family before their own demands. Even a squalling baby had to wait for attention when dinner was nearly ready. The 'ex-babies'—toddlers displaced from the limelight by a newcomer—were sometimes 'left to shift and forage for themselves'.[42]

> Too young to go out alone, with no one to carry it now the baby had come [the ex-baby] lived in the kitchen, dragging at its mother's skirts, much on its legs but never in the open air.[43]

Self-sufficiency and co-operation were encouraged early, for hard-working mothers could not give their children constant attention and care. As settlement worker Reginald Bray observed:

> Actions which disturb the home and cause annoyance to the family are forbidden; for example the noisy and dirty child is punished, and quarrels in the house are discouraged.[44]

This may have been especially true for girls, in training to follow the example of self-sacrifice attained by their mothers. (When a little girl was asked by a lady in about 1889 how she would define love, 'unhesitatingly she replied, "It's going errands"'.)[45] Older children's help was an obvious resource, though it did not sit well with middle-class views either on infant care or on keeping childhood free of responsibility.

So although the general pattern was for babies and toddlers to be indulged, from the age of around four, even in quite prosperous families, the long climb towards adult responsibility was apt to begin. Where daily life was precarious and babies followed hard on each other's heels, the three or four-year-old was already required to help at times, and was certainly not likely to be spoilt.

Ups and Downs

Insecurity in some degree was the general experience of the London working class. Although life was most precarious among the casual poor—unskilled, irregularly employed, and engaged in a daily struggle for subsistence through all means available to them, no family can have felt invulnerable even when possessed of steady income and good health. Economic factors, the life cycle, and hazards of life and work all played a part.

When Charles Booth attempted his grand classification of the London population he discovered that it was difficult to portray 'so shifting a scene', but noted that 'as in photographing a crowd, the details of the picture change continually, but the general picture is much the same, whatever moment is chosen'.

> I have attempted to produce an instantaneous picture, fixing the facts on my negative as they appear at a given moment, and the imagination of my readers must add the movement, the constant changes, the whirl and turmoil of life.[46]

Booth endeavoured to analyse his London crowd by fitting its members into categories which he constructed mainly on the basis of male employment. The casual poor constituted classes A ('the lowest class—occasional labourers, loafers and semi-criminals') and B ('the very poor—casual labour, hand-to-mouth existence, chronic want').[47] These numbered 354,444 people, and made up respectively 0.9 per cent and 7.5 per cent of the total London population.[48] Those in class B, Booth said, were 'ill-nourished and poorly clad', more or less always 'in want', but mostly not (or only sometimes) in immediate distress.

> From day to day and from hand to mouth they get along, sometimes suffering, sometimes helped, but not always unfortunate, and very ready to enjoy any good luck that may come in their way. They are, very likely, improvident, spending what they make as they make it, but the improvidence of the poor has its bright side. Life would indeed be intolerable were they always contemplating the gulf of destitution on whose brink they hang.[49]

Those in his next categories, C and D ('the poor—including alike those whose earnings are small because of the irregularity of employment, and those whose work, though regular, is ill-paid'), if not 'in want' still had 'an unending struggle' to make ends meet and no possibility of saving against still harder times. These constituted another 22.3 per cent of the population. (The families in M. Pember Reeves' 1913 study for the Fabian Women's Group, *Round About a Pound a Week*, fell into this group.) Thus 30.7 per cent of the London population (or 41 per cent of the working class), his classes A to D, Booth classified as 'in poverty', with at best 'means...sufficient, but...barely sufficient, for decent independent life', and not always that. Most of them, some 400,000 perhaps, were dependent on casual work.[50] The rest of the working class were in categories Booth called 'comfortable'. Class E included most artisans and other regular wage-earners, along with the 'best class' of street sellers and small dealers, most small shopkeepers, and some small employers; and class F the best-paid artisans with some superior warehousemen and lightermen, and foremen. Together classes E and F made up 51 per cent of the total London population and 59 per cent of its working class. Being 'regularly employed and fairly paid', they at least might seem safe from the insecurity under discussion.[51]

Tidy categories and proportions ignore the ups and downs which families went through over time, Booth's 'whirl and turmoil'. There was little margin for savings or insurance at the best of times (except in class F, and in E if the children in a family were not too numerous); and small chance of cushioning major blows like the injury or illness or death of a parent or other wage-earner, or even the relatively minor difficulties caused by temporary unemployment or sickness.[52] Work hazards, poor health provision, advancing age,[53] the fluctuations of the trade cycle (despite an overall context of rising prosperity), and the particularly precarious and seasonal character of much London employment,[54] all threatened family security.

Booth recognized this vulnerability:

> The position of the class may be secure—some set of men and their families must hold it—but that of the individual is precarious. For the wife and family it will depend on the health, or habits, or character of the man. He drinks or falls ill; he loses his job; some other man takes his place. His employment becomes irregular and he and they fall into class C, happy if they stop there and do not drop as low as B. Or it may be the woman who drags her family down....Marriage is a lottery, and childbearing often leads to drink. What chance for a man to maintain respectability and hold up his head among his neighbours if he has a drunken wife at home, who sells the furniture and pawns his clothes? What possibility of being beforehand and prepared to meet the waves of fortune?[55]

Drink was indeed a danger, from which church or chapel and temperance beliefs protected some, but not all, for 'rough' culture was not restricted to the casual poor. Men's customs during and after work tended to involve drinking;[56] and many workers drank to counteract heat or other disadvantages of their work, from skilled and well-paid men such as glass-blowers, coopers and metal-workers, to laundresses toiling for endless steamy hours. Long-term alcohol addiction was not unusual, especially among men. It meant the continual erosion of their wages, with the result that other family members went short: when, as Booth put it, 'the children do not receive a fair share, and in truth are poorer than their homes'.[57] It might also mean higher levels of violence in the family.[58] And it brought the risk of disaster: loss of permanent work, whether through dismissal or through drink-related accident or illness.

Of course unemployment could happen for other reasons too, to skilled as well as unskilled:

> it may be that trade shrinks, so that for a while one man in ten or perhaps one in seven is not wanted. Some must be thrown out of work. The lot falls partly according to merit and partly according to chance, but whatever the merit or the lack of it, the same number will be thrown out of work. Thus we see that the 'common lot of humanity'...is cursed by insecurity against which it is not easy for any prudence to guard.[59]

The impact of disaster on a skilled man and his family could be dramatic. In a boilermaker's family in 1882 the father 'had become an imbecile through shock, despair and depression at losing his job'; the mother, though 'a frail woman', was selling whelks in the street, to supplement 2s. 6d. savings club money and weekly poor-relief of 2s. and two loaves of bread. They still could not manage, and the eleven-year-old son was sent to Barnardo's Stepney Home (and thence later to Canada as a child emigrant).[60] A prosperous Enfield family in the 1870s slid into poverty after illness struck the father, a highly-paid gunmaker. ('Except when work was slack' he had earned the huge sum of £4 5s. a week; and they 'always had a girl to mind the baby'.) He was progressively incapacitated by rheumatism, with months in hospital which used up their savings, and it was only through a charitable intervention that they recovered even the meagre security of 15s. a week, after the wife had been helped to train as a midwife and get steady work with the Royal Maternity Charity.[61] Will Crooks's father, a ship's stoker in the 1850s, lost his arm and his livelihood in an accident, and in spite of the mother's valiant efforts the father and the five youngest children eventually (when the Guardians refused further out-relief) had to spend a period in the workhouse. Crooks himself, though a time-served cooper, later had a long spell out of work because of his reputation as an agitator; his own family ended up in the workhouse.[62]

Among applicants for remission of school fees in the mid-1870s were men incapacitated by illness or accident (or their widows) who appear to have belonged to one of the more 'comfortable' groups: for instance, a shipwright crippled with rheumatic gout; a wheelwright unemployed after an accident; a cooper eight months off work with a diseased arm; a blacksmith eight weeks out of work; a chandler's widow; the widow of a coffee-house keeper; a boilermaker ill and out of work nine weeks (though with 14s. weekly from a savings club); an ironmoulder out of work seven months (club money 8s.); and an engineer with failing eyesight.[63] Instances of furniture and clothing being sold for subsistence, also fairly frequent, again suggest a fall from comparative prosperity. And the admissions to

Greenwich workhouse analysed by Geoffrey Crossick, although predominantly from the unskilled and semi-skilled, nevertheless include an
important proportion of skilled men (27.4 per cent in 1864, 24.1 per cent
in 1867–70, and 20.8 per cent in 1871–2). Disaster, as he says, 'was always a
real possibility even for the most secure of artisans'.[64]

Families which escaped dramatic vicissitudes and disaster would still go
through phases where the balance of earners to dependents must almost
inevitably spell poverty. This was analysed by Rowntree for a labouring
man's life.

> The life of a labourer is marked by five alternating periods of want
> and comparative plenty. During early childhood, unless his father
> is a skilled worker, he probably will be in poverty; this will last until
> he, or some of his brothers or sisters, begin to earn money and
> thus augment their father's wage sufficiently to raise the family
> above the poverty line. Then follows the period during which he is
> earning money and living under his father's roof; for some por
> tion of this period he will be earning more than is required for
> lodging, food and clothes. This is his chance to save money. If he
> has saved enough to pay for furnishing a cottage, this period of
> comparative prosperity may continue after marriage until he has
> two or three children, when poverty will again overtake him. This
> period of poverty will last perhaps for ten years, i.e. until the first
> child is fourteen years old and begins to earn wages; but if there
> are more than three children it may last longer. While the children
> are earning, and before they leave the home to marry, the man
> enjoys another period of prosperity—possibly, however, only to
> sink back into poverty when his children have married and left
> him, and he himself is too old to work, for his income has never
> permitted his saving enough for him and his wife to live upon for
> more than a very short time.[65]

For women the cycle was similar but not identical. At all ages their earning
power was less and the disposal of what they earned more subject to others'
demands or needs. When still living with their parents but earning a wage,
like their brothers they contributed to the family purse which their mother administered, but they would end up with less spending (or saving)
money than their brothers—with a smaller proportion of a smaller total.

In the first years of marriage, while husbands were at the peak of their
earning power, wives were increasingly handicapped by child-bearing and
rearing, least able to earn for themselves (though working hard), and most
dependent.[66] Wives controlled the family purse, but this 'power' brought
no privileges, only anxious responsibility for stretching scant resources. It
was often exercised with complete self-abnegation; everyone else's needs
were put first and women made do with minimum expenditure on themselves, eating least and working most.[67] Their energy and self-denial were

the first lines of defence when poverty advanced; their health and vitality were often the first casualties. Children, especially daughters, were the reserves (mobilized under strict discipline should co-operation falter), but their contribution was made in labour not abstinence. If food was short it was 'not the husband and children, but the mother' who made her meal of tea and scraps and pretended to have eaten before the rest came home.[68] Relief came as the older children entered employment (though, depending on the balance of age and gender in the family, that might entail a greater burden of domestic labour for the mother), and this period of prosperity was shared by both parents so long as the husband was still in work, the wife still had her health, and they were still together. Even a widow might not be badly off at this stage if there were no young children and she could go out and earn without paying for child care.

In old age the experience of men and of women again diverged. There were more elderly women than men. They were less likely to have any savings, insurance policies, or claims on trade unions or benefit societies. More of them were managing on low incomes: in 1892 a 'Test Census' of people over sixty-five estimated that 59 per cent of those living on ten shillings a week or less were women.[69] More of them turned for help to the Poor Law authorities: 31 per cent of women over sixty-five did so in the course of 1892 in England and Wales; to 26.9 per cent of men.[70] But they did so less readily, according to witnesses before the Royal Commission on the Poor Laws (1905–9).[71] More women managed to stay out of the workhouse: 'The old man who is left without friends is more helpless than the woman, and betakes himself earlier to the workhouse or the sick asylum'.[72] During 1892, of those who received outdoor relief (bread and a contribution towards the rent, which enabled them to survive outside the workhouse), 25.1 per cent were women and 15.6 per cent men. Conversely, men made up 11.3 per cent of those in England and Wales who were 'indoor paupers' (workhouse inmates) at some point, and women only 6 per cent.[73] As restriction of out-relief was observed more harshly in London than elsewhere at this time the percentages were different, but the contrast remained: 'no less than 30 per cent of the old men are on the indoor list and 18 per cent of the old women'.[74]

Women's relative earning power increased in old age. It was harder for men to get work as their strength and stamina declined, especially in the city,[75] but women's skills remained useful.[76] They took in sewing or other outwork, or washed, cleaned or minded children for relatives or neighbours. Being used to a lower standard of living than men, having less need or expectation of extras such as alcohol or tobacco, and being accustomed to looking after themselves and to making the money stretch, they could also manage better on whatever pittance they earned.[77] Again, their greater usefulness and lower expectations made relatives or neighbours more ready to take them in, which gave them a choice beyond going into the hated workhouse or living alone, though it also carried risks.[78] The resident grandmother, according to a slum priest, was often 'the drudge of the whole family, minding the baby and the little children even when her head is splitting'.[79]

Grown children may also in some cases have felt a greater sense of obligation towards their mothers.[80] Mothers often figure in the autobiographical literature as heroic and self-sacrificing, deserving more than could ever be done for them in return. Fathers seldom loom as large or evoke such loyalty, especially if their response to stress in earlier days had involved much drink or violence.[81] In old age such men no longer inspired fear, but they were not always forgiven. In an 1883 Bromley case noted by Booth the adult children supporting their mother refused to keep their father because they said 'he ill-treated her and spent his money in drink'; and the father had to go into the workhouse.[82] As earning grew more difficult, assistance of some kind became more important. Out-relief, as even Poor Law Guardians recognized, was 'usually inadequate if it were not supplemented from other sources'.[83] Sometimes 'daughters in service and sons at sea' managed a regular allowance; but 'casual assistance in money or kind, or the providing of houseroom' were 'much more common'.[84] Regular visits were often the occasion for taking presents of food or small sums of money, picking up and returning washing, and doing household jobs.[85] Charity was the only other resource, but it was never enough for chronic need.[86]

Women's consciousness of their insecurity is disclosed by the gigantic success of 'pension teas' in the 1890s: packet tea which instead of a bonus or a free gift offered the promise of a pension.

> Advertised in all working-class quarters, pension teas entered home after home like an epidemic of measles, especially as the swiftly-accumulating profits allowed the first claims by widows to 'life pensions' temporarily to be met. The disillusion came with the natural maturing of further claims.

By 1905, when the company's 'delusive and reckless promise of impossible pensions' was denounced in the law courts (bankruptcy ensued), 'half a million women had become purchasers, and 19,000 widows were calling for a fulfilment of obligations'. 'Like all charlatans, the promoters of this scheme traded upon a real need.'[87]

Economic insecurity, then, was widely known in the working class, even if only as a threat. Although we may accept Booth's estimate that around 41 per cent of the working class lived in poverty while 59 per cent were 'comfortable', we must also recognize that more were affected by poverty at some point in their lives than fell within the category at any one time.

> The proportion of the community who at one period or another of their lives suffer from poverty to the point of physical privation is therefore much greater, and the injurious effects of such a condition are much more widespread than would appear from a

consideration of the number who can be shown to be below the poverty line at any given moment.[88]

Poverty was most directly experienced in childhood and in old age;[89] and it had implications for people's standard of living, for the stability of their living arrangements, for their approach to life, and of course for the experience of childhood itself. The following chapter examines the ways in which households responded to individual or family 'ups and downs' by moving on or by reorganizing.

4. *Children outnumbered adults in Providence Place (Bakers Row, Finsbury), where about fifty people lived in ten two-room houses which backed on to a factory wall.*

2
Where the Poor Lived

———◀◆▶———

Moving On

HOUSING ALWAYS reflected the changing economic position of the house-hold. Rent was a major item in the budget of the poor, even though the standard of their housing was low. It was significant, therefore, that it could be varied, both by changing quarters and by reorganizing the house-hold.

In the last four decades of the nineteenth century evictions and demo-litions for urban improvement steadily forced working people out of the old central districts of tenements and workshops. Imposing thoroughfares like Kingsway and Aldwych cut swathes through densely packed 'rookeries', and streets and courts were replaced by roads, railways below ground and above, stations and marshalling yards, wholesale markets, department stores, schools, law courts, police stations, offices for local and national gov-ernment, and model housing (intended for the poor but rarely within their reach). The resulting clearances cut through or levelled old densely popu-lated neighbourhoods and displaced many thousands of people, without rehousing them. Between 1853 and 1901 more than 76,000 people were displaced. The population of Finsbury, Holborn, the City, Westminster and St Marylebone dropped steadily; Shoreditch and St Pancras were affected a little later. Adjoining districts gained population (see Table 2.1). Even where buildings were not demolished, offices and warehouses competed for the space and rents went up.

Until the 1890s and 1900s, when cheap transport improved, municipal housing began to be built away from the centre, and there was some decen-tralization of industry, working-class families had little choice where to live. As the campaigning journalist George Sims explained in *How the Poor Live* (1883), they could not leave the crowded central districts 'because they must be where they can get to the dock, the yard, the wharf and the ware-houses without expense'.[1] New suburbs like Peckham, Hackney, Kilburn, Holloway, Forest Gate and Walthamstow were full of streets freshly erected by speculators for the lower-middle and upper-working classes. But work remained concentrated in Clerkenwell and the City, and the cost of travel,

Table 2.1:   Population change in inner London 1851-1911.
(In thousands; L/G = Loss or Gain.)

Borough	1851	1891	L/G	1901	L/G	1911	L/G
Group A: declining by 1901							
City	128	38	(−90)	27	(−11)	20	(−7)
Finsbury	125	110	(−15)	101	(−9)	88	(−13)
Holborn	96	67	(−29)	59	(−8)	49	(−10)
Marylebone	158	143	(−15)	133	(−10)	118	(−15)
Westminster	244	202	(−22)	183	(−19)	160	(−23)
Shoreditch	109	124	(+15)	119	(−5)	111	(−7)
St Pancras	167	235	(+68)	235	same	218	(−17)
Group B: gaining till at least 1901							
Stepney	239	285	(+46)	299	(+14)	280	(−19)
Islington	95	319	(+224)	335	(+16)	327	(−8)
Hackney	54	200	(+146)	219	(+19)	223	(+4)
Camberwell	55	234	(+179)	259	(+25)	261	(+2)
Kensington	44	170	(+126)	177	(+7)	172	(−5)
Wandsworth	40	156	(+116)	232	(+76)	311	(+79)
Paddington	48	136	(+88)	144	(+8)	143	(−1)
Fulham	12	92	(+80)	137	(+45)	153	(+16)

Based on H. Llewellyn Smith (ed.), *New Survey of London Life and Labour*, 1930,
pp. 74–5.

whether in fares or in the time it took to walk, was often too high for them
to move away. Workmen's trains, though cheap, did not always run at the
right times or serve the right places. Gareth Stedman Jones, in *Outcast
London*, explains the importance of 'the smallest difference in the cost of
living' in this context.

> The lack of women's work in the suburbs, the lack of cheap mar-
> kets and the cost of eating in coffee-shops meant that any married
> man with a family would have to earn over 30s. a week before he
> could afford to move out.[2]

Moreover, decisions about housing were generally made by the wives, and
it was hard for them to investigate suburban lodgings:

> these overburdened women have no knowledge, no enterprise, no
> time, and no cash, to enable them to visit distant suburbs along the
> tram routes, even if in their opinion, the saving of money in rent
> would be sufficient to pay the extra outlay in tram fares.[3]

So although a working-class presence did steadily grow in boroughs like
Islington, Camberwell, Hackney and Fulham, where rents were lower and
conditions likely to be more desirable, the families which moved needed at
least one steady and well-paid wage-earner, and not too many children. For
others the balance was tipped against moving out (or in favour of moving

back) by other factors—costs besides rent,[4] or the inconvenient timing of trains, or neighbourhood ties of various kinds.[5] Those who did move out were therefore likely to be more financially secure. As Booth remarked, it was:

> only the man whose position is assured who can treat railway or tram fare as a regular item of his daily budget, to be saved out of rent, or set against the advantages of happier surroundings for children, fresher air and better health.[6]

Migrants to the suburbs were also more likely to be native Londoners or English immigrants to the city. Irish and foreign-born Londoners were generally at the poorer end of the spectrum, and likely both to settle and to stay where they already had contacts, that is in the central districts.[7] Certain London districts were continuously identifiable as Irish even though 'the cast of characters changed constantly'.[8]

But even if their households did not move out to the suburbs, many children did not spend their whole childhood in one place. Moves were very common, and 'nomadic' and 'migratory' were terms often applied to the poor. School logbooks abound with references to the turnover of pupils resulting from 'removals'. The headmistress of Webb Street School (Bermondsey) in 1888, defending her school against a threatened penalty for low attendance rates, pointed out that it had 'suffered through the demolition of houses' and that 'the neighbourhood being a poor one, the inhabitants were very migratory'.[9] Booth noted that in many districts of London 'the people are always on the move; they shift from one part of it to another "like fish in a river"', and quoted a Bethnal Green school visitor who found that nearly half of the families on his books removed in a single year (1,450 out of 2,720 children).[10] Such 'capricious migration' was an administrative problem for the London School Board: quarterly lists of attendance fines outstanding show that over half the parents moved before payment (let alone attendance) could be enforced, and not all were subsequently traced.[11]

The restlessness of the poor was observed with incomprehension by those whose own homes were comfortable, and for whom moving house involved upheaval and expense. It was literally foreign to them, and invited association with the exotic (as in 'The Nomad Poor of London'), the uncivilized and irrational ('capricious').[12] It was also threatening. For a Walworth clergyman, the children of people who were

> wanderers like the Arabs of old, dwelling in tenements instead of tents...[formed] no attachment to any habitation or any locality....No teacher, no local magnate, no clergyman stands out as the familiar figure of their childhood.[13]

The home was supposed to provide essential stability in society, giving material form to the emotional comfort and moral support of the 'family',

with which it was inextricably linked, so nomadism and the inadequacy of
poor homes were alarming. The socially-concerned and successful doctor,
Sir James Crichton Browne, addressing a conference on the welfare and
protection of children in 1902, asserted that 'the very poor can scarcely be
said to have a home, but move on through a series of tenements, dirty lodgings, damp cellars or close-packed warrens'. Their temporary abodes, he
said, were 'without any touch of beauty or attraction'.

> Comparatively few of the working classes settle down and let their
> own affections and those of their children take root, but [most]
> are extremely migratory in their habits, even when migration is
> not necessary to follow work, and waste considerable sums of
> money in moving, on small pretext, from place to place.[14]

Before examining some of these 'small pretexts' it is worth challenging the
doctor on several points. First, if lodgings were so dismal (and other evidence confirms that they often were), it is hardly surprising that they
inspired little affection and were abandoned without reluctance. Second,
affections within the family might well be strengthened by frequently moving on together. Third, the cost of moving was seldom high for the poor,
and its economic implications were certainly calculated to the last farthing.
Finally, moving was generally rational and often necessary; the attribution
of perverse nomadic urges is unwarranted.

There were many possible reasons for moving. A major one was the
pursuit of employment.[15] Again, this comes up in school logbooks. An early
entry in the one for Gainsborough Road School (Hackney)commented on
the number of schools which the newly registered pupils had already
attended—generally for only a few weeks—and explained: 'this probably is
the result in great measure of the parents moving from place to place to
procure work'.[16] Transport development, suburban expansion and a whole
range of urban improvements all required intensive short-term labour in
particular localities. So navvies and other construction workers, with some
of those who provided services for them, moved around to follow opportunities of work.

The history of Battersea illustrates the link between employment and
settlement. In the 1850s Battersea was a district dominated by market gardens (which employed many Irish men and women), fringed by boatyards,
and with pockets of manufacturing. From the 1890s it was fully urban, an
industrial and residential quarter. Its population rose from 11,000 in 1851
to 169,000 in 1901. But within that massive expansion there was continual
turnover and mobility. Market-garden workers were first joined then displaced by building workers, who from the late 1850s were working on the
construction of new bridges (Chelsea, opened 1858; Lambeth and the new
Westminster, both 1862; Charing Cross railway bridge, 1863; Albert, 1873);
on the embanking of the Thames (1864–70); on new railway lines, viaducts
and bridges (including the notorious Clapham tangle of competing lines),

junctions and stations (Victoria, 1860; Charing Cross, 1864); on new residential and public buildings, as in Westminster; and in Battersea itself on the streets of speculative housing which rapidly devoured the old market gardens and the drained marshes.

By the 1890s the casual building workers had largely moved on. Battersea's residents now included artisans and clerks (concentrated in certain streets),[17] railwaymen and the others who found work in and around the stations, marshalling yards, train sheds and depots, wharves and warehouses, along with laundrywomen, gasworkers, and employees at the cabyards, at big riverside works like Price's candleworks, Doulton's pottery, or Plumbago Crucible, or in the factories of the Wandle valley.[18] Not all Battersea residents worked south of the river, however. Refugees from clearances on the north side were likely to travel back to Westminster, Pimlico or Chelsea for their work,[19] while shop assistants, clerical workers and theatre people from the West End often found it convenient to live south of the river.

A smaller-scale example of a change in population because of work was documented by research on the 'Island', a group of streets north of Hackney Downs built in 1870 to house workers constructing the new Enfield branch line of the Great Eastern Railway. Many of those first Islanders were already leaving by the mid-1870s; and a second generation identifiable in the street directories of the mid-1880s had mostly moved on by 1891. (Booth at that point referred to this 'curious patch' of poverty as 'Navvies Island'.) A more stable population was achieved only from the turn of the century.[20]

Specific local factors produced endless variation in the sequence and form of change. The rough north-Islington street, 'Campbell Bunk', intended by its developers to provide single-family houses for artisans and clerks, came instead to be dominated by houses in multiple occupation which in the 1870s to 1880s sheltered 'the workers needed to build Holloway and nearby suburbs', 'railway workers, both uniformed servants and labouring navvies', and skilled workers migrating from the inner city; then from the 1890s an unskilled poor population attracted both by cheap rents and by the local availability of casual work.[21]

Pursuit of work could also involve moving on a seasonal basis.[22] The fringes of London offered harvest, market-garden and brickfield work in the summer, when much London employment was slack, whereas winter opportunities were better in the city, whether for work (with exceptions like the building trade) or for charity. Seasonal movement is noticeable at a school in Tottenham (then just outside London), where the head regularly noted the loss of pupils whose parents left the district in October and November. ('Have lost several little girls removed to London, parents seem to dread the winter here.')[23] Walthamstow, too, attracted regular summer visitors. It had a neighbourhood known as little Bethnal Green because of the way its inhabitants had 'reproduced the characteristics of East End life'

(including 'the same constant shifting'), and in spring it was not unusual
to see:

> a small procession of weak-kneed broken-winded hacks or jaded-
> looking donkeys dragging their weary length along the Lea Bridge
> Road, drawing carts laden with household goods of a rickety and
> heterogeneous order; or returning by the same way 'when the
> leaves begin to turn'.[24]

Large numbers of London children were involved in the annual migration
to the hopfields in the late summer, but this was only an excursion: the parties which moved out to Kent laden with cooking and sleeping equipment
returned to their London homes after a few weeks, when the hops were all
picked.[25]

Variations in family income or household composition were often a
reason for changing house. When income shrank through illness or unemployment, leaving even less margin for rent, somewhere cheaper had to be
found. The cheapest housing was of course the worst, and those who occupied the most filthy and dilapidated rooms were the most transient of all.[26]
Conversely, if family income improved (perhaps when a child left school
and started work, or when one of the wage-earners found a better job), the
mother looked for a place whose rent might be higher but which had fewer
disadvantages—which was less damp, or had more light, better cooking
facilities, easier access to water, fewer stairs, or a less intolerable smell.
Some smells were peculiar to a house, relating generally to drains or damp
or to an occupant's work. Others, inescapable, were industrial or sewage
smells and dominated the neighbourhood. The smelliest trades and plants
were inevitably located in the poorest districts, and were reflected in local
names, such as 'Stinkhouse Bridge' in Poplar. In a letter in 1869 'a stranger
to these parts' complained that thrice in eighteen months he had 'been
obliged to shift my quarters in search of a locality without...a stench'.[27]
According to the Camberwell social worker, Alexander Paterson, however,
the smell of the slum was itself inescapable, 'the constant reminder of
poverty and grinding life, of shut windows and small inadequate washing-
basins, of last week's rain, of crowded homes and long working hours'.[28]

Moves, or contractions or expansions of the space rented, might be
made within the same house if relations with the owner were good and if
alternative or preferable space was available when finances forced or permitted change. Even within a single house different rents were charged.
Front rooms cost more than back, and the more stairs the cheaper—a little back attic was therefore the cheapest of all, though sometimes the
disadvantages of basement rooms also brought down the rent.[29]

When lack of work locally was not the reason for moving, nor a better
job elsewhere, there were important advantages to staying at least in the
same neighbourhood, if not in the same house.[30] The local network played
a central part in day-to-day survival when times were difficult. You knew or

would quickly hear on the grapevine where to go for cheap or free food and fuel, who would give you credit, where there might be homework given out or a child wanted for errands or child care, what firm was taking on hands, how to get a reference or charitable help or a 'hospital letter' (for free medical assistance) when it was needed, and what strings might be attached. Neighbours helped one another in an intricate weave of reciprocal favours, given and paid back over time as need arose.[31] Those who moved too far jettisoned the confidence and credit they had built up in their local network and with local shopkeepers.[32] They had to start from scratch, learn a new district and establish a new set of connections.[33] If they belonged to an ethnic or religious minority it made social and economic sense to stay near compatriots or co-religionists. If they lived near relatives, to move risked loss or reduction of kin support, both given and received. These considerations were especially important for women, with their responsibility for day-to-day managing, their irregular patterns of employment, and their strong family ties.

Sometimes people moved because they were behind with the rent or other payments, which could mean a furtive flitting of the kind celebrated in Marie Lloyd's much-loved song, 'My old man said "Follow the van"'.[34] Belongings were few enough to allow a rapid decamping, often with a borrowed or hired market barrow. (The greengrocer whose cart was used when the Rolph family moved from Southwark to Finsbury Park in 1903 displayed a chalked notice in the shop saying 'Move with us by Moonlight'.)[35] Alice Lewis, born in Fulham in 1898, recalled a moonlight flit when her mother was behind with payments on a sewing machine.[36] Sometimes the move was not planned, though perhaps not unexpected. Thomas Morgan, born off the Blackfriars Road in 1892, his parents being 'known as the two biggest drunkards in Waterloo and Blackfriars', recalled that they were:

> never long in one place you see....We moved from place to place I know because my mother was always thrown out. Many a time I've gone home, come home from school as a child until about seven— six, seven, eight—I've come home from school with all the other boys and girls and find the furniture out in the street...[If you missed a week's rent] and if you hadn't got the two weeks' rent— out! They'd put your furniture out in the street. Course nearly everybody only had one room. If you'd two rooms you thought you had a mansion.[37]

Children probably found the moves and the uncertainty difficult, though complaints are infrequent. The family of Alice Linton, who was born in Shoreditch in 1908, 'seemed to move around quite a lot but mostly in the same area'. She had recurring nightmares (still even occasionally in her 70s) of returning from school 'and standing in a strange street with no idea which house was mine and...nobody about to tell me'. She was able to stay at the same school, but the time it took to walk there varied with each move.[38]

Declining fortunes would be reflected in a series of moves, with or without evictions and moonlight flits. As funds, credit and hope were progressively exhausted along with anything that could be sold or pawned, ever cheaper and more wretched accommodation would be tried. Charlie Chaplin recalled such a sequence during a particularly poor phase of his childhood in the 1890s, when 'we kept moving from one back room to another; it was like a game of draughts—the last move was back to the work-house'.[39] The same could happen even in a less marginal domestic economy. V.S. Pritchett's parents, in the 1900s, 'rarely stayed in one house for as long as a year'. He realized later that:

> almost every time we moved house Father had lost his job or was swinging dangerously between an old disaster and a new enterprise, that he was being pursued by people to whom he owed money, that furniture had 'gone back' or new unpaid-for furniture had 'come in'.

By the time he was twelve his mother was saying that they had moved fourteen times, and when his father, offended, said she exaggerated, 'she counted up on her fingers and said she now made it eighteen'.[40]

Families without financial difficulties also moved: most housing was rented, so it was easy enough. According to Graham Balfour, writing on Battersea for Booth, there was a quite 'superior' group of people, 'respectable but restless', whose delight it was 'to go into the newest houses for a year or two, until they have worn off some of the first splendours, and then away they go to pastures newer still'.[41] Or a family whose fortunes were rising would move to progressively better neighbourhoods, perhaps as part of the process whereby the 'respectable' separated themselves from the 'rough'.[42] Or 'respectable' families would move on if the character of their street began to change, 'shunning—it may be for their children's sake—the bad language and drunkenness that are engrained in the habits of the newcomers'.[43]

Reasons for moving could be social or emotional, too: the result, for instance, of rows with the landlady or the neighbours, perhaps over the use of shared facilities like the wash-house and WC, or over the performance of shared duties, like cleaning common areas, or over unequal borrowing, or children's activities, or noise.[44] Booth reported a rebuke which amounted to 'amend your ways or go', given by a landlady to a tenant whose drunken ways were causing hardship to his children and nuisance to others.[45]

Local hostility could be incurred by whatever was considered scandalous behaviour. What was acceptable would vary with group and locality, but would be recognizably consistent. According to a clergyman familiar with poor London neighbourhoods early in the century:

These people have their own code. It differs largely from ours, but it is a code, and infractions of it were intensely resented by the people themselves. A beaten wife did not matter, but a beaten child always excited the keenest anger and molestation. A man and woman would live together as husband and wife, and while the partnership lasted would be true to one another, but a man who deserted a woman and child must quit the neighbourhood.[46]

Similarly, in Poplar there were 'only two crimes—neglecting the children, usually because of drink, and a woman going "loose" with another man (it was less serious for a man to go with a woman not his wife)'. If neighbours could not get such culprits to 'pull themselves together', ostracism would follow.[47] In general, brutal treatment of children was deplored. In Greenwood's 1866 novel, *True History of a Little Ragamuffin*, a drunken father is prevented from beating his son by other drinkers, the publican (whom he knocks over for intervening) and the potman (who smuggles the child out).[48] It might be hard to stop a violent parent in full flow, but sometimes the police were called;[49] and neighbours sheltered abused children, surreptitiously fed the hungry and neglected, and reported brutality.[50] Fear of being reported as well as direct intervention or ostracism might drive away the violent parent conscious of local censure.[51]

Neighbourhoods could also combine against outsiders. In the middle decades of the nineteenth century the Irish were the chief victims of xenophobia; by the turn of the century poor Jewish immigrants had joined or even to some extent replaced them in this position. Walter Southgate remembered of the Hackney street where he grew up in the 1890s that while the many Irish neighbours, and the few Welsh or Scots, 'had been assimilated into our community life',

we had no Jews or 'foreigners' living among us. They would have had a rough reception and their life made a misery had they attempted to live in 'our street'.[52]

An incident reported in 1901 suggests that Southgate's prediction was not unfounded: when a Jewish family tried to move into a largely Irish dockland street, people poured out from every house, smashed up van and furniture, and routed 'the unfortunate foreigners'.[53] Feared or actual prejudice (especially if language and culture reinforced the difficulties) meant that those objected to would gravitate to any neighbourhood where they were tolerated, and build up their own community.

Disadvantages in a new home sometimes surfaced after the move. Florence S. remembered that her Deptford family stayed only three weeks in one place, in about 1910, because her mother ('I think she was a puritan') didn't like the constant coming and going between the nearby pub and a men's urinal opposite their house.[54] But unhappy associations also drove people to move, and another daughter's illness and death there may have been more significant. When A.S. Jasper's sister and her husband lost

their first child with pneumonia in Hoxton in 1914, they moved because
'the place they had gave too many memories of the baby'; while Dolly
Bolton, in *The Island*, recalls that in 1915 'we moved...after my father died,
because my mum felt she couldn't stay in that house'. With one of Mrs
Jasper's many moves, when misfortune had dogged the family still more
persistently than usual, 'she reckoned the house had a curse on it'.[55]

Some recollections attribute to mothers a restlessness, an urge to
move, which was seen (if not articulated) as irrational, but which can be
interpreted as part of their endless struggle against impossible conditions.
Mrs Mack, for instance, fourth child of her mother's seven in Hackney in
the 1900s, recalled that her mother moved 'almost every time we had a new
baby', and she referred to the last house, where they stayed longest, as a
defeat for her mother.

> Mum couldn't move any more, she had to stay there...that was the
> last place that Mum moved to, she met her Waterloo there, she
> had to stay there whether she liked it or not.[56]

Such mothers, forever toiling to achieve a clean and comfortable home
against all the odds, were perhaps seeking an illusory perfection.
Somewhere there must be rooms without bugs, black-beetles, mice or rats,
free from leaks, draughts, peeling wallpaper, cracked ceilings threatening
collapse, ineradicable smells, rotting floorboards and temperamental
chimneys. Some day they would find a house with taps indoors and with
copper and lavatory that weren't shared, with an easy-going landlady and
rent they could afford, close to market, school and work, with good neighbours, a street that was lively without being too noisy, and a cornershop that
was understanding about credit. Meanwhile, when one place became intolerable, they could at least move out and try again.

Versatile Households

When illness or lack of work brought destitution close, it was possible to
apply for help from the local Poor Law authority, the Board of Guardians.
They would assess the circumstances of anyone who applied, and offer out-
relief (a basic supply of bread and help with the rent) or a place in the
workhouse, the institution which housed the destitute and the penniless
infirm. Hostility to the workhouse was widespread, and going into it was
very much a last resort.[57] But outdoor relief was often conditional. A widow
with young children, for instance, would commonly be told some must go
into the workhouse, on the grounds that she would not be able to manage
with more than one or two.[58] In Lambeth in 1911 a sixty-three-year-old
widow with an unemployed son of thirty-one was told she could not have
out-relief 'until her big son left her and fended for himself'.[59] Such conditions on help might also be imposed by other charitable bodies: Annie

Kaplan's mother, widowed in 1911 with six children, at first had 12s. a week from the Jewish Board of Guardians.

> But then they wanted to take away Becky and Hymie [to the Jewish orphanage at Norwood]....My mother said 'If four'll starve, six'll starve. If I have a piece of bread for four, I'll have a piece of bread for six....No, I'm not giving anybody away. However it'll be', she says, 'we're all happy together'....So they stopped the money.[60]

According to Mrs Hilton, who ran a much-publicised crèche in Poplar, such requirements resulted in great hardship: 'Doubtless the children would be better cared for in the house, but mother cannot be forced to give them up'.[61] Some years later, in similar vein, she wrote:

> The dread of the [Poor Law] Union seems universal, and we have often been astonished at the privations cheerfully endured rather than break up the 'home', as they term it, although to outward eyes it is desolate enough.[62]

The mothers' reluctance was about the break-up of family as well as home. Separations were imposed in the workhouse (adult from child, sister from brother, wife from husband). Wider hostility was also generated by the unpleasant and humiliating aspects of life inside.

Neighbours would try to protect children from being sent there by providing temporary refuge, as in a case used by George Sims to show that 'the charity which robs itself to give to others', was 'nowhere so common as among the poor':[63]

> In one wretched room we visited there were six little ones home at the midday hour from school.
> 'You have six children?' I said to the woman.
> 'No, sir, only four; these two little ones ain't mine—they are staying with us.'
> I imagined that they were children of a relative, and questioned the woman further, wondering how she cared to crowd her little den with extra visitors....These two extra mouths the good soul was feeding belonged to children whose mother, a widow, lived in a room above. For an assault on the police she had been sent to prison....[The children] would have starved or been taken down to the workhouse, but this good creature went up and fetched them down to be with her own children and made them welcome, she washed them and dressed them and did for them what she could, and she intended to keep them if she was able till the mother came out.

As Grace Kimmins, a settlement worker in Bermondsey in the 1890s, observed, 'if a woman dies it is seldom, for a while at any rate, that the children are allowed to go to the "house with the big gates"'.[64]

It was not unusual for a child to join another household, sometimes as an arrangement of mutual convenience, often as a result of crisis or bereavement.[65] Applications for the remission of school fees in the mid-1870s reveal cases of orphaned children adopted by cousins, by older sisters, and by grandmothers, themselves not in easy circumstances.[66] Babies whose fathers did not acknowledge or support them were often taken in by the maternal grandparents or other relatives so that the mother could find work, especially if she was a servant.[67] For other reasons, too, it could be desirable to farm a child out for a time at least: for example, extreme crowding or illness at home,[68] the need for a mother to earn,[69] bad feeling between a child and a parent or step-parent, or some other tension, perhaps between the parents.[70] But where crisis was chronic and there were children they would probably be dispersed, and some might end up in the workhouse.[71]

The general flexibility of living arrangements and the open character of the family made it relatively easy to fit in an extra child. Beds were normally shared, and expectations of privacy were low (see next chapter). In a household with children one more might not make much difference; or indeed a harassed mother of only small children could be grateful for an older one to help. Older relatives or neighbours living alone were pleased to have company and someone to help with chores and errands, whether on occasional visits or semi-permanently.[72] (Arthur Newton, who used often to stay with a childless aunt at weekends, recalled that 'she became rather possessive toward me, a fact that caused a few words between my parents and them'.)[73]

Extra adults were also incorporated—a grandparent, an aunt or uncle, more distant relatives, even someone without blood ties—for longer or shorter periods. Sometimes their help was needed, perhaps because of many small children,[74] or because of illness. (When the mother of C.H. Rolph was terminally ill with cancer in 1908-9, her sister and mother took turns to stay and look after invalid and family.)[75] Sometimes their contribution to the rent eased the budget or even staved off eviction. Related or not, extra adults were likely to contribute to rent and food; if female they would also, or perhaps instead, provide domestic help. Young women bookfolders in the 1900s often lived with relatives, making 'fixed weekly payments...for board and lodging', which however might be reduced when work was slack or waived when they were out of work. 'Even when being made in full they do not always represent the actual cost of accommodation and living'.[76] Like other female household members, co-resident grandmothers, for instance, they probably gave a hand with chores and child care.[77] Sometimes, too, a child could sleep with an aunt or a grandmother, thus relieving the pressure on beds.

Household members who were technically—to the census-taker or the sociologist—servants, lodgers or visitors,[78] might still be more or less part of the family. They ate with the family, even when paying for their food; and might be helped by them if times were hard.[79]

It was not unusual for a quasi mother-son relationship to develop between young working lodgers and their landladies. In the artisan family described by Thomas Wright in 1867, Mrs Jones had a 'motherly regard' for Charley, the young journeyman who lodged with them: 'as is often the practice of this class with their landladies—he calls her mother; and he strikes her as being like what her first-born boy would have been like had he lived to be three and twenty'. He took Sunday dinner with them, when the presence of other visitors would have been 'an impertinent intrusion'.[80]

Motherly relationships also sometimes followed the kindly act of taking in a homeless young adult. When William Nn's father (born in 1868), was left homeless at sixteen by his mother's death, he slept rough around the docks.[81] Then he was befriended by a postman, whose mother, 'old lady Webb', made him one of the family. ('In later life', wrote William Nn, 'our two families lived and worked together as one.') The pattern was repeated in the next generation, when Mrs Nn took in a homeless fifteen-year-old found by one of her sons. 'While with us he became one of the family, sharing all our poverty, but he was happy because he had found a home.' He stayed with them till he married, and 'visited Mum right up to the time of her death, he thought the world of her'.[82] (The incorporation of young men did have its risks, though: when a Hoxton mother took pity on a young man who 'had a rough home life', and 'let him have a room', he got her daughter pregnant.)[83] Mrs Nn's responsibilities and her family—eight children—might seem already enough, with a poorly paid husband who worked for the East India Company at 24s. a week but sometimes was on half-time for weeks together. But she was always helping 'with food and little bits of clothing' the old couple who rented a room in the same house, and who were called 'Nanny and Grandad Foster' by the children. After 'Grandad' died the old lady scraped a few shillings by doing mangling (on Mrs Nn's mangle) and taking neighbours' parcels to the pawnbrokers. Sometimes, when this was not enough, she went into the workhouse, and then Mrs Nn would somehow find the half-crown to get her out again. When 'Nanny' died in the workhouse and had to have a pauper funeral, Mrs Nn was very upset.[84]

Sometimes households would merge and pool their resources. Short-term doubling up might follow an eviction, for instance: if the evicted family had nowhere to go neighbours took them in at least for a few nights till they found somewhere. George Sims reported such cases:

> Quite recently in a house of four rooms in Foxley Street, Bermondsey, there lived a man, his wife, and ten 'children', the latter ranging from four to twenty-four years in age. Yet, when a case of eviction occurred near them, they took in the three children of a poor woman who was unable to find shelter. The same hospitality I have known extended by a family of eight occupying two rooms.[85]

Desertion or bereavement also sometimes led to doubling up, not always short term. When Mary H.'s mother had been deserted in Liverpool by her seaman father in the 1880s and (after six months in the workhouse with her three small children) set off to London to find him, she and another deserted woman took a room together.[86] And in the very poor dockland district of Ratcliff in 1888 a widow with four children took into her one room 'a newly-made widow with four little ones'.[87] In a case recalled by Arthur Newton (born in Bethnal Green, 1902), Mrs Jaggard, when her brother's wife died, took in the brother and his numerous children: 'they all moved into one house and she reared the lot, with her own husband, brother, brother-in-law, two families of children—something like twelve or thirteen persons'.[88]

Relatives often helped each other in hard times by sharing their homes.[89] The minutes of the London School Board for the mid-1870s provide examples of the possible combinations. Some were joint households of women, where a woman with children but no husband lived with a single woman, often a sister or mother. They might merge their earning power, as washerwomen, for instance, or making matchboxes, folding envelopes, or doing other homework.[90] If a daughter moved in with a father and he was in work, she would share and perhaps supplement his earnings while keeping house for him and any children. (Thus Ellen Hollingrake, in Greenwich in 1873, whose engineer husband had gone to Peru the previous year but had not been heard of since, along with her two children lived with her father, a labouring man. He made 14s.–15s. a week, to which she could add two or three shillings earned by cleaning.)[91] If a daughter moved in with both parents, she might go out to work, leaving any children with the grandmother, or she might help in the house. In other cases second marriages combined 'broken' households. (From today's standpoint the advantage is often questionable, as when the result was a household with two eleven-year-olds, two nine-year-olds, and two seven-year-olds, plus another three offspring of the new marriage.)[92] Or grandparents might be present as dependants, like the blind grandfather in the family of a temporarily unemployed cabman, Edwin Thorpe, in Chelsea in 1875, which also included nine children. (Three, however, were earning, and contributed 18s. a week to the family budget.)[93] Or a child might go to live with a grandparent, to provide help and company.[94] Or sisters and brothers might have joint households, with various arrangements as to finances.[95] This general flexibility resulted from the perpetual insecurity of working-class life.

The variety of domestic arrangements which London children knew was not peculiar to London. People in the rest of the country had similarly flexible answers to the needs of friends and relatives, or to their own problems. In Northampton just before the 1914–18 war, it was found that out of 693 households only thirty-one conformed to the 'so-called "normal family"' of man, wife and three children; and so great was the variety of household forms that there were '330 distinct groupings'.[96] Links between London and the country also led to comparable arrangements, temporary or longterm. London families took in provincial newcomers, related or otherwise connected. Or they sent children who were poorly for visits with relatives, to breathe a bit of country air and regain their colour.[97]

For many children, then 'home' and 'family' were less fixed than in middle-class thinking. Home was wherever they currently lived, and perhaps represented a set of functions and relationships as much as a place. 'Family' included the larger set of relatives and did not necessarily describe the household, which might well have members who were not their immediate family or not family at all. The composition of a family group could change over time, and children did not always stay in the same household.

THE OLD ROOM IN SLUMLAND.

THE NEW ROOM IN A MODEL DWELLING.

5. *An idealized view of the transition from slum to 'model' dwelling: the new housing was not designed for large families, who could only move on to another slum.*

3
Close Quarters

The Housing Problem

RATES OF overcrowding were high both in the old districts, where clearances crammed those who stayed into fewer houses, and in the adjoining districts, which received many of those displaced. As rents rose, people had to pack in ever more closely.[1] In the East End space and air were 'everywhere at a premium', with every open space built over, and even gardens and yards filled in with tenements or workshops.[2] In Stepney and Bethnal Green housing was strained by industrial expansion (for instance by the big breweries) and by the influx of some 4,000 Jewish refugees from eastern Europe. The central and eastern districts of Finsbury, Holborn, St Marylebone, Shoreditch, Whitechapel, Bethnal Green, and St Pancras were those named most often in late nineteenth-century calculations of overcrowding.

Wretched housing was linked with children's poor attendance and poor performance at school by a London School Board inspector, T.M. Williams, in his 1883 report and in letters to *The Times* in 1884.[3] He published supporting calculations on how families of the children on the elementary school schedules for his area were housed—in one room, two or more, with separate figures for each of his district's divisions.[4] Since it took in quarters as diverse as Seven Dials and St Giles or Bloomsbury and Holborn (all very central and crowded) on the one hand, and select Islington neighbourhoods like Canonbury and Barnsbury or new suburbs like Stoke Newington and Tollington Park on the other, his breakdown throws interesting light on the differences (see Table 3.1).

Williams concluded from his data that there were 'at least 60,000 families in London whose houses consist of one room only'.[5] London had 112,388 one-room tenements with more than one occupant, according to the census of 1891, of which over 100,000 had two to six people living in them, and another 1,000 had seven or more.[6] (See Table 3.2.) Children were no doubt present in most.

Williams also argued that children from such homes would mostly attend schools run by the Board rather than voluntary (church) ones.

(This fits with Booth's findings on the greater relative poverty of Board
school children.)[7] As a result, he continued, some schools in his area had
a much higher proportion of children from one-room homes than the
average for their district—60, 70 and 80 per cent rather than 40 or 50.[8]
These children did not come only from really poor families. Pressure on
housing meant that 'the artisan who is not really poor is yet poorly housed;
the labourer who is poor, but not very poor, is yet very poorly housed'.[9] But
if the number of families in one-room tenements does not accurately
reflect poverty, it does provide some measure of how many children lived
'crowded' (two to a room or more).[10] Thousands of London children
undoubtedly grew up in crowded homes.

Table 3.1: Housing and schoolchildren in Finsbury Division, 1884.

District	Number of children	Families living in		
		one room	two	three
St Giles:	5,224	58%	28%	14%
Bloomsbury				
+ Holborn:	7,639	45%	45%	10%
Lower Clerkenwell				
+ St Luke's:	17,746	30%	33%	37%
Upper Clerkenwell				
+ St Luke's:	6,112	7%	38%	55%
Lower Islington:	37,015	10%	40%	50%
Upper Islington:	14,778	12%	39%	49%

Source: T. Marchant Williams, *The Overpressure of Poverty and Drink, and the
School Board for London*, 1884, pp. 4–11.

Table 3.2: One-room tenements and number of
occupants, London 1891 and 1901.

Number of occupants	Number of tenements	
	1891	1901
one	60,114	60,421
two	44,766	48,341
three	29,005	23,680
four	16,111	11,279
five	7,409	4,001
six	2,871	1,257
seven	879	384
eight	231	103
nine	72	39
ten	27	10
eleven	10	3
more	7	6
Total	172,502	149,524

Source: Census figures quoted Booth, *Final Volume*, pp. 4–5.

How was lack of space experienced? Statistics do not tell us what people felt or how they managed. But by combining information from various sources, including oral and written memoirs, we can draw some conclusions: about mobility, for instance, as we have seen; about the use of limited space and its implications for children, and about the relation between family, home and neighbourhood.[11]

Too Little Room

Life in cramped conditions bore hardest on the mother, who was responsible for daily routines relating to child care, meals, washing, cleaning and sleep. (Although children were her auxiliaries in all this, their best contribution was often to take themselves and younger siblings off outside.) The greater her efforts to keep things clean and tidy in a room or rooms that were in constant use, the harder was her burden of work and anxiety.[12] In winter, coal fires meant continual deposits of soot on every surface—'the soft, gentle shower of dirt, which falls, and creeps, and covers, and chokes',[13] and which insinuated itself from outside even when no fire could be afforded indoors. In summer, open windows and the children's comings and goings let in flies and dust along with not-so-fresh air.[14]

The strain was probably worst when the home doubled as workshop. The mother who combined domestic responsibility (caring for the very young or the sick or the old) with earning was always badly paid, whether she did laundry, or sewed shirts, or took in other kinds of outwork. Such work was done only by those with little choice, who were also the poorest, in the worst housing, and had children. The addition of yet another function put still further pressure on their wretched homes. In the washerwoman's home draped 'maidens' (clothes horses) blocked off the fire, festooned washing lines were strung across from wall to wall and the heavy smell of damp clothes was everywhere.[15] Mangling—putting wet washing through a wringer, which allowed a woman to earn at home even if she had no facilities for washing—was less damp and steamy but still took up space. In the home of a Stepney woman described in 1892, 'the mangle half fills the kitchen, while the parlour and the passage from the front door are often blocked with bundles of clothes'.[16]

The homeworker's materials had to be stacked up somewhere, and she probably required at least a table and maybe other surfaces. Pasted paper bags or boxes, or newly painted toys or flowers, dried on strings across the room or spread out on the floor. Where the fur-puller with her blunt knife plucked the long hairs from rabbit skins to prepare them for hatter or furrier, the air was thick with hairs: 'the baby drank in the fluff with its milk, the children ate it with their bread and scrape'.[17] In the artificial-flower maker's and the paper-colourer's rooms, powdered paint dust (sometimes containing arsenic and other poisonous metallic colourings) hung in the air.[18] The brushmaker's family choked on dust from horsehair and bristles; occasionally it gave them anthrax.[19] And the glue used by brush and box-makers and for other homework staples had to be melted for use: it was of bone or fish origin and released as it simmered a pervasive and lingering stink, which in winter combined with fumes from paraffin lamp or open gas-lights to produce an overwhelming foetid fug.[20]

Children joined in the work if they could help, but otherwise were best out of the way. Arthur Harding described the effect of his mother's work making matchboxes when he was a baby and later:

> Our home in Keeve's Buildings was very crowded. The floor being the drying ground for the matchboxes, there was no room to move about. The matchboxes had to be spread out to dry and you could-n't afford to tread on them. I used to be put in a box outside the door, or sent into the street with my sister Mighty. My mother monopolized the table with the paste for the matchboxes...there was no room for you inside....[Then when he was older:] Immediately you got home from school at four o'clock you were naturally a wee bit hungry. But mother would be busy at the table, and the floor was covered with matchboxes. You couldn't go in while the performance was going on, so directly I got in she would say 'Get out'. Sometimes she would chuck me something to eat— she would give me perhaps a couple of slices of bread, put it on a saucer and say 'Go on outside,' and I'd eat it on the street.[21]

Even without the extra problems of homework, mothers often wanted the children out from under their feet. Household work was more easily done without them, and less quickly undone. As Alexander Paterson, Camber-well settlement worker in the 1900s, remarked (though we need not accept his slurs about disorganization and the demoralizing effects of tea):

> Children in large numbers prove a little trying to the unmethodi-cal mother, whose nerves are not fitted by tea and late hours to endure the constant strain of their presence. The rooms are very small, and closely packed with furniture. Crawling infants, grasp-ing at everything with sticky and destructive hands...tumbling up and down the stairs, and crying loudly till smacked into silence, are really found to be rather 'in the way'.[22]

House-proud mothers sent children out, like the 'spotless' mother of Ethel V. (born Whitechapel, 1895). When her children came home from school she would give them a cup of tea then send them out to play 'because she wanted to clean the house or do something with it' and 'couldn't do it while we was there—there wasn't enough room'.[23] Or there might be a sleeping baby or someone sick or a shift-working adult not to be dis-turbed.[24] Or the mother herself might want to get out for some fresh air and space and company.[25]

Space and cost restricted provision of even 'basic' furniture, and increased housekeeping difficulties.[26]

> There are not enough chairs, though too many for the room. There is not enough table space, though too much for the room. There is no wardrobe accommodation other than the hook behind the door, and possibly a chest of drawers which may partly act as a larder.

Some furniture was improvised, with orange and soap boxes used for cupboards, chairs and cradles, or their dismantled planks put up as shelves or recombined in ingeniously. Some pieces served several purposes, or could be folded away when not in use. In the 1850s, Spitalfields weavers made the most of their space (often a single room, workshop as well as home, which held at least one huge loom) by using 'what they call turn-up beds, which form drawers, boxes and tables in the day, and are taken down at night', and by fitting 'a bed under the loom for the children'.[27] Or a truckle bed could be 'rolled under the big bed in the daytime'.[28]

Sleeping arrangements were usually the greatest problem. In extreme poverty people slept on the floor, with old clothes to soften it: descriptions of slum rooms often mention the heaps of rags in them, or sick children lying on rags. Or they had mattresses stuffed with straw or horsehair or flock,[29] on the floor or even on a bedstead.

By the 1890s chair-beds were coming into use in households which could afford them.[30] Arthur Harding recalled how when improving circumstances allowed his family to move (in 1902) from the very rough Gibraltar Buildings into a cottage nearby:

> We got rid of the bloody mattresses...they was alive with vermin...we bought another completely different thing, a chair-bedstead. Completely new...it was the first proper bed we had, before then the children had to sleep on the floor.[31]

Folding beds were used too. In a 1900s Fulham household parents and grandparents slept in one bedroom, children in the other. The eldest child still 'living at home and the last to come in at night...would pull out an iron folding bed and sleep in the kitchen not to wake the others'.[32]

In one-room living, arrangements for the night and in the morning were complicated.[33] The Naylor family, seven of them in one room in Chelsea in the early 1920s, had one 'proper' bed, shared at night by the two elder girls and used for sitting during the day. Then, 'taking up most of the wall opposite the window was an iron contraption of Edwardian vintage...a huge double bed that folded into three sections, secured at the top by an iron hook'. Three more 'bunks' were contrived in the remaining space:

> Our two chairs were tied together for Joey, with the scrubbing board along one side to keep him from falling out. This

contraption was pushed alongside Mum's bed. Joey had a pillow
for his mattress and a little square cushion from the pram for his
head. My bunk was Dad's armchair with the wooden back let down
flat. As I didn't need a mattress, I got a pillow and a blanket and
Mum's outdoor coat on top. Poor old Georgie had the saggy one,
with knitted wire like chain-mail looping its way over the folding
iron frame.

During the day the bedding was stowed away in the big folding bed, so
when they spread the beds they also had to distribute pillows and covers,
and to work on 'the huge dollop of shapeless flock mattress' 'until the
lumps were shared out more or less evenly'. In earlier single-roomed
households, the task of getting ready for the night (with or without folding
beds) must have been comparable. And in the morning the makeshift beds
and pallets had to be folded and somehow put away.

Even when families had more than one room there was rarely enough
space.[34] Rooms still had multiple uses; furniture was insufficient and
crowded; bed-sharing inevitable. As Maud Pember Reeves commented:

> It is difficult to say whether more furniture or less furniture would
> be the better plan in a home consisting of three rooms. Supposing
> the family to consist of eight persons, most people would be inclined
> to prescribe four beds. As a matter of fact, there will probably be
> two. In a double bed in one room will sleep father, mother, baby
> and ex-baby, while in another bed in another room will sleep the
> four elder children. Sometimes the lodger granny will take a child
> into her bed, or the lodger uncle will take a boy into his, but the
> four in a bed arrangement is common enough to need attention.[35]

Nor was it an elastic one: 'in cases of illness it goes on just the same....
Measles and whooping cough just go round the bed as a matter of course.
When a new baby is born, the mother does not get her bed to herself'.[36]

Extra beds required more bedding and expense, and so took up precious space. While children were young, they could pile in together, four
or six to the bed, top and tail. But in a large family, even with several rooms,
beds still sometimes overflowed into the kitchen. Lilian Westall in 1905 was
one of eight children under fourteen who lived with their parents in a
shared terrace house in Kings Cross. They had two bedrooms, and a front
room which was kitchen, living room, and bedroom. 'It held a bed, sofa,
table, half-a-dozen chairs, a wash-stand, [and] an open grate on which my
mother cooked all the meals....'[37] Alexander Paterson observed:

> There is no sharp distinction between what is and what is not a
> bedroom. Where homes are small and families are large, there
> must needs be a bed of some sort in every room. Nearer the sub-
> urbs may be found some parlours that have never known bedding,
> but by the riverside there is not space for such niceties.[38]

Kitchens and parlours were still slept in only if there was absolutely no alternative. Use of the kitchen, the centre of activities, either limited evening
sociability, or postponed bedtime for the bed's occupant(s). In the home
with a parlour, every effort was made to preserve it from daily use and keep
it as a sanctum of respectability and tidiness.[39] With 'a sacred room where
the blinds hang down all day and there are antimacassars', the father 'need
not always have his children with him', and had 'less need for the public-
house'.[40] In the Finsbury Park terrace where C.H. Rolph, a policeman's
son, lived with his family in 1906, every one of the three-storeyed houses
had a 'little-used front parlour'. The back parlour between that and the
kitchen 'was often...used as an extra bedroom': upstairs were three small
bedrooms, but 'there were usually a lot of people to be got into them,
including grannies, lonely aunts, and lodgers'.[41]

Preserving Decorum

By at least the turn of the century many families had rules for all but the
youngest, to protect modesty through separation of the sexes.[42] Washing
was one problem. Bathrooms were rare. Luckier families, with access to a
copper in a scullery, used that, either filling it and heating the water spe-
cially, or re-using the water from the final rinse on wash day.[43] For those in
upstairs lodgings with no water laid on, bath-night meant endless trips by
the mother and older children with jugs, basins or buckets, and the long
business of heating the water in kettles and pans, to fill a galvanized iron
tub in front of the fire.[44] In a mixed family, as the children grew older, there
would be one night for the girls and one for the boys.[45] If the budget
allowed and there was a local public bath, fathers and older children (especially wage-earners) went there for a weekly hot bath. Mothers went
occasionally,[46] but they were reluctant to spend the twopence on themselves.[47] Finding time was a problem, too, even for a bath at home: 'when
the husband and elder children are at home there is no space; when they
are out there is no-one to mind the little ones and answer the door.'[48] The
desire for privacy could be another obstacle, though here attitudes varied,
and it is hard to generalize confidently.

Some women felt strongly about exposing their bodies, even to family:
Mrs Mack's mother, in a poor Hoxton household in the 1900s, 'wouldn't
even wash her feet' in front of the children.[49] In Arthur Harding's very
poor and rough Bethnal Green family, 'many a time when I was a boy my
mother and sister used to wash their selves with practically nothing on 'em.
It was nothing to me'; 'there was a different mentality at that time...there
was no shame'.[50] But his recollection is that it is not specific about age.
Once he was no longer a boy, or when his sister was adolescent and perhaps
shy, there may have been more avoidance and embarrassment. Again, it
may be that his sister was more self-conscious, and secured privacy where

she felt the need (for instance around menstruation), in ways of which he was not aware. In many families dressing and undressing was not to be done in front of the other sex, at least after puberty: 'you couldn't even pull up your stockings without going into the bedroom'.[51]

After they were 'too old'—presumably around puberty—boys and girls were if possible given different bedrooms.[52] If they had to share a bedroom, they would probably be in different beds (though Arthur Harding shared with his older sister till they were both adult), and the room was sometimes divided by an improvised curtain. Grace Foakes (born Wapping, 1908) shared with a sister and three brothers, so her mother 'divided the room with a large clothes horse covered with a sheet, to separate boys from girls'; and similarly in Albert Cullington's childhood (Hackney before the First World War) the bedroom was divided by a rope with a curtain over it.[53] In Tommy Morgan's childhood, spent in a series of one-room homes around Blackfriars in the 1890s, a sheet on a line divided the children and the parents.[54] When James Fulljames (born Camberwell, 1910) grew 'too big to sleep with my sisters in the back room' he was given a little bed in a corner of his parents' room, 'with a sliding curtain on a rail to give it some privacy'.[55] In some cases these separations were taken seriously enough for mother and daughter(s) and father and son(s) to share room or even bed, rather than parents together and mixed adolescent children together.[56] A further reason might be the mother's wish to reduce sexual contact with her husband, perhaps to avoid pregnancy.

Bedtimes

Many children went to bed late. In some cases there was no-one to send them, especially if their mothers went out to work and they had no elder siblings left in charge. Laundry and factory work seldom finished before eight;[57] office-cleaning went on later still.[58] Some children were locked out because their mothers feared fire.[59] In other cases it was easier to keep the baby quiet if older ones stayed out; or no-one cared; or it seemed pointless to insist on a rigid bedtime with a wide-awake child and distracting noises. Or in spite of admonitions they stayed out anyway, either not noticing the time (clocks were scarce), or prepared to risk retribution. Such children had more freedom than adult workhouse inmates: Jack London, investigating the casual ward of Whitechapel workhouse, was kept awake for hours after the obligatory seven o'clock bedtime by 'the voices of children, in shrill outcry, playing in the street...till nearly midnight'.[60] Sometimes, too, it was work that kept them up. If the mother took in outwork they could be helping till late; or if they worked as street sellers they kept going till their stock was sold or there was no-one left to buy. On Saturday, at least, they might go on till past midnight.[61]

It was different in the respectable streets of the new suburbs, at least in winter.[62] Mr C. recalled of his childhood in Bromley-by-Bow:

> In the winter time we wasn't allowed out once you got home. Not in the dark....Summer times we could go out and play till it began to get dark. Then 'all in'. You could hear them calling their kids from all over the place. They knew their cry. They knew their call. And round they'd come dashing....I think all the kids was abed...of a night time eight o'clock in that street. You never 'ear a child after about half past seven or eight of a night. All abed.[63]

Early bed combined what was considered best for the children and what suited the parents: there was little room for play in homes in the working-class suburbs, and harassed mothers and fathers wanted evening peace and quiet.[64] Early bed was also part of respectable culture. It was a practice found where the mother was an ex-servant, where Sunday School, Band of Hope and church or chapel were part of the weekly routine and children had special Sunday clothes, where thrift, regularity, and hard work were admired and practised. It was usual in the families of artisans, shopkeepers, clerks, and the like, but also among poorer people who espoused those values.[65] It was a way to assert respectability when you and your family were striving to maintain standards above those of the neighbourhood, like Mrs Bartle's mother in Poplar, or the Hanrans in a Paddington mews.[66]

In poor neighbourhoods, by contrast, 'they all go to bed late': eleven o'clock was normal, according to evidence presented to the 1902 committee enquiring into children's employment.[67] 'Bedtime is when the public houses close', wrote Mary Tabor. 'The hours before that are the liveliest of the twenty-four, and they swarm about undisturbed until then.'[68] Only round 10.30 or 11 p.m. did the numbers of children fetching beer to take home from a pub near Fitzroy Square in 1897 fall off.[69] In seventeen essays written by Whitechapel boys of ten to fourteen on how they spent Saturday, ten boys identified bedtime: none went before nine, three between nine and ten, four between eleven and twelve, and two later still.[70] (Saturday was the latest night, because of work in late markets, visits to the music hall or other outings, or because the parents stayed out.)[71] The child of an East End vicar envied such freedom:

> Upstairs there was always Nanny's reassuring presence, ready with my supper bowl of sugared bread and milk, and outside the street lamps burning brightly, the shops and public houses lit up as usual, the traffic rumbling by, the children yodelling piercingly to each other from one street corner to the next—lucky children who never seemed to have to go to bed.[72]

For Nanny herself, both as a member of the respectable working class and as overseer of middle-class convention, such children's late hours were no doubt evidence of neglect.[73]

Adults accustomed to households whose children retired early to the
night nursery found such lateness especially shocking. For them adult life
and child life had to be kept distinct, just as rooms had to have specialized
functions. It was not only physically bad for children to go short of sleep, it
was morally wrong for them to keep the same hours as adults and to be
seen out and about after the proper time. Children out late in the street
affronted their sense of social order. This helps to explain the pitch of their
indignation, and the focus on 'parental irresponsibility' to the exclusion of
other possible factors. One writer invoked fears of racial degeneration and
called for a law to protect children's sleep:

> this need of sleep is recklessly ignored: mere babies are taken
> shopping at all hours of the evening, and tiny children are kept up
> late in order that they may sing at Band of Hope concerts. I once
> went at eight o'clock p.m. into a London school to speak to the
> caretaker and was astonished to find the whole place alight and
> alive with children dressed as fairies, and prepared for a concert
> only then about to begin....It would be a blessed thing for children
> if the ancient English laws relating to the Curfew and the early
> putting out of lights were in force today, and such laws would prob-
> ably do their elders no great amount of harm.[74]

Today television and poor parental discipline are blamed for bedtimes 'getting later', with the assumption that it is a new thing for 10 per cent of
ten-year-olds to be 'not even indoors by nine p.m., never mind in bed'.[75]
The supposition is unwittingly based on a practice which is relatively recent
and has never been universal.

Sleeping was difficult in these poor homes. If they did go to bed early
there was noise to contend with, and in a single-roomed family probably
light as well, at least in winter. Women's work often went on late into the
night. The drowsy child was lulled by sounds of continuing adult activity—
washing up, perhaps, or the drone of the sewing machine or the click of
knitting needles, or even the fire being poked or the ashes riddled. The lul-
labies of the washerwoman's child, according to Patricia Malcolmson, were:

> The thonk of the heavy wooden box mangle, the hiss of irons, the
> thwack of the dolly, the slosh of washing, the quiet swish of linen
> on washboards, of scrubbing brushes on heavy fabrics, the splash
> of seeming oceans of water, mingled with muttered curses...[76]

Other sounds were less soporific: coughing if anyone was poorly, a fretful
baby crying, a returning father not sober enough to keep quiet, perhaps
arguments or anxious accounting, comings and goings and talk on the
staircase or in adjoining rooms.[77] Even where the house was quiet, a child
used to daytime involvement in the street world must have found it difficult
not to listen to passing steps and voices, to speculate about who it was and
where they were going, to envy the friends still out there. Sudden noises

outside could jolt sleepers awake. In the rough court where Thomas Wright and his family reluctantly sojourned in the 1860s, night was 'made hideous...by wife-beating, the return home of drunken men and women, occasional midnight flittings, and the incessant barking of a number of dogs chained up...'[78] Even the state of the house could interrupt sleep, for instance when the onset of rain meant buckets were needed beneath a leaky roof. One child was woken by 'a face full of plaster' when the leg of his mother's bed went through a rotted floorboard above.[79]

Shared beds were another problem. Even with beds of their own, children in the same room often keep each other awake. Restless bedmates, or fights over the distribution of space or covers ('half the bed and all the clothes'), made it hard to get off to sleep. Nightmares or bed-wetting disturbed everyone, not just the sufferer. Improvised beds didn't always suit, either. Marie W., a child in Hoxton before the First World War, 'never really got a proper night's rest' on the sofa in the parlour: 'all I was doing was picking myself off the floor where I'd just rolled off', and the black-beetles which infested the room also kept her awake.[80]

In summer the bed-bugs, endemic in poor districts, bothered everyone.[81] Despite preliminary bug-hunts, more always emerged to inflict their silent attack, and the victims woke, itching and burning, and continued the hunt—'in the summer it was murder', 'didn't have any sleep, we used to be up all night. You couldn't sleep'.[82] Bill Jones (born in Hoxton in 1900) recalls the hazards of this sleepy pursuit:[83]

> the house was full of bugs, which—in spite of all the desperate attempts to keep them down with candle flames and disinfectant— seemed to grow bigger and bigger. It was a nightly occupation for my brothers and me, awakened by bites, to chase the bastards up the wall. During one of these nightly excursions I almost managed to burn my brother Dave to death; he lay on water bags in the hospital for weeks.

In hot weather some people slept outside to escape them, on balconies or in courtyards or even on the street pavements, on beds of newspaper. (This still happened in the 1920s, as Fred Davey recalled from his childhood in the very rough Waxwell Terrace, Waterloo.)[84]

After late and disturbed nights early mornings were caused by others setting off for work, the fire being raked out and lit, street sounds, or children's own early responsibilities, for lighting the fire or getting breakfast, going on errands or doing jobs.[85] On Sundays, however, all was quiet and the roads deserted, 'save for the few who hurry to church' and the occasional paper boy or milkman.[86]

'Late to bed and early to rise is unfortunately becoming the rule', thought Medical Officer of Health, George Newman.[87] The eugenist researcher Alice Ravenhill agreed, and concluded her report on the hours of sleep enjoyed by children in town and country by proposing three steps:

a public campaign 'to bring the subject in all its seriousness before the parents and guardians of child life in this country' and to promote 'more intelligent methods of child rearing'; 'improvement of the housing of the people'; and 'strict enforcement of the law relating to the employment of child labour'. 'To regulate the clock of child life' was 'a great undertaking' but its object, 'namely the welfare and nervous stability of the nation', deserved 'sustained and untiring efforts'.[88] The conditions of daily life in poor and overcrowded homes and the need of the children's contribution were placed in a context of national efficiency, with little compassion or understanding and much moralizing. This is a shift of emphasis from that in an 1890s pamphlet published by the Society for the Propagation of Christian Knowledge, where mothers were advised 'to put your young children to bed at a fixed time every evening; this will give you rest and quiet as well as being good for them'; moreover, 'husbands would sometimes prefer staying at home in the evening if their homes were quiet and tidy, and free from soap-suds and tired fretful children'.[89] From a closer perspective, the settlement worker Reginald Bray wrote anxiously of the irritability and excitability of the children of the poor. Lack of sleep, which he does not mention, presumably contributed to the state he describes.

> When a number of people inhabit a few rooms peace and order take wing, leaving behind a ceaseless babel of noise. With boys and girls varying in age, from the baby to the child about to leave school, and indulging in their respective amusements, nothing else is possible. From lack of calming influences there is a constant strain on the nerves which renders those living in this way highly irritable, and the child develops a highly strung, excitable nature.[90]

It is hard, in the 1990s, to decide how far to trust such judgements. Most people expect and often have a relatively large ration of space and the opportunity for privacy and perhaps quiet. So we easily accept the assumption that living hugger-mugger without space or quiet or privacy must result in strain and irritability. We see bed-sharing as a problem, except when it is chosen by a couple, for we associate it only with sex. But when expectations are different, so too is experience.

Old people remember the comfort of shared warmth,[91] or how funny it was when the bed collapsed, or how lonely it was to be in a bed on your own for the first time.[92] Their enduring loyalty and affection for the brothers and sisters with whom they shared cramped quarters, and the warmth of their recollections of family life (and of those members not born into it), are often remarkable. Nor is this simple nostalgia or whitewashing. They do not forget hunger, cold, shabbiness and the rest. But other memories—of family and friends, of games and work, of things that happened to them, sometimes of school—matter more. Contemporary observations also suggest a fear of being alone and a pleasure in company which, whether adaptation or cause, must have made the crowded homes more tolerable.[93]

These overcrowded homes, with their minimal facilities for the ordinary processes of daily life and minimal space for their multiple functions, were not conducive to the domestic scenes envisaged in the dominant ideology as essential to family life. They did nevertheless provide a focal point for the family, even if its members (except perhaps the mother) spent a good deal of their time away from them, and even if the location of the home often changed.

It is not safe to infer from overcrowding that family relationships were warped or diminished. On the other hand they were probably affected. The role of the mother in the family may well have been strengthened by the temporary and inadequate nature of the home. Probably, too, children's earlier independence was reinforced both by their involvement in domestic responsibilities (it was hard to keep them completely ignorant of 'adult' concerns such as money and work) and by the time they spent off on their own.

Neighbours

During the day one way to reduce the strains of overcrowding was to turn the children out into the street, where they had plenty to occupy them and were out of the way.[94]

The friendliness of working-class children was remarked on as 'evidence that the poor use their children well and...that this treatment is extended to the children of others', for 'experience has taught them to anticipate kindness at the hands of all they meet'.[95] Children were used to care and supervision from people outside their immediate families. They would also know a good many people by sight and by name—those in the same building or court, and most of those in the same street or block, and some further off again. Their behaviour was partly shaped by awareness of the standing and expectations of everyone (child and adult) in the immediate neighbourhood, and of how they were likely to react. So from an early age they commonly possessed 'the child's acute perception of all that happens in his neighbourhood, that queer assortment of fragments of knowledge about events and peoples which is ready to overflow in a ceaseless stream of words'.[96] Their world extended well beyond the walls of their own small home.

Adult supervision had an informal, collective quality.[97] In street or court, 'mothers looked on as they idled at their doors'; in model dwellings the balconies were 'seldom without groups of gossiping women'.[98] Whoever was at hand—passing by, looking out the window, talking at the door, sitting out on doorstep or pavement chair while knitting or sewing or preparing vegetables—administered comfort, threats or scolding as required, no matter whose the children. They watched for children's safety, too: when a Waterloo woman one evening in 1901 saw a stranger pick up

a local six-year-old out on an errand, she called '"haven't you got your butter yet, Mary?"' and the man threw the child down 'damn quick and away
he run'.[99] Many children's pleasures were hazardous, and passing adults
cautioned them and kept watch when they could.[100] One dangerous sport
was swimming: boys dived and swam in canal, river and lake, wherever they
could reach water, which often also involved evading police and other
adults.[101] Mr N. and his friends in Wapping played on the river steps, and
'the old rowboat watermen used to keep their eyes on us...in case the tide
turned and took us away'. (Once he was swept away all the same, but swam
and landed further down stream.)[102]

    Formally as well, child care was often shared by neighbours, especially
when mothers were ill or working and had only little children, with no
older one to put in charge, and no nearby relatives to help out. A wide variety of arrangements existed. To take children for a few hours or overnight
during their mother's confinement was one common favour. Mrs Bartle
(born in Poplar in 1882) remembered that:

> When any poor woman had a new baby all the kids had to turn out
> of the bedroom while she had the baby....P'raps a neighbour
> would take these poor little kids in and keep them till the con-
> finement was all over, and then they'd all go back again. I
> remember distinctly one morning going to school and a little
> school girl said to me, 'My mother had a baby last night—my
> mother's got a new baby. And we all went out—we went up to Mrs
> So-and-so's, and we had tea and bread and butter in the night, all
> night, we had tea and bread and butter'. They thought that was
> wonderful.[103]

Even where relations with neighbours were relatively distant, this kind of
help was available in times of crisis. Grace Foakes's stern and moody father
discouraged any social relationships; yet when her mother was in labour
Grace was sent to fetch a neighbour; and later, when her mother went into
hospital to have a tumour removed, 'offers were made for each of us [the
five children] to stay with a different neighbour'.[104] Daily child-minding,
especially of babies, was also sometimes provided by neighbours. For a regular commitment payment was expected, unless the mothers were
particularly good friends or had some understanding by which the favour
could be returned. (See Chapters 5 and 6.)

    Just as responsibility for children spilled out beyond the family and
house, so other aspects of domestic life involved frequent or occasional
mutual help which continually blurred the distinctions between immediate
family, non-resident relations, and friends or neighbours. 'Friends', as in
earlier days, could overlap with family, and the many references in case-his-
tories of poverty to 'assistance from friends' probably meant both relatives
and friends. Certainly, neighbours were sometimes relatives.[105] In Katherine
Buildings, for instance, a model block near Tower Bridge, in 1885–9 'about

thirteen per cent of the adult women and six per cent of the adult men had kin living in the buildings'.[106] In a settled neighbourhood, ties of blood or marriage could link almost everyone in the street.[107] With new arrivals, common origin extended the web of obligation beyond neighbours and kin. Irish migrants helped each other, for example.

> Irish neighbours contributed money for funeral expenses, if the dead person's kin could not raise enough. Neighbours loaned money and kitchen utensils, helped orphans to find jobs and lodging, attended wakes and weddings. Newcomers were given a corner of a room in which to sleep and helped in their search for work.[108]

Membership of a minority religious or political group had the same effect.

Neighbourly help overlapped with the obligations of kinship and other ties, but it did not depend upon them. It was probably easier to ask help of an unrelated neighbour—someone you saw constantly and were on good terms with—than of a relation, even a close one, whom you seldom saw or had fallen out with.[109] Perhaps most important was that help from neighbours could be reciprocated, and therefore was easiest to ask for and to accept. In the early 1870s a report on Poor Law administration commented on the practice of collections made to help widows, by neighbours or at the dead man's workplace, and continued:

> Indeed...what amounts to interchange of charitable assistance among the poor in London is not uncommon...they assist each other to an extent which is little understood, and for which they receive little credit. It is scarcely possible to conceive a form of charity which combines so completely its highest reciprocal benefits, with the absence of the mischief so frequently incident to almsgiving.[110]

This kind of help was not almsgiving and could be accepted without shame, because it was part of a network of reciprocal favours, given and received amongst people who were aware that on another occasion positions might be reversed. But the reciprocity was generalized: time and labour were not carefully accounted. You helped (if you could) because it was the right thing to do, and in the hope that support would be forthcoming whenever you in turn might need it.

> As long as one person has anything to share, they are willing to share it. Hungry children are given meals, simple and rough it may be, but the starving can always secure help from neighbours in distress, for the poorest never know when their turn to starve may not come.[111]

The sense of obligation could also override previous hostility: a district nurse visiting a Hammersmith woman with heart disease, in 1892, found that the washerwoman next door had sat up all night supporting her so that she could breathe, though for several years 'their only conversation had been unprintable abuse from their respective back doors'.[112]

Such help was short-term, to tide people over until things improved and it was no longer needed, or until 'a better arrangement could be formed'.[113] If, instead, the crisis proved chronic, the support of 'friends' would be insufficient and major change inevitable: children farmed out, an invalid taken to hospital, an old person, or at worst even the whole family, admitted into the workhouse.[114] Joy Parr's research on the children in Barnardo's orphanages shows that typically admission followed not from a single crisis in their immediate family, but from a series ('deaths, illnesses, quarrels and lost jobs'), producing 'a breakdown in the kin tradition of mutual help'.[115] Neighbours' help also—and perhaps sooner—had its limits.

Adult access to neighbourhood support varied with the neighbourhood and with the family's local history and standing.[116] A quarrelsome woman might find herself cut off from the women's network through which news of need and mutual help were disseminated. A drunken or gambling man would find it harder to borrow money in an emergency.

But children's need, once known, evoked immediate response in a variety of forms. The annals of the dockland Ratcliff Crèche provide one example of collective support: twelve women working in a bottle warehouse in 1882 supplied between them two shillings a week so that the two children of a friend and workmate could sleep and be cared for at the Crèche while she served a six-week gaol sentence for fighting.[117] Bowls of soup or stew were often supplied by neighbours, especially for children, if they knew a family was in difficulties.[118] M. Loane, district nurse of long experience, dismissing the common argument that prosecution of wife-beating men would deprive the family of support, observed that in fact such children were 'kept alive by the labour of the mother and the charity of the neighbours', both of which would operate as well or better during the husband's enforced absence.[119] Women also colluded to avoid trouble from husbands, hiding children or each other when violence threatened.[120] According to one unusually open memoir, men arriving home drunk would sometimes 'attempt to molest their daughters'.

> Before the wives of these drunken men would open the door they took the precaution of locking their daughters in the room. If they had no room with a lock and key they would pass the girls over the back walls for the neighbours to look after them until the husband had slept it off.[121]

Sometimes an anxious neighbour put children's welfare before deference to parental 'rights' or territory: a woman in 1890 was so concerned at the way a neighbour left her baby alone and hungry all day that she regularly went in and suckled it, to be abused by the mother later on for interfering.[122] In other cases the mother was only too grateful for neighbourly help, as Mary P., who was born in Hackney in 1903, recalled:

And mother used to say to me, 'Poor Mrs Somebody next door.
She's got no food in the house'. So mother used to have a good
old nourishing stew, and she used to cook it in a big saucepan with
a handle both sides. And I was the one to take it in to Mrs
Somebody next door. And she'd say 'Oh, thank you ever so much!'
and she used to feed the kids. And one day mother never had
enough for her neighbour. And four o'clock came and she
knocked on my mother's door and she said 'Do you think you
could give me some food?' She says, 'The children have got nothing,' and Mother felt so ashamed, she said she would buy sufficient
in future for the person next door. You didn't count the cost, you
just did this....This is how the poor would help the poor.[123]

The mother of Mrs Bartle (born in Poplar in 1882), on the other hand,
always keen to distinguish herself from the rest of the street in general and
her feckless drunken neighbours in particular, refused this sense of obligation; according to her daughter she 'wasn't well off enough to help
anybody anyway'.[124]

'Borrowing', also normal, was different. Its conditions were understood: the woman who borrowed too often without paying back risked
having requests refused, at least when they were a question of convenience
rather than emergency. Clothes were borrowed—a clean apron when
respectability needed to be asserted, a crepe hat or gloves for a funeral,[125]
baby clothes, or even a bed. (Mrs C., another Hackney woman, remembered a neighbour telling her mother, 'I'll lend you my bed and you can
have your baby in it'.)[126] Requests for the loan of small quantities of food—
a pinch of tea or sugar—were most common of all.

When a woman was 'confined' (in childbed) or sick, neighbours did
washing and shopping, minded her little ones, and sent round food.[127]
They took turns sitting up with an invalid in need of constant care, or kept
each other company then or in watching a corpse.[128] In the same spirit of
kinship or neighbourly help, as we have seen, households took in extra
members or even combined forces.

Children's experience of household and neighbourhood, especially
among the very poor, was often then a fluid one. The boundaries of the
household were relatively permeable. Neighbours in the same house or
street sometimes shared responsibilities and resources. A child, or an old
person, might sleep in one house and eat in another. The willingness to
integrate children and young people into other households can be partly
explained by the young age at which they started to be useful—from at least
the age of five or six. (See Chapter 10.) Pity and maybe affection for the
particular children, and friendship for the mother, were also likely to have
an influence. And, finally, there was a general sense that institutional care
was a last resort and that responsibility for children extended beyond the
family and concerned neighbours as well as parents.

6. East End boys enjoying a battered 'horse' tricycle, no doubt rescued after rejection by its previous owner.

4
Beyond Four Walls

———◄◆►———

'The Streets Were All Alive'¹

INDOORS, OBSERVED Maud Pember Reeves of poor homes in Kennington, there were 'no amusements...no books and no games, nor any place to play the games should they exist'. This may be an overstatement, but her comment that 'wet holidays mean quarrelling and mischief and distracted mothers' rings true;² and homes did, as we have seen, serve many functions without proper space for any of them.

There was in fact some playing inside homes, and some children used to visit each other to play. (Medical Officers of Health blamed this for helping to spread epidemics.)³ If there were no books and no 'games' of the bought variety, such as snakes and ladders, games could still be played. Some street games—like those played with cherry 'oggs (cherry stones), cigarette cards, five-stones or knucklebones, marbles, even—could be played inside too. An 1890 painting shows children playing 'Oranges and Lemons' in a rather sparely furnished room.⁴ Games of imagination could be played anywhere. In 'Ghost in the Copper' the 'mother' 'washed' at a 'tub' made by a chair; and other chairs across a corner made the 'copper', behind which the child playing ghost hid ready to scare the 'child' helping with the wash.⁵ Or chairs and tables might become ships, trains or market stalls. Sometimes it was best to find somewhere out of the way, like the 'ideal retreat' recalled by James Fulljames: under a big square table 'covered with a heavy cloth that hung down almost to the floor'.

> Many an intrepid jungle explorer crouched beneath its shade, waiting with cap-loaded gun to blast the head off a fierce marauding tiger or a pouncing lion. Tiny night-gowned mums had scolded whole families of dolls beneath its solid top before being routed out...and hustled off to bed.⁶

Even where household circumstances and a tolerant mother did sometimes allow of indoor play, children soon learnt that they were freer outside and preferred to get out. In bad weather, or if required to stay within earshot, they played on landings, stairs, and balconies, in hallways and passages.⁷ In

East End tenement blocks, a visiting nurse observed, 'the children all play on the stairs, so it is easy to make friends with them'.[8] Because there was no room indoors, Mrs C. (born Bermondsey, 1893), recalled:

> we used to get on the stairs in one another's places. Get up there say, with dolls' clothes and all that sort of thing...plait one another's hair.[9]

The pull of outdoors was always strong, and street and court in poor neighbourhoods were exciting. Many children spent most of their time there, with home merely as base.

> Swarming up and down the doorsteps or camping out in the roadway, are countless numbers of puny, dirty children....They live in the roadway; it is quite safe from accidents, for there is no traffic; nobody thinks of passing through...wet or dry, hot or cold, the children swarm up and down, eat and drink, play and even sleep, from each morning to late at night...[10]

The street offered a range of pleasures: the company of other children and all the regular street games, for example.[11] Smooth paving stones or asphalt were good for marbles and 'buttons' or hopscotch; walls were used for ball games and for chalked cricket stumps and goal-posts; with some road surfaces you could even drive in cricket stumps.[12] If you could get a length of rope,[13] you could fix swings from lamp-post to railing, or skip, or from the lamp-post bar twist two ropes tightly together and play 'string-twist-'em', clinging dangerously as the ropes untwined.[14] Even bad weather brought possibilities: sailing improvised boats in the rainwater flow, or when it was icy making slides,[15] or endless games with mud, like those observed by Norman Douglass in the years before the First World War:

> Of mud you make PIES, and BRIDGES, and STICKING BRICKS (against a wall), and MUD-CARTS (played with a tin-can), and WELLS, and TUNNELS, and FLOWER POTS, and CASTLES—in fact anything you please. There's nothing like mud, when all is said and done, and it's a perfect shame there isn't more mud about, nowadays; or sand, at least. You should see them go for it, when the streets are up.[16]

In summer hot children (the boys often naked) cooled off in the spray of the water carts which sprinkled roads to lay the dust, 'dancing and shrieking happily', sometimes with 'a mother walking indulgently by the side of the cart and carrying dry clothes and a towel'.[17]

Streets were busy with the comings and goings of neighbours and the passing of street vendors and performers (especially in the evening or at the weekend). There was competition for street space:

> a football descends, like a bombshell, on a group of girls intent on the thrilling amusement of hopscotch, and tiresome pedestrians ruthlessly break into the most exciting skipping exhibition...[18]

Horse-drawn traffic meant something untoward could always happen—a runaway horse, an overturned van, a collision, a stubborn donkey exasperating its master, or a row between drivers. Braving the driver's whip if he caught sight of them, children used 'to run behind the carts and to hang on to the tail-board or slide along', or be towed on roller skates.[19] They 'sprang in hordes, apparently from the pavements, whenever anything in the least out of the ordinary occurred.'[20] Street music from barrel organ or hurdy-gurdy would bring them to dance. 'Sometimes a gang of navvies...would commence a free show for the populace', lifting and striking in rhythmic pattern to break up concrete with their fourteen-pound hammers.[21] Children watched fascinated as the steam roller 'ground all the small granite pieces to a flat surface that made a metal road surface'.[22] Or a fire engine thundering past, 'a kind of pied piper', summoned 'from every side street...an unresisting troop of delirious children to add their shrill voices to the general roar, and their small persons to the hurrying crowd'.[23] Saturday night was still more exciting. Fights were more likely;[24] and drunks declaimed or quarrelled ('we had our favourite drunks'),[25] and if violent might be carried off by the police strapped to a special barrow 'to the delight of all the boys following along hoping the fellow would burst his straps and put up a fight'.[26] In quieter streets and courts even the passing of a stranger was an event, evoking comment and speculation at least, or perhaps jeers, or attempts to wheedle alms or to earn a tip by guiding or other help.

If you could not be down there, the street still provided entertainment. Eileen Baillie, in her nursery in a Poplar vicarage, knelt on a chair at the window,

> and there, for all my waking hours, was my theatre, puppet show and pantomime in one. From breakfast-time until winter dusk when the curtains were drawn, or the reluctant bedtime of the long, light summer evenings, there was always something to be watched...[27]

She was excluded from street play by her class, but though lonely was 'never dull for long, with such an outlook'.

For the alert and enterprising the street was full of opportunity. You could earn the odd copper; grab coal fallen from a delivery cart (indeed perhaps encourage it to fall); collect broken boxes for fuel; or pick out 'specked' fruit and vegetables rejected by the seller but still edible. Rejected fruit at wholesale markets was a staple for the 'children of the gutter', according to a lurid account by Greenwood:

> they will gather about a muck heap and gobble up plums, a sweltering mass of decay, and oranges and apples that have quite lost their original shape and colour, with the avidity of ducks or pigs.[28]

The materials for games and constructions were largely found: cherry stones, for instance, were collected in the wake of cherry-eaters then used as missiles in a miniature game of skittles played with a two or three-inch screw stood on end; the 'first contestant to knock down the screw would take all the stones on the ground'.[29] Other games used shells or tins from the rubbish (often salmon cans), bones, bits of broken china, or stone which would chalk. As settlement-worker Alexander Paterson explained:

> The London child has not far to look before he espies a likely play-thing. A couple of milk-tins and a piece of string, or a fish-bone and a nail will suffice. All the impossible combinations left by the street cleaner are at his service.[30]

Carts and toboggans were made from soap-boxes and the wheels of old prams, or 'a rusty old tea-tray' drawn along by a string.[31] Kites were produced from torn-up newspaper and string, balls from scrumpled newspaper bound with string, or sawdust or even a stone bound up in rag: none of the materials were bought. So foraging and improvization ('*bricolage*') was an important part of children's street life, and the basis of their cultural economy.

Many entertainments and activities, especially for girls, had to be compatible with child care. Toddlers were plonked on step and kerb to watch or play, or pulled into a ring game. Babies were carried, their interminable weight only partly taken by the shawl wrapped around nurse and charge and pinned in place. Or a home-made pram (usually a soap-box on wheels), or simply a box, held one or more babies while their young elders were busy.

Those who were not thus shackled—more of them boys—ventured farther off. Anything might happen, as in the critical but vivid description of the 'aimless wandering of a child down the street' by Camberwell settlement worker, Reginald Bray:

> He is dodging now this vehicle and now that; he is halting now to gather up dusty treasures from a coster's barrow providentially upset, now to watch a herd of bullocks swept into the slaughter-house; here he is pressing urgently into the heart of a drunken quarrel, there he is flying from some shopkeeper whose wrath his pleasing amenities have aroused; at one moment he is clambering up a lamp-post, at another he is pouring the vials of his contempt on a stranger whose innocent appearance suggests an impotence to harm; here walking, here running, here idling, now laughing, now crying, now shouting, he drifts in gentle aimlessness down the roadway.[32]

As children grew older they ranged farther, exploring, foraging, avoiding adult oversight by distancing themselves from the immediate locality of home. On the fringes of the city there were orchards, fields, woods, commons, marshes and wasteland to explore and raid. Some remained even as

the city expanded: the extension of the East End left the Lea Valley relatively undeveloped and its marshes and streams drew children from both
sides, while the survival of Epping Forest provided a huge and exciting
resource for those within reach.[33]

In the congested central districts open spaces were fewer, and of a different kind. From the 1860s increasing efforts were made to create space
for children to play. Reformers like Octavia Hill (directly and through the
Kyrle Society) and the Barnetts of Whitechapel campaigned for playgrounds in their efforts to regenerate poor neighbourhoods.[34] In the City,
the gardens of the Temple were opened to 'small fry' for a while each day
in 1870, and the *Pall Mall Gazette* appealed for similar concessions at
Lincoln's Inn and Gray's Inn, for 'the health of the children who come
hither from crowded courts and alleys'.[35] Some central churchyards were
opened for play; there were swings by the turn of the century in 'Itchy
Park' (the former graveyard of Christchurch, Spitalfields); and most districts had small playgrounds and recreation spaces.[36] Lambeth Palace
Meadows were opened between May and September for children with tickets given out by the local clergy.[37]

Poor quarters were short of parks. As Bray remarked in 1901, 'vast
tracts...in both North and South-East London' were 'so far from any parks
that the child has to journey more than a mile to reach them'.[38] But such
expeditions were often undertaken. Children made their way to Victoria
Park, South Hackney (in use from 1845) even when they could not afford
a tram fare either way and were trailing tired younger ones or pushing a
laden pram. From Whitechapel it was about four miles there and back: 'a
fair walk, but it was worth it'.[39] Victoria Park offered wide expanses of grass
to run and play, cricket, bands, open-air speakers and a lake with swimming
and boating.[40] Even a small patch of 'park' with forbidden grass could also
give much pleasure, as Grace Foakes recalled of the little park in Wapping
where she and her sister used to 'spend all morning running and dancing
about in bare feet', savouring 'the feeling of bare feet on warm asphalt'
even as they longed for grass.[41]

Parks and playgrounds had their disadvantages, however, especially for
poor children. Some playgrounds separated girls and boys,[42] and all were
dangerous for truants, as school attendance officers checked them.[43] An
1890s attempt to open school playgrounds for children's use on Saturdays
was only partly successful, whether because of associations with school and
the presence of the caretaker, or because the street held more attractions.[44]
Parks were not ideal either:

> For one thing, the keeper is always coming up in the park and
> interfering; next, they can't find kerbs and paving stones there;
> next, it makes them wild to see other boys with bats and things,
> when they have none.[45]

So the freedom of the street was often preferred: 'the Park belonged to the

Park Keeper, the street to the Children, and not only their street, but every street'.[46]

Other play spaces were found by wandering children, even in densely occupied districts. They invaded work sites, like a Kentish Town mews timber-yard where they improvised see-saws.[47] Or they slipped into unconverted graveyards, like that of St John's Church, Hackney, where in the 1890s Walter Southgate and his friends played hide-and-seek among the gravestones.[48] They overran temporary waste sites where older buildings or other uses were giving way to new development. When a circus and menagerie vacated some empty land in Dalston, in 1898, children took it over. (Ten of them, aged three to ten, contracted typhus, perhaps from ticks left by the menagerie.)[49] Empty houses drew them, too; and children left their mark on them. Clara Grant recalled of Poplar at the turn of the century how hoardings and palings gave scope for budding artists, and how condemned houses would 'display an extraordinary being and the warning "Do not enter. Ghost will appear. This is the ghost."'[50]

Everywhere there were corners to which children laid claim. On hot days they congregated near drinking fountains.[51] After dark they gathered outside pubs, where 'the lights are bright, the pavement is carefully mended and smoother for marbles and other games', and under lamp-posts.[52] Ethel V. (born 1895) and her friends used to play on the stairs of the old Bishopsgate station, where they could watch the trains, or else nearer home in the courtyard between the blocks of the 'model dwellings' built by philanthropic housing trusts to shelter the poor.[53] In Westminster, a statue of Queen Anne standing 'in a very dilapidated condition' in Queen Anne's Gate was incorporated into a game:

> the children of the locality...were accustomed...to call upon the statue, by the name of Bloody Queen Mary, to descend from its pedestal, and on receiving, naturally, no response, to assail it with missiles.[54]

When pedestrian subways were opened to help people across the busy roads which converged at Elephant and Castle, they became a 'playground for riotous hordes of children' who 'came from all parts of the district'.[55]

Some children ranged quite widely. Even the well-brought-up Leah Manning 'had a compulsive habit of wandering', and would follow 'circuses, German bands, organ grinders with their monkeys, above all funerals'. (She lived near Abney Park cemetery, Stoke Newington.) Once, she followed an organ grinder 'away from our nice respectable neighbourhood and into the jungle of little back streets, where children played all day on the pavement', and took off her boots to dance with the little girls 'whirling madly in the road, tattered petticoats and tangled curls flying joyously'. The boots were gone when the music stopped.[56]

Rough and Respectable

In the neighbourhood, and even beyond, adults exercised authority over children who were not theirs, and could ask them for services such as running an errand. Their right was not absolute, however. The little reward (a sweet, a slice of bread or a coin) often given to a child who ran an errand suggests recognition of a favour rather than exertion of a right; while discipline could lead to rows between adults if later deemed unjustified or excessive.[57] It was safer to report (or threaten to report) any offence to a parent.

Adult authority, generalized outside the family to varying degrees, enforced standards of behaviour. Some communities had tighter networks than others, and clearer rules; some laid more stress than others on how children should or should not behave; and expectations would be more easily enforced in some (the more settled or homogeneous) than in others.[58] There were always people, too, even in relatively stable communities, who were outside the local networks, who (like Mrs Bartle's mother) held themselves aloof or who broke with local convention and were excluded.[59] It took time for recent arrivals, whether country people or people from other countries, to adjust or to be accepted, and some were more readily accepted than others. Difference of religion or origin kept some apart, whether by their own choice or through local rejection; so did family pride, or teetotalism, or, conversely, rougher ways than were locally approved. In districts with a wide cultural range a general adult consensus was unlikely, which increased the risk of friction. Generally speaking, adults expected recognition of their authority at least from children whose parents were linked to them by friendship, work, kinship, or co-residence.

Adult concern or intervention justified itself as enforcing 'proper' behaviour. 'Taking no notice' of an adult request (for quiet, for instance, or for help or respect) was one offence which infringed the proper relation between child and adult, and 'running wild' could be another. The limits were different for boys and for girls. Mrs Jones (born 1903), as a young tomboy in Poplar, fell foul of local assumptions. The neighbour who told her father how his daughter had been towed up the road on roller skates by eight boys rightly expected the father to find that unacceptable. (When he took her skates away, though, the boys clubbed together for another pair and took turns to keep them overnight for her.)[60]

Definitions of propriety were particular as well as collective. The family's cultural identity, in interaction with their economic situation, affected such varying aspects of children's experience as how much and when they were kept at home or allowed out, how young they started work and what at, who held how much authority, and the degree of difference made between boys and girls.[61] The variations of cultural identity are endless and their origins hard to pin down. They were influenced, for instance, by where the parents came from, how old they were, their own experiences, whether and how they were religious, what social groups they belonged in, and their relations with neighbours and workmates. A father who had been a soldier was likely to expect a more disciplined, timetabled and hierarchical family than one whose employment varied with season and opportunity. A mother who had been in domestic service would want household tasks done the 'proper' way, and have clear ideas about how the family should dress and behave, individually and as a group. Those who had been brought up to religious observance (especially chapel) were stricter about Sunday behaviour, even if they no longer attended any service.

All this may be summed up in the key word respectability. In the late nineteenth century this came increasingly (and sometimes contradictorily) to embody aspirations and concerns both about self-respect and about self-presentation.[62] It implied some acceptance of bourgeois ways, even if reshaped to fit the possibilities of working-class life.[63] At the same time, it retained earlier overtones of artisan independence.

Everyone knew the difference between 'rough' and 'respectable', but since the boundaries were not fixed they could be subjectively interpreted. Almost no-one saw themselves as not respectable.[64] The factory girl whose bold and gaudy style made domestic servants look down on her as rough, saw herself as respectable so long as she observed the conventions of her group; other distinctions were probably more important to her.[65] Self-respect survived unscathed when the 'self-improving artisan' lapsed into 'the time-honoured role of the English workman on a spree' during a carefully planned excursion with his wife; and a respectable married woman could get away with occasional (though not regular) intemperance.[66] Nor would the married woman who went out to work agree that her respectability was thereby compromised, despite the indispensability of the housekeeping and dependent wife for the ideal respectable family. For some women pawning was shameful; and in middle-class perceptions the pawn shop stood 'next door to the public house and over the way to gaol'.[67] But it was not confined to the poor and desperate: housewives who could afford it made purchases in good times with an eye to their pledgeable value, and used pawning to tide them over slack periods.[68] Letting children work for money or accept free meals, finally, was unthinkable for some, however poor, and for others a perfectly acceptable adaptation to hard times which in no way compromised their respectability.

So although the rough-respectable dichotomy was widely recognized, the distinctions are not simple. First, the terms were used to describe both behaviour and identity. Second, they concerned both subjective identity—how people saw themselves, which overlaps with self-respect; and social identity—how they were placed by other people, whether neighbours and equals, or charity workers, teachers, pawnbrokers and others with power over them.[69] Observed behaviour, that is, was used to define others as respectable or rough. But someone with a strong sense of self-respect could engage in non-respectable behaviour without jeopardizing their subjective respectability, as in the examples above. Third, definitions were disputed and shifting; they lay on a spectrum rather than being opposite sides of a coin. Class entered into the dispute, as when a respectable cook's traditional appropriation of kitchen surplus ('perquisites') was called theft by her employer;[70] and respectable behaviour was sometimes adopted to impress social superiors and seem 'deserving'.[71] The respectable role, as Peter Bailey points out, was 'assumed or discarded as easily as the collar which [for men] was its symbolic accessory'.[72] Finally, the labels did not tidily match economic or social status.[73] 'Rough' ways were often part of a plebeian culture to which artisans and shopkeepers might well belong unless claimed by chapel and temperance;[74] while low wages and misfortune did not erase the desire for respectability, even though they made its conventions harder to observe.

Children were much affected by respectability. They soon learnt the distinction between rough and respectable, both to place others but still more because they were caught up in the identity and image of their own family: respectability was 'a family enterprise'.[75] It required display, whether of property (clothes—especially Sunday best, a parlour and its furnishings, pictures and ornaments) or of ritual and behaviour (the family meal, going to church or chapel, the Sunday excursion or walk). A home-cooked Sunday dinner, for Charlie Chaplin, 'meant respectability, a ritual that distinguished one poor class from another'.[76] (This conviction was strengthened by the contrast between his own precarious family life and the comfortable routines of more prosperous relatives.) Children's clothes and conduct signalled the family's financial standing and, still more important, the efforts of the mother. Women, as Ellen Ross argues, 'embodied respectability, or the lack of it'.[77] The assertion of respectability through domestic competence took on a special importance for the married woman who did not go out to work. Her pride in home and family, and in children especially, paralleled the skilled man's pride in his craft.[78] Her self-respect was achieved and maintained through her children's appearance and conduct, showing everyone that she took good care of them and was training them well. Even if money was short she saw that they were regular and punctual at school and at Sunday school, that they had good manners, polished boots, tidy hair and clean pinafores, and that they observed restrictions on their play, especially on Sunday.[79] Allen Jobson (born in Anerley, South London, in 1889), from a deeply Methodist family, recalled his mother's achievement:

> remembering where we lived, the little my father [a lame shoe-maker] earned, and our close proximity to the seamy side of life, there is little doubt that we should have joined the great unwashed. It was our mother who kept us all on the upgrade.[80]

Generally speaking, the more respectable a family was or wanted to be, the more strictly it was run. Ideally, it had regular meals, where all members, or

most, were present at the table, to be served by the mother and ruled, usually, by the father. ('Never allowed to speak at the meal table. And we had
to say our grace before we had our meal. And we wasn't allowed to put our
feet on the pins of the chairs. Please and thank you...')[81] Its children were
well-mannered and they did not swear, or anyway not in front of adults.[82]
They had to ask if they could go out, say where they were going and with
whom, and accept conditions about how far they went and when they came
back.[83] They were seldom allowed to visit other children's homes or to
invite others in.

Rough children, on the other hand, could go anywhere, including in
and out of each other's houses; they could play with anyone ('we sorted out
ourselves, didn't we');[84] they could come in to eat at any time, or feed themselves from fried-fish or pie-shop or shellfish stall; it did not matter if they
went barefoot or got dirty; and their language might be coarse.

The respectable mother saw 'rough' neighbours as having 'no control'
and letting the children 'simply run wild'; she stigmatized them as people
who 'didn't care' and told her children not to play with theirs.[85] Her children were less independent and more strictly ruled. They had mealtimes
and bedtimes (as we have seen), and a time by which they had to be indoors.
They had explicit responsibilities within the household, chores which they
regularly had to do before being released for play. Their work was 'helping' rather than earning (see Chapters 9 and 10). If there were boys as well
as girls a clear difference was probably made (providing age allowed) in
the work allotted to each—though this varied from one family to another,
both in the extent of differentiation and in who did what.[86]

Respectability demanded that the mother control her children's movements, especially the girls', and keep girls' work (and dress and interests)
distinct from boys'. But the poorer she was, the harder it was to maintain
such restrictions and demarcations. If every penny was needed, it was
tempting to let a child—even a girl—take a job even though it meant loss
of supervision. Allowing a child to run errands after school for a shop or a
neighbour, or to clean steps or do other domestic work, could bring in a
few pence, with perhaps a supplement in food. Most such work was only an
extension of what the girl already did at home, and the mother could try
to make sure that the employers were respectable. Again, when toddlers
were underfoot or bored, why not let an elder sister or brother take them
out? Or when the mother was busy and tired, it made sense to send a child
when something was needed from the shop, and risk her dancing to a
street organ with unsuitable friends, or straying too far, or loitering to
watch a drunken fight.

The difference between the 'respectable...people trying very hard to
bring up their children decently' and 'the people who just didn't care' was
recalled by Mrs Bartle (almost ninety when I recorded her in 1971) with an
emphasis which had probably been her mother's.[87] She was born in Poplar
in 1882, the late child of an Essex couple, her brothers and sister a good

deal older. Her father was a seaman (he became a mate) on coastal trips, much away but back quite often. Her mother, 'a very ambitious woman', according to the headmistress of the daughter's school,[88] did needlework for the church, sewing surplices, or sheets and baby clothes for the maternity bags they lent out, and sometimes she also did machining at home for a local factory where they made suits. (This was respectable homework, whereas her neighbour, who had seven children, drank and fought with her husband, machined mackintoshes.)[89] In their street, Northumberland Street, most of the doors stood open; 'the kids just used to tumble in and out of the passage all day long, and their pals used to run in and out with all their dirty boots and everything'. But her mother 'wouldn't have her door open', and 'kept us well away from a lot of the children, as far as she could'. Her father fixed a swing in the back door, where she used to sit reading on holidays or in the evenings after school.[90] She did sometimes go on errands, to fetch milk from the cowsheds near Bow Common (where she didn't like the smell, the dirt or the rough manners of the cowmen), or to the sawmill at the bottom of the street for twopennorth of waste wood for the copper, or to the shop, and then she could seize a bit of freedom. Down the road lived a fervent street preacher who held forth on one street corner while his drunken wife abused him as fluently on the other:

> Well, that was a treat for me to get out Saturday night and see those two. But I had an awful job to dodge my mother...I used to do my mother's shopping, and if I could forget something that I knew she wanted, then she'd say 'all right, you'd better run and get it, but don't be long'. And of course if I was longer than usual I could always say I was kept waiting, there were a lot of people in the shop....I'd got no conscience—if I thought I'd get away with something I didn't care.[91]

Another stolen treat (after they moved to South Hackney when she was nine) was possible sometimes on a Sunday, when if she went to a nearby church instead of the one where her brother was organist, she and a couple of other girls would 'sneak out before the sermon':

> We used to go into Victoria Park where this fountain was, go round where the speakers were, and there used to be a man there reading most horrible stories out of the penny novelettes....How my mother never found out, I don't know, because she could find out anything, my mother could....I should have got blood and thunder if she'd known. We used to love those stories—Murders and all sorts of terrible things.[92]

Although she was prepared to defy some restrictions, there were others which she respected. 'Kids used to dance round the barrel organs—of course I didn't'; and she never joined the children who followed Salvation Army processions and made fun of them.[93] Perhaps these carried too much risk of discovery and retribution—being 'sent to bed early or deprived of some little treat—or 'she used to give me some good hidings, you know'.[94]

If a child was at all inclined to break rules (and many elderly women recall stolen freedoms and treats), her evading supervision depended not only on her parents, but also on the extent of local support for their rules, and how likely it was that word of wandering or other infringements would get back.[95]

Also important to the child's freedom was how the parents, especially the mother, were occupied. Only a home-keeping mother could insist her children remain in sight of the front door. If she went out to work they necessarily had more autonomy. Even at home, if she did paid work she would be less able to enforce strict rules: time and money were lost each time she interrupted her stitching, ironing, pasting or folding. On the other hand, children were themselves restrained by work. Some had chores to do before they could play; others spent most of their waking hours out of school 'helping' parents or neighbours with housework, homework or children, or working in shops and on stalls (see Chapter 10). The poorer the family, and the older the child, the more such help was needed, and the briefer the time for play or mischief.

Girls and Boots

In some circumstances a girl of spirit could attain a considerable degree of freedom. Gladys B. was brought up in Hackney at the turn of the century; her parents ran a small greengrocery business.[96] She had a brother close to her age, but she did (and liked doing) many jobs which might have been left to him. She helped with deliveries, either on foot with a basket or with her father and his cart; she cared for the horse in the evening; and sometimes she went with her father in the early morning to the wholesale market at Covent Garden to hold the horse while he was off buying. She described her father as very strict, but his rules do not seem to have discriminated between her and her brothers: all had to keep silence at meal times if he was there or be struck ('he'd just clip us'), and all had to be in by a set time, though when he was out they sometimes coaxed their mother into giving them longer. On Sundays they could not play out, and after church they had to go for a formal walk with their parents, with no playing around. But on weekdays after school, with her stern father off on his rounds and her mother tied to the shop, Gladys would often get away to play with her brother and his friends, 'the poorer boys'.

> I never played with a doll or anything like that. I was a tomboy you see then. What they did I did....Anything the boys had, I wanted.

She was more hampered by her girl's clothes than by rules or inhibitions about what girls should do. She recalled going scrumping for apples on

Hackney Marshes (where in those days there were farms) at about the age of eight:

> they climbed some fences or railings with spikes on and they got chased by some farmers and of course I was the one left behind. I went to jump down, and I had on one of those frilly pinafore things on. And I got caught on the spikes, didn't I. Did he tan my bottom through the railings!

She didn't remember being encouraged to see more of girls, whom she played with only at school.

> No, no, I suited myself. If they did I wouldn't have taken any notice, I'm sure of that....I thought it much more sporting playing with the boys. The girls seemed to be insipid to me. Babies.

She shocked her father on one occasion, when she and the boys made a 'grotto' with bits of broken glass from the pile of discarded bottles at the glass works, and she was put in front of it, cap in hand, to beg pennies—'remember the grotto'—with a tale of distress. 'It was lovely. Till my father caught me. He said it was dreadful begging in the streets. Us having the greengrocer's shop.' But even then his anger was at the begging, not because she, a girl, was playing in the street with boys.

Gladys B.'s mother may have been more apprehensive about the young tomboy: she certainly drew the line at buying her the boy's boots which she coveted. This too was partly a question of status. Poor girls had hobnail boots, because they lasted longer and could serve whichever child they fitted.

> I had to have the old brown side button-up boots and my mother took me to a boot shop once to get some new boots, and of course we considered ourselves a bit better-off—having a shop, you see—middle class. Anyway, I saw all these hobnail boots hanging on strings....Oh, I'll have a pair of those, I don't want those other boots—And I didn't get any in the end, naturally...I said, no, I want those or none at all. Cause I knew all the other boys would have them. We could afford them, but I never had any at all. And I used to borrow the boys' boots to kick along the kerb, and make these sparks. Lovely...

This family conflict over boots may be contrasted with one recounted by Grace Foakes in her memoir of a childhood in Wapping in the 1900s. She too was an active child, and particularly enjoyed sliding along behind carts, an amusement which wore her boots out too fast for her father's liking. So he took her along to get new boots, and to her horror insisted on boy's ones.

> My tears had no effect on him and boy's boots I had, fitted with tips and blakeys. As soon as we got home he put studs in the soles.

Oh! the noise they made. I felt terrible. The other children
laughed, and I cried myself to sleep for many nights....I need not
tell you that this lesson taught me to be careful with my next pair
of girl's boots.[97]

The contrast is in the girls' own attitudes as well as the parents'. One
demanded a boy's freedom, regarded herself almost as a boy ('I knew all
the other boys would have them'), and longed for the privilege of wearing
boys' boots.[98] The other could not defy convention, saw her boys' boots as
a punishment for behaving too like a boy, and could not wait for the boots
to wear out so that she could resume her proper appearance.

Of course two girls in the same family might have reacted almost as differently, and one can generalize only with caution. But one possible
explanation hinges on the poverty of Grace Foakes' family and the relative
prosperity of Gladys B.'s. Although generally speaking a girl's freedom was
likely to decrease as her family's status improved, if she was rebellious, prosperity gave her more chance of getting away with it because the family
standing was already assured and did not have to be confirmed by its members' comportment.

The child of a Wapping dock labourer, by contrast, if the family were
to keep themselves distinct from their less scrupulous neighbours (as her
father wanted them to), had constantly to prove their respectability by her
appearance and behaviour. Grace Foakes could envy the boys their freedoms, like playing out in the evenings, or in summer swimming in the
Thames, but she did not try to join them. ('How we envied them but, being
girls, how could we too enjoy this game? There was no answer...') She
played with other little girls, and defied rules only in quite minor ways, like
taking off shoes and stockings in the park on a Saturday morning to enjoy
the feel of warm asphalt under bare feet, or on Sundays smuggling out a
ball in her knickers so that she and her sister could have fun bouncing it
on their supposedly sedate Sunday walk.[99]

The determination of a parent to achieve respectability even though
desperately poor was likely to restrict daughters in a number of ways.
Playing barefoot like any urchin was out: Eliza H. 'got a bashing' for that,
though her mother was probably also anxious about the risk of the shoes
being stolen.[100] A scant supply of clothing kept them indoors or even in bed
while things were mended or laundered: they couldn't be seen in torn or
dirty clothes.[101]

Grace Smith was brought up in Kentish Town in the 1900s. Her father,
a cab driver, died before she was born, and her mother worked early and
late at washing, cleaning and cooking to support the two children. She was
a proud woman, a church-goer, who set great store by their being nicely
dressed and well behaved. Money was always tight, but Grace remembered
how once when a neighbour gave her a copper for running an errand, her
mother said that it was her duty to help so she mustn't accept rewards, and

sent her to give it back. Nor were she and her sister allowed to take jobs after school as some of their friends did, though sometimes their mother kept one of them home from school when she needed help. Her insistence on a proper appearance meant that instead of putting them into the hard-wearing boots their school friends wore she scraped and saved to buy good quality soft button boots (like the ones Gladys B. resented so much), and then stopped them playing in the street for fear the boots would wear out too fast: just the opposite of Grace Foakes' experience.[102]

This concern for the boots was probably reinforced by the desire to keep the girls away from undesirable companions in the street. According to settlement worker, Reginald Bray, in 1901:

> the more thoughtful parents dislike, and rightly dislike, their chil-
> dren to be exposed to the influences there [in the street], and prefer
> to keep them at home. This is especially the case with girls.[103]

C.H. Rolph, son of a policeman who 'thought we were a cut above artisans', preferred 'living as a street urchin, with other urchins as my boon com-panions'. He had been allowed early on to play in the street 'because there was nowhere else within a reasonable distance where children could com-munally play'; and he continued, though his 'street companions were a constant source of disapproval among the family, worrying my father, puz-zling my mother, and provoking in my elder brother Harold, who went to better schools, a profound distaste'.[104]

Hazards of Respectability

Families which hid their poverty might fare worse than those with less pride. They had prohibitions against accepting help and against cadging or foraging ('picking things up in the street'), and their children would be less street-wise.[105] Both adults and children were handicapped not only by ignorance and inexperience, but also by embarrassment and family rules.

But to keep children off the street, whether or not it protected their morals, might jeopardize their health, at least where income levels were low.[106] According to a school medical survey in 1906, 'the survivors of the slum children at the age of five are as a rule sturdier and quicker than the more carefully nurtured children'. In schools attended by 'children of the well-to-do artisan, the clerk, and small shopkeeper', on the other hand,

> the children are often over-clothed, coddled and pampered, and
> lymphatic conditions from want of exercise, enlarged tonsils, ade-
> noids and anaemia are essentially the troubles of these better-class
> schools.[107]

Girls' lower standards of nutrition and their greater liability to anaemia and poor eyesight, recorded in the 1890s and 1900s, were attributed to

their being outside less and having less exercise.[108] Among candidates for
Junior County Schools in 1908 (children of about eleven, not from really
poor families), 11.4 per cent of the girls were found to be anaemic, 'a much
greater proportion than among the boys...probably due to the greater confinement to the house...'[109] That they consumed less protein than boys was
probably a factor; and likewise their larger share of domestic work.

The difference as to eyesight was particularly striking. In 1908, 75 per
cent of the schoolchildren with poor or bad vision were girls. The causes
were said to be 'purely social': boys played more in the open air while girls
were more confined to the house; and girls' eye-muscles (already at a disadvantage) were further strained by needlework, which boys did not do.
Needlework, of course, included household darning, mending and making, probably often done in poor light, as well as sewing classes at school.

The quest for respectability set happiness at risk as well as health, especially in a poor family. It involved a constant effort, especially by the
mother, to keep up standards by hard work, thrift and vigilance. Emphasis
on privacy and 'keeping to themselves' cut women off from neighbourly
help.[110] If one parent set more store by respectability than the other, or
defined it differently, tensions and clashes ensued, especially over drink,
which concerned not only appearances but the family budget. 'No figure
among the poor is so much commended as the hardworking...drudge who,
in spite of a drunken worthless husband, keeps her home together and
rears her children respectable', wrote Anna Martin, settlement worker in
Bermondsey.[111] Such women, and their children, often paid a heavy price,
especially if from shame they tried to hide the husband's drinking.

For children, maintaining respectability posed other problems: they
were torn between the fear of maternal wrath and the desire to avoid rejection by their friends as 'stuck-up'.[112] And being too well-dressed was
hazardous. William Nn (born Poplar, 1896) went out in his new sailor suit
but did not get far before: 'the big boys held me down and cut off all the
buttons and stole my whistle'. Other times, they would grab the pork-pie
hats his mother made for him and his brother, 'pee into them and throw
them back to us'.[113]

Grace Foakes' parents had high standards. They were often very poor,
but her mother made sure that the girls were neat on Sundays, with special
dress and black stockings, and their hair clean and crimped.[114] She was 'too
proud to send us to the charity school', in spite of the free clothes and
boots it provided. Most Wapping people took for granted that you added
to a precarious living anything that chance might offer in streets or docks.
But she 'was a very honest woman and would go without rather than take
what was not hers'. When her son William came home proudly laden with
tomatoes, his jersey bulging and his pockets crammed, but would not tell
her how he had come by them, she threw them away.

Telling us to watch, she turned to William and asked him to

open the slide which led to the 'shoot'. She picked up the tomatoes one by one from the table and dropped them through the
shoot. Poor William! it was a hard lesson, but Mother explained that
we must follow her example and never take anything that did not
belong to us.

Their much harsher father would have reinforced the lesson with a beating, as he did most brutally on another occasion with her brother Robert.
He was a stern, unsociable, hardworking man, who allowed no visitors ('my
mother could never have a neighbour in for a cup of tea or a chat, and we
could not ask our friends in either'), did not drink or smoke, and 'saw to
it that the children learnt the meaning of work'.

He would not borrow or lend, nor allow my mother to do so. In
our household his word was law and nobody dared dispute it.

His rules and the mother's scruples made their life harder, impeding—if
not preventing—the neighbourly help and friendship which could alleviate
some of the hardships of poverty. His hostility also cut the mother off from
her relatives. Only old Aunt Amy, whom he disliked for her 'dirty' snuff-tak-
ing (and her 'borrowing'), came to the house if he was out. The mother
would then urge her to stay for tea and to take no notice of his moods.

'I Was a Terrible Tomboy'

The atmosphere in such a family seems far removed from the robust independence possible for Gladys B., whose father, though she thought him
stern, liked company and drink and from affection treated her more like a
son, and whose mother could be persuaded to indulgence and anyway put
more into looking after shop and house than into overseeing her children's behaviour.

How far girls internalized the constraints of respectability varied a
good deal. Some (like Gladys B.) broke rules whenever they could get away
with it. Others would break out in some ways but not in others. Mrs Bartle,
who escaped to the excitement of the street whenever she could, nevertheless 'didn't often play with boys because they were so rough'.[115] Ada S.,
whose father was a brewery worker in Bethnal Green, accepted the values
of her parents but chafed at some of the restraints. Her playmates in
Buxton Street in the 1880s and 1890s were 'all nice children like ourselves',
whose fathers also 'nearly all worked at Truman's Brewery...or else they was
a policeman'. Even so, there were some who were brought up less strictly,
who were allowed to dance to the street organ, as she would have liked to,
and 'One or two of them wasn't so good—I mean...wasn't brought up like
us. My mother was very particular'.[116] Ada still had a fair amount of freedom, and took advantage of it. Her sister, who was handicapped by poor
health ('she couldn't run about, and would mind the children'), seems to

have resented this, and told their mother whenever Ada overstepped some
limit.

> I did everything my brother did. My sister used to say 'Mum, look
> what they're doing...' I used to like to play with the boys. I liked to
> play with boys. I used to play marbles with them. Always played
> with boys, I did. I did everything but over-back [leap-frog]—I
> mustn't do that. Wasn't allowed to do that. Cause my sister'd come
> round and tell my mother...I'd get a thrashing then for misbehav-
> ing.[117]

To play with boys was to define yourself as a tomboy, especially as you grew
older. That had to be locally acceptable: to yourself and the boys you
joined, to street and court opinion, and to your parents. Unfortunately evidence on the subject is scant until the latter end of our period, when oral
sources can be used. It is difficult to tell how definitions of and attitudes to
the tomboy varied with locality and decade. There is an attractive picture
of one in Soho in the 1860s ('Dick Lapintosh'), in the autobiography of a
religious worker, 'Mother Kate':

> her family was...French and her name was really Labertouche. I
> forget what her Christian name was (Pollie or Annie or some-
> thing), but she was called Dick because she looked so like a
> boy—and always played with boys. She was a square, sturdy, impu-
> dent-looking person of eleven or twelve, with bright yellow hair,
> saucy blue eyes, and cheeks like a Normandy pippin. She cared for
> nobody, and could fight any boy her own weight, or more, if nec-
> essary.[118]

In this case the use of a boy's name (by her family and friends, not only by
Mother Kate) suggests that she was regarded as crossing a boundary: her
boyish behaviour was accepted, but marked her out.

A Jewish tomboy in about 1910 'had a fine vocabulary of swear words',
but her disapproving elder sister reported to her mother (in Yiddish):
'Hoodela said that little word beginning with eff', whereupon 'Hoodela
was duly chastised'.[119]

The presence of tomboys shows the existence of approved gender
roles, and suggests that labelling was used to push girls back in line. But it
also reveals resistance, at least as a transitional phase. The upper limit for
permitted tomboy behaviour, like sanctions against it, varied with the class
and family situation. In an 1890s girls' novel, *Her Own Way*, motherless
childhood and companionship with her widowed father have created a
middle-class tomboy, but eventually he takes alarm and sends her to boarding school to be tamed ('You'll never be a lady, Kitty, at this rate').[120]

For most working-class girls the earliest pressures against tomboy
behaviour were material ones. Their time was not their own, because mothers needed their help. They often had younger children in tow, which

made it harder to join in boys' games and activities. (Girls' games were joined by children of any age, while boys over about eight ranged further afield and their games tended to involve competition between peers.) By the 1900s at least, when clean and tidy looks were increasingly demanded of girls at school and more generally, anxiety about clothes and appearance also began to inhibit. The white pinafore was an impediment not only because of its loose shape, but also because it had to be kept clean. Perhaps, too, girls were more careful than boys to avoid damaging or soiling their clothes, especially as they grew older, because laundry and repair were their work. It rarely fell to boys to wash or mend their clothes.

Being a tomboy, then, was a phase, though not all girls went through it. It was more likely if you had brothers close to your age, if you were not an elder girl in the family, or, still more, if you were a youngest. Delicate health, child care obligations, fear of rough boys ('they used to like to pull our hair'),[121] or identification with feminine activities ('they were real girlish girls, they were, not like me—I was a tomboy')[122] could all inhibit it. Increasing domestic responsibility and the approaching end of childhood, with the prospect of jobs, new status, and courtship, were likely to bring the phase to an end.

But the zest with which octogenarian ex-tomboys recall those years is striking. 'Oh, I was a terrible tomboy, I'm afraid!' is said in a celebratory tone, not an apologetic one. That contradiction between words and tone, that sense that the years of relative freedom from the restrictions of girlhood were a golden age, suggest that their transition to conformity may have been reluctant. For such girls the discovery and acceptance of the social implications of their sex was a long-term process. It happened within a social context which included the family but was also larger; it was likely to involve a sense of loss and restriction; and it was not tied to the biological event of the onset of menstruation.[123]

7. Orange Street school, Southwark.

PART 2

Home Versus School

8. *Kindergarten provision at the Hoxton Mission crèche, 1900. Children in such nurseries were often bathed and put into special clothes for the day.*

5

Caretakers or Schoolchildren?

————◆————

A Novel Principle

CHILDREN'S USEFULNESS after the age of five or six (especially as 'caretakers' of those still younger) was taken for granted in much of the working class before and after Forster's Education Act of 1870.[1] So, too, was their transition from dependence to responsibility and even wage-earning while still children. In the poorest families their time and labour was indispensable. But their help was valued and encouraged whatever the family's economic situation.

Even where a father was able to meet all the money needs of his family without help from wife or young children, as the youngsters reached eleven or twelve they often joined him in supplying cash or labour for the family. (They might, exceptionally, train as apprentices or pupil teachers, if the family could afford the investment and if contacts and aptitude allowed.) Sometimes the need was greatest at home, in domestic labour or a family enterprise. On leaving school a daughter or (less often) a son then stayed and helped in the family rather than taking a job. Most often, they found a job and put all or most of what they earned into the family exchequer. If a girl went into resident domestic service (more likely in districts with a middle-class presence than in East or inner South London), she usually kept in touch with her family, visited them on her days off and perhaps handed over some part of her wage.[2] But whether employed or helping with housework, child care, or family enterprise, whether living at home or out in service, many daughters stayed within the family economy in one way or another until marriage, sometimes for ten years and more. The even greater crowding of already cramped homes which could result was not important beside the security of having several wage-earners.[3]

In most of the working class a contribution would be needed from an earlier age, though when and in what form would vary, as we shall see. For working-class children, 'real life' was not the future but the present. Work and responsibility were not the separate province of adults, but co-existed with growth, with play and with school; they anticipated full adulthood, sometimes by many years. As Alexander Paterson wrote of Camberwell in the 1900s, 'the difference between a child and an adult is everywhere regarded as one of degree rather than of kind'.[4]

Following the Act in 1870 and successive local bye-laws, compulsory education in London required children to be in school for five hours every weekday from the age of five, for a period of five years (later extended to eight and then nine).[5] As had been predicted in debates on education in the 1850s and 1860s, this obligation clashed with working-class parents' needs and expectations. And 'school pence', the fee to be brought in on Monday morning by each child, put new pressure on the family budget just as school reduced the child's contribution.[6]

Ruling-class opinion was not united behind compulsion.[7] Some took the hard line, that children who were not in school already, under the voluntary system, were either running wild, or were at work. If they were running wild, there was danger to present and to future social order; if at work they needed to be rescued from exploitation by lazy and avaricious parents and to be given a more appropriate experience of childhood. Compelling them to attend school was therefore necessary and desirable.

Others had doubts. Some thought early employment the best training for the children of the poor, and school a waste of time for them; some wanted their labour. Others did not approve of making parents send children to school against their wishes: it was unjustifiable interference with individual rights.[8] Others again were concerned at the economic results of such compulsion for poor families.

Enforcement of the new law was to prove difficult on a number of counts.[9] Amongst them was compassion when parents pleaded poverty. Some magistrates constantly dismissed or adjourned school attendance cases, or inflicted only nominal penalties.[10] This led to acrimonious and indignant complaints from the School Board Visitors, whose responsibility it was to check why children were absent and to press charges when they thought fit.[11] In January 1874, for instance, Saunders, Visitor for Finsbury Division, denounced Vaughan, the Bow Street magistrate:

> During the last three months I have taken out at that court thirty-three summons and only obtained one conviction, and that was simply costs, and yet some of the cases had been summoned two and even three times before—but the Magistrate will not enforce the penalty, so that the people do not mind being summoned, and compulsion has very little effect in the neighbourhood of St Giles and Drury Lane.[12]

The magistrate explained that the parents' poverty and ignorance 'rendered it very desirable that a large measure of patience and forbearance should be exhibited'. It was not surprising, he said, if parents did not at first comply with an Act which 'had introduced a novel principle, unintelligible to many of that class, which deprived them of the means of eking out a scanty subsistence by the labour of their children'.[13] Such patience and forbearance were still being exercised well after the principle had ceased to be novel. At the School Attendance Officers' Conference in 1900 the complaint that 'magistrates don't do their duty' was still being made, and an occasion was cited when a Poplar magistrate had dismissed every one of the seventy cases he heard.[14]

The problem was not an easy one, especially in the early years, and attendance officers themselves could have qualms about strict enforcement. The anonymous 'Riverside Visitor', writing in 1872 on his work as a School Board Visitor in a South London riverside district (probably Deptford),[15] expressed their dilemma. He regarded it as right and 'to the interest of humanity and national policy' for children 'of tender years' to be withdrawn from labour and sent to school, but he also recognized the hardship involved for parents and for children.[16] The factory inspector Alexander Redgrave noted the difficulty for employers as well as for poor families;[17] and he too favoured a soft approach. In his view, the Elementary Education Act of 1876 (which extended the provisions of the 1870 Act) 'restricted the manufacturer in his supply of labour, and deprived the parent of the earnings of his children'. It must therefore 'be enforced with tenderness, and both parties led up, rather than driven, to compliance'.[18]

A clash resulting from 'tender enforcement' occurred in Wandsworth three years later. The local superintendent of school visitors angrily accused Mr Paget, a magistrate, of always adjourning his cases, with the result that it was 'absolutely useless to attempt to enforce the compulsory attendance of children...in that part of my district within the radius of Wandsworth Police Court'. Paget denied having said as he dismissed a case that the absentee child in question 'was being better educated by following his costermonger father's cart in the streets than if he were at a Board School'.[19] He asserted his right to exercise discretion and not 'be dictated to by the School Board officers'; and explained that his repeated adjournments had 'secured better attendance of the children without the necessity of convicting the parents'.[20] (Two years later Paget was again under attack, from representatives of the Latymer Road Mission who thought it 'very hard' that the magistrate should 'take the part of unruly boys'.)[21]

The extra work involved in School-Board cases may have irritated magistrates in courts which were already busy. Dismissals (and even adjournments, which were more common) would be one way to get through a heavy load with greater dispatch, and might encourage the school authorities to be more selective in their prosecutions. In the same year, two Clerkenwell magistrates complained to the Home Secretary of having had 500 school-attendance cases in three months, pointed to 'the amount of misery involved' through 'the fines and imprisonment consequent upon the issue of so many summonses', and suggested that their number could with advantage be reduced.[22] The situation was not substantially relieved, however, till 1891, when Justices of the Peace were empowered to hear School-Board cases and fees were abolished in Board schools.[23]

Little Nurses

A major task for children, which often conflicted with the demands of school, was the care of younger brothers and sisters. Almost every description of life in London's poorer quarters included some reference to 'little mothers' nursing, watching and playing with their infant charges. Jules Vallès, a Communard refugee in the mid-1870s, writing from London for a Paris paper, commented on the number of big sisters 'being mother' ('*qui font la maman*') on doorsteps and pavements with babies in their arms.[24] Nearly thirty years later, in *Living London*, George Sims described the same thing, in 'a frowsy little street with most of the doors ajar':[25]

> At the open door sits a girl of eight...a typical 'little mother' of the London doorstep....She is nursing a heavy baby who is perhaps a year old. She talks to it, soothes it, hushes it to sleep, rocks it, dandles it when it wakes up, and kisses its poor little face again and again. But every other minute her attention is distracted by the conduct of a sister, aged four, and a brother, aged five, who are also under her guardianship....Because she is the oldest of all that have come, all that will come after are hers to tend and hers to watch. By the time she marries and has children of her own she will be a woman weary of motherhood.

The perspective indicated by the phrase 'little mother' is of course a middle-class one. Such children were not taking over their mother's job, nor anticipating their own future. They were doing a job which belonged to them. Although it was delegated by the mother, its delegation was expected and taken for granted. It was a matter of labour resources:

> with the increase of the family there creeps in the system of subcontracting....The mother hands over the baby to the older children, the older children to the younger...[26]

Looking after the baby was one of the easiest jobs to delegate, whether briefly to a small child ('Aggie dear, will you hold the baby while I put the potatoes on?'),[27] or more or less entirely to an older one. The delegation might not be acknowledged by authority, however: 'Harriet Pedding, a cleaner at a common lodging house, whose husband has been in the Infirmary about three months, has to leave six children ages from three to twelve totally *without care* during the day' (my italics).[28]

Children generally took pride and pleasure in their responsibility, and they were good at it. As settlement worker Alexander Paterson pointed out:[29]

> They do not grudge the duty as a hardship, and in fact, it does not tie their movements very much, for they take the baby with them wherever they want to....They have more delight in the position than their mother would probably be able to find, and, as a rule,

are patient and good-tempered, and unselfish, even when the baby is exceptionally tiresome.

The relationship was often a very close one, if with cuffs and scolding as well as hugs and praises. The babies were theirs, and only outsiders used inverted commas for the attribution. ('We had to allow the older girls to bring "their babies"', wrote Muriel Wragge of a Hoxton play-centre in the 1900s.)[30] Children who had no babies of their own, like Ethel Page in 1900s Poplar, found it easy to get substitutes, whether to earn a penny or 'for the sheer joy of possession—I liked to pretend the babies I minded belonged to me'.[31]

Supervision and distraction were demanding:

the faithful nurses, whether girls or boys, fight and bravely win a hard battle when they turn from ball, skipping rope, hoop, or marbles, and remain the spectators of games in which they long to join, because they will not neglect the helpless infants intrusted to their care.[32]

But mostly child care could be combined with play, in street or yard, or even park, if there was one in reach. Excursions were encouraged when serious work like washing was under way at home. Mrs Layton (born in Bethnal Green in 1866) recalled enjoyable trips to Victoria Park:

My fourth sister and I always stayed away from school on washing day to mind the babies. In the summer it was real sport, because so many people did their washing on the same day, and everybody had large families and generally kept the elder girls, and sometimes boys, at home to mind the little ones. We used...to go out all together with our babies and prams into Victoria Park....We would picnic on bread and treacle under the trees in the Park and return home in the evening a troop of tired but happy children.[33]

Often older children had entire charge of their babies. They did not simply take them out of mother's way when she was busy, but dressed, washed and perhaps fed them, entertained them, lulled them to sleep when they were tired, comforted them, and dealt with any emergencies. Arthur Harding was 'brought up more by my sister than I was by my mother. My earliest recollection is of being taken round by her'.[34] 'Little mothers' were familiar figures at the Children's Hospital in Hackney:[35]

Sometimes one of these tiny little 'grown-ups' will walk into the hospital holding by the hand a child...and she will busy herself keeping the little one quiet, soothing her, or scolding her, just like a mother, while the doctor is finding out what is the matter.

The 'little mother' was not necessarily a girl. Child care was more a girl's job, it seems, but boys often did it. Opening a series of articles on how to look after babies, in *Girls' Own Paper* in 1881, the writer felt obliged to talk about 'young nurses' rather than 'little mothers' so as not to exclude boys, because she saw 'almost daily such pleasant pictures of small boy-nurses in the exercise of their vocation'.[36] Such glimpses occur in various sources. The magistrate, Montagu Williams, in 1892, describing a cricket game on waste ground in Bethnal Green, observed that:

> Two of the lads had been sent out in charge of baby sisters whom they have deposited on a neighbouring doorstep, towards which, while snatching the fearful joy of an innings, they direct an occasional glance.[37]

Among 'typical cases of absenteeism' cited in School Board records figure two twelve-year-old boys domestically engaged. One, in 1893, was:

> kept at home entirely to look after house and younger children, all over three, whilst father and mother, two elder brothers and a sister are at work, father saying 'I want him, and I won't send him for you nor anyone else'.

Another, whose father was at work all day and whose mother was delicate (this often meant tubercular), was being 'kept at home to mind the baby'.[38]

Reports by religious workers also reveal boys looking after younger children and the home.[39] The Boys' Evening Shelter in Latymer Road, Notting Dale, set up by evangelical mission workers to keep boys of nine to fifteen off the street, had to be open to all ages because 'so many boys are nurses and caretakers of younger boys and sisters'.[40]

Memories show that in the absence of an eldest girl a boy could be 'nursemaid in chief'. Jack Welch was six when his sister Ada was born in 1909, and 'staggered about with her in my arms like a proud dad'. Soon he was 'well versed in the art of nursing a baby, feeding it with a bottle of Glaxo, and changing nappies when needed', and by 1915 'had four brothers and sisters under my command'.[41]

Glimpses of child care by boys can also be found in local authority records. The report of an anthrax investigation in Bermondsey in 1896, mentions a thirteen-year-old washing his six-year-old niece's face and taking her for a walk over Tower Bridge; and cases in a Southwark outbreak of enteric fever in 1900 included a boy of nine and a girl of two who played frequently together, the little one being left with her grandmother all day while her mother was at work.[42] Reports of accidents and fires also show boys in charge, as where a Poplar two-year-old left with her brothers died in a fire caused by the nine-year-old's trouble lighting a cheap oil lamp.[43]

Sunday-school-prize 'waif novels' are also suggestive. The central figure was often an older child who, whether girl or boy, both provided for and nurtured a younger one, and so broke with ideological prescription both for age and sex. In *Froggy's Little Brother*, for instance (set in London in 1873), when Froggy and his brother are orphaned Froggy supports them both, sweeping a crossing and carrying people's bags for pennies. He finds it increasingly hard to cope, and Benny falls ill. They are discovered by charitable visitors too late, and Benny dies. Froggy, heartbroken, is taken to a kindly orphanage, where at first he mopes. But he is given fresh hope and will to live when a new little orphan arrives at the Home, whom he is allowed to take as his special charge—in effect, to 'mother'.[44] The fraternal behaviour being presented and approved involves solicitous care and responsibility, as well as affection. Waifs in other such books often strike the reader less strongly as 'boy' or 'girl' than as 'child'. With the reduction in actual waifs the genre gradually petered, and publishers increasingly distinguished between books for girls and books for boys, both categories portraying more stereotypical behaviour by each sex.[45]

Crèches and Baby Rooms: no 'opening the way to socialism'

The 1870 Education Act empowered local School Boards to provide for children between three and thirteen, and to propose local bye-laws for compulsion between specified ages.[46] London's bye-laws, approved in December 1871, made attendance compulsory for children from five to ten and in most cases till thirteen, at least half-time. But the 'young nurses' were enrolled at school without alternative care being organized for their charges, and the warning in an 1872 Charity Organization Society report: 'the School Boards will have great difficulty in enforcing the compulsory clauses until some means exist for disposing of the infants'.[47]

The only organized daily child care was the charity crèche, run in connection with church or mission, or funded by subscribers and patrons. The best documented was Marie Hilton's in Ratcliff (Stepney), which from 1870 kept going for over twenty years, and took as many as 100 infants at a penny or two a day.[48] This was a recent innovation: in London before 1870 there were probably a dozen at most.[49] It was seen as a French import (following a Mr Marbeau's initiative in 1844),[50] necessary not only to save babies from 'the tender mercies of incompetent child-nurses' but also because 'education in its highest and best senses is inseparably connected with the early years of infancy, though no instruction, strictly so called, may be attempted'.[51] They were few and far between. W.G. Howgrave's 1872 report for the Charity Organization Society identified only twenty-three in the whole of London, and named several districts which had none. He suggested that the School Board should set up its own, attached to schools so that overheads would be lower and infants could be delivered by older children as they arrived at school.[52]

The London School Board did attempt this, but it met with legal difficulties. As the Education Act charged School Boards with educating children over three, expenditure on children under that age could be challenged. An unfavourable legal opinion in 1872 made the London Board refuse to take over a crèche set up in Mile End New Town in 1868.[53] But in

1873 the Board convinced the Education Department that because 'the elder girls are constantly kept at home to take charge of the younger children, and are consequently unable to attend school with any regularity', it was necessary 'to devise some means by which they could be set free to attend school'. The Department then approved the setting up of 'Baby Rooms', where infants might be left during school hours, at schools where it seemed necessary.[54] Orange St school, in Southwark, was one: the headmistress later recalled that they were 'obliged to open a crèche' because the girls were 'staying so much at home to look after the babies'.[55]

By 1879, twelve had been opened.[56] But auditors challenged the costs of equipping them, and the challenge was eventually upheld by the Local Government Board, so no more were set up. The decision was affected by current criticism of the Board as extravagant and over-ambitious, but it also revealed conflicting approaches to the question of child care.

The School Board and the Education Department were prepared, on the basis of experience, to accept infants as the inevitable adjuncts of the older children. They argued that if children were kept at home 'to take charge of their younger brothers and sisters whilst the parents are necessarily at work', they could secure the education of the older children only by providing for their charges. One note from an Education Department official even maintained that baby rooms were as justifiable as cloakrooms:

> I do not see why these Babies may not be regarded as cloaks or bonnets for which provision must be made.

The Local Government Board, like the auditors, refused to accept this argument. They considered infants the responsibility of the mothers, and censured the School Board for providing Baby Rooms 'not...for the purpose of education, but merely for the purpose of relieving the parents of the care of their infants during school hours'.[57]

The argument that mothers ought to be looking after their children did not enable them to do so. Many working-class wives contributed cash to the household budget when it was needed, either by going out to work for odd days and weeks (or more regularly), or by taking in washing or outwork. Women raising children on their own, like the many widows, would have no choice. The mothers whose need was served by the crèche run by her Haggerston convent were evoked by an Anglican sister, Mother Kate:[58]

> The door of the day nursery begins to be besieged a little before eight o'clock, and you see pale, worn looking women leaving their children there before hurrying to their day's work in the warehouse or factory.

George Sims, in 1883, described a crèche he visited, where forty infants were looked after 'with motherly care by a kind-hearted creature whose lot I do not envy'.[59] They had a low table where they played or ate their bread and butter (brought from home), and a long bed where eight or ten at a time could rest and 'forget their baby troubles'. He deplored the veto on more School Board crèches, and saw the crèche as:

> a boon and a blessing to the poor woman who going out to work has a choice of keeping an elder girl at home to nurse the baby and be summoned for it, or locking the said baby up alone in a room all day.[60]

Subsequent attempts by the Board to reopen the question failed to break down opposition. 'Is it not opening the way to socialism to give them these rooms in which to have their babies nursed?' was the indignant response when Baby Rooms were advocated by a School Board witness to the 1887 Cross Commission on education.[61] Existing crèches survived, but without funding they depended on voluntary contributions to cover running costs.[62]

There was no immediate mushrooming of private crèches to fill the gap, though existing ones were praised as liberating 'little Annies and Maries' for school.[63] In the 1880s and 1890s their number did slowly grow,[64] but never in proportion to need. One run by Wesleyans cared for 100 children a day, at the West London Mission, in Soho, where 'many deserted wives, widows and poor women…[were] compelled to be the breadwinners of the family'.[65] By 1904 there were still only fifty-five crèches in all London. Seven boroughs had none—Battersea, Bethnal Green (where a School Board one closed in 1903), Fulham, Greenwich, Paddington, Poplar and Woolwich. Provision depended more on the supply of philanthropic resources than on need; and 'some of the districts either totally unprovided for or with inadequate provision' were also 'amongst the largest, poorest and most densely populated'. Moreover, only nineteen of the London crèches allowed unconditional entry; and twenty-five excluded illegitimate children, thus denying access 'to those unfortunate mothers and infants who need it most'. 'Crèche babies' remained 'only a teacupful out of an ocean…of babies who ought to be crèched'.[66] Predictably, it was still the case in 1904 that:

> one of the most frequent defences heard…when school attendance cases are being dealt with, is that the mothers must earn their children's livelihood, and that to enable them to do this the younger children must be looked after by the older ones.[67]

Although existing crèches met a need, at least if their hours were long enough and their location useful, they were not universally popular. It was normal practice for children arriving at the crèche to have their own clothes changed for ones kept in the crèche, and often also to be bathed.[68] Mothers who considered they kept their children neat and clean anyway would find these procedures insulting;[69] and some would also have seen the emphasis on baths and (later) fresh air as cranky and even dangerous. In other cases, even if clean clothes and baths were not the rule, the child had to be clean and tidy enough to be accepted. This meant yet more to be done in the rushed start to the morning; inevitably, too, there was friction over what 'clean and tidy' meant. A friend or neighbour, on the other hand, would 'take them as they are without raising objections'.[70] It was noted in 1904 that 'in Notting Dale mothers frequently prefer to pay 9d. a day to neighbours and find the food rather than use the two excellent crèches where for 6d. a day a child gets proper food and care'. Quite plausibly, 'dislike of supervision or regulation of any sort' was given as the explanation.[71] But crèches may also have been rejected for standards which were too low: the minority report of the Poor Law Commission noted that many were 'overcrowded, ill-ventilated, dark, dirty and foul-smelling'.[72]

The philanthropic basis of most crèches probably also caused difficulties. The Infant Nursery at Latymer Road Mission was dubbed the 'Mission to Babies',[73] but some crèche organizers saw them as missions to mothers, and aimed through them to reform working-class domestic practices. Their reports stressed the 'skilled' care provided for the children. The Stepney crèche took in local girls to help, but first, 'day after day, with wonderful patience and skill, Marie Hilton drilled and trained them till they became trustworthy nurses'.[74] Such emphasis on 'training' and 'skill' no doubt gratified servant-employing subscribers, but of course they denied the validity of the child-care skills and experience which mothers and local helpers had already. Reports made constant reference to clean and wholesome premises profesional support and proper food, contrasted explicitly or implicitly with home conditions and care. In daily practice, great tact would surely have been needed, especially from lady volunteers, for harassed mothers not to have felt exasperated and resentful.[75]

Cost was a further problem. Crèches were not cheap to run. The writer W. Pett Ridge recalled that the Babies Home and Day Nursery in Hoxton ('which I ran') cost about a thousand pounds a year.[76] None of those inspected for the *COS Reporter* in 1872 was self-supporting, and Howgrave calculated that to cover 'fixed expenses, such as rent, coals, gas, matron's salary, etc.' would be possible only with a regular attendance of twenty children, each paying fivepence a day. (This allowed threepence a day per head for feeding them.) He thought this rate, or even sixpence a day with a reduction for other children from the same family, 'would not be oppressively heavy'.[77] But the object of self-sufficiency conflicted with other aims. Only one of the crèches visited by Howgrave charged over fourpence, even when they provided food without extra payment. Mrs Hilton's crèche charged only threepence,

> to induce parents to send their children so that the latter may come under the influence of the Crèche, and become in future better members of society than they are likely to prove otherwise.

In practice crèches had to keep down their fees or they would not be used. The gap was closed by donations, obtained privately from patrons and their friends, or solicited more widely through circulating printed reports and getting publicity. Even the subsidized fees were nevertheless too high for some. The records of child emigration agencies are full of cases where widows had to surrender their youngest children to Homes because they could not afford crèche or other child care but had to earn.[78]

Schools, by contrast, were free and plentiful. Even without Baby Rooms many schools were under pressure to allow children to come before they were the official minimum age, which was three.[79] The headmistress of an infants school in Homerton told the Cross Commissioners how parents 'often bring the little things to me under three, and beg of me to take them'.[80] School Board records show children under three in school, though their numbers steadily diminished. (They were probably rising three; and they were most numerous, not surprisingly, in the poorest schools, like Nichol Street in Shoreditch or Orange Street in the Borough.)[81] Members of the Wheeler family in Camden Town in the 1870s all started school early: 'I suppose when I first went to school I was two years old and a half, as soon as they'd take me, or Mother would put a year or so on my age'.[82] According to Clara Grant, who taught in Bow in the 1900s:

> The legal age of admission to school was three, but as a copy of the registration certificate cost 3d. very few mothers could buy it....Indeed, it was more convenient not to have it, since no head teacher could then demand to see it, and children toddled in to school at two and a half or even less.[83]

The headmistress of Saffron Hill school, Clerkenwell, ran into trouble in 1889, when alterations she had made in the age entries in her register were challenged and she was criticized for having children in classes inappropriate to their age. In her defence she wrote:

> when the women get work to do, they will foist a child on an Infant teacher when it is not much beyond two....If teachers are to be vilified on the age question, all teachers in very low neighbourhoods will have to look to their laurels.[84]

Other heads were sterner: Mrs Mansfield of Darby Street school, Southwark, reported refusing admittance to 'babies one and a half or two years old'.[85]

Sometimes teachers turned a blind eye. In the early 1900s Grace S., whose widowed mother was washing to support her and her sister, was unofficially allowed to attend Holy Trinity Infants school (Kentish Town) when only two: she was not registered, but her sister brought her every day. (She was shy and for some time never took off her hat and coat.)[86] Similarly a classroom described in 1903 held at the back 'a big girl with a baby on her knee—a chubby little fellow of about eighteen months, sitting quiet, as good as gold, while the girl attends to her lesson'.[87] But that solution required the good will of the teacher and the good behaviour of the baby, and was presumably resorted to only in emergency.

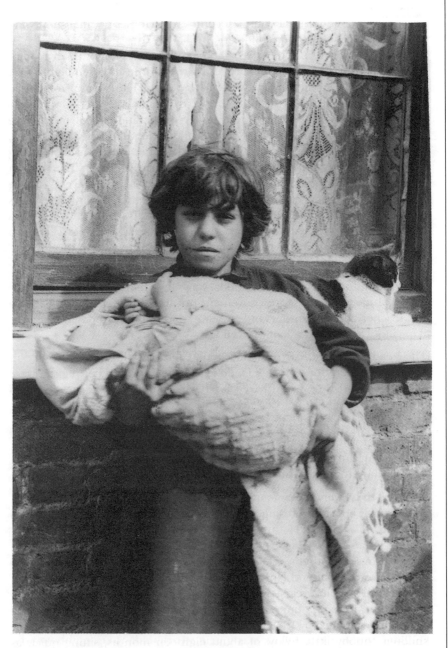

9. Girls often spent a good deal of time looking after younger children.

6
Needed at Home

———◆———

Minding the Little Ones

IF MOTHER or older children could not care for infants during the day, and if there was no crèche to take them, what were the alternatives? The occasional father took charge if his wife was in work and he was not, or if his hours were different, or if she was ill.[1] Another member of household or family might be available: most likely someone whose age or poor health made it hard for them to get work—often a grandparent, if one was part of the household or lived nearby.[2] A sister just released from school might be kept at home rather than sent to work. Old and young might combine forces, as in a family of Drury Lane flower-sellers in 1889, where a forty-five-year-old mother of six cared for the babies of her two eldest daughters with the help of her youngest.[3] A child might go to a nearby relative, perhaps a married sister.[4] Of working mothers surveyed in a turn-of-the-century report, half regularly left children with relatives.[5] Sometimes—how often we cannot know—children were locked in for the day or, if older, locked out.

The more prosperous mother—a shopkeeper, for instance, or perhaps an artisan's wife—engaged a 'nurse', a girl who had just left school, to look after the baby during its waking hours. (Mrs Layton did this at ten, in Bethnal Green in 1865.)[6] Wage-earning mothers could not usually afford this arrangement. Sometimes neighbour or landlady obliged for the odd day, but for more she would have to be paid.[7] Sometimes there was a local child-minder, most often an older woman who kept herself by taking in infants for money.[8] Child care could consume a third or a half of the earnings of a woman who worked for wages. As a child-minder in 1885 observed, she did not make much out of her charge of sixpence a day for each of the three babies she looked after (supplying their milk and food), 'but the women only earn 1s. 6d. to 2s. themselves'.[9] Nearly thirty years later, in a case noted by Clementina Black, a woman who earned eleven shillings for four days' work was giving nearly half to a neighbour who charged 1s. 2d. a day to mind her two small children.[10]

The need was often an irregular one. Some women's employment was casual—now a day washing, now a day cleaning, now a few days in factory or workshop during a rush. Some women had regular part-time work, three or four days a week in a laundry, for instance. Or a woman doing homework needed time, perhaps several hours, to go two or three times a week to the warehouse with the finished trousers (or sacks or matchboxes or whatever) and to collect the next lot of work. Or the prospect of a heavy wash with toddlers underfoot loomed. So 'twopence or a cup of tea to some old woman or little girl to mind the baby for a few hours', was 'an item which you may find in the poorest budget'.[11]

Where the older children already looked after the younger ones outside school hours, it was tempting to save those coppers by keeping a child at home for the odd morning, or afternoon, or both. This, as we shall see, was the pattern of girls' absence from school. It was on girls that the burden of child care chiefly fell, and girls whose attendance was most affected by the lack of crèche facilities.

Under some circumstances, domestic need was officially recognized. It was possible, for instance, for an older child to become a half-timer, combining school and work like the child workers of the northern mill-towns.[12] In London in the 1870s this was in principle allowed only when a child was 'beneficially and necessarily at work', and she or he still had to attend for ten out of twenty-five hours a week changed in1879 to five out of the ten weekly attendances.[13] Many half-timers were said to be employed in household work.[14] Others again did industrial work, usually in small workshops or domestic outwork, though Bryant and May's match factory used some half-timers in the 1870s.[15] Teachers disliked the arrangement.[16] For half-timers were often irregular even in the attendances they were supposed to make; they were unsettling in their effect on other pupils and harder to get through examinations. They also depressed the attendance rates to which government grants were keyed, and so, under the payment by results system, could lower the teachers' salaries.[17] In London official policy was to phase out half-time attendance, and half-timers dwindled from 2,417 in 1879, to 1,873 in 1889–90, to 693 in 1893, to 88 in 1899–1900.[18] After that it was formally abolished in London.

There were however informal arrangements about half-time attendance, such as would escape the official record. Harriet ('Mighty'), the sister of Arthur Harding, born in 1882, was the mainstay of her crippled mother long before she was permitted to leave school and start full-time work. She looked after her young brother and sister; she went to and from the Bryant and May depot to return the matchboxes her mother made and collect materials for new ones; she shopped; she foraged; she traded, she washed; she ran every kind of errand. To combine all this with full-time school was not possible. So three days a week, her brother recalled:

> Mighty, instead of going to school, would hop it. My mother came to some arrangement....They didn't want to summon her, my mother being a cripple, so they made this special arrangement— twice a week she went to school and the other days she had off.[19]

This was probably not official. A later example can certainly not have been sanctioned: half-time had been formally ended in London when Mrs M., who was born the eldest of seventeen in Hoxton in 1896, was permitted at twelve to go half-time so as to help at home. Her mother had new twins, four babies needing bottles, and a broken arm; so her grandmother, who 'went to ask', presumably made a strong case.[20]

A child approaching the age of release and not behind with school work could sometimes get complete exemption from further attendance, if the authorities were persuaded that her services or her earnings were really needed. Such exemptions were ratified with phrases like: 'Children's earnings required owing to poverty of parents'; 'Required at home owing to special circumstances'; 'Wanted to go to work'; and so on. But poverty and special circumstances had to be extreme for exemption to be granted, and the age and standard demanded rose steadily. In the school year 1894–5, 1,205 children were excused from attendance, most over twelve and in or above Standard Four. Next year the Board stopped exemption for children under thirteen, and allowed it between thirteen and fourteen only for those who had attended regularly for five of the six preceding years. Eight hundred and forty-six children were excused in 1896–7. They stiffened the requirements still further in 1898, and the total was down to 313 by the end of the decade.[21] The exceptional cases where exemption was granted show how desperate the need had to be; moreover, most of these girls had only two months to go before they could leave anyway, and often they were in the highest possible class, Standard Ex-Seven. Here are examples:

Ellen Pearce, 13 years 10 months, Standard Five, mother widow... parish relief; one elder girl earns 7s., total income 12s. 6d., rent 5s., two children younger.

Florence Plummer, 13 years 10 months, Standard Seven, father deserted family, mother unable to work, eight children none over school age, rent in arrears, family living on charity and will probably go into the workhouse, two children invalids.

Ruth Card, 13 years 6 months, Standard ex-Seven. Father...ill...five younger children, girl has offer of situation in confectioner's shop at 3s. a week with board and lodging.

Nelly Kempton, 13 years 10 months, Standard ex-Seven, mother dying of cancer...required to attend to home.[22]

The threshold of desperate need set by the authorities bore no relation to the family's perception of need, especially as it was linked to age and formal attainment not to crisis. Parents were unwilling to cede priority to the demands of school. At a sitting of North London Police Court in 1891, the sixty parents summoned for not sending their children to school included:

> Several poor widows who complained of having to go out to work
> and keep six or seven children, without having the privilege of the
> services of the elder children 'nearly fourteen years of age' who
> might assist in the maintenance of the family.[23]

It was hard for parents to accept an edict which threatened the natural
(often the only possible) resort in domestic emergency, that daughter
should stand in for mother, or son earn a wage. The girl herself, or the boy,
might also regard school as an irrelevancy to be escaped from as soon as
possible, and want to play more part in the family economy. A Putney
father in 1902, was found guilty of falsifying his daughter's birth certificate
to justify her absence from school. He claimed the daughter had done it
herself, which she confirmed, and that he had genuinely thought her fourteen anyway.[24] The magistrates, who fined him five pounds or a month in
prison, presumably did not believe that a 'child' would have initiative or
skill enough for the forgery, let alone that she could want to abandon
childhood for an adult role so soon. (They might also have doubted his
casual attitude to exact age, unthinkable by then among those more liter-
ate or more exposed to bureaucracy.)[25] It is quite possible, however, that
father and daughter spoke the truth.

Older girls might well put home before school, and be backed up by
parents, particularly mothers. Sometimes, it seems, they effectively left
school before the permitted age. In the 1890s, Maidstone Street school, in
Haggerston (a poor part of Hackney, bordering on Bethnal Green), suffered 'very irregular attendance, especially among the elder girls',[26] and
one headmistress there made lists in the logbook of persistent absentees
the school visitor was to pursue. These show that some children were not
just irregular: they never came.[27] In one list of thirty-four girls (6 Sept.
1895), twenty names were starred, to indicate, according to the head, that
'the parents refuse to send, and in many of these cases the children are at
work'. One had missed nineteen school weeks, another eighteen, two
more seventeen. Others had showed up only sporadically over periods as
long. Another list, of twenty-one names (3 March 1896), showed girls who
in the previous eleven months had managed respectively fifty-two, fourteen, fifteen, ten, thirty, forty-seven, twenty-four, sixty, sixty-six and eighty
out of a possible total of over 400 morning and afternoon sessions. Most
of these, and those who had attended least, were from Standards Four and
above, so probably between eleven and thirteen years old.[28] In the whole
list, too, the majority were from standards above Four. (Other lists gave no
indication of standard or age.)

Similar cases figure among the 'typical' absentees listed in School
Board records, like these from Hackney in 1892:[29]

> Girl aged 12 in Standard Two....Absent 12 months....Parents say
> 'Old enough to leave school', 'Won't send any more'. They have
> removed five times since Christmas; when found they remove

again before action can be taken. The last fine is still outstanding
as the present address is not known.

Girl 12 absent 13 weeks. There is no father, and the child is kept
to mind the baby while the mother goes out to work. The child is
the oldest of four.

'Typical cases', and occasional lists for one school (I have not found data
as clear in other logbooks)[30] over five years, are of course no basis for statistical analysis. But annual school returns show that Maidstone Street
school was not the worst girls' school in Hackney for attendance, and
Hackney's average attendance rates were close to the average for London.
In other poor schools too, then, there may well have been girls marked
absent on the register more often than present.

Overall, however, the most common pattern for girls—in contrast with
boys—was to turn up during most of the week but miss two or three mornings or afternoons.[31] This is suggested by a School Board return in 1899,
where figures for the last quarter of 1898 were analysed to show the weekly attendance of boys, girls and infants.[32] In those three months only 17.5
per cent of girls managed ten out of ten attendances a week, while 23.9 per
cent of boys did. Among boys, 59.2 per cent made nine or ten attendances,
and 22.3 per cent made seven or eight. Among girls, 46.4 per cent made
nine or ten, 35.6 per cent managed seven or eight, and 7.7 per cent (as
opposed to 2.5 per cent of boys), only six. The infants' rate (influenced, of
course, by still other factors)33 was lowest for full attendance (13 per cent);
for eight attendances and under, it was almost the same as the girls'. The
most striking disproportion is in the figures for nine attendances out of
ten, a level achieved by 35 per cent of boys, 33.5 per cent of infants, and
only 28 per cent of girls.[34]

Girls, then, were more likely to miss attendances than boys, and more
of them missed more. More boys would miss a single morning or afternoon; more girls would miss two, three, or more, but especially three.

School logbooks confirm this. At a poor school newly opened in Upper
Holloway, the headmistress deplored girls' irregularity.

17 Feb 1873 Numbers again small....Parents say they would be glad
to send but their girls' services at home cannot be dispensed with.

10 July 1873 It seems almost impossible to induce the parents to
make an effort to send their girls regularly—they are kept at home
for everything.[35]

Illness at home kept the girls away as nurses. When the head of
Gainsborough Road school (Hackney) in 1885 asked the attendance officer why girls' attendance was more affected by a prevailing sickness than
boys', she was told that the girls, being 'more useful in the house', were
'wanted to nurse the sick ones'.[36] If their mothers were ill themselves, or in
childbed, girls not only nursed them but took on running the household.

Mothers engaged in homework, as many wives of unskilled men were at times, valued their children's help on the work, or as messengers with it once finished, or with the baby; and when under pressure they kept them home.[37] The girl was unlikely to protest, and indeed might make the decision herself: she knew as well as her mother what was needed.

Child care was often the immediate cause of girls' absence, to free the mother for other work, to replace her if she was ill, or to cope with emergency. Heads of girls' schools noted poor attendance on days when infants' schools were shut for vestry elections, as this 'necessitated many girls staying away to look after their younger brothers and sisters'.[38] When an epidemic closed the Stepney Crèche in 1880, the School Board visitor came daily to ask when it would reopen, 'almost beside himself as the children are staying at home to nurse babies'.[39] In Southwark in 1872 lower enrolment of girls was blamed on the insufficiency of school places for infants.[40]

Washing days were notoriously bad for attendance, and everyone understood why. As a settlement worker put it:

> One fully appreciates how tempting it is to keep Mary Jane at home, at least on washing day. Perhaps there are six little ones, one of them a small baby, and twins of eighteen months.[41]

At one school, lessons from Wednesday afternoon were moved mid-year as it was local washing day, and the many girls who regularly missed those lessons might fail their exams.[42] Elsewhere Monday posed the same problem, with the additional disadvantage of being the day when the week's fee was due.[43] Friday was bad too. ('It seems almost impossible to secure a satisfactory attendance on Friday afternoon', wrote a headmistress in 1874.)[44] It was the hardest day for homeworkers, when money had to be accumulated for the weekend. It was the day when casual cleaning work could most easily be had. And even mothers who did not do paid work were more likely to keep back their children on that day 'to tidy up the house'. By the 1890s a special effort was being made in some schools to make Friday afternoons attractive, with extra time for play, visiting lecturers, sometimes experimental science lectures (as a show, however: girls did not study science—see next chapter) and even a street organ engaged to play in the school yard for half an hour.[45]

The Double Standard

The pattern of girls' irregularity was a difficult one to deal with; but the authorities scarcely tried. They held that 'needed at home', as an excuse for absence, 'must, under the circumstances, be accepted as reasonable'.[46] Efforts to provide school-based child care had failed; legal enforcement was unrealistic if only two or three attendances a week were missed. It is not surprising to find a fatalistic tolerance of such absence.[47]

There was some attempt to keep absence for domestic reasons within limits, though enforcement varied in this respect as in others. In 1874 a School Board committee on attendance problems took evidence from the superintendents of visitors in each division of London. In Chelsea, the practice was 'occasionally [to] excuse the attendance of a child over ten for one day a week, where it appears that there is a large family to wash for, and a baby is to be cared for'. In the City, an elder child was sometimes allowed to stay and help if there was illness at home. In Hackney, up to fourteen days' absence was allowed if the father was out of work or the mother ill. In Lambeth, half-time was granted if there was 'great poverty' and the child had passed enough standards. In Marylebone, the mother's confinement was accepted as an excuse for absence, for girls.[48] Whatever the theoretical limits, they were probably applied with some flexibility. Florence H., in Bethnal Green in the 1890s was brought up by an elder sister because of her mother's death. She often took a note saying that she had 'had to stay at home and mind the baby'; this would be accepted, she later recalled, as long as she 'didn't stay away too much'.[49]

In general, for girls, 'the necessities of domestic life' held good as an excuse.[50] In 1900, Sir Charles Elliott of the London School Board, writing to *The Times* on the attendance question, divided reasons for absence into three groups: 'excusable', 'doubtful' and 'inexcusable'. In the first category he placed 'retention at home on account of illness of some member of the house whether for infectious disease or...confinement of mother, or accompanying mother or little brother or sister to hospital, etc.'; in the second, 'helping mother' (the excuse, he said, 'most frequent of all'), and in the last, being employed at home more than twice a week.[51]

Twice a week, that is, could be tolerated, even at the level of statistics and official pronouncements.[52] The individual teacher or attendance officer, knowing particular circumstances and seeing no alternative, might often condone a still higher level of absence. A Deptford teacher around 1900 regularly put up with losing one of her eight-year-olds: the harassed mother (a widowed washerwoman) would call through the classroom window at Frankham Street school, ' "Come on out, Liz, I need you", and the teacher would say, "All right, you'd better go then," and let her'.[53] In the same way, a teacher might tolerate lateness, and even try to cover it up, because she knew what a child had to do before school. Children who arrived after 9.30, when the registers closed, were supposed to be recorded as absent. But Board inspectors complained of inaccurate records of lateness: 'It is impossible to get some teachers to see that in registering facts, sentiment has no place'.[54] Self-interest may have played some part, however: teachers would be reluctant to inflate the number of 'absentees' by including late-comers, since this ultimately affected their pay. Heads, with less personal contact with the children and more stake in successful discipline, might be stricter. Some conducted real campaigns on punctuality.[55] Being unpunctual, like being irregular, was affected by home circumstances and the parents' attitude to school—both how much the child's help was needed, and how seriously the parents took the demands of education.[56] Again, as with irregular attendance, girls were affected the most.

Girls definitely found it harder to get to school on time. The question of punctuality was explored by a School Board inspector in a report in 1883. During a sample week, he calculated, 71 per cent of boys and only 51 per cent of girls were marked early (that is, arriving before nine o'clock, when classes started). In five girls' schools, he added, 'less than a third were marked early'.[57] When a system of rewards for regular and punctual attendance was set up in 1887, the number of reward cards given to boys was consistently about 30 per cent higher than that for girls (see Table 6.1).[58] HMI Nickal's evidence to the Cross Commission confirmed the unpunctuality of girls, especially in poorer schools. He was asked whether in 'schools generally' many children missed the first lesson. (The question was prompted by concern about scriptural instruction, which always came first.)[59] He answered, 'Yes, in girls' schools'; and submitted as examples figures on punctuality at a range of schools. In two very rough and poor schools 31 per cent and 38 per cent of the girls arrived before the first lesson began, about 20 per cent missed it altogether, and the rest were present for some of it. At another school, poor but 'of a little better description', 51 per cent were on time, and 12 per cent too late for any scripture instruction. At a school with a slightly higher fee (twopence instead of a penny), long established but in 'a rather poor crowded neighbourhood', 52 per cent were on time, 23 per cent present for most of the lesson, and 10 per cent too late. Even at a 'comparatively new school in an outlying district', 4 per cent missed the lesson and 15 per cent were late. It was only in a few of the best schools that 90 to 95 per cent were on time and none missed scripture 'habitually'.[60]

The reward-card statistics, show that although rates varied between neighbourhoods, girls' punctuality was never up to boys'. Boys even in the poorest School Board divisions received more reward cards in 1887 than the girls of any division, with the exception of Greenwich, whose girls outdid the boys of Chelsea, Finsbury, Marylebone and Hackney.[61]

This difference was rooted in the division of domestic labour.

Table 6.1: Reward cards for punctuality received by boys and by girls, 1889-94: number of cards awarded shown as a percentage of average attendance.

School year	Boys	Girls	Difference
1889–90	93.9	61.6	32.3
1890–91	86.9	57.4	29.5
1891–2	83.7	54.2	29.5
1892–3	85.9	56.5	29.4
1893–4	93.0	62.9	30.1

Source: SBL School Management Committee, Annual Reports.

Although both boys and girls ran early morning errands, boys' other work before breakfast mostly took the more regular form of delivering newspapers, milk or bread. These rounds made them tired for school but they were less likely to be late. Some witnesses before the 1902 Committee on children's employment maintained that children with regular employment were regular at school, neither absent nor late, whereas 'those who work at home are the worst'.[62] Girls' usual task to get younger children dressed and fed and take toddlers to infant school or crèche affected afternoon as well as morning punctuality. Small children are hard to hurry; and the task could be onerous. Workers at the Stepney crèche in 1895 noticed a child who every morning brought 'an infant she was hardly able to carry', and then went back to Whitechapel (perhaps a mile) for another child, old enough to walk much of the way, but whom she carried a good deal so as to get to school herself. (They provided 'an old perambulator, to ease the child's labours'.)[63] So the unpredictable last-minute demands of child care and domestic crisis contributed to making girls late more frequently than boys, as well as to keeping them away more often.[64]

But girls' lateness and absence for domestic reasons were not tolerated by the authorities simply because they could not be helped. Other factors were involved. Although in their notion of the family children were dependent, duty to the family and the authority of the father (and behind him the mother) were also central precepts. Legislative restriction of employment had already undermined the right of parents to their children's earnings. Further interference with parental prerogative was not acceptable to everyone.[65] In 1899, in a Parliamentary debate whether to raise to twelve the age at which half-time exemption was allowed, many expressed reluctance to impinge on parental rights.[66] One rural member (Mr Jeffreys, North Hampshire) thought the law should be left as it was.

> Why should not parents in the poorer classes of life treat their children as we do in our class of life? If the parents think that a girl, having passed her Fourth Standard, can leave school and help her mother in the house and attend to the smaller children, why not entitle them to do so? Why not have more confidence in the parents? In a similar way, if a boy passes the Fourth Standard, why should he not leave school to help his father in tending cattle or scaring birds?

The member for Birkenhead, Sir E. Lees, thought employment of a child of eleven was the lesser evil if the alternative was that the mother should go out to work. That the claims of family sometimes came before the claims of school was a view held even by some members of the London School Board: the system of awards for regular attendance was criticized at a committee meeting in 1900 because it meant that 'children have been sent to school or insisted on going when their highest duty was to their home'.[67] Such general sentiments had a long heritage. They survived most tenaciously, however, when combined with ideas about gender difference.

Girls were consistently absent more than boys (see Table 6.2). Yet problems of attendance were discussed largely in terms of boys. In 1886–7, the average attendance rate for boys' schools under the London Board was 82 per cent; for girls' schools it was 76 per cent, a difference of six points. The difference varied with the fee charged by the school, and so, presumably, with the poverty of the families concerned. Table 6.3 shows the variation.

Table 6.2: Attendance percentage for boys, girls and infants, by London School Board Division, 1886–7.

Division	Boys	Girls	Infants
City	68.3	72.8	77.5
Chelsea	82.5	76.9	77.7
Finsbury	81.1	75.7	76.8
Greenwich	85.2	79.6	77.7
Hackney	81.2	76.2	76.0
E. Lambeth	84.1	78.8	75
W. Lambeth	84.1	78.8	75.8
Marylebone	82.6	75.5	75.3
Southwark	82.9	70.5	76.8
Tower Hamlets	82.6	74.9	74.2
Westminster	81.4	75.2	74.5

Source: SBL *School Management Committee Report,* 1886–7, Table R, School Returns.

Table 6.3: Percentage of average attendance according to sex and fee in London Board schools, 1886–7, and difference by sex.

Fees	Boys	Girls	Difference
4d+ (32 schools)	86.6	83	3.6
3d (114 schools)	85	78.4	6.6
2d (233 schools)	81.8	75.8	6.0
1d (57 schools)	78.2	72	6.2

Source: Constructed from SBL *School Management Committee Annual Report,* 1886–7, Table R (School Returns).

The problem of improving attendance was initially presented by the school authorities as one of efficient scheduling and better enforcement. The need was for conscientious attendance officers to make sure no children went unrecorded and to pursue truants, and for co-operative magistrates to enforce the law even when it conflicted with 'their idea of what it should be'.[68] This approach dominated the 1870s and early 1880s. Other explanations did begin to be heard ('the poverty, the sickness, and the home needs of the parents....I really do find scarcely an unreasonable excuse given'),[69] but the stern allegations about defiant truants, inadequate enforcement and irresponsible parents continued to be frequent.[70]

At the same time, in the drive to improve the general average the lower attendance of girls was not much remarked. One inspector, Mr Ricks, reporting on 1875-6, observed that, 'In general the attendance of boys is better than that of the girls and infants', and without comment on the girls went on to explain the irregularity of infants.[71] Mr Noble, for South London in 1877, listed sixteen schools with 90 per cent attendance, and fourteen with attendance below 70 per cent. In his first list there were twelve boys' schools, two girls' and two infants'; his second comprised eleven girls', two infants', and one mixed.[72]

Inspector McWilliam's report on attendance and punctuality in his South London division in 1883 tabulated attendance rates for three years (see Table 6.4). His accompanying comment was that:

> The fact that the regularity of the girls keeps steadily below that of the boys and infants, shows that it is home cares rather than indifference or defiance which is the cause of much of the irregularity.[73]

He offered no solution, and passed on to discuss at rather more length the problems of boys' absence.

Table 6.4: Percentage attendance McWilliam's schools 1878, 1880, 1883.

Week ending	Boys	Girls	Infants
6 Sept. 1878	83.4	77.3	80.5
10 Sept. 1880	80.5	75.3	80.5
26 Oct. 1883	83.2	76.8	77.3

Source: SBL *Minutes,* 20 Dec. 1883, p. 185.

The polarized assumptions (truancy versus domestic need) also influenced punishment. Albert and Olive, brother and sister whose father made chairs in a domestic workshop, had to take a barrow-load of chairs to the wholesaler twice a week in their dinner hour. When the delivery was from Bethnal Green to London Fields, a manageable mile, they were all right. But sometimes they had to go three miles to Bermondsey, with the risk, too, of delay if Tower Bridge was letting river traffic through. This made them late for afternoon classes. At Albert's school the head waited on the stairs and caned all late-comers without excuse or exception. Olive, in the girls' school, was never caned.[74]

Attempts to establish different causes of absence in different groups were made for a School Board committee set up in 1890 to investigate attendance. Its printed proceedings include a report from the Committee of Representative Managers of London Board Schools, whose chair, William

Bousfield (himself previously a member of the School Board), argued that:

> everything really depended...upon the character of the parents. Where the parents were in steady employment and of steady habits themselves, regular attendance was as a rule secured....The difficulty really existed with the children of parents who were of irregular habits, or who were constantly out of work.[75]

This distinction between regular and irregular work slipped easily into an assumption about moral regularity, both here ('steady employment and steady habits') and in the classification presented for the Committee by the School Managers. Children attending London elementary schools were divided by it into three categories, which are worth quoting at length:[76]

(a) Those of parents fairly well off.
   (i)   These generally attend well...except:
   (ii) Infants, who do not attend unless quite well and the weather is fair.
(b) Those of parents who are poor, but in regular work and of regular habits.
   (i)   Infants are entered early and attend well.
   (ii) Girls attend regularly as a rule, but are liable to be detained to take care of younger children, for home washing, in cases of illness, etc.
   (iii) Boys attend regularly as a rule, but leave school early to get work.
(c) Those of parents in irregular work, such as costermongers, dock labourers, etc, and of the idle and dissolute.
   (i)   Infants are often entered early and attend better than other children of same age, the school being regarded as caretaker.
   (ii) Girls are often most irregular. The mother's earnings are frequently larger than the father's and the girls are kept at home to look after babies and children, or are sent to beg in the streets, sell flowers, etc.
   (iii) Boys are generally very irregular. Parents of this class have often no control over their children, though they encourage their begging and getting odd employment. From this class comes the great bulk of truants, street arabs, crossing sweeper boys and young criminals. The whole of this class are more migratory in their habits than the others...

In their model, then, the children of the well-off attended well. The regularly employed were respectable, and their children attended well even if they were poor, except that sometimes the girls were needed at home—which was not incompatible with their being respectable. The irregularly employed were (actually or potentially) idle and dissolute, and their children, except the infants, were very irregular. Comparison of the model with attendance figures confirms some of their observations (such as the high attendance of the infants of the poorest class), but it also brings out important distinctions obscured by their concern with moral ordering.[77]

Detailed comparison is made possible by the attendance returns given each year for all Board schools in the reports of the School Management Committee. Individual schools often had a marked social character, established partly by the nature of the district they served, and partly also by the level of the fee charged. (The system of charging different fees at different schools was one way of reassuring better-off and respectable parents that their children could be accommodated in the Board system without being exposed to rougher ways.)[78] Such differences can be illustrated from the account given by Mrs Bartle (born in Poplar in 1882, her father a coastal seaman who became a mate) of the two schools she attended. The first, Thomas Street, charged sixpence, a very high fee.[79] She recalled it as:

> really very superior...some of the better-off children used to go to Thomas Street. And of course there were tradespeople's children as well...'

> When my mother went to register my sister there ('cause my sister went before I did)...the headmistress of course told her it was sixpence a week, and she asked mother what father's position was, and mother told her...and she says, I think you're a very ambitious woman.[80]

When they moved, the mother's sights had to be lowered, and the girl went to Sydney Road, Homerton: a 'terribly rough school', where pupils fought in the street with Irish children from a nearby Catholic school and the fee was twopence. School Board statistics record high attendance rates at Thomas Street and low at Sydney Road.[81]

Using school fees as a guide to the approximate social standing of the school, we can explore the classification offered by the School Managers through one year's average attendance rates for the boys, girls and infants of London Board schools, according to fees charged.[82] (See Table 6.5.)

Table 6.5: Average attendance for boys, girls and infants, according to fee, 1886–7.

Fee	Boys	Girls	Infants
4d+ (32 schools)	86.6	83	79
3d (114 schools)	85	78.4	76.8
2d (233 schools)	81.8	75.8	77.1
1d (57 schools)	78.2	72	76.8

Source: Constructed from SBL *School Management Committee Annual Report*, 1886–7, Table R (School Returns).

In 1886–7 the thirty-two schools with a fee of fourpence or above may
be taken to represent category (a) in the Managers' list; the 114 threepenny schools and the 233 twopenny schools their category (b), and the
fifty-seven penny schools their (c). It should be noted that nearly three-
quarters of the children were in twopenny and threepenny schools. Table
6.5 confirms that attendance improved with prosperity, but it also shows
that girls' attendance was always, at each level, lower, and that in poverty it
deteriorated more than either boys' or infants'. The girls' rate drops by 11
points (from 83 to 72 per cent) between the fourpenny school average and
the penny; while the boys' rate falls by only 8.4 points (from 86 to 78.3 per
cent), and the infants' by a mere 2.3, from 79 to 76.8 per cent.

The difference between boys' and girls' attendance was least (3.6 per
cent) in the schools which charged fourpence or more. (At sixpenny
Thomas Street it was only 2.3.) In the other three groups it was 6.6, 6.0 and
6.2 per cent. It is significant that there was always some difference. It is also
interesting that the School Managers' analysis did not take note of it: they
made no distinction between girls and boys in their category (a); in (b)
they implied girls' greater absence but did not dwell on it; while in (c) they
gave reasons for boys' and girls' respective absence rates without remark-
ing that girls were absent more. Yet the annual statistics of the Board make
clear that it was a difference which could be seen everywhere.

The lower attendance rate of girls, if noted at all, was attributed to
home cares, with no suggestions on how to improve it. Boys' absence continually drew comment; it was defined as truancy and attributed to
indifference and defiance; and various ways to control it were tried. Special
roving Street Visitors were assigned to search 'streets or open spaces, markets, railway stations' for truants. Girls' absence was not seen as truancy;[83]
homes were not searched in the same way, and girls ('necessarily required
at home more than boys') were relatively immune from pursuit.[84] More
boys than girls were sent to mend their ways in Truant and Industrial
Schools;[85] and probably the parents of absentee boys were more prosecuted and more punished than those of absentee girls.[86] The School Board's
1890 inquiry into attendance discussed the subject almost entirely in terms
of truancy, and took evidence from thirty-nine headmasters and only three
headmistresses.[87] (No children or parents were called.)

An 1880 case reported in *Social Notes* suggests that domestic responsibilities were also a less acceptable excuse for boys.

> A poor woman in the house I live in has three children, two are
> babies, and one a boy of eleven years....The woman's husband
> gives her 12s. to pay rent and provide food and clothing with. To
> nurse the babies she keeps her boy from Board School now and
> then, when she has a chance of going out to earn a shilling or two.
> For this crime she was summoned before the Board-school
> Committee, who treated her explanation with contempt and
> would not allow the boy's absence for even half a day...[88]

'A boy ought never to miss an attendance, unless there was not an elder girl in the family', was the opinion of Mrs Hickman, School Visitor for the City and Westminster, in 1890.[89] Girls' absence, by implication, was to be condoned. If, at each level of enforcement, tolerance was more likely for girls kept at home than for boys, then, where there was any choice, the tendency for domestic responsibilities to fall on girls would be confirmed.

By the end of the century attendance rates had generally improved. The gap between the girls' rate and the boys' had narrowed to 4.2 per cent but was still there,[90] and it continued to be obscured and excused by the double standard. Girls' lower attendance, Spalding explained in 1900, stemmed from their 'greater usefulness in the domestic economy'. In his summing up he effectively ignored the difference:

> It cannot be considered unsatisfactory that more than half the total roll (50.7 per cent) should make perfect, or almost perfect, attendances, having regard to the many hindrances to regular attendance. These arise from the impossibility that infants should not often fail, from circumstances beyond their control, to attend school; the need for occasional help in the household from the girls; the squalor and destitution of many of the homes from which the children come; and the unavoidable absences on account of illness, not only of the children actually suffering, but also of the children living in houses where there is infection.[91]

Again, girls' domestic duties are given as contributing to absence from school, but the extent is not remarked on. 'More than half the total roll (50.7 per cent)...make perfect or almost perfect attendance', so the composition of that 50.7 per cent is forgotten: 59.2 per cent boys plus 46.4 per cent girls plus 46.5 per cent infants equals 50.7 per cent children.

The usefulness of school, then, was perceived as different for girls and for boys by those concerned with the provision of elementary education, whether at the level of the individual or of social and national interest. Boys were to be workers and citizens, and needed schooling to discipline and educate them. If they came from 'irregular' families which were irresponsible about sending them to school, this was especially important. Girls' intended future was domestic. So the call of domestic obligation was more properly made to girls, and its fulfilment was more properly the responsibility of girls. If girls did not attend regularly it meant that family need was being put before education. But for girls this was ultimately as it should be: as women they would not be citizens, their work would be in the home, and they should indeed put the family first. Thus the double standard undermined the formal equality of educational provision.

10. *Teacher and class in the Isle of Dogs, 1897-8. The number of attendance medals and the 'best clothes' show that these children came from relatively comfortable working-class homes.*

7

A Centre of Humanizing Influence

The Infant School

WHAT WAS children's experience once they got to school, and was it the same for girls and for boys? It is not always easy to discover. First, the experience of children—girls or boys—is not the central focus of the mass of administrative data which is the obvious source on education in Board schools. Second, official records often do not distinguish between girls and boys; and (as we have seen with attendance) they contain statements apparently relevant to both which in fact refer only to boys.

The major differences of syllabus are relatively easy to document and will be discussed in Chapter 8. Text books too can be examined: most were intended for both boys and girls, but assumed they would have different interests and futures.[1] For classroom practice and experience, the best source, after autobiography, lies in the logbooks, or school diaries, kept by head teachers. Logbooks tell us about teachers' expectations of the children, of each other and of the parents—especially where these clashed. They show the working out in daily practice of the general rules set out by the Board; and from their accounts of the exceptional we can read off the norm. Moreover, the logbooks of girls' schools are also a source where, for once, 'children' can confidently be interpreted as 'girls'.

The classic London Board school of this period, still to be seen today, had three floors, and each housed an autonomous department: Infants (both sexes up to seven or eight years old), Girls, and Boys. One of the major tasks of the Infant School was to prepare children for more serious work in the 'Standards' later on.[2] Before anything, however, the three-year-olds starting school had to acquire 'the rudiments of cleanliness and behaviour'.[3] Most, but not all, could walk; most could talk, 'but as a rule imperfectly'.[4] They did not all have full control of bladder or even bowels; and starting school might set back those who did. William Nn (born in Poplar, 1896) recalled of his first day that:

all the children who were going to the school for the first time were crying, including myself, and nearly every one had messed themselves before they had reached the school gates.[5]

'Much of the house-training' of small children, according to C.H. Rolph, was done by the long-suffering teachers. His own first remembered school lessons concerned bootlaces.[6]

'Habits of neatness, order and obedience' came next.[7] 'Both for the sake of the infants themselves, so much neglected and mismanaged in their homes, and still more for the sake of the efficiency of the other schools',[8] children had to learn to accept the teacher's authority, to keep still during lessons, and not to talk or to move around without permission. These aims were not easily achieved: complaints of talkativeness and fidgetting, unruliness, disorder and inattention recur in the logbooks. The school room was organized for surveillance and discipline, with the children seated in rows ('facing mutely towards the source of knowledge')[9] on long fixed forms, sometimes without backs, which rose in a tier on the steps of a construction called a 'gallery'. Children suffered from confinement, discomfort and fatigue: small wonder if they were restless. After several decades, galleries went out of fashion, and low movable tables or dual desks were recommended, with space for games in the middle of the room. But change was slow, and keeping still and quiet did not get easier.

In these 'Babies' Rooms' children from three to five learnt 'to speak clearly, to understand pictures, to recite the alphabet and to march to music'.[10] They learnt to count and to recognize letters and figures, then, using sand-boxes or slates, to form them.[11] Edward Ezard recalled how, at a Battersea school in the early 1900s, he 'pored over pot-hooks and hangers on the first steps of the literacy road and counted coloured balls on the rods of ball-frames as an introduction to numeracy'.[12] Progress was monitored, even at this early stage:

> This morning I examined the Babies' Class and found them very backward in every subject, only five exhibited a knowledge of letters, their writing and Figures were very bad, and the children were fidgetty...

wrote a headmistress in 1878.[13]

On graduating from Babies' Room to Infants' Class, they continued along the same lines, marched to music and learnt songs, practised writing and some drawing, and learnt to read simple words. Richard Church, who started at Surrey Lane Infants school in the late 1890s, saw his time there as proof of 'children's infinite patience'.

> Slowly and laboriously I learned the alphabet and the spelling of two-letter words, sing-songing them in a class of sixty infants, following the red-tipped cardboard pointer in the teacher's hand, as she wrote the symbols on the blackboard....Would an adult sit from

8.50 a.m. until 12, with few breaks, at a hard wooden desk, with a spit-rubbed slate and a shrieking pencil, tonguing out pot-hooks and hangers, content to make no seeming progress, day after day; and then resume the dusty and evil-smelling task from 1.40 to 4.30? [14]

Besides basic skills they were daily taught the all-important 'religion and morality'. This was especially serious in church schools, with formal prayers and church visits, and religious instruction, usually by a local clergyman. There in the catechism the child was taught class as well as religious values, praying 'teach me to do my duty in that station of life to which it has pleased God to call me'. Religion might be brought into other subjects too. An 1833 book (by a bishop-to-be), probably used for decades in church schools, drew on the Bible for arithmetic examples:

[Numeration] The children of Israel, were sadly given to idolatry; notwithstanding all they knew of God, Moses was obliged to have three thousand of them put to death for this grievous sin. What digits must you use to express this number?...

[Subtraction] When Abraham was eighty-six years old, Ishmael was born; and when he was a hundred years old, Isaac was born; what was the difference between the ages of his sons? [15]

In church and Sunday schools, both in town or country, such traditional teaching no doubt persisted. Board schools (following the sectarian battles of the 1850s and 1860s) gave non-sectarian though Protestant instruction, mainly through Bible stories; and there was continuing radical pressure for more secular emphasis.

Teachers also taught 'the phenomena of nature and of common life', [16] generally by giving 'object lessons' on familiar articles or animals. This meant that the teacher held up an object—say, an apple—(or with something less easily produced, a picture, or a stuffed example), [17] and asked the children what they knew or could observe about it. To whatever they offered, the teacher then added further information about its origins, distribution, use, and so on. A list of object lessons in a Rotherhithe school in 1886 included Horse, Cow, Sheep, Fox, Elephant, Tiger, Pins, Needles, Chairs, String, a Slate Pencil Box, Bread, Chalk, Salt, Chairs, a Blacksmith's Shop, the Human Foot, Sun, Rivers, and a Letter. [18] The imparting of 'facts' was a long-standing pedagogical tradition, formalized in the monitorial system of 'interrogation', and satirized by Dickens in the first chapter of *Hard Times* (1854). Object lessons, a reforming alternative to the rigid cramming methods of the monitorial system, were meant to encourage observation. In theory, they allowed open and flexible teaching. In practice they could confuse, as Joseph Ashby recalled from his village schooldays:

There were object lessons now and then—without any objects but with white chalk drawings on the blackboard—an oil-lamp, or a vulture, or a diamond might be the subject. Once there was a lesson

on a strange animal called a quad-ru-ped—cloven-footed, a chewer
of the cud; her house was called a byre (but in Tysoe [his village] it
was not); her skin was made into shoes and from her udder came
milk. It burst upon Joseph that this was one of the creatures he
would milk after school, part of Henry Beasley's herd.[19]

Object lessons were not confined to infant classes; but with older children
the principle was only loosely observed. At a Lambeth school in 1896, for
example, they covered activities or abstractions like Minding Baby
(Standard One), and Punctuality, Tidiness, How to Light a Fire, and
Cleanliness in Homes (Standard Three): impossible to hold up before the
class or pass round. (Standard Two, more appropriately, studied Soap.)[20]

Girls began their long domestic training in the infant classes. First they
learnt needlework or knitting drill, rehearsing without needles how to sew
and to knit. To assist memory and co-ordination, the teacher might teach
them to sing:

> Hold the needle up on high
> Now peep through its little eye
> Let the thread so neatly lie
> Straight upon the desk.
> [tune 'Men of Harlech'][21]

Then they progressed to the use of actual needles, first 'pricking and
sewing cardboard'.[22] Boys too learned needlework in the 1870s, but during
the 1880s (especially with developing emphasis on vocational instruction,
sex-specific of course) drawing came to be regarded as more suitable for
them than sewing and knitting. Only a few schools let the boys continue
with needlework and the girls 'share the drawing lessons given to the boys',
and by 1902 the rule was that 'In all schools...boys should learn to draw and
girls to sew'.[23] When Miss Semphill, the Board's Needlework Instructress,
tried to convince the Flint Street headmistress in 1884 that boys should
learn sewing and knitting too, she was rebuffed.[24]

Under the influence of Friedrich Froebel's ideas, action songs, simple
'hand and eye' exercises to improve co-ordination, and activities intended
to stimulate observation and imitation were introduced already in the
1870s.[25] But his principle for kindergarten exercises, that children learn at
their own pace through stimulus and discovery, had as little chance as his
emphasis on spontaneity and movement. They were negated by the large
classes (double and treble Froebel's ideal of twenty-four children to a
teacher), the galleries (which filled the room and prevented movement),
the timetables, and the teachers' lack of Froebelian background.
Kindergarten occupations, according to an 1893 Circular to Inspectors,
were often:

> treated as mere toys, or amusing pastimes, because they are attrac-
> tive for children, and the intellectual character of the 'Gifts of

Froebel' is disregarded, whereas the main object of these lessons is
to stimulate intelligent individual effort.[26]

Nor had Froebelian emphasis on the equal and complementary importance of school and home in education much chance in Board schools,
given the conflicting interests of school authorities and parents, and the
cultural gulf between them. It is questionable, too, how far the rather
mawkish Froebelian songs and games were appropriate—in his terms—to
children who knew little of country delights, or indeed of urban middle-
class nursery ones either. A whole new set of texts and songs were needed
for these children.[27]

In any case, kindergarten songs, games and exercises were merely
tacked-on additions. Everyday teaching in the Board schools, whatever anyone's ideals, was geared to discipline and mechanical acquisition of basic
literacy and numeracy. The aim was to advance the whole group of children to the next stage, of standards and examinations.[28] Where senior
departments were overcrowded, a Standard One class might have to be set
up in the Infants to prepare them for examination in basic reading, writing
and 'number'.[29]

By the turn of the century, ideas about the importance of freedom of
movement, play, and individual learning had gained ground. At the same
time more and more stress was being placed on the importance of moth-
ering.[30] Infant schools then came under double attack. Some argued that
children under five (or even under seven) should not be in school at all,
but with their mothers. The 'home-developed' child, according to Rosalie
M. Munday, one of the women school inspectors who prepared special
reports on schoolchildren under five published in 1906, was better educated than the 'little scholar', 'though he has not directly learnt any of the
three Rs'. While the latter was 'all day one of sixty or more units', with no
personal attention, the former could prattle with mother, go shopping with
her, stroke cats, shell peas, run around, have a nap, and enjoy attention
from visitors.[31] Others pointed out that poor mothers could not always give
their children this kind of stimulus and attention, and that working-class
home conditions were often cramped and unhealthy. They argued that
infant schools were necessary for the proper development of the children
and (some added) the sake of the race.[32] But even those who defended the
principle agreed that the practice was deficient.[33] They criticized poor provision and use of space, insufficient movement, exercise or fresh air, rigid
methods, excessive discipline, lack of 'joy' and affection, and a totally inappropriate approach. 'Little children are subjected to military rather than
maternal influences' wrote Miss Bathurst, another inspector:

Individuality is crushed out, spontaneous qualities are checked,
and at three years old children are forced to follow a routine only
suitable to a far later age.

She advocated 'national nurseries' till six and a gradual introduction to school; women inspectors and doctors; and more Froebel training.[34] No-one suggested a return to dame schools, though these had supplied a kind of schooling much closer to what was being recommended, with a home-like atmosphere, 'maternal' teaching, relaxed attitudes to punctuality, attendance and discipline, and plenty of individual attention.[35]

The arguments against infant schools at this point, reinforced by topical fears that the nation's health was degenerating, were so influential that in 1905 the Board of Education empowered local authorities to abandon provision for children under five, and numbers did so.[36] (Exclusion had the merit of reducing costs and so pleasing the rate-payers.) The consultative committee set up by the Board to consider the question nevertheless ended up supporting the principle of local-authority nursery schools.[37] It recommended many changes, however. The curriculum needed to be greatly modified, lessons made shorter, and classes smaller. Light movable furniture should replace the galleries, there should be facilities for sleeping, and 'great latitude' should be exercised in regard to attendance.[38] It was also suggested that motherly women should be employed to help the teachers with the smaller children.[39]

The early twentieth-century critique of how children were treated and taught in school focused on the infant school, because it was powered by a vision of younger children as a distinct category: no longer babies, but still in need of motherly care and not ready for real school. But for Edmond Holmes, in his passionate *What is and What Might be* (published in 1911, soon after he resigned as Chief Inspector of Schools), the whole education system was to be criticized. In particular, it was tainted by the demand for mechanical obedience and based on 'complete mistrust of the child'.

> For a third of the century—from 1862 to 1895 [the period of 'payment by results']—self-expression on the part of the child may be said to have been formally prohibited by all who were responsible for the elementary education of the children of England, and also to have been inhibited *de facto* by all the unformulated conditions under which the elementary school was conducted. In 1895 the formal prohibition of self-expression ceased, but the *de facto* prohibition of it in the ordinary school is scarcely less effective today...and the old regime, though nominally abrogated, overshadows us still.

For teachers trained under the old system could not easily escape it.

> The teacher who has been deprived by his superiors of freedom, initiative, and responsibility, cannot carry out his instructions except by depriving his pupils of the same vital qualities.

By his standards, the infant schools were perhaps freer than those to which the children moved on.[40] The tyranny of examination work was less grave, attendance was not legally enforceable, and confrontations with authority were probably also less fraught, if only because the teacher was likely to be more secure in her authority over a younger child.

Girls or Boys

The transition from infants' to boys' or girls' department meant physical separation and a new school identity as girl or boy rather than infant. This segregation was taken seriously by the London School Board, though it might not have been. In 1840 the Committee of Council on Education 'supported the principle of co-educational teaching on the Scottish model, with the boys and the girls sitting on alternate benches in four separate classes, according to their proficiency in the three Rs'.[41] Matthew Arnold, as a school inspector in the 1850s, thought separation by age (with infants under a mistress and older children under a master) was more important than separation by sex, so long as playgrounds were distinct. He suggested that the 'British' schools (those of the British and Foreign School Society) lost 'by their anxiety to separate the boys from the girls', and so compared badly with Wesleyan ones, which followed the system he advocated.[42] And he held that girls educated with boys benefitted by 'that very correctness and stringency which female education generally wants'.[43] Scottish Robert Louis Stevenson, in 1881, deplored segregation on more general grounds: 'the little rift between the sexes is extraordinarily widened by simply teaching one set of catchwords to the boys and another to the girls'.[44]

But the School Board decided early on that infants' schools were to be mixed and senior schools separate; with 'Female Teachers only normally employed in Infant and Girls' Schools'.[45] By the early twentieth century arguments for co-education began to gain support, among both liberals and some imperialists,[46] and model mixed schools like Fleet Road in Hampstead operated successfully.[47] Parental views in general cannot be ascertained, but in 1895 when St John's (church) school, Walworth, merged its boys' and girls' departments most parents accepted the change.[48] Official commitment to separating the sexes remained.

In one rather extreme expression of anxiety about contact between boys and girls, a writer (in 1878) argued for total separation in classroom and playground because 'girls of the lower orders' lacked 'the habits of modesty which appear to be almost instinctive in our own' and both boys and girls needed to be taught 'the first principles in thought and conduct from teachers of their own sex'.[49] A more pragmatic assumption was that boys should be kept apart because they were tougher and rougher.[50]

Separation started as the children arrived: there were usually two entrances (sometimes three), with GIRLS AND INFANTS over one doorway, BOYS over the other: and 'woe betide any boy or girl who went in to the wrong gate'.[51] When the girls at Cottenham Road school, Holloway, had to use the boys' gate for several days while theirs was inaccessible because of work on the drains, the headmistress released them fifteen minutes early every day, so that 'the girls were away from the school premises before the boys left school'.[52] Playgrounds were also separate, divided not only by a wall, but by rules against approaching the frontier, or talking or even looking across it.

Each of the three groups had its own cloakroom indoors, with a 'Lavatory [for washing hands] and a Hat and Bonnet-room',[53] and outside separate ranges of water closets or 'offices'. 'The uncivilized way' in which the boys in a Tottenham school were using their 'offices' shocked the school managers' clerk in 1882. ('Her Majesty's Inspector thinks, and the Board thinks, too, that little things like these are an essential and important part of a boy's education.')[54] At V.S. Pritchett's rough Camberwell school around 1908, as no doubt at countless other schools, boys used to stand, 'a row of us, in the stinking school jakes, happily seeing who could pee the highest'.[55] William Nn (born 1896) recalled of his Poplar school that the 'two tiny toilets' provided for the boys (whose average daily number he reckoned at 484) were 'crowded out after school', so that many boys, instead, 'rushed into the street and lined up along the curb'.[56] At home, segregated facilities were unknown but urgent need with someone else in occupation all too familiar, since any provision was shared with other households.[57] Boys (and probably little girls) made use of handy drains or corners when in a hurry to pee.

Although they shared a school building, boys and girls—as Frederick Willis remembered of the 1890s—were 'poles apart'. In his school, a fairly superior one, the boys accepted this.

> It was an unwritten law that boys and girls should keep apart, and unless a boy had a sister at the same school he acted on the assumption that girls did not exist. If he displayed any interest in them he was regarded as a 'cissy' by his schoolfellows.[58]

Any girl seen walking with him would in turn 'be seen as a tomboy and not quite nice'; mixing was 'considered bad form'.[59] Peer-group pressure, then, in his recollection, reinforced the separation imposed by the school. This no doubt varied to some degree with age and with class stratum and culture. An anecdote from the novelist Pett Ridge records opposition to being split up amongst an audience of East End children at a free pantomime performance at the Britannia Theatre, Hoxton: when the girls were directed to sit downstairs, the boys up, the boys held back, and one protested, 'What? Ain't we going to sit alongside our tarts?'[60]

Before they started school children were not likely to meet segregation from siblings and playmates of the other sex, nor any stigma attached to mixing. Boys and girls (as we saw in Chapter 1) were dressed alike till boys were 'breeched', when 'off came the petticoat and dress, and knickers took their place'.[61] This happened between three and six, sometimes only after they started school.[62] Younger girls and boys shared a common experience of daily life at home, even if later more domestic help was expected of girls and more freedom (and perhaps food) given to boys. They played together a good deal at least until the age of eight or nine. Then they began to diverge, and girls, usually with younger children of both sexes in tow or joining in, played hopscotch, skipping, ball, and singing games; while boys, though often with tomboys among them, tended to play or roam together in groups (see Chapter 4).

Divergence in both syllabus and classroom experience became more marked after infant school. Richard Church (born 1894) recalled the change from women teachers to men, when he was eight. It made:

> a difference that affected every aspect of life. Everything and every relationship became less personal and more formal and official.

He found the male teachers 'administrative, legalistic, inexorable, reluctant', and the new environment bewildering.[63] Although girls moving up would also find more was now expected of them and work was harder, their teachers were still women, and discipline and the style of teaching probably changed less. The recurrent assertion that boys 'needed' the firm hand of a master suggests that masters were seen as exerting tougher discipline, and that older boys were supposed to need it.

Classes were generally large. Many schools had rooms intended for seventy, eighty and more: Maidstone Street, Hackney, in 1898–9 had two rooms for ninety-six and two for seventy-two which could be thrown together to hold 144. Even a superior (sixpenny) school might have classes of fifty to sixty.[64] Schools were allowed to register more children than there were places for, because of the expected shortfall in attendance. (Infant departments could enrol up to 20 per cent more; for older children the margin was 15 per cent.)[65] So in many schools irregular attendance was in some ways a good thing. Logbook complaints about poor attendance sometimes coincide significantly with comments on good order and progress, and obviously a smaller class meant more effective teaching for those who did show up. Good attendance, on the other hand, meant overcrowded classrooms. Nor were large classes only a Board-school problem: a Catholic school in Peckham in the mid-1870s had room for 125 children, but an enrolment of 170 of whom 165 attended regularly; while in an Enfield church school (St Andrews, Sydney Road) in 1897, Florence Dugdale, the future Mrs Thomas Hardy, taught a class of eighty-eight.[66]

Pressure was acute in the early 1890s. Fewer children would now escape enrolment or the vigilance of the truant officers, and levels of attendance had improved. But under the Moderate party's domination of the School Board fewer new schools had been built, as Progressive SBL member Lyulph Stanley (closely involved in the expansion of school provision between 1876 and 1885) pointed out in 1893.[67]

Teaching a class of sixty or more can never have been easy, especially when many missed two or three days or half-days a week, and pupils came and went as they moved house and changed schools. Individual attention was necessarily limited, and generally the class was dealt with as a block. This made quiet essential, and it was sought by continual admonition.

> Such phrases as 'Don't talk', 'Don't fidget', 'Don't worry', 'Don't ask questions', 'Don't make a noise', 'Don't make a mess', 'Don't do this thing', 'Don't do that thing', are ever falling from [the teacher's] lips. And they are supplemented with such positive instructions as: 'Sit still', 'Stand on the form', 'Hold yourself up', 'Fold arms', 'Hands behind backs', 'Hands on heads', 'Eyes on the blackboard'.[68]

The tendency was for teaching methods to be mechanical. As with the infants, repetition and rote-learning were staples. These were joined now, despite the inspectors' protests, by simultaneous reading or reading in turn with no regard for sense:

> the school makes known its existence to the ear as soon as to the eye by the dolorous chant proclaiming to the passers-by that d,o, spells doo, and g,o, spells go. The spelling lessons and the simultaneous reading lessons in the lower schools absorb an inordinate amount of time, much of which is absolutely wasted; but what is even more serious, they...create distaste for reading altogether. It seems scarcely credible, but even now in some schools the children are taught to read one line at a time without any reference to the sense.[69]

Even when reading was not done syllable by syllable, or line by line, and attention was paid to the sense, the pace was slow and the content of the readers uninspiring. Here, for instance, is a passage entitled 'The Boy and his Top':

> A boy and a girl. The girl has a doll for a toy. The boy has a toy too, but it is not a doll that he has. Girls have dolls, but boys do not have dolls for toys. The toy that the boy has is a top. The boy will hit his top with a whip, and then the top will spin.[70]

Books for the higher standards, which often doubled as texts for history or geography, or anthologies for 'English', could be more interesting. But teaching was often no better, because under the system of 'payment by results', too much (the government grant to the school, and in turn the teacher's salary) depended upon impressing the inspector on the day of the annual examination. He heard each child read a passage from the reader, and passed them if they could do it correctly and with tolerable fluency. So to prepare them, to ensure that everyone really knew the books from which they were to be tested, teachers took classes through them again and again, till some children knew them by heart.[71] Any initial interest could hardly survive such repetition.

The large classes were hard on teachers, especially when a single hall accommodated several lessons. Even with a glass partition teachers of adjoining classes were in competition: 'in the middle of sums you would be distracted by the geography and history going on a yard or two away'.[72] A throat specialist in the 1880s found a type of throat inflammation so common among teachers that he named it 'Board School Laryngitis', and wrote a monograph about its special features. He attributed the complaint to classroom conditions and faulty vocalization, and remarked that women teachers' training should include voice projection, since they could not make their voices carry.

> Seventy or eighty pupils in a classroom are common....Sometimes there is more than one class in a room....Many of the schools [are]...in noisy thoroughfares...the teachers soon acquire a habit of shouting, or, as is frequently admitted, of screaming at their pupils.[73]

Elsewhere, he recounted the case of a ten-year-old girl with similar throat problems. The child's favourite game, according to her mother was to be 'schools', in which she liked to play teacher: 'she do yell at 'em proper, Sir, so that I fair wonder how she gets sich a voice from her little chest'.[74]

Large classes were commonest in the lower standards, partly because the top ones were depleted during the course of each year by children leaving as they reached the age of exemption, and partly because teachers were reluctant to jeopardize next year's success rate by promoting children who might fail. Some children never managed to work their way up through the school, but stayed in the lower standards.[75] They included the 'delicate', who missed school because of illness. Deaf or short-sighted children could also fall behind, their handicap often not even identified. (Children with unrecognized ear infections were scolded for inattention.)[76] The short-sighted, especially numerous in poor schools and among girls, might be unable to see the blackboard.[77] If difficulties with hearing or sight were recognized (more likely as school medical inspection spread in the 1900s) some help was possible.[78] But for children with other learning difficulties there was no special teaching yet: they stayed in the lower classes with those whose irregular attendance and lack of interest held them back. In a very poor school in Hackney, where children missed school often, the 1893 inspector's report noted excessive numbers in the lower standards:

> There are 184 girls in or below the First Standard, though there are only twenty-two girls in the school below eight years of age. There are 132 in the Second Standard, of whom only thirty-two are under nine. In the lowest class of fifty-two a majority of the girls were said to be of defective intellect.[79]

Such imbalance was especially obvious in girls' schools, probably because of their more irregular attendance; so girls' overall progress was worse than that of boys, though this rarely evoked comment. (See Table 7.1)

Table 7.1: Percentage in each standard of the children on the school rolls, in 365 boys' and 365 girls' departments of Board Schools, March 1887.

Standard	Boys	Girls
Below One	0.2	0.2
In One	18.1	20.4
In Two	21.8	23.3
In Three	19.8	20.3
In Four	17.5	17.1
In Five	13.0	11.4
In Six	7.2	5.6
In Seven	2.4	1.7

Source: SBL *Report of School Management Committee* 1886–7, Return X, p. 424.

Individual schools were graded by the examiners for their 'tone' and discipline, and the standard achieved seems to have varied quite considerably. Local culture probably accounted in part for this. Amongst the roughest and poorest, children's share in responsibility often meant that parental discipline was relatively weak. Robustly self-sufficient children, not used to unquestioning obedience, did not always accept school discipline easily. But the competence of the head also played a part: schools often received different assessments under different heads, even though the character of the neighbourhood had not changed.

Habits of Obedience

Children were expected to behave respectfully to their teachers, 'with yes ma'am and no ma'am and if you please ma'am: I remember her standing over me to make me say, if you please'.[80] The entrance or departure of an adult was saluted by the class rising; and the children had to form orderly lines for entering or leaving classroom or school, often to set words of command. 'What they said, went', recalled Mrs M. of her schooldays in Hackney in the 1900s: 'We'd no more than flying in the air back-answer the teacher.'[81] Other children were less daunted—or perhaps more provoked. A girl at Garratt Lane school in 1884 struck the headmistress; and in 1886 a nine-year-old was caned at Walnut Tree Walk school for slapping her teacher's face; while complaints of extreme insolence and insubordination are to be found in almost any logbook.[82] A change of teacher or even of head sometimes followed, but it is never clear whether the teacher gave up in despair, or whether higher authority deemed her incompetent.[83]

Obedience was a recurrent theme in the readers approved for use in the schools, along with diligence, punctuality, patience, tidiness, gratitude, and thrift. The message was often direct—'The Little Dove' presented as an example (in obedience, innocence, cleanliness, and even gratitude);[84] or a passage entitled 'Obedience'; or a dialogue like this:

Mistress: What do you come to school for, Mary?...
Mary: To learn to read and write and sum.
Mistress: There is something else that I hope you will learn. What is it?
Mary: I don't know.
Mistress: Then I will tell you. You will, I hope, learn to be obedient...[85]

And it was parents and teachers who were to be obeyed, as adults, 'because we are older, and therefore wiser, than you can be'. Or a story might point the same moral—in one, a disobedient boy plays with fire while his mother is out and accidentally burns down the forest; in another, Mary loses a canary promised her 'if she is good' by opening a box she was told to leave—the bird flies out and escapes.[86]

Drill, which was mainly done by boys and which, apart from the infants' marching to music, was the only form of exercise in school until the mid-1880s, was advocated as 'an aid to securing and maintaining discipline'. It had produced 'a great improvement in the behaviour and carriage of the boys', according to one inspector. He wanted 'to see all movements in school, as well as in the drill-ground, executed at the word of command' and he recommended 'that girls as well as boys should participate in the benefits of drill'.[87] The Swedish drill subsequently developed for girls was much less militaristic, though it had its own discipline; and it was taught by women trained in gymnastics rather than ex-sergeants.[88] The official syllabus of physical exercises published in 1909 was 'designed to suit children of all ages and both sexes', and showed the influence of the childhood lobby in its stress on 'developing in the children a cheerful and joyous spirit', but retained the disciplinary objective. Its effects were to be twofold, 'physical and educational': it was to improve the children's general health, but also make them acquire 'habits of discipline and order' and respond 'cheerfully and promptly to the word of command'.[89]

The system of delegated authority, with monitors passing on to smaller groups the instruction they had received, was already being replaced in the 1860s by simultaneous or 'class teaching', as promoted in the training colleges. In Board schools this meant teachers had either to hold the interest of the large class while teaching, or to employ devices like chanting in unison or written exercises to keep them out of mischief. If the whole class could not be occupied, it was common to tell the children to put hands on head or to fold their arms. This last was denounced as 'injurious' by the Superintendent of Physical Exercises for Girls and Infants Schools.[90] But teachers clearly found it too useful to surrender: within very recent memory arms were still being folded so as to keep idle hands under control and show that no mischief was going on.

When an individual offended, the first sanction was disgrace—perhaps simply by scolding. With infants, according to one teacher, 'even taking their names down punishes them: they don't like the disgrace'. She also kept them in after school if they were late, but only for 'about three minutes, when they begin crying and I then let them go'.[91] Or the child was sent to wait outside the door (with the risk of further punishment if the head came past), or to stand in the corner or on a form, perhaps with pinafore over head for extra humiliation. In a mixed class a teacher could try to 'bring a rebel to shame by making him sit with the girls'.[92] Standing in the corner was often 'quite enough' punishment according to one headmistress, who called her children 'very sensitive': it was sometimes even enough punishment for the bigger girls. 'Or sometimes they are sent to my private room, and they dislike that very much indeed. They feel the disgrace.'[93] Some teachers held that the moral effect of disgrace was stronger than any other punishment, at least on older children, and advocated punishment books and systems of good and bad marks.[94]

Control was also achieved through ferocity. 'I cannot stand it: the girls are spoken to there as you would not speak to cats and dogs at the Grey Coat [school]', one student teacher told her ex-headmistress.[95] George A., born in 1904, remembered little caning at his school but a frightening atmosphere, and one teacher who 'drove things into your head by fear'.[96] A common weapon was 'the cheap, petty malice of sarcasm' denounced by Ethel Mannin as the 'last refuge of the schoolteacher brand of stupidity'.[97]

Incentives and positive reinforcement were also to be found. Frederick Willis and his classmates were rearranged every month according to their position on the marks sheet:

> the top of the class was nearest to the fire...and the bottom right out in the cold. As I always managed to accumulate a respectable number of marks I was always warm, and I suspect it was this bodily warmth that gave us intellectuals ascendancy over those who led an Eskimo existence in the far-flung outposts of scholarship.[98]

Some teachers used little rewards of sweets or other favours. On a larger scale, logbooks record many instances of rewards, usually promised in advance. Nosegays were given by a visitor to the 100 best behaved scholars; sweets promised by the Needlework Inspector to all who learned to sew nicely (everyone in fact received sweets, and there were eleven pinafores for the 'very best'); a trip to the zoo rewarded children for 'having done best work for Her Majesty's Inspector';[99] and for regular attendance there were various treats—extra recreation, sweets, teas, apples and hot cross buns, Christmas cards, library books, tickets for Magic Lantern shows and other treats, and permission to attend the swimming class. (The obverse of the reward, deprivation, was also used, as when a four-year-old at Deptford Park Infants school was punished by having to push the rocking horse while others rode.)[100] Such tactics appear more frequently after the mid-1880s. This may reflect the limitations of the records, but a shift toward a softer approach is suggested by an 1891 Board circular which recommended that extra play-time be promised (and given) as a reward for regular attendance.[101]

For more serious offences detention was used, especially to punish lateness, but sometimes also for disobedience or unruliness. It was discouraged by the Board, however, at least by the 1890s, and if used was not to last over half an hour.[102] Its punitive effect was reinforced by the child's fear of trouble at home, either because late return caused anxiety, or because it delayed jobs that the child had to do after school. But for the same reasons detention might also bring an angry parent to school.[103] Sometimes a child was shut up during school hours, perhaps to cool off. The School Management Committee in 1888 investigated a case in a Tower Hamlets school where a girl locked in the lavatory by the headmistress tried to escape through a window, fell twenty feet and fractured her skull. The committee found 'No undue harshness in the Head's treatment'.[104]

Physical punishment was common, though not always officially sanctioned: slaps, pinching and tweaking, pulling the hair, and throwing chalk or other missiles were all resorted to, and 'a great deal more shaking and pushing than there ought to be'.[105] The children's impression of all this is suggested by a 1900s description of Spitalfields girls playing 'School':

> [the game] seems to be the merest excuse to slap and rap and poke and hustle and shake without parley or discrimination. The mock scholars howl in an agony of protest....But their elders are relentless, and the play proceeds grimly, and amid much wailing, until every form of punishment is exhausted.[106]

Ethel Mannin recalled of slappings that 'they would make one's arm sting and the red mark would stay for a long time', but that inflicting them made the teachers look silly ('with their hair flopping up and down...and their faces going as red as the smacked arms'). For her, much more shame attached to being caned.[107]

The cane was permitted and used, even on 'infants'. It was expected to be more necessary with boys.[108] In boys' schools, according to Lowndes, 'every sum wrong, every spelling mistake, every blot, every question which could not be answered as the fateful day of examination drew near, was liable to be visited by a stroke of the cane'.[109] At a mixed school in suburban South London in 1912, the 'crowd was kept in order by the cane', and 'girls got it as much as the boys'.[110] Overall it seems to have been less freely used in girls' schools, though there is little comfort in a note from a new head at Garratt Lane in 1883: 'somewhat improved. No corporal punishment today'.[111] Girls' punishment may also have been less severe: a 'pointer', which hurt less than a cane, was often used to give 'handers' to girls.[112]

Most of the women members of the London School Board opposed use of the cane. Honnor Morten, Rosamund Davenport Hill and Helen Taylor (who linked it to wife-beating) did so with particular determination.[113] There were teachers, too, who opposed corporal punishment altogether; and a handful of schools (girls and infants overwhelmingly) where it was not used.[114] Winchester Street Girls school, Pentonville, for example, was run 'entirely without corporal punishment' in the 1880s and 1890s, and although it had 'very poor rough children' secured good exam results and high attendance. Its head believed in persuasion and rarely issued summons for non-attendance.[115] But many others regarded corporal punishment as indispensable, or, at least, like the headmistress of a school attended by 'rather well-to-do' children, suggested that the discipline of the school 'would not be quite as healthy' without it.[116] An Islington teacher in 1880, 'in despair' with an especially noisy class, blamed her difficulties on the head's refusal to cane the girls she sent out for punishment. The head, she complained, said that 'every other means should be tried before I do so'.[117] According to the Education Department:

> the more thoroughly a teacher is qualified for his position, by skill, character and personal influence, the less necessary it is for him to resort to corporal chastisement at all.[118]

Caning was officially limited in various ways (more as time went on); it had to be administered under agreed conditions and recorded in due form.[119] This produced recurrent protest from teachers.[120]

In one London school in the 1900s the girls found an effective way to deal with a teacher whose punishments went beyond official limits:

> They were spiteful to you in those days, you know. You only had to be late or give a cross look, and I remember this teacher, she caned this girl for something. And I said to her, 'If she hits you again like that', I said, 'scream at the top of your voice and don't leave off. Scream, scream, scream.' Well, she got a whacking after that and the teacher hit her across the wrists. Well, all the faces come out the street, out the class doors. She never stopped screaming. Mind you, she was in pain. And then the caning stopped. After that you only had your name put in the punishment book.[121]

Potential offences were legion: talking or laughing, eating a sweet or an apple, passing notes, having trouble with a sum or other task, arriving late, writing with the left hand, smiling at the wrong moment ('insolence') failing to bring a note to account for an absence,[122] trying to explain why you were late or protesting your innocence when accused of something ('lying and insolence'), helping a friend ('talking', or even 'cheating'), using vocabulary of which the teacher did not approve ('bad language'), writing on walls, or even, in church schools at least, missing Sunday School or attending a rival service.[123] Children were punished for infringing a code of behaviour which was new to them and must often have been quite incomprehensible. It is not surprising that sometimes memory of the punishment rankles even in old age:

my sister, a year older than me, she give me a piggy-back in the playground and the teacher caught us. And I had a couple of handers for that. And me name put...in the book. Just because she gave me a piggy back, I ask you![124]

Sometimes caning was the desperate resort of a teacher scarcely coping. Ethel Mannin recalled how a headmistress caned a child who was already hysterical:

> The girl was caned as a point of discipline; she had refused to submit to the corporal punishment, kicked and screamed, and the thing had developed into a tussle between the child and the head mistress. The child was finally expelled as being unmanageable and for gross insubordination, the head mistress took three aspirin, had a cup of tea, and went to lie down in 'the teachers' room' feeling herself a martyr.[125]

Parents, Teachers and Punishment

Parents did not always agree with the teachers' definition or treatment of offences. A Marylebone mother, 'very angry' after her child had been punished for scribbling on the doors (100 lines 'for such a little thing'), took her child away.[126] A Kennington girl was removed by her mother after having been made to wear a label saying 'thief' (she had taken another child's hat); and after a Deptford child was given three strokes of the cane for stealing a shawl, her elder sister came to the school and was 'most abusive'.[127] Perhaps the little thieves thought—and their families accepted—that they were 'just borrowing', while at school a sterner line was taken. With the many punishments for rudeness and insolence, where we always have only the teacher's version, the child's quite different understanding of events might be accepted at home. Or perhaps, as one historian has suggested, indignant support at home was won by some slight distortion of events.[128]

Protests at punishments recur in the logbooks, most often by mothers, but also by grandmothers, sisters and fathers. Detention, we have already seen, might result in an angry visit to collect the child. In some cases, like those of theft, above, or over accusations of untruthfulness or impertinence, elders came to complain about the charge, and did not admit an offence. On other occasions (perhaps with girls especially) they considered the punishment excessive.[129] At other times again they challenged the teacher's right to punish at all, let alone so harshly.[130]

But they seldom won satisfaction on visits of complaint. Now and then a teacher was reprimanded.[131] More often, the head stood firm and maintained that the punishment had been deserved and not excessive. This frequently escalated the complainant's anger. Mere abuse became 'bad' or 'obscene' language. If it ended there, the child or children might be excluded from school pending an apology from the parent. Sometimes it did not end there. At Wilkin Street school in 1898, for example, a girl was given one stroke with the cane by her teacher, Miss Leggett, for rudeness. Next day her mother came and 'struck at Miss Leggett with a rolled-up apron and threatened that she would wait for her outside and would also come up to the school and cane her across the face'. A charge of assault was brought, and the magistrate, fining the mother, said she had acted very foolishly: 'Teachers must not be assaulted in this way in the course of their duty.'[132] This appears to have been the line usually taken by the courts, though the *Schoolmaster* was always accusing them of being too soft.[133] The threat to cane the teacher across the face suggests that the stroke the child had received may (perhaps accidentally) have landed there, but the rolled-up apron does not suggest premeditation or even much danger.

Mrs Elizabeth Leopard, when she came to school and gave the teacher 'one on the face', was accused of acting 'in a spirit of revenge'. Some were indeed clearly vengeful, like Mrs Selina Pierpoint, who (along with her own mother) came to school, seized the headmistress, and ordered her daughter to take the cane and cane her.[134]

It was not unusual after disputes over punishment to send the child to another school: probably this was the best course when feasible, though other schools might not take a child when there was a dispute. Even if complaints were taken to the School Managers, or raised on the Board's School Management Committee, in the final decision the teachers' version was almost always believed against that of children and parents, and the punishment vindicated.

Behind some of these confrontations there was perhaps a class difference in attitudes to corporal punishment. After all, at public schools in this period upper-class boys endured floggings as part of their education, and their parents accepted it, or what they knew of it. A writer in the *Globe*, dilating on the frequency of brutal assaults by parents on teachers and calling for more severity of punishment, noted the difference:

> The working classes seem to have taken up with a fixed idea that while it is most right and proper for the offspring of the well-to-do to be subjected to corporal punishment at school, their own children are far too tender skinned to be treated in that way.[135]

Similarly, a magistrate at Worship Street Court in 1902 said that 'parents of children in the Board schools...were too prone to complain of any punishment inflicted, whilst in higher circles the matter ended with the master and the boy'.[136] As we have seen already (Chapter 2), the view was often expressed in the middle class that working-class parents gave their children too much latitude and 'spoiled' them. The point where punishment was judged excessive may well have come sooner for poor parents and children than for teachers and magistrates. A School Manager told a School Board committee in 1902 that: 'The parents object to corporal punishment generally altogether...of course here and there are exceptions'. Another witness, a Superintendent of Visitors, said that parents would punish their children 'as much as they like themselves', but would not allow a teacher 'to put a finger on them'; while another (also a superintendent) suggested that the 'better class of parents' minded more about the efficiency of education, but 'the poorer classes attach all importance to the kindly treatment of their children'.[137]

It may also be that, for parents who had not been won over to the idea of school but recognized that they could not keep their children away, the children's sufferings at school were hard to stand. Struggles over discipline may have been a rearguard attempt by working-class parents to assert their rights as parents, unfortunately, however, in just the area where they were deemed least fit.[138] Solidarity with their children came more easily than with the teachers: the common interests of adults against children could not automatically be established across class, since the parents and teachers, in spite of their shared adult status, were not equal in authority. It should be added, however, that there were also cases where parents called on the school to support their authority; and where any punishment given at school was liable to be repeated at home. With time this pattern may also have gained ground.[139]

In any case, discipline was recognized as a general issue, not just a matter between individual parents and teachers. When anger at a particular teacher or school spread beyond one or two families to a neighbourhood,[140] it could build up into collective action to terrify or beat up a brutal teacher.[141] A Bristol case suggests how local support could be expressed: when a woman whose boy had been brutally beaten was fined £20 for assaulting the teacher, local women 'made a collection, then went and fetched her out of prison with rosettes and white hats on'.[142] Opposition to corporal punishment probably helped the candidature of Edgar Andrews, a labourer elected to Wanstead School Board in 1889, though it resulted in his bankruptcy: he was successfully sued for libel after alleging that excessive and improper punishment had been inflicted on local children.[143]

School authorities, likewise, because of the missionary function attributed to schools, placed such conflicts in a larger context. As the next chapter will argue, discipline and order in school were about discipline and order in society. They were about class.

11. *Training for a domestic future (housewife or servant?): laundry, Tennyson St school, Battersea, 1907; and housewifery (cleaning flues) at Barnsbury Park school, 1908.*

8

Beacons of Civilization

---◀◆▶---

Shame and Pride

IT WAS COMMON in nineteenth-century political discourse to present education as a 'civilizing' force, and to contrast the discipline and order of the school with the chaos surrounding it. In the early days of 'ragged schools', indeed, the chaos was even in the classroom, where 'unruly pupils' were responsible for 'deafening noises, catcalls and stone-throwing', broken lights and all kinds of mischief.[1] But even 'little wretched schools' in 1860s slum courts might be claimed as 'bright centres of civilizing influence and of Christian education'.[2] Once school was compulsory, with state sanctions to back its authority, order was more easily maintained inside, and the civilizing glare grew stronger.

Board-school discipline extended outside the school walls, to the parents themselves. In the children's reading books, parents, as much as teachers or more, were owed respect and obedience. But the parents in those stories were worthy cottagers or undefined middle class. The parents of Board-School children, by contrast, belonged to the urban working class, and often to its poorer, rougher parts. They could not be patronized like cottagers; but nor, of course, could the teachers see them as equals.[3] Class overrode the shared adult status. Parents were part of the problem which schools were supposed to be helping to resolve.

Enforcement of education exposed parents to visits of enquiry by attendance officers, to prosecution, to fines if found guilty, and to prison or to having their goods seized if they could not (or would not) pay. They were not welcome or expected at the schools. When they did come, as we have seen, it was in anger and anxiety which were unlikely to be assuaged. If frustration drove them to be abusive and violent, a constable would be called; assault charges probably ensued, followed by fines or imprisonment.

Poor parents were assumed to threaten the order of the school. At a Holloway voluntary school, in 1897, an electric bell was installed so that the head could summon help, 'so frequent and annoying had the visits of irate parents become'.[4] In 1903, when fire broke out at a Clerkenwell school, the

133

fire-bell was rung and the children were led out to the playground. There
they stayed, the gates locked to keep out the crowd of 'anxious and excited mothers' who had heard the alarm and rushed up. 'Near riots' reported
on two subsequent occasions also probably originated in a clash between
parents' anxiety for their children and teachers' fear of parental indisci-
pline.[5]

The education of working-class children was presented as their rescue
from the abyss. Teachers were missionaries, who visited daily from the
'quintessentially lower middle-class areas' where they lived.[6] Schools were
'oases in the desert of drab two-storied cottages'; they were 'tall sentinels',
their three storeys towering over 'the squalid homes around...like benefi-
cent giants holding aloft the beacon of religion and civilization'; they
provided havens of peace amidst squalor, 'bright, airy and specklessly
clean', with flowers and 'good pictures'.[7]

Socialization, more than the imparting of knowledge or skills, was the
point of this schooling. The children were to be 'broken in'. The value of
school life for 'the lowest class of children' was 'quite inestimable', wrote
Helen Dendy, in 1895, in a collection on 'the social problem', but it 'consisted less in the actual information imparted than in the discipline and
order which is enforced'; 'the habits of order and obedience which they
are learning' were 'their one chance of civilization'.[8]

With order and obedience, and carrying the same moral overtones,
went cleanliness. Together they took priority over any other instruction. As
the chairman of the London School Board put it in his annual address in
1874:

> Tens of thousands of children are in our schools who are, I regret
> to say, grossly ignorant and utterly uninstructed, and the only
> thing we can do is to look to their cleanliness and give them habits
> of order and promote their regularity of attendance...with good
> schools and most efficient teachers...the results are sure to follow.[9]

We have already seen something of the training in orderly habits. The question of appearance was closely connected: it became the visible proof of
educational success or failure.[10] Frederick Willis and his schoolfellows at
the turn of the century were trained to combine moral and physical spruce-
ness:

> We were taught to be God-fearing, honourable, self-reliant and
> patriotic; to be clean and trim in our appearance, to be smart in
> our walk and actions, and always walk in step with a companion. I
> remember a master saying, 'Never slouch, walk like soldiers'. The
> best of us tried to follow this advice, and although our clothes may
> have left something to be desired, we made a brave show with
> clean collars, clean boots, well-brushed hair, and shiny faces when
> we assembled for morning prayers.[11]

In many schools, the teacher's 'first morning task' was to check that hands and faces were clean.[12] Children who did not meet the standard were sometimes sent home—another frequent source of friction with mothers. According to the social worker, Anna Martin, schools were 'veritable harrying machines....If a child turns up dirty or untidy the mother is ruthlessly called to account'.[13] Head teachers made sure that the pressure for cleanliness was kept up: the logbooks often record warnings about untidy appearance or hands not washed in the dinner hour.[14] Inspectors assessed schools on their discipline and tone, which included the appearance and manners of the children. They were not expected to report favourably unless satisfied:

> that all reasonable care is taken, in the ordinary management of the school, to bring up the children in habits of punctuality, of good manners and language, of cleanliness and neatness, and also to impress upon the children the importance of cheerful obedience to duty, of consideration and respect for others, and of honour and truthfulness in word and act.[15]

Neatness, however desirable, could be hard to achieve. More effort probably went into girls' appearance: they were said to manage best, if encouraged. An inspector in 1885 noted that 'in good girls' schools, however poor the children, they soon learn to make themselves neat'.[16] They had an advantage in the pinafore, easily washed (if less easily starched and ironed), and able to 'hide sad deficiencies'.

> The girls everywhere, on account of their white or pink washing aprons, and other patches of colour distributed about their garments, have a more cleanly and smarter appearance than the boys.[17]

But photographs from Board schools usually show some girls without a pinafore, and certainly the perfect one was seen only in superior schools or on special occasions. Mrs C., in Hackney in the 1900s, only had a clean pinny on prize days, when a friend used to bring her one, 'starched and ironed...so I would look as good as anyone else, you know'. Her school encouraged effort:

> Sometimes we didn't hardly have any shoes on our feet...had to make do, and me, I used to polish mine up, and my teacher used to say....'Now look at her, she's got old shoes and yet she's got a bit of polish on them' and she used to stand me out in the middle of the classroom, you know.[18]

Making an effort, or achieving the easier kinds of improvement (as to dirty faces, for example),[19] had to be regarded as a success. It was often all teachers could hope for.

For in the circumstances of many children's lives, especially during the

early years of Board schools, it was not easy to look neat. Any clothes not
being worn or washed would more probably serve as bedding than be folded or hung away; while hairbrushes and toothbrushes were 'extras' rarely
owned. Water for all purposes had often to be fetched in from an outside
tap or even a street standpipe (and the slops carried out again), and in
many poor districts it was turned on only for part of the day, at least before
the 1890s. Washing was a weekly burden, clothes in short supply, and not
all mothers had time or inclination for extra washing to meet the new and
exigent standards being set at school, even if they were prepared (as all
were not) to make an effort for Sunday or the Sabbath.

Children wore clothes which had known a good few previous owners,
more or less adapted to fit their particular requirements. Where time and
skill allowed, all kinds of contriving went on, both to produce needed garments and to prolong their life. Patches were normal—'all we asked was
that the patch should be a reasonable match to the rest of the material'.[20]
Whether passed down or bought from rag stalls, old clothes never died.
Women and girls unpicked the seams of jackets, dresses, shirts, skirts and
coats, then 'turned' them (remade them inside-out) so as to hide where
they were worn or stained, or used good parts for some new purpose altogether.[21] They ran up frocks and underclothes from old flour sacks; knitted
endless scarves, socks and jerseys, often recycling wool unravelled from
something else, and 'made down' adult trousers for smaller fry. (When V.S.
Pritchett, aged eleven, needed trousers for a new school, his mother raid-
ed his father's wardrobe, found 'a pair of trousers of the kind commonly
worn with morning dress', and vengefully cut them down. She knew 'she
couldn't get a penny out of him for our clothes' and her own poor childhood had taught her these skills.)[22] The universal black or brown
'stockings' (knee-length socks) would be given new feet—often uncom-
fortable—the old ones could be darned no more.[23] Marie W. and her
Hoxton friends patronized a market stall which sold refooted stockings:
'sound' ones were all the same colour and cost a penny, while halfpenny
ones had feet which didn't match. The few who had sound stockings on
both feet would show them off, especially during drill or dancing classes.[24]

The biggest problem was boots. Many a poor mother might feel that
'"want of boots"' would be found written on her heart', wrote 'Riverside
Visitor'.[25] New boots cost several shillings, so old ones had to last as long as
possible.[26] If someone (usually a father or son) knew how to mend the family boots on an iron 'foot', and if there was money for 'a few coppersworth
of leather and a card of blakeys', the cobbler's fees could be saved.[27]
Cheaper temporary repairs were managed with paper or cardboard and
glue, and concealed with a coat of blacking. Many children wore ill-fitting
and worn-out boots, perhaps tied on with string;[28] and in winter those
whose families could not muster the skill and materials for home repairs,
or the money to pay the cobbler, missed days of school when their boots
gave up. Bare feet, though getting less common, did not disappear. C.H.

Rolph, in Finsbury Park before 1910, 'always had barefoot schoolmates', though none amongst his friends; and Wallie Easey (born Stratford, 1907) recalled of his Manor Park school from 1912 that 'forty to sixty per cent of the children would come without shoes all the year round'.[29] This point is important: while bare feet in summer could be a choice, no-one preferred to go without shoes in the mud and slush of winter.[30]

The 'Rules for Teachers' in 1893 stipulated that schools had to admit barefoot children, which implies that some teachers had been excluding them: this in turn suggests either that they were more exceptional than before, or that teachers thought they went barefoot by choice, not from necessity.[31] A school trying to establish or defend a reputation as respectable would no doubt discourage barefoot children; while at one already known as 'rough' they would hardly matter. Charitable organizations or individuals, or the school authorities themselves, often tried to help with boots to improve attendance.

School and teachers had the power to exert control over the children's appearance: whatever the home circumstances, it was they who defined the acceptable. In Finsbury in 1878 two children were excluded from their school because they were said to smell intolerably of fried fish. They lived above a fried fish shop their father ran, so presumably the smell settled invincibly in their clothes. Their mother protested against the exclusion. But it was upheld by the Education Department, with the helpful comment:

> It is the duty of parents not only to send their children to school,
> but to send them in such a state of cleanliness as to prevent their
> being a nuisance to other children.[32]

In Southwark in 1888 there was a conflict of another kind between parent and school. A father complaining to the School Management Committee about a teacher's conduct to his daughter enquired whether there was any restriction as to how children should wear their hair. The local managers reported that the child was 'an object of mirthful comment' on Friday afternoons (her hair may have been in curling papers, as in a similar case some months later); and pronounced 'that the Mistress acts correctly in endeavouring to ensure that each child should attend seemly in condition and appearance'.[33]

A perennial obstacle in the schools' crusade for seemly condition was that of headlice, endemic in poor, overcrowded districts. Thomas Gautrey recalled the problem in his memoir of a life in education:

> Some mothers were indignant at receiving requests for their girls
> to be sent to school with clean heads. Their outraged dignity led
> them to visit the schools and even to assault the mistresses. I had
> on many occasions to intervene and advise such mistresses. In one
> month four mothers were prosecuted for personally assaulting
> mistresses.[34]

Gautrey here implies that the resentment was provoked by the mere demand for 'clean' hair. One reason for it, however, was probably the equation by the authorities of headlice and dirt, and their euphemistic, but insulting, reference to 'clean' or 'dirty' heads rather than to infestation.[35] Headlice flourish in clean hair, too,[36] and mothers who knew their children's hair to be freshly washed were puzzled and indignant when told it was dirty. Another source of resentment was no doubt the attaching of stigma to the condition. For a great many people headlice, like the omnipresent bed-bug, were an inevitable nuisance rather than a personal disgrace. Anyone with hair of any length would have trouble with them, as women teachers themselves were dismayed to find.

This made it more of a female problem: older boys' heads were commonly shaved, or, like men, they wore their hair short, while segregation at school might protect at least the boys without sisters. Boys' strong peer culture also helped them resist being shamed. During head inspections at a poor South London school attended by eight-year-old Victor Pritchett in about 1908, 'as the inspector cracked the lice and dropped them into a basin of water beside him, the lads would grin or wink proudly at us and we would laugh back'. So far from rejecting them as dirty, Pritchett was attracted by their cheerful insouciance and fellowship: 'One half wanted to find a louse oneself, but Mother was good at combing out the nits.'[37]

The measures taken by the authorities aroused indignation. The schools did not confine themselves to stimulating a sense of shame and demanding 'clean' heads: they also cut the children's hair. Gautrey quotes a letter to the headmistress from a mother who saw this as one more in a series of official attacks:

> I should like to know how much more spite you intend to put upon my child for it is nothing else. First you send the Sanitary Inspector and I have my home taken away, then my husband has to get rid of his few rabbits and chickens, and now you cut the few hairs my girl was just beginning to get so nice....I know she had no need to have her hair cut off as it was washed with soft soap last night. The child is thoroughly heartbroken.

A more conciliatory mother quoted by Gautrey was sure that she had succeeded in getting the headlice under control:

> Please Miss B....if the nurse looks at Agnes' head she will find that it is quite all right. There might be one or two nits [the eggs] but I think she will find they are dead. Her father is not half going on about it, as he has seen me doing her hair dinner times, tea times, and at night.[38]

In the 1900s systematic inspections for headlice began, carried out by nurses rather than teachers. The children identified by 'Nitty Norah' as verminous would be given a white card to take home, with instructions to treat the head with sassafras oil, carbolic or paraffin.[39] At the end of the week any children not now certified 'clean', were segregated (they 'sat at benches together, shamed outcasts', and were referred to as 'the dirty girls'),[40] and given a more urgent, red card. If there was no improvement after several weeks of warnings and visits, the child could be excluded from school and the parents prosecuted, though this step was rare.

In 1908 cleansing stations were set up, to which children could be sent (after warnings) to be disinfected and perhaps shorn.[41] This was 'a great disgrace', according to Grace Foakes, even in her poor Wapping school: on return such a girl would be shunned. Obviously, there had to be enough 'clean' girls to shun the minority of 'dirty' ones, so this may mean that the infestation rate was decreasing. Or again it may have been a way for one group of girls in a mixed school to establish superiority.[42] Even the superior were vulnerable, however: everyone 'lived in great fear' of going to the cleansing station.

But this fear was not only about being stigmatized as dirty. Girls wore their hair long: 'it was an unheard of thing...to cut a girl's hair. Only girls with dirty heads had their hair cut'.[43] Cropped hair meant loss of a central feminine attribute; it was also the mark of the children in orphanages and other institutions. So it was a double attack on the child's identity—as a girl, and as someone with home and family. It was also an attack on the mother, if the association of headlice with dirt and rough ways was accepted, since her child's shorn hair then declared her uncaring or incompetent.[44] Older girls, accustomed to sharing responsibility for the well-being and reputation of the family, might also feel impugned as their mothers' auxiliaries.

It is not surprising, then, that mothers and daughters were themselves increasingly caught up in the campaign against headlice; even though compliance with the new demands did not necessarily mean acceptance of the stigma. The girls probably wanted to avoid segregation with 'the dirty girls', to keep in with their friends and, most important, not to lose their hair; while the mothers' concern was to maintain respectability and avoid attention from the authorities. But whatever their reasons, meeting the new demand took time. Mothers had to pay continual attention to their daughters' hair. Grace Foakes recalled what this meant:

> every day, without fail, my mother would undo our plaits and comb through our hair with a small-tooth comb. If we so much as scratched our heads, she would stop whatever she was doing and look to see if we had picked up anything. Each Friday night at bath time she would wash our heads with soda water [washing soda was used to soften water] and sunlight soap, and then plait it into many plaits. These would not be undone until Sunday, when they were loosed, crimped and shining.[45]

So the battle against headlice, even more than the schools' other demands, had the double effect in many households of adding to the domestic work-load and increasing both mothers' and daughters' concern with appearance. The care lavished on girls' hair—the week-day plaits, the watchfulness, the washing and brushing—not only kept it clear of headlice, thus proclaiming respectability; it also produced Sabbath beauty, which became a further aim in itself. Moreover, both the concern and the effect emphasized divisions among children: they still further differentiated girls from boys, and they separated off the 'clean' from the 'dirty'.

The insistence that children should attend school clean and neat (and without headlice or other vermin) had both immediate and long-term aims. It was intended to produce cleaner, healthier schoolchildren, to improve conditions in school (not least for teachers) and to improve the reputation of the schools by showing what they could achieve.[46] It was also to bring about a transformation of the conditions of working-class life. 'The repulsive habits of many of our neglected children' were to be eradicated so that the next generation would be better brought up.[47] This snatch of dialogue from a children's game overheard and recorded by the writer William Pett Ridge suggests how teachers must have been continually on the alert:

> I'll be the schoolmistress, standing 'ere, and you be the children standing on the edge of the pavement....
>
> Tell me now, Minnie Gibson—and leave your nose alone, miss—who was John the Baptist?[48]

Some of the teaching was more subtle, intended not only to correct habits, but to create a new consciousness, new standards, new self-respect, and it was directed particularly at girls. This was partly done by playing on the sense of beauty: as with well looked-after hair, effort expended on cleaning and tidying could be expected to produce an aesthetically satisfying result. In the school textbooks girls were presented as sensitive to flowers and the beauties of nature; it was girls who were to take a modest pride in their appearance (though neatness and effort were stressed, not show); and it was women whose pride would be to keep their homes and their children neat and clean.[49] Even ambition was depicted in terms of cleanliness, in this sentiment from a lesson entitled 'Getting on in life':

> If you are a housemaid, it is 'getting on' if your rooms look clean-er and fresher, your fire-irons brighter, your steps whiter, your whole house neater than other people's.[50]

The neat appearance of the teacher herself was also an important model, at least where she had a good relationship with those she taught. For one Woolwich girl of ten, around 1906, her teacher was 'my ideal type of woman. She dressed well—her things were dainty and nice—clean—and her shoes—and I thought I'd like to be like her when I grew up'.[51] Girls who thus responded to the attractions of 'daintiness' internalized the new standards of appearance and behaviour. But the attempt to live up to them, or to transmit them to their families, might well lead to frustration and a conflict of loyalty between school and home. Or the impossibility of ever matching the model could produce a sense of inferiority. If the new ways were superior, those who failed in them felt shame. Results for the children might also be divisive. When a Peckham child commented on the dirty neck of her Maypole dancing partner on Empire Day, he told her to mind her own business. (Her father later agreed, pointing that the boy might live with his granny who might not see very well!)[52]

Some teachers had no qualms about exploiting such feelings, and brought a missionary zeal to the civilizing task. Mrs Burgwin, for instance, headmistress of a very poor school in South London, told the members of the Cross Commission in 1887:

> I feel very strongly that the girls that I turn out of that school will never be content to lead the same kind of life as that which their mothers have led.

She saw the school as 'a centre of humanizing influence', and claimed that it had already achieved great changes in the neighbourhood. Where formerly:

> You could...hardly bring a person down that street without a blush of shame; the people did not think of putting window blinds up,...[they] made the street the dustbin of the place, and certainly their language was shocking. Now...provided the people are sober, whatever quarrel may be going on, and they will be using bad language, if they see a teacher coming up the street they stop....Some Christmases ago I sent a new short curtain to every house, to give it a bright appearance for Christmas day, and now the people feel a sense of shame in various ways...a woman will borrow a neighbour's apron to come and speak to me so that she may come up looking clean. I felt it my duty, if one came up to me dirty, to tell her that she should have enough self-respect to wash her face before she came to speak to me.[53]

The writer George Sims had a similar view of the effects of education, and already in 1883 was claiming that the young mothers were 'a race far ahead of the older ones', having just 'got the benefit of the Education Act before they were too old', so that now they were reaping the benefits of 'those principles of cleanliness and thrift which the Board School inculcates'.

> These young women...live in a better way; their room is tidier and cleaner, there is little coquetry in them, and they have a sense of shame which renders them excellent service. They are anxious about their children's education, they recognize the advantage the discipline and instruction have been to them, and the general tone of their lives is in every way a distinct advantage on the old

order of things. I quote these facts because they so fully bear out
the theory that education must be the prime instrument in changing the condition of the poor for the better.[54]

Whether coercion or manipulation was used to impart it, then, and whatever the obstacles to meeting its standards, 'civilization' was undoubtedly
on the hidden curriculum for girls. What was on the open one?

The Girls' Curriculum

The widely held view that education was to transform the working classes,
with its corollary, implicit or explicit, that future mothers were to be the
vehicle of change, had been used in 1851 as an argument for getting more
girls into school:

> considering how vast an influence is exercised by the female char-
> acter upon the general disposition of society, it cannot but appear
> of very great importance that the future wives and mothers of the
> people should be qualified by sound and healthy education, con-
> tinued for the longest practicable period, to exert a softening and
> an elevating influence upon their partners and their offspring.[55]

As more girls were drawn in to inspected schools, and with compulsion
after 1870, it also influenced the content of girls' education as opposed to
boys'.

Before education was made compulsory, schools with state subsidy
often had fewer places for girls and fewer girls than boys attended school;
those who did were taught less (particularly in arithmetic); and went less
regularly and for shorter periods.[56] Private day schools had more girl
pupils, but the category ranged from young ladies' academy to neighbourhood dame school, so the total is harder to use.[57] Working-class children
often attended dame schools, which were run by working-class women or
men (often elderly) in their homes, to make a living. Such teachers had no
formal qualifications, and their level of education was variable, though not
necessarily as poor as their detractors—the advocates of systematized state
schooling—maintained. They were usually relaxed about regular attendance and punctuality, and so better suited for children, especially girls,
who might be 'needed at home'. Domestic demands probably also cur-
tailed girls' school years. Even when family culture and finances favoured
education, boys were more likely than girls to benefit. Thomas Okey (born
in an artisan family in 1852) recalled that his elder sisters were withdrawn
from school at eleven 'to assist in the work of the home', while he himself
stayed on till twelve, and his brothers went on to secondary education at
Bishopsgate Institute.[58]

Women teachers before 1870, if trained at all, were given a different
syllabus from men: with 'fewer and easier' subjects, and without 'the sub-

jects...intended for the general refinement of the students' minds'. (These included Euclid, Latin, Physical Science, Mechanics and English Literature from Chaucer to Milton.) Unlike male counterparts they studied domestic economy during their two years, with a syllabus which included clothing, food, cooking, laundry, the duties of servants, household expenses of a labouring man and his family, savings banks, the nature of interest, and practical rules, personal and domestic, for the preservation of health. They also had to fulfil needlework requirements.[59]

Needlework—as had long been the case—was considered an essential part of a girl's education. Matthew Arnold's reports on elementary schools in the 1850s and 1860s stress its importance, warning that it must on no account be neglected for other subjects:

> The importance to a poor family that the daughters should be skilful in needlework is obvious to all; yet their ignorance of it is something incredible.[60]

In the Revised Code of 1862, failing to teach girls plain needlework was one of the few offences for which a school could lose its government grant.[61] All women teachers had to be able to teach it. To become pupil teachers girls needed 'a written attestation from the school mistress and managers that they possess reasonable competency as seamstresses'; while each year during their apprenticeship they had to demonstrate progress in needlework, as well as in the subjects taken by boys.[62] Their arithmetic syllabus was easier; and they and their teachers were paid less.[63]

After 1870 female pupil teachers went on having to show themselves competent seamstresses, and to satisfy the inspector of their annual progress in needlework.[64] The achievements expected in arithmetic were still less at every stage for female pupil teachers than for male.[65] Training college syllabuses, though extended, remained narrower for women, particularly with regard to science, and needlework was always an essential requirement.[66] In the schools themselves there were differences both in the subjects taught and in the standard of teaching, especially in arithmetic.

The Education Act of 1870 made no distinction between boys and girls, both being equally required to attend school. 'Equality of provision of educational facilities' was strongly advocated by the progressive and influential Lyulph Stanley (Board member from 1876-85, and subsequently member of the Cross Commission) in 1879: he argued that it was against the national interest for half the population to remain without education.[67] But in practice, as we have seen in previous chapters, segregation was normal after seven, and there were differences in methods of discipline and the enforcement of attendance. Moreover, the Education Department's annually revised Codes and London School Board policies maintained and even extended differences in the curriculum for girls and for boys.[68]

Through the allocation of grants, the Education Department fixed minimum standards and subjects: grant was paid according to the number

of children at each school who satisfied their inspectors in the required
subjects (Reading, Writing and Arithmetic), and in one or two 'specific'
subjects from an approved list. There were two levels in the School Board's
scheme of education, too, but its initial list of basic subjects was more ambitious, as Table 8.1 shows. The Board's programme, on its own admission,
set forth 'what is ultimately desirable, rather than what is at present attainable'.[69] In practice, during these first years, the syllabus in most schools
consisted of the three Rs, with singing and drawing, religious instruction,
needlework for girls, and sometimes (more often for boys) drill.[70] Later
attempts to broaden the syllabus tended to fall foul of the Board's
'Moderate' party, who opposed both principle and expense.

Table 8.1: Basic and optional subjects in London Schools, 1871, according to
   the Education Department's Code requirements and the SBL scheme.

1: Basic subjects

Code	London School Board
Reading	Morality and Religion
Writing	Reading, Writing and Arithmetic
Arithmetic	English Grammar and Composition (senior schools)
	Mensuration and Principles of Book-keeping (senior boys' schools)
	Systematized Object Lessons, embracing in the six school years a course of elementary instruction in physical science
	History of England
	Elementary Geography
	Elementary Drawing
	Plain Needlework and Cutting Out (girls' schools)

2: Discretionary Subjects

Code	London School Board
Geography	Algebra and Geometry
History	Any extra subject recognized by the New Code
Grammar	
Algebra	
Geometry	
Natural Sciences	
Political Economy or any definite subject of instruction	

Source: SBL *Minutes,* 28 June 1871, p.16. See also Spalding, *London School Board,* pp. 91–6.

The 'ultimately desirable' wide-ranging syllabus proved even less attainable for girls than for boys. They were often more handicapped, as we

have seen, by irregular attendance. Some suffered more than their brothers from hunger, ill-health and tiredness, since often they fared worse for food and carried more responsibility outside school.[71] Domestic instruction consumed much of their school time, expectations of what they could achieve were probably pitched lower, and their teaching was still likely to be inferior by prevailing standards.[72] Arithmetic in particular was constantly said to be worse taught to girls.[73] Their work was called 'old-fashioned and mechanical', and said to rely 'on memory rather than understanding'.[74] (These were faults which their inadequately trained teachers probably shared.)[75] Girls' 'natural inaptitude for dealing with the various processes of arithmetic' was advanced as explanation by one inspector (Mr Williams); elsewhere the blame was put squarely on poor teaching; or on household duties.[76] But the most common and most convincing explanation lay in the time which girls had to spend on needlework, when the boys would be doing more sums; and this tied in with the assumption of a domestic future for girls. (Mrs Burgwin, headmistress of Orange Street school, thought girls should not have to learn tables of area and capacity: 'I quite agree with the boys learning those tables, but I do not think they are of much good to girls'.)[77] For the same reason the Education Department tolerated a lower standard in arithmetic from girls, which of course confirmed the vicious circle of low expectations in one field because of large demands in another.[78]

The Board early decided that plain needlework and cutting out should be included among essential subjects for girls.[79] The importance attached to needlework and other domestic instruction was undoubtedly girls' greatest handicap, not only in arithmetic but in all their school work. In 1873 sewing took up at least a quarter of the school hours devoted to secular instruction: five to seven hours a week, according to a committee on needlework instruction that year. The committee recommended that a limit of five hours a week be set, and suggested needlework classes from 2.15 to 3.15 every afternoon.[80] Later that year the Board, 'desirous that a greater encouragement should be given to the practice of Needlework in their schools', asked the Education Department to make it a grant-earning subject,[81] and Needlework was recognized under the Code. In 1875, when a new system of 'class subjects' was introduced, it was one of them, along with grammar, history, geography and later drawing and elementary science. This meant that if all the children in a class passed creditably when the inspector examined them in the subject, the school was eligible for a grant calculated according to their number. So if garments were still unfinished as the examination approached, other subjects were sometimes displaced, or needlework invaded the time given to other subjects, as children could knit or sew while listening.[82]

The new system did not resolve the imbalance: indeed it made it worse. If needlework was to be essential for girls but not done by boys, either boys must do an alternative subject, not done by girls, or girls would have less

time than boys for other school work. Matthew Arnold, by now an experienced inspector, thought that making needlework a class subject was a
mistake.

> Taking needlework as a class subject for girls means dropping as a
> class subject...either grammar or geography. They certainly ought
> to learn both, and needlework besides, and if they do not take
> needlework as a class subject, they still learn it; whereas if geogra-
> phy or grammar is not taken by them as a class subject, it is in most
> cases, I fear, not learnt by them at all.[83]

Arnold's fears were fully justified. Where girls took needlework, boys took
geography or 'animal physiology' or, later, drawing or science.

The same difficulty arose with the 'specific' or optional subjects which
could be taken in the higher standards. The 1876 Code stipulated that
every girl presented for examination in one of these must take domestic
economy. So in schools which presented children in only one specific subject, girls would have domestic economy as their only option, while their
basic class subjects would already almost certainly include needlework. If a
second specific subject was offered to girls, it was usually English. To give
an example, the inspector's report for Hackney and Tower Hamlets in 1877
showed that 5,920 boys and 3,219 girls were being taught 'specific' subjects.
The boys did a range of subjects, with English Literature, Animal
Physiology, and Physical Geography the most important; the girls overwhelmingly did Domestic Economy and English.[84] In following years the
choice of subjects changed, but the pattern remained the same: year after
year the specific subjects most often taken in boys' schools were Animal
Physiology, Mechanics and Algebra; while in girls' schools they took
Cookery and Domestic Economy. 'All other subjects, compared with these,
are but infrequently taken.'[85]

Until the late 1880s, as we have seen, boys in the infants' schools were
taught knitting and needlework as part of manual instruction—training
hand and eye; but then drawing lessons began to take their place. For older
children drawing was made a 'class' subject from 1886, and in boys' schools
lessons were compulsory.[86] Girls were taught in about equal numbers at that
point, but the standard of teaching was worse,[87] and when the Science and
Art Department raised the standard required for the examination and put
more stress on technical drawing, many girls' schools stopped teaching it
in the upper standards.[88] Drawing instruction for boys was to prepare them
for 'the after-walks of life': 'as teachers they will be better able to demonstrate and illustrate a lesson to a class; as carpenters, builders, engineers, or
workers in any handicraft, they will possess the very useful power of being
able to make a working drawing'.[89] Mrs Burgwin favoured a separate, 'more
artistic' scheme for girls because 'the girls like pretty things', with the more
scientific and mechanical work, 'leading up to the workshop', left to the
boys.[90] But as one of the drawing instructors pointed out, since drawing was

a necessary skill for teachers, and such a large proportion of pupil teachers were girls, it was essential for drawing to be more systematically taught in girls' schools.[91] After new regulations in the 1890s dropped Solid Geometry from requirements for the drawing examination, leaving 'Freehand' and 'Model', girls' schools took it up again.[92] The difficulty may have been standards of arithmetic—teachers' as well as pupils'—rather than preference for the pretty and artistic.

Scientific subjects were almost completely denied to girls.[93] When Elementary Science became a class subject, in the 1880s, no girls took it (nor at first many boys); by the 1890s, when it was more established as a subject, a few girls' schools taught it, but three times as many boys' schools did. (Lack of teachers was no doubt an obstacle.)[94] It was the same with specific subjects: girls never took Mechanics or Chemistry; they almost never took Algebra, Physics or Mensuration, and only a tiny proportion took Animal Physiology or Botany.

As an experiment—and partly also as a bait in schools with poor Monday and Friday attendance—a course of scientific lectures with demonstrations was given for several years at a dozen schools.[95] The girls privileged to attend were said to be very interested, even in some cases to have shown 'a remarkable aptitude'. Moreover, the lecturer reported in 1894, he had been told 'that all who attend find the advantage of it in their Domestic Economy lessons'.[96] A colleague later spelt out the usefulness of scientific education respectively for girls and for boys, in his account of a science course taught to both. It started with the relative densities of solids and liquids:

> For girls this knowledge is useful when testing the purity of many liquids in the household, and for boys in the detection of the alloying of metal. The course proceeds to deal with the general effects of heat upon matter. The girl here obtains...a correct idea of the principles of ventilation, the construction and use of clinical and household thermometers; and the boy can learn at what period of the frost his father's waterpipe bursts....Boys and girls are then encouraged to take up questions of evaporation, of distillation and filtration...the girls, at the same time, can be taught to observe the most favourable atmosphere as regards moisture, for drying and airing clothes...[97]

Most girls would receive scientific instruction only in their domestic economy lessons, largely theoretical at first, though intended to cover such useful topics as the composition and nutritive value of different kinds of foods, and how to choose and prepare them; how to warm, ventilate and clean the home; and general rules of health and the management of the sick-room.[98] An inspector in 1877 criticized their irrelevance to daily life—instead of 'lessons on...albumen, fibrine, casein etc.', the children should be taught about 'the cleansing of drains', 'the evils of keeping rotting refuse in dustbins close to the windows', and the care of cuts, burns, colds and simple diseases.[99] From the 1880s this approach also led to a more practical emphasis in needlework, and to the introduction of other practical work.

In needlework, fine work and embroidery were criticized as inappropriate to the girls' needs and damaging to their eyesight; while the Code's requirements were challenged as excessive.[100] In the late 1870s, by the end of Standard Four girls should have made a shift, a petticoat, a nightshirt, a nightdress, a full-sized youth's sock and girl's stockings, a man's shirt or a girl's frock, and a full-sized boy's knickerbocker stocking. Usually the teacher 'fixed' (cut out and prepared) the work for them to sew. Those who were taught to cut out learnt to produce 'any undergarment ordinarily required' in families of their class (a potential source of embarrassment for the all-male inspectors).[101] As undergarments were not universally worn among the poor and rough, an unstated aim was probably to encourage an unfamiliar habit. The general intention was to equip girls to dress themselves neatly (and according to their teachers' ideas of what was appropriate), and to meet family responsibilities, rather than to prepare them for work in the sewing trades. After pressure by teachers and negotiations between the Board and the Education Department, the Code for 1884 and subsequent years reduced the needlework requirements so that they contained 'no more work than can be fairly mastered by any girls' school in which four hours weekly have been devoted to this subject'.[102] (Reorganization of the preparatory work also relieved the teachers of much of the burden of 'fixing'.)[103] Material was not to be 'so fine as to strain the eyesight of the children', no embroidery was to be used, and the garments (fewer, but still including some for other members of the family) were to be of 'plain simple patterns, showing intelligence and good workmanship, but without elaborate detail'.[104] During the following decade, under the influence of the Board's lady needlework inspectors (especially Miss Heath), the trend away from 'sight-destroying microscopic stitches' and 'elaborately worked garments' continued, and there was increasing emphasis on teaching the girls to cut out (using paper patterns) and on the simple and practical. From 1892 children were encouraged to bring mending from home.[105] Favoured (and expert) pupils might also do sewing for their teachers.[106]

Laundry teaching was also introduced in 1889, and centres were set up where older girls were taught techniques of washing and ironing along with 'some simple facts of chemistry'.[107] They mostly practised on clothes brought from home, or even from neighbours,[108] but a stock was also kept at the centres. Some teachers sent 'their own articles to be washed and ironed and thus [gave] encouragement and practice'.[109]

Cookery was made a grant-earning subject in 1882, in the hope that it would become part of the ordinary course of instruction, since 'after the three elementary subjects and sewing' no subject was of such importance for 'the class of girls who attend elementary schools'.[110] It competed with needlework (though other subjects probably lost in the end): a class in Battersea in 1885 had to be given an extra hour a week for Needlework because they were 'missing so much for Cookery'.[111] The Board had started cookery instruction even in 1875, with classes held at a school near Euston to serve Finsbury and Marylebone, and at a Blackheath school for Southwark and Greenwich.[112] In 1878 it was decided to create a network of cookery centres and by 1882 there were already twenty-one functioning centres in London. Five years later there were forty-nine, and more planned.[113] As with needlework, the importance of cookery instruction for girls was scarcely challenged. (One attempt was made, in 1884, by the Board's strongest feminist, Henrietta Muller. She wanted the School Management Committee to find out how many girls of what ages took cookery, and for how many hours, and also to consider 'whether cookery is, properly speaking, an educational subject'. But her move was blocked.)[114] On the contrary, numbers continued to rise. In 1889 15,154 girls completed a course of instruction; in 1891, 17,527, in 1893, 22,025, and so on.[15] Each course (by 1902, at least) involved forty hours of teaching a year for each child, sometimes concentrated into eight hours a week, sometimes spread out.[116] Such statistics, however, as Lowndes drily notes, convey nothing about the quality or relevance of the teaching.

Housemaid or Housewife?

Cookery classes were advocated not only as technical education, part of the swing towards the practical which brought in kindergarten handwork and 'Slojd' woodwork and prepared boys for a useful future in industry, but also as part of a larger campaign, again justified on national grounds, to encourage thrifty domestic management. The same general arguments had been made already for other domestic instruction, but cookery acquired special importance. Sixty per cent of a workman's wage went on food, argued Fanny Calder of the pioneer Liverpool School of Cookery:

> knowledge and capacity in this department mean health, thrift, comfort and saving; so that efficient instruction in this branch of education seems likely to have a more direct effect on the welfare of the people than any other subject in the timetable of our girls' schools....Moreover, if the wife finds her interest and occupation in thrifty housekeeping, there will be neither time nor inclination for the objectionable afternoon occupation of gossip on the doorstep or forming drinking parties indoors.[117]

In the rhetoric of the time, the family was in decay, and the national well-being therefore threatened, but if women could be taught to be good cooks and housewives all might yet be well. Their men would be tempted home by the prospect of a tasty meal, pleasingly served in a bright, clean room, so they would not go to the pub. It would be concocted thriftily out of next to nothing,[118] and no money would be spent on drink, so wages would go further. Family life would be saved, and the good of the country therefore secured. As a Standard Six girl declared in 1894, in a competition essay on temperance:

> People do not drink so much if there are light and comfort at home. It is necessary for girls to learn to cook so that their husbands and friends may not have to go out to get a good meal.[119]

A writer in the *Contemporary Review* in 1904 argued that cookery (for girls) was more important than the three R's, or indeed than needlework, because 'it has directly to do with the preservation of health, the comfort of home life, and the prevention of that curse of civilization, drunkenness'.[120] Barnardo, according to an early account of his work, understood that 'a thrifty girl is a benefactor to her country, while a slattern is a burden to herself and others'.[121] Cookery teachers thus had a responsibility to the nation. In 1900, in the same vein, the Inspectors of Laundry and Cookery Work urged teachers to develop a 'missionary spirit', because:

> on their earnestness and zeal depends the result for which the Government is willing to pay so large a sum, namely the increased comfort and health of the homes of the people, due to greater thrift on the part of the women and a better knowledge of how to economize time, labour and money.[122]

A rather less lofty argument was also put forward to support domestic instruction, namely its value as a training for domestic servants. Lord Brabazon saw it as a simple question of supply and demand:

> while a mass of girlhood is going to ruin in London and our large towns from absence of training and want of honest occupation, there is extreme difficulty in finding a supply of properly trained servants....I can only account for it by the want of any system for transforming the slatternly girl of the slums into the neat and tidy domestic servant....Why could not cookery and housework form an essential part of a girl's education? How much more important for the starving girlhood in London to be fitted for domestic service than to know the height of the Himalayas or the names of the Plantagenets...[123]

By such people the work of a servant and of a working man's wife were seen as similar, one or other of them the destiny of all working girls. The same training was to qualify the girls for both, fitting them for 'their true sphere, home' in whichever role. 'That girls are not taught housework while young and still capable of being taught is the main cause of the incapacity of our domestic servants and working men's wives', argued Miss May Elizabeth

Headdon, of the Association for the Promotion of Housewifery (founded in 1886 at a drawing-room meeting in Earl Fortescue's London residence). Before the unenthusiastic Cross Commission in 1887 she advocated the Kitchen Garden system:

> In fitting our girls for their after life, as wives, mothers, and ser-
> vants, we would begin with the little ones before they lose the
> natural womanly taste for domestic work which is always seen in
> very little girls; and by a practical development of the
> Kindergarten system, we would teach them by means of small
> models, songs and object lessons, the rudiments of housework.[124]

She wanted such instruction to be a compulsory part of every girl's educa-tion, which the Commissioners thought 'a little despotic'. They saw small advantage in expenditure on models to train the children in work they would (and should) learn at home.[125] They may also have been uneasy with her emphasis on domestic service. Although it was often assumed that ser-vice was not only the most likely but the most desirable occupation for girls to take up on leaving school, comparatively few London girls went into ser-vice, at least in the houses of the wealthy.[126] For rate-supported schools to give girls compulsory training as servants would be politically ill-advised, though success stories about satisfied employers of Board-School products were all right.

The emphasis in London schools in the 1890s, then, was on 'helping girls to become better housewives in the future, and more intelligent mem-bers of society generally', rather than on preparing them for domestic service. The aim was to combine theoretical and practical work so as to produce:

> a deft and ready practical knowledge of the application of the
> essential principles underlying the making of the home, its eco-
> nomical management, and the maintenance of the health of its
> inmates.[127]

Teaching equipment in cookery centres was from the first to consist of 'such appliances as are suitable for the ordinary artisan's home, with the addition of a gas stove',[128] and on the whole the dishes taught were simple ones which could be made without elaborate equipment. (In 1891–2, for instance, they included potato soup, rock cakes, meat cakes, fruit pudding, invalids' cakes and jelly, meat pies and patties, pea soup, stewed beef and rice, apple dumplings, rice buns, shepherd's pie, toad in the hole, semoli-na pudding, mince meat, oatmeal buns, seed cake, meat pudding, bread, Christmas pudding, sausage rolls, and fig pudding.)[129] The syllabus was criticized both for being too narrow, by those who expected it to prepare for domestic service, and for being too wide, by those aware of the limited resources of working-class homes. Certainly some of those dishes would at times have been beyond the means or the facilities of the ordinary working-class household. Moreover the underlying assumption was of a family meal cooked by one person. In many families this might happen only once a week, and the degree of preparation which cookery lessons assumed would have been quite strange. On the other hand, cookery in domestic service not only demanded wider experience and a larger repertoire, but also would be closed to a London girl who had just left school. In a household with only one servant, the girl would be a skivvy. She would clean, run errands, mind babies, and do all the odd jobs, but she would not be entrusted with cooking. And where there was a larger staff, the girl would come in at the bottom, and the cook's position would be one of jealously guarded eminence, not to be aspired to by a mere kitchen maid for some years, if at all.

This ambiguity—housemaid or housewife—also affected the teaching in the housewifery centres set up in the late 1890s for the instruction of older girls from the surrounding schools in the scientific principles and practice of cookery, laundry and housework. The girls attended for five half-days a week, leaving the other five for instruction in 'the ordinary school subjects.[130] Again, 'it was not intended to allow these classes to resolve themselves into places for training girls for domestic service'.[131] But an account by Charles Morley of a visit to the Bethnal Green centre described teaching suggestive of service and a concept of housewife developed with servants as the pattern. Morley reported that the centre was 'not developed as a manufactory for the production of servants...but a school for the raising of the standards of workers' houses', nevertheless he presented both possibilities. (Pretty Selina, 'a little maiden with a mob cap and a nice print apron', blushes when asked by the teacher to give an account of the week's work 'supposing you had a nice little home of your own'; while 'Mary Roxbury, of a plainer cast...proposes domestic service as her career in life'.)[132] The house which they were learning to look after, though supposed to be 'furnished and fitted as a model workingman's house',[133] was more spacious and better equipped than the ordinary poor London home. Mary had to sweep a carpeted room in stages:

Place the furniture in the middle of the room or the passage.
Remove the ornaments.
Pin up the curtains.
Cover the furniture with a dust-sheet.
Open the windows top and bottom.
Sprinkle the carpet with tea leaves [to lay the dust].
Use a short stiff brush to finish sweeping, and take up the dust on a dust pan.

Paraphernalia and ritual alike are more suggestive of domestic service than of the homes these children knew.

Such training pointed either towards service, or towards a new kind of housewife, the dependent housewife of altogether domestic function. This

new model for the working-class woman was an elaboration of the diligent
and thrifty manager hoped for in earlier decades, whose home-making
efforts were to keep her husband from the pub. In the new version her role
as mother came first. In the early twentieth century, during a wave of concern that Britain's imperial and industrial pre-eminence was being
threatened by high infant mortality and the low level of working-class
health, it was argued that working-class mothers were the problem, and
'education for motherhood' was presented as a panacea.[134] Now the future
mother had to be taught the right way to care for babies as well as the right
way to sew, to cook, to do laundry and housework and to run the home. At
Myrdle Street (Higher Grade) school, Stepney, in 1909, weekly lessons on
the theory of infant care ('the baby's sleep, airing, food, teeth, ailments,
dress, formation of habits, intelligence, playthings') were supplemented by
visits to a nearby day nursery, where the girls were shown how to undress,
bath and put to bed infants and little children, and how to prepare and
give a bottle.[135] Such instruction had support in the highest quarters. Even
if it meant paying less attention to 'what is commonly called booklearning',
announced the Secretary to the Board of Education in 1910, the teaching
of older girls should be 'more definitely directed towards arousing interest
in, and increasing the knowledge of, the ordinary routine of domestic
housecraft, including infant care'.[136]

Throughout this period there was a gulf between the classes on questions of domestic practice and especially child care, which resulted from
both economic and cultural differences. Middle-class certainty that there
was only one right way of doing things was reinforced by the growing pro-
fessionalization of medicine and social work; and allowed social problems
to be explained in terms of the inadequacies of the working-class family
and its domestic practices. Following this diagnosis, the obvious prescription was to alter working-class practice. It was for this reason that domestic
instruction, both theoretical and practical, took up a substantial part of
girls' time at school and was often presented as the most important part of
their education, while other subjects, especially science, might be given a
domestic content or rationalization. But by the same token, the theory and
the practice which were considered so essential for girls were not usually
thought necessary or even desirable for boys.

12. Outdoor washing over brazier, with clothes line behind steam.

PART 3

---◆---

Working or
Helping?

13. Children's work took many forms. Kindling wood once chopped and bundled could be sold door to door from a home-made barrow like the one here used in play and child care.

9

Children, Work and Independence

———————————◀◆▶———————————

MANY CHILDREN worked in the second half of the nineteenth century, though the patterns of their work and how it was seen were changing. It was an economic unit to which children as well as adults contributed earnings and unpaid labour, in a ratio which varied with age, sex and family needs and which itself was changing during these decades. Many London wage-earners lived by seasonal or irregular work, on wages which left no margin for saving or for emergency. Their children shared in the daily struggle; they were prepared for adult life through participation, not through the segregated education favoured by the well-to-do. If death or want crippled the domestic unit, or if they left it to escape internal discord, children in the middle decades of the century might fend for themselves from nine or ten; by the end of the century this was less common.

Children's Work in the Mid-nineteenth Century

Until the 1870s London children might enter full-time employment as young as six or seven, though between ten and twelve was more usual.[1] A parliamentary enquiry in the 1860s found them occupied in domestic manufacture (often combined with housework) and in a variety of workshops. They worked in the production of shoes and many items of clothing, of 'trimmings' for furnishings (they threaded beads, or wound silk for the older workers who made fringes, tassels, pompoms and the like), of matches and of furniture.[2] They were also employed in street selling, in service (both domestic and in shops and workshops), and for delivery and errands. Children of the very poor worked the streets. They sold low-priced wares; swept mud from street crossings so that elegant shoes and trailing skirts would not be dirtied; and found scores of ways to earn or wheedle coppers from monied adults.

The young watercress seller who talked to Henry Mayhew in about 1850, through her mixed contribution of cash, labour, and the food provided by employers, probably earned most of her own keep. Mayhew's account of their meeting is worth examining, for despite his mediation as interlocutor and scribe it brings us unusually close to the views and life of a poor child.[3] She lived in Clerkenwell with an older sister, a younger brother and sister, her mother, who did cleaning, and her stepfather, a scissor grinder. At eight, she had a work history already.

> On and off, I've been very near a twelvemonth in the streets. Before that, I had to take care of a baby for my aunt. No, it wasn't heavy— it was only two months old; but I minded it for ever such a time—till it could walk. It was a very nice little baby, not a very pretty one; but, if I touched it under the chin, it would laugh. Before I had the baby, I used to help mother, who was in the fur trade; and if there was any slits in the fur, I'd sew them up. My mother learned me to needlework and to knit when I was about five...[4]

In season she went down to Farringdon Market in the early morning, between four and five, to pick up her watercress. Then she sat on a doorstep and made it into the bunches which she sold over the next few hours, mostly to shops. She usually took threepence or fourpence besides renewing the stock money for next day's supply; she had once even made a shilling. On getting home she scrubbed out their two rooms. ('I puts the room to rights: mother don't make me do it, I does it myself.') Each Friday she went to a Jewish family to look after the fire and snuff the candles, tasks forbidden them during their Sabbath. They fed her well:

> I have a reg'lar good lot to eat. Supper of a Friday night, and tea after that, and fried fish of a Saturday morning and meat for dinner, and tea, and supper, and I like it very well.

Her wage, a penny-halfpenny, went either to her mother or into a savings club for her clothes:

> It's better than spending it in sweetstuff for them as has a living to earn. Besides it's like a child to care for sugar sticks, and not like one who's got a living and vittals to earn. I ain't a child, and I shan't be a woman till I'm twenty, but I'm past eight, I am.

A girl's first work was often as a nursemaid. As soon as she was strong enough, she would be 'keeping guard over the younger children' for her mother, or 'lent out to carry about a baby to add to the family income by gaining her sixpence weekly'.[5] Next she obtained 'a little place'. One girl Mayhew talked with had found a place as a 'servant-of-all-work' when just eleven. An Italian couple gave her a shilling a week and her tea 'to clean the room and nuss the child'; she took her dinner at her grandmother's.[6] Mrs Layton, seventh child of a government clerk whose large family spelt poverty, recalled her first job in 1865:

> When I was ten I went to mind the baby of a person who kept a small general shop. My wages were 1s. 6d. a week and my tea and 2d. a week for myself. I got to work at eight in the morning and left at eight at night, with the exception of two nights a week when I left at seven o'clock to attend a ragged school.[7]

This was a typical first full-time job. She went home to sleep; she kept only a small share of her wage and was paid partly in kind; her work was as general auxiliary to her mistress (besides caring for the baby she worked in the shop); the pay was low and the hours were long. She mentions a visit to the shop by her aunt which is also significant: the first job was generally local and the employer someone known through family, neighbourhood, work or friendship, so relatives could observe how things went. She left the job because her mistress wanted her to give up the evening classes. The decision was apparently hers, without consultation: 'the conflict ended by my refusing to work for her, and so we parted'.[8]

Older children sometimes found work on their own, usually within range of home. The street labour markets of Bethnal Green included one for girls and boys from about nine to sixteen. Early in the week the children waiting to be hired would seldom number less than forty or fifty, though 'in former years' there had been many more.

> The children are hired by the week, the wages ranging from 1s. 6d. to 2s. 6d., with 'twopence for myself' and tea. No character is required on either side. The girls are engaged principally for the purpose of taking care of infants while the mothers are at work; the lads are usually employed by the weavers and others, the hours of labour being from seven or eight a.m. to eight or nine p.m., sometimes less and sometimes more.[9]

At twelve or thirteen the alternative to factory or workshop employment was domestic service, as daily nursemaids,[10] or maids-of-all-work. Live-in jobs were preferred when there was tension or overcrowding at home.[11] East End or Irish girls had no hope of the 'good' jobs in households of higher social status, where several servants were kept, pay and prospects were a little better, and work might be lighter.[12] They were handicapped by prejudice (English or Welsh village girls were supposedly more docile and hardworking); and they could not afford the necessary outfits.[13] A possible option might be service in prospering Jewish families: the Jewish households where Mr N. (b. 1899) was Sabbath goy 'nearly always had an English girl servant', usually between twelve and fifteen (his own age) and often from a school he too had attended.[14] In districts where rich and poor lived in proximity, such as Paddington, local girls had more chance.[15] A well-placed relative, or church or school, permitted useful connections with housekeepers, clergymen or ladies, and thus recommendations to jobs and help with clothes. In poor districts girls who looked strong enough were taken on in lodging houses, pubs and eating houses, or in the households of local shopkeepers and anyone else who could afford domestic help. Children leaving orphanages and workhouse schools were often placed in jobs of this kind,[16] which meant long hours and heavy work. The 'child-servant who drudges from morning till night in some house where only one servant is kept' was called a slavey (for obvious reasons).[17] Besides endless scullery work, preparing and clearing up meals, she had to 'take up the carpets, scrub the stairs, wash the babies, wait on the boarders, carry the children out for an airing, make the beds, black the grates, and run messages'.[18] Carrying water and coal fell to her, also lighting and keeping in fires.

Little Women and Street Arabs

Middle-class adults of the mid-nineteenth century were less shocked by working children (especially servants) than by street children and their independence.[19] When Mayhew recounted his meeting with the young watercress seller, he emphasized her pathos and precocity. His opening remark was that 'although only eight years of age [she] had entirely lost all childish ways, and was, indeed, in thoughts and manner, a woman'.

> There was something cruelly pathetic in hearing this infant, so young that her features had scarcely formed themselves, talking of the bitterest struggles of life, with the calm earnestness of one who had endured them all. I did not know how to talk with her. At first I treated her as a child, speaking on childish subjects; so that I might, by being familiar with her, remove all shyness, and get her to narrate her life freely. I asked her about her toys and her games with her companions; but the look of amazement that answered me soon put an end to any attempt at fun on my part.[20]

Whether unconsciously or for dramatic effect, he exaggerated her shocking precocity. Despite that 'look of amazement' when he broached 'childish subjects', later in the account she spoke of knowing a great many games, and of playing honeypots and kiss-in-the-ring with the girls in the court. With her early-morning start, though, she was often too tired to play, and she always went to bed at seven, which cut down playing time. She had playthings, presents from her Jewish employers. Asked about dolls, she said she'd never had one, adding 'but I misses little sister'. (Till recently the two had shared a bed: a doll was presumably just a substitute to cuddle at night.) The look of amazement can as plausibly be attributed to surprise at being asked about toys and games by such a person—adult, male, and a gentleman—as to ignorance of play or of fun.

Her account is sturdy and matter-of-fact, and it belies Mayhew's suggestion that she had endured 'the bitterest struggles of life'. She knew cold,[21] fatigue, hunger, and the occasional punishment ('mother don't often beat me; but when she do, she don't play with me'). But she spoke warmly of her mother ('I always give mother my money, she's so very good to me'), and was grateful that she had removed her from school 'because the master whacked me'.[22] She also spoke affectionately of her little sister and of her aunt's baby whom she looked after, and appreciatively of her open-handed Jewish employers. She was proud of what she could do: 'I am a capital hand at bargaining...they can't take me in'; 'I know the quantities

very well'. Her rejection of sweets as childish was an assertion of the will to
be strong and responsible, as was doing housework ('mother don't make
me do it, I does it myself'), or her endurance of cold ('I bears the cold—
you must'), or her refusal of tears ('No, I never see any children
crying—it's no use'). Mayhew conveys dismay at this child who proudly
took on the burden of adult responsibility, insisted that she was not a child,
felt no shame about her situation and expected acceptance or even respect
rather than pity or alarm.

It was exactly her strength and self-sufficiency which he assumed his
readers would find shocking. They would expect children to be childlike:
that is, dependent, vulnerable, needing safeguard from responsibility and
from adult concerns, especially from the dangers and corruption of the
public world. Precocity was not admired as it had been fifty years before,
when Hannah More's Kate Stanley (a fictional model for the upper-middle-
class child), gave up picture books at seven, and on her eighth birthday
declared: 'today I give up all my little story books, and I am now going to
read such books as men and women read'.[23] In prevailing ideology by the
mid-nineteenth century, precocity and sharpness were unnatural, even
dangerous,[24] and a working child, still more an independent one, was a
contradiction. In real life, however, such contradictions were plentiful.
Most children, even in families, did not live that ideal of the well-to-do.
Moreover, their early experience of waged work and responsibility
equipped them for emergency while their coeval 'betters' were still in the
school-room. Thus a twelve-year-old might assume the domestic functions
of a mother (see below); children who lost both parents sometimes managed to survive together;[25] and children who ran away, whether from
hunger or from being mistreated, might pull through alone.[26]

These extreme situations produced two contrasting representations of
the child-as-adult amongst those whose children were always children. The
first, domestic and mostly female, involved responsibility for others.
Charley Neckett, in *Bleak House*, is an example. She took charge at thirteen,
when her mother died in childbed, then on her father's death went out
washing and cleaning, helped by neighbours who kept an eye on the two
little ones and found her jobs. Dickens combines admiration for her with
a strong sense of wrong that responsibility and work should be shouldered
by such a child: the word 'little' recurs constantly. Similar scenes recur in
Dickens' novels, and in other popular writing of the time. They abound in
the Sunday-school-prize waif novels.[27]

The 'little woman' was an emotive figure for middle-class readers. arousing admiration, indignation and pity. By taking charge she was defending
the family, asserting the importance of close ties between its members and
the need for older ones to protect the younger. She was heroic. But her heroism was a sign that things were wrong—it should not be necessary or indeed
allowed. She was pathetic, because in that same vision of the family children
and females were essentially dependent, not responsible.

The antithetical figure, the ragged street boy, provoked fear as well as pity.[28] Shaftesbury, in a parliamentary speech in 1848, deplored the condition of 'the naked, filthy, roaming, lawless and deserted children in and about the metropolis', whose numbers he put at 30,000.[29] Street children were highly visible. Boys and girls, emerged from slum courts and rookeries to scratch a living in busy streets and public places—wherever work, charity or pickings might be available.[30] They swept crossings, ran messages, held horses, called cabs, carried bags, guided strangers, and they turned cartwheels, sang or whistled for coppers.[31] They buttonholed passers-by with importunate pathos or cheek, hawking their wares—fruit, flowers, matches, lights for cigars, or cheap toys—and always hopeful that a tender-hearted or liberal customer would overpay.[32] Others scavenged as mudlarks along the Thames at low tide, or were employed in the dust-yards to sift refuse for what could be recycled.[33] Or they picked over market waste for anything still edible; hungrily watched those who could afford to eat and might throw them coin or crust; and stared into food shops till bought off with scraps or driven away.[34] They seized any opportunity to earn money or food, and any chance to help themselves from an unguarded stall, shop, cart or pocket.[35] Some became skilled pickpockets and thieves.[36]

Survival was hard alone. To belong to a family, their own or one they lodged with and perhaps worked for, assured food and shelter even when takings were poor or illness struck,[37] though runaways had sometimes fled relatives who beat them for bringing back too little. Those who slept rough often had companions. A fictional ragamuffin in the 1860s, newly runaway, was shown the ropes by two other boys, who taught him how to find shelter and how to get a living, and invited him to go partners: 'you works with us, and you grubs with us, and you lodges with us'.[38] For a novice such sharing was critical; for old hands it was insurance against sickness and bad luck.

Shaftesbury's estimated 30,000 certainly included many children with homes. The well-to-do seldom distinguished between street children with regular work and those with none, or between those who slept rough, who paid for a lodging, or who belonged to households. All were lumped together, condemned by appearance and behaviour alike. They were arabs, urchins, scaramouches, guttersnipes; 'a wild race', 'nomadic', 'a multitude of untutored savages', even 'English Kaffirs' and 'Hottentots'.[39] The labels tagged them as heathen and uncivilized, alien to order and progress.

For those who believed that children belonged in protecting families, street and home were in total opposition. The street stood for danger and corruption, and no child with a proper home would be freely allowed there. Without a home, or with a deficient home, a child had no sanctuary from the dangers of the street, and no domestic counter to its corrupting influences. So any child who picked up a living in the streets risked moral contamination. With girls the fear, explicit or not, was of their being on the street, not just in it. Moreover, such children were not only in danger, they were themselves dangerous. All these children who lived by their wits with minimal adult support or control were a threat to society. They eluded (and so challenged) 'natural' adult authority, indeed even preyed on the adult world, in a hand-to-mouth freemasonry of petty thieving and sleeping rough. Such youngsters swore, smoked, gambled, exchanged coarse repartee, begged, stole—all improper for children. And girls too did these things; some groups sleeping rough were mixed; and in the worst lodging-houses a dozen children might sleep 'squeedged into one bed...some at the foot and some at the top—boys and girls all mixed'.[40] With 'natural' rules of both age and gender thus breached, all morality and order were imperilled.

From the 1870s onwards, vagrant children could less easily elude adult authority. Their night-time lairs were cleaned out by police and philanthropists.[41] Nine-year-old Arthur Harding had been sleeping rough for about three weeks in 1893 when police with a lantern found him in an empty house; and around 1890, when Charlie Chaplin and his brother were noticed asleep near a night-watchman's fire (their stepmother, drunk, had turned them out) police took charge of them, made the stepmother take them back, then sent in the NSPCC.[42] The daytime haunts of children seeking pence, food or fun were watched, both by philanthropists [43] and by the school-attendance officers who patrolled the streets and courts,[44] though some sharp children learnt how to feign ringworm or to tell convincing stories of infectious disease at home. At stations ('the best place to beg' because of 'all the country people coming up, frightened of what they might meet')[45] policing became more strict, and while carrying luggage between bus, cab and train still paid, it grew harder to cadge. Children found to have no 'proper' homes were placed under alternative care and discipline. Booth noted the growing pressure on the children of the very poor, 'the street arabs'. Many, removed from their parents, were in pauper or industrial schools, or in Homes.

> Some are in the Board schools, and more in ragged schools, and the remainder, who cannot be counted, and may still be numerous, are every year confined within narrowing bounds by the persistent pressure of the School Board and other agencies.[46]

Rescue stories, exciting or pathetic, but always improving, filled the reports of charitable organizations and the pages of children's Sunday-school prize books and magazines.

Street children with homes were vulnerable because parents who let their children 'run wild' must be either neglecting or exploiting them, and in any case neglecting their duty as parents.[47] In the combined interests of order, hygiene and child protection, official intrusion into the home was increasingly given legal sanction. Truancy officers (after the 1880 Education Act) could pursue their quarries indoors. Sanitary officers checked homes for smallpox and other diseases; common lodging houses had regular nocturnal visits; and from 1888 they could also enter canal-boat homes and register the age and sex of all living on board so as to combat overcrowding and immorality.[48] At the same time the fast-growing lobby against cruelty to children extended definitions of cruelty and neglect and of 'unfit' parents.[49] By 1880 children might be taken into official custody on three grounds: if parents could not control them; if parents were teaching them to be 'depraved and disorderly'; or if parents were in prison.[50] Legislation in 1880 and 1885 allowed their removal to Industrial Schools if any part of the house was used 'for immoral purposes';[51] while Acts on Prevention of Cruelty to Children (1889), Poor Law Adoption (1889), and Custody of Children (1891) added further grounds for removal, mainly based on children's right to reasonable treatment and the parents' duty to provide proper care. Interpretation of what was reasonable and proper of course lay with the authorities.

By the early twentieth century the street arab was recast as waif, as victim rather than threat, a vanishing anachronism. Children belonged at school and in home or Home, not in workplace or street; and home had to meet certain standards. The compulsory schooling initiated with the 1870 Education Act assisted this process of redefining childhood; it reinforced and was reinforced by restrictions on their employment.

Investigating Children's Work, 1890s–1900s

In spite of the campaign against street independence and the introduction of compulsory school, adults and children throughout the late nineteenth-century working class continued to expect children to share in work.

Even in the most secure and prosperous sector, among artisans, older children helped with younger, girls joined in most domestic work, and boys had set tasks (such as Saturday cleaning of knives and boots) and were sent on errands.[52] If either parent—or both—worked in a domestic workshop, the children helped: they did odd jobs and errands at first, then learnt by assisting, and took on more as they became more competent. Arthur Newton (born in Hackney in 1902) recorded how in his shoemaker grandparents' backyard workshop:

> the family, one by one as they became old enough, were taught their craft. The girls were taught by my grandmother to do fitting or machining, and the boys were taught to cut and round soles, channel them and sew. All began this at a very early age, some time before they left school.[53]

Work for the household and work in the workshop were regarded as training, in necessary skills and in proper habits. The same attitude sanctioned regular jobs on Saturday or before or after school, for boys anyway. The children who worked most regularly belonged, it was said, even in the 1900s, to 'respectable and fairly well-to-do people who put their children to work to teach them habits of industry and to keep them from bad street habits'.[54] Such children found their own jobs; they valued their increased pocket money and (according to Frederick Willis) thought 'the art of getting a living', was learnt 'in the world, not in schools'. In his fairly comfortable circle, 'the most enterprising boys made a tentative plunge into commerce long before they left school'. The most genteel boy delivered bottles of medicine from the doctor after school; others delivered 'papers or milk at the break of day'. The initiative for getting a job was entirely theirs.[55]

Children's domestic help and earnings also enabled a secure but not prosperous family to present a bolder face. The anxiety of the better-off parent to spend more on clothes often resulted (according to Edith Hogg, of the Women's Industrial Council) in 'serious overwork to the little body in tidier clothes'.[56] In some families looking respectable was of overriding importance, perhaps to impress the charitable as 'deserving', or to assert local superiority, or with a view to securing better prospects for the children later (a letter of recommendation for a steady job in service for instance, or an apprenticeship).[57] In such cases children's earnings—as well as their domestic labour—helped to maintain respectability rather than threatening it, so long as jobs were regular and local and did not involve hanging around the streets.

For many people, however, certainly for those caught in the daily grind of poverty, children's work was not primarily a question of moral training or apprenticeship, nor of maintaining appearances, but of necessity, immediate or imminent. The more small children there were, the more joint effort was required to keep the home together, and children took part in that effort as soon as possible, even at four or five, though older children, of course, had most to do. Every little helped, and their contribution might become indispensable. Just as parents took for granted the right to their children's labour, so children recognized the need for their work: it was the natural thing. Children were also 'pleased and proud to be in a position of partial independence'.[58] Transition to adult status involved a mounting contribution to the family budget.

But if children's work in this family context was still needed and accepted in the late nineteenth-century working class, in middle-class opinion it was neither acceptable nor as easily ignored as before. Pressure groups, like the Women's Industrial Council (WIC) and the Committee on Wage-Earning Children, worked hard to document and publicize it and to abolish or at least limit it.

The Women's Industrial Council's survey in 1896–7 took fifty-four sample schools, 'representing different conditions of poverty, of industry, and of population', and asked teachers for numbers of children earning 'a wage, however nominal'. The replies varied in completeness and precision, but suggested that out of 16,000 boys and 10,000 girls about five per cent (729 boys and 523 girls) worked for wages. But by their own admission the overall average masked higher percentages for older schoolchildren; and they were forced to conclude that there were far more children casually employed than the terms of their enquiry could reveal. The evidence on girls alluded 'with increased emphasis and frequency' to children employed:

> not strictly as wage-earners, but to help in the house of neighbours
> or relations for food, stray articles of clothing, and casual coppers.
> In one school, where only twelve are returned as regular wage-
> earners, 'nearly all' are said to be employed as above described.[59]

This survey was used for intensive lobbying of public opinion and the authorities.[60] WIC representations stimulated a London School Board enquiry (1898), a parliamentary return (on the labour of children at elementary schools in England and Wales) in 1899, a report to the Public Control Committee of the London County Council (1900), and the major Interdepartmental Committee on Children's Employment Out of School Hours (1902), set up jointly by the Board of Education, the Board of Trade, and the Home Office.[61] The WIC had a useful ally in the idiosyncratic Conservative MP, John Gorst, Vice-president of the Privy Council's Committee on Education, who spoke and wrote powerfully on education and children's work. When presenting the 1899 parliamentary return he supported the WIC's contention that the available figures underestimated child labour, and in particular represented 'a very small portion of the girls actually at work': the 'painful and disappointing return' was also an incomplete one.[62] Out of 1,014 London Board schools, 831 had replied, and their returns recorded 21,755 boys and 9,052 girls as working. This was about seven per cent of average attendance, according to the chairman of the London School Board.[63]

These figures were none of them much more than guesses based on narrow definitions of work. The real question, as Edith Hogg noted, went beyond that of wage-earners, and the figures collected were 'little more than an index to the habit of working school children generally'.[64] This was above all true of girls. The returns, however inadequate, provide a starting point. Tables 9.1 and 9.2 ('Typical Returns from Girls' Schools' in the 1899 School Board report) illustrate the information they supply. Regent Street school, Greenwich (see Table 9.1) served a poor district and was classified as a 'school of special difficulty'. Before fees were abolished in 1891 it charged only a penny a week, and had almost the lowest average attendance in that division (66.5 per cent). Maidstone Street, in Haggerston (Table 9.2) also charged only a penny; but its attendance rates were a little higher (72.3 per cent), and closer to the local average.[65] The returns suggest that children in Haggerston engaged in various forms of homework, whereas in Greenwich only domestic work was available. They show more Haggerston children working, able to earn more and at higher rates. They show more Greenwich children receiving food in part-payment.

But the returns leave a number of questions unanswered. Does the absence of homework on the Greenwich list really mean none was done? Certainly some women will have taken in washing and mangling, with which children helped. Moreover, Greenwich in 1903-4 had sixty-six firms which reported employing outworkers, and 287 addresses of local out-workers (too few of course).[66] Wherever there was outwork, children were involved either in the work itself or in associated errands (see next chapter). In nearby Woolwich and Plumstead, where women outworkers were employed by Slazenger's to stitch the coverings onto tennis balls, children delivered them. (C.G. Perkins, for instance, aged ten in about 1911, helped the old lady next door by carrying 'six dozen balls in partitioned boxes' to the factory—'two and a half miles each way on my little legs once a week for tuppence'.)[67] It is unlikely that no children in Regent Street school helped mothers, neighbours, or relatives with mangling or washing or out-work errands, even if none figure in the return.

Another question concerns seasons. The crackers which four Haggerston children made, and probably also the bonbons, were for Christmas: this was the best-paid work in the returns, but it was seasonal. It cannot be assumed that such well-paid work was available all the year round.

Table 9.1:   Return on children's employment out of school, showing hours and pay per week, from Regent Street Girls' school, Greenwich.

Name	Age	Standard	Occupation	Hours	Pay
LC	12	5	Housework	21	1s 6d
MM	13	3	Housework	34	1s 2d + food
ED	10	4	Housework; errands for aunt	24	2d–3d
RW	10	4	Housework; minds baby	31	1s 0d
EC	9	3	Errands	30	1s 0d
BM	11	4	Errands	39	6d
GD	9	3	Errands; minds baby	27	6d
RG	10	3	Minds a baby	25	6d
KD	10	3	Errands and housework	37	4d
BN	12	5	Housework	25+	6d
JM	13	5	Errands; minding children	19	1s 6d
EM	13	4	Housework	25	1s 0d
LH	13	4	Housework; minds baby	31	6d–9d
LJ	11	4	Housework; errands	37+	1s 0d + food
AH	13	4	Minds baby	22+	2d + food
LC	11	4	Housework; minds baby etc.	30	10d or 1s 0d
AA	10	4	Errands; minds baby; washes up	27	1d + dinner
FJ	10	4	Errands; minds baby	32	3d + dinner
FW	10	4	Errands; minds baby	21	3d

Source: SBL *Report of School Accommodation and Attendance Committee*, 'Out of School Labour by Schoolchildren', 1899, pp. 12–13.

Again, does the absence of domestic work on the Haggerston list really mean the girls did none, whether at home or for neighbours? Or does it mean that the teachers collecting information did not ask about it, or discounted it, or that the girls themselves thought that it would not count so did not mention it?

The same question arises about part-payment in food. The girls in the Greenwich school who reported receiving food were all but one from Standard Four: perhaps in the other classes (and throughout Maidstone Street school) no-one thought of mentioning it. Food often supplemented or even replaced the low wages paid to children. Those who did baby-minding and housework would at least be given tea and perhaps bread, with marge, dripping or jam, and if the employing family ate more they might share it. What they had might not amount to much, in quality or in quantity, especially if their employers were hard-up or mean,[68] but it still helped

Table 9.2:   Return on children's employment out of school, showing hours and pay per week, from Maidstone Street Girls' school, Hackney.

Name	Age	Standard	Occupation	Hours	Pay
JG	11	4	Crackers for mother	25	2s 4d
RN	13	4	Luggage hats for bonbons	22+	2s 6d
AH	11	4	Rub down and button boots	26	1s 2d
FR	11	4	Artificial flowers, helps mother	24	1s 0d
RW	11	4	Minding baby for lady	22+	1s 6d
FC	9	4	Fetch errands for dressmaker	26	10d
EM	10	4	Sewing shoes for aunt	34	2s 0d
EM	12	5	Minds lady's baby	24	1s 0d+food
RG	11	5	Minds 2 babies on Saturday and goes to shop	25	8d–9d
BO	10	6	Goes errands for lady	24	6d
PH	12	6	Cracker work	35	2s–3s
RU	12	6	Minds lady's 2 children	20	1s 0d
ES	11	6	Bookwork for grandmother	22	1s 6d
JT	10	6	Makes babies shoes, helps mother	30	6d
RO	11	5	Bonbon work (when not at school, which is very frequent, does double work and earns 8s a week)	40	4s 0d
CY	11	5	Minds lady's baby	25	6d
FS	12	5	Minds baby	30	9d
EC	13	5	Minds aunt's baby	23	3d–6d
EW	11	5	Minds lady's baby	31+	1s 2d
GO	12	5	Minds lady's baby	27+	6d

Name	Age	Standard	Occupation	Hours	Pay
EB	11	5	Does mother's mangling	20	6d
EN	11	5	Fetch lady's errands	21	9d
BB	12	5	Scour, damp down + polish boots	21	1s 0d
AM	10	5	Stay work	20	3d-4d
ET	11	5	Bone fanning, help mother	27	1d
KF	12	3	Sews buttons, inks and buttons up boots; goes to shop for mother	30	1s 1d from man for going to shop for mother; + 2d from mother
KS	9	2	Helps aunt with crackers	26	1d
EF	8	3	Minds lady's baby	20	2d
EB	10	1	Crackers for mother	30	3d

Source: SBL *Report of School Accommodation and Attendance Committee*, 'Out of School Labour by Schoolchildren', 1899, pp. 12-13.

to relieve demands on the resources at home. Walter P. (born in Whitechapel in 1903) recalled how he and his brothers and sisters each had a round of Jewish households in the Brick Lane district of East London, where they would light fires on the Sabbath, and the reward—as for Mayhew's watercress girl—was often a piece of fried fish and a slice of rye bread. They either ate it at once, or brought it home for supper to be greeted gratefully by their mother: 'What good children you are!'[69] Children who worked on street stalls or in shops which sold food were given surplus or substandard stock—'specked' fruit, cracked eggs, ageing vegetables, broken biscuits or stale bread—for family consumption.

The rates of pay given in both returns are also problematic: do these sums consistently show what the child earned altogether? It was not unusual for an employer to pay the mother, who then handed on something to the child. Where an eleven-year-old had done thirty-nine hours of 'errands' for sixpence, or twenty-two hours of child care for twopence and food, it seems likely either that the work was done within the family economy (for mother or aunt perhaps), or that the mother was paid more than the coppers given to the child. Conversely, a child who earned four shillings making bonbons, or two or three shillings at crackers, was probably expected to hand most of that over to her mother. All these uncertainties make it hard to generalize from such figures. On the other hand, it is useful to have some indication of the variety of outwork done around Maidstone Street (Christmas crackers, elaborate sweet wrappings, boots and shoes, artificial flowers, dressmaking, laundry and stays). And the catch-all categories in the Greenwich return demand exploration (see next chapter). The information assembled for the enquiries of the 1890s and 1900s then, though a

prime source, must be used with care. The origins and methods of the
enquiries, and the assumptions of those who collected and analysed the
material, all had their effect on the findings. This can be seen in the tendency to accept only paid work as work, the invisibility or discounting of
domestic work, the ambiguous reported rates of pay, the emphasis on overwork, and the failure to examine the context in which children worked.

Investigation and discussion of working-class childhood around the
turn of the century was carried out by people whose own experience and
definitions of childhood were middle class, whose acquaintance with other
views was limited and rarely sympathetic, and who took for granted the
superiority of their own ways. For them, as indeed for us today, child labour
was exploitation of the helpless, and adults who profited by their work,
whether employers or parents, must be prevented and denounced.
Moreover, these investigations into children's employment were made
when England's economic and military supremacy was being challenged,
in trade by Germany and the United States, then in empire by the Boers. A
new sense of insecurity provoked examination of the nation's assets, with a
wider definition and a longer perspective than had been usual before.
Children acquired an enhanced importance, both as future workers, sol-
diers and sailors, and as parents of the next generation.[70] Efforts to improve
children's condition still drew on humanitarian rhetoric, but the discovery
that children's health and training had national significance gave such
efforts a new political credibility and even urgency.

These assumptions were common ground in 1900s discussion of children's employment. But they still left room for confusion, about how long
a child was a child, and, still more, about what constituted work.

The investigators expected children's work to be bad: heavy, exhaust-
ing and exploitative. They collected cases of long hours and low pay, and
discounted what did not fit their definitions. For the 1899 School Board
enquiry, teachers were asked how many children worked more than nineteen hours a week. The concern was therefore with excessive work, but no
effort was made to gauge what would be normal and how the two were related. The 1902 committee asked witnesses mainly about overwork and
ill-health. One, Ella Holme, a school manager in Southwark and Bermondsey,
prepared her evidence by asking teachers to find out from children how
many were earning. She then checked their figures by visiting the children's
homes. Out of thirty-five girls whom she checked, she dismissed twenty as
not proper wage-earners: they were just 'running errands for neighbours at
odd times'. In such cases, 'it was not work at all: the children like to make
themselves out rather important'.[71] She was of course in a position to impose
her definition of work, and to exclude theirs.

Comparable difficulties may be glimpsed in a conversation with children which a journalist reported in 1899. Jimmy Towler, a twelve-year-old
with 'the restless eyes and the unkempt look of the average little street
Arab', was not very regular at school, but said earnestly that he only stayed

away to sell papers—'I never do a mike'. Susan Nasmyth, another twelve-year-old, earned about half-a-crown a week by running errands, scrubbing steps, cleaning windows, and so on, but 'I don't stop away from school 'cept it's to do this....I never goes "mooching", sir'. 'Mooching' or 'doing a mike', like playing truant, carried with it a charge of idleness against which they wanted to defend themselves. Although they were missing school, they were not taking time to themselves; they did not deserve reprimand.

Like others, Susan Nasmyth was very suspicious of her journalist inter-rogator. ('They thought I was a School Board officer, to whom it was a dangerous thing to vouchsafe too much information.') She parried and evad-ed many of his questions, with monosyllables, with counter questions, like 'What's that got to do with you?', and with straight refusals: 'Find out then'.[72] Questions about the activities of children echoed the prying of the School Board Man, whom few parents or children could face without anxiety. (Eliza H. was 'terrified of the school board—we only had to see him—although I never stayed away'.)[73] Suspicion hampered the investigators, whether they were ladies of the Women's Industrial Council, journalists, or the authori-ty figures who collected evidence for the 1902 committee—teachers, school managers, clergymen and the like. Such wariness, greater still in adults who had already discovered the endless capacity of authority for interference, probably also explains the discrepant estimates noted by Ella Holme: 'The children generally gave more hours than the parents did; but they are gen-erally more to be believed than the parents'.[74]

Discrepancies revealed by returns to the 1902 committee were some-times substantial. In one poor school, in Hackney Wick, a twelve-year-old estimated that she spent twenty-eight hours a week on housework; her moth-er said seventeen. (The father was a house-painter, the mother took in washing, and there were six children, two of them earning.) An eleven-year-old said she spent twenty hours a week doing housework and helping her mother make crackers; her mother called it nine. A thirteen-year-old with an unemployed father reckoned she put in sixty-one hours a week at house-work and making matchboxes with her mother; her parents only admitted to nine; and in another case the parents denied altogether the forty-seven hours their daughter said she spent in housework and helping her father, another house-painter.[75] Reticence increased. Committee members:

> heard from more than one witness that where enquiries were car-ried on long enough to arouse the attention of the parents it became impossible to get satisfactory answers to questions;—the same result would probably ensue on a larger scale if a new return were called for after the propriety of employing children at all is known to be in question.[76]

Difficulties arising from class and age difference were not the only source of bias in the investigation of children's work. Five male civil servants com-prised the committee conducting the 1902 inquiry, and they took evidence

from head-teachers, school managers and visitors, administrators, social
workers, and clergymen. Most responses on the subject of domestic work
(not raised with every witness) displayed indifference and ignorance. The
Rector of Poplar had limited his enquiries to children employed for wages,
and did not include girls, who were only 'going errands for their mothers'.
He agreed, when asked, that girls did much work at home for their parents,
especially on washing day; but he clearly saw this as outside his scope and
beyond intervention. A West Ham headmaster was simply vague. Domestic
work was 'a delicate subject to approach'; some of his boys were 'compelled' to do it; he had no particulars about girls, though they were 'no
doubt engaged very largely' in washing; and he feared that to investigate
'cases of overwork in domestic work' 'would require a number of officers
to ferret out the truth of the statements'.[77] Ella Holme, South London
school manager, thought many girls were drudges, and no better off for
working at home than those who were out earning:

> An enormous amount of unpaid domestic work is done, more
> especially by girls....Girls are more tractable than boys, and are
> more easily made into drudges. Boys are more likely to work for
> money or to run the streets.[78]

She did not see how information could possibly be collected or classified.
Others were daunted by practical questions. Miss Neville, St Pancras school
manager and Charity Organization Society visitor, recognized that girls
were 'heavily worked in their own homes', but doubted whether they could
be protected by legislation; while Poplar headmistress, Mrs Desprelles,
thought it impossible to prevent children from helping their parents.[79]

Paid domestic labour was almost as difficult to detect or to quantify as
unpaid work done at home. Witnesses to the 1902 committee who mentioned domestic work at all mostly lumped paid and unpaid together. Sir
Charles Elliott, who represented the London School Board before the
committee, had chaired the Board's own enquiry (1898–9), which was limited not only to paid work but to cases involving more than nineteen hours
a week. In his view domestic work was intermittent and 'not usually severe';
and 'to enquire into the hours when it begins would require such inquisi-
tion...'[80] But as Edith Hogg pointed out in 1898, although the far larger
number of girls listed as 'uncertain as to the number of working hours'
made findings 'less precise and informing', their 'uncertain hours may be
generally taken to mean long hours'.[81]

Adelaide Anderson, with other women factory inspectors, criticized the
1902 enquiry for its bias towards boys. They were concerned about 'errand
running for girls; dinner carrying long distances to parents and other relatives between morning and afternoon attendances; stupefying domestic
drudgery for girls of school age...' They recommended study of the educational and physical needs of girls in any occupation; and noted critically 'how
much more consideration has been given in detail to the needs of boys than

of girls'. Though more difficult to investigate, it was as important:

> apart from any question of physical strain to the girls themselves, immense economic injury is done to the community by the bad habits acquired by girls from nine to twelve years of age...kept much at home to do untaught housekeeping for their family. I hardly think it possible that mis-employment or over-employment of boys can in any direction be found, bad as it is, to be so opposed to the interests of society and of the individuals as this is...the girls remain stunted in every way in their domestic calling, or drift into one of the many overcrowded unskilled industrial occupations.[82]

The enquiries concentrated on paid work, which was more typically done by boys. For girls, the distinction between paid and unpaid work was hard to make, and in terms of demands on their strength not very relevant. 'The wage-earners among the girls do not seem to be distinguishable from those who are merely domestic drudges', noted Edith Hogg:

> while the boys accept employment largely in order to earn a little money, the wages are a subordinate consideration in the case of the girls. It seems to the mothers only natural that a girl should help to clean or baby-mind; and if there is no need of her services at home, then she can 'oblige' a neighbour...she may get six-pence...but if only twopence or threepence were offered, she would do the work just the same.[83]

(This may also mean that girls had lower expectations of sharing in anything they did earn.) Much of girls' work defied precise definition or quantification. The hours were 'indefinite and varying';[84] so were their tasks. The Women's Industrial Council's 1896 study of schoolchildren's work stressed that girls' hours of employment were 'more difficult to ascertain, their occupations being mostly "minding baby" and "fetching errands"'; and that 'the great majority of girls [were] worked, and often hard worked, at home'.[85] 'Errands', 'helping', 'minding baby', and 'housework', the next chapter will suggest, described most work done by girls.

Work in the home was less visible than the long hours of children selling papers, delivering milk, or working in barbers' shops; and it seemed almost impossible to assess, let alone to regulate. But its invisibility was surely increased by the fact that the official enquiries were structured and headed by middle-class men with little notion of housework or child care even in their own homes as women performed and supervised such work.

The most difficult to gauge is the extent of children's work, particularly girls'. The enquiries concentrated on paid labour, and, in effect if not in intent, on boys; and their evidence, as was suggested above, also has limitations of other kinds. Their estimates as to the number of children working, within their various definitions, by no means coincide; in some cases it was admitted that true figures were impossible to obtain.

14. Matchboxes for firms like Bryant and May were commonly produced at home in the East End. Tray and case had to be folded, edges pasted together and labels stuck on. Pay was by quantity, so the more hands the better.

10
Patterns of Children's Work After 1870

A S SCHOOL enforcement became more effective, full-time work was possible only for children who had satisfied the school authorities. Some found regular part-time jobs, helping with early morning milk deliveries or in shops after school and on Saturdays. Others picked up casual work. But although such paid work preoccupied investigators, as we have seen, it was a small part of children's contribution to the domestic economy, especially as real wages rose and it became easier for adult and teenage earners to supply family needs. Many working-class children did not do paid work, but all supplied domestic labour and a good few contributed in kind, whether by foraging for food and fuel or by finding some of their food independently. They made themselves useful in many ways, most obviously with the care of younger children, housework and shopping, but also through other unpaid labour—for instance in domestic workshop or home industry, or at a family-run shop or stall. This chapter examines the range of their work for the family.

Work Around the House

Most children were their mothers' auxiliaries in the incessant round of cleaning, cooking and service in the home. What and how much needed doing depended on the size and composition of a household ('you can guess how much there was to do with fourteen of us...it used to be hard'),[1] its accommodation, and the domestic budget. Other factors were how neat and clean its members had to look at work and at school, how dirty clothes got at work, and what standard of housekeeping was attempted.

Young children meant work. Babies, in endless cycle, needed changing, feeding and settling to sleep. Toddlers had to be dressed and washed, given meals, and put to bed.[2] Children over three had also to be got off to school. If appearances mattered, their hair had to be brushed; it might also be checked for nits. Eliza H., eldest of seven in a 1900s dockland family, as soon as she came home from school had to clean all the boots, then 'plait

all their hairs'. On Saturday nights she bathed them all. She lit and filled
the copper to heat water with which to fill a tub before the fire; she washed
and dried each child in turn, brushed their hair and braided multiple
plaits (about fifty altogether!) to make it wavy; she emptied the tub (by
scooping bucketfuls and tipping them outside); then she settled them all
in bed. (When they were all asleep, about ten o'clock, came her reward:
'I'd go up the pub and just open the door...if my mother was there she used
to get me a cake'; and she would play with friends for a while.)[3]

Besides attention to their physical needs, little ones needed to be
entertained, responded to, taken out, kept from danger or mischief, and
sometimes comforted. The smallest ones had to be carried. Soap-box carts
and prams (even if only 'an old vehicle, some old broken-down thing')[4]
provided relief; and made it easier for child nurses to join friends at play.
Sometimes a group went to the park together. Mrs Layton recalled how on
wash-day mothers clubbed together to hire a pram, and children crammed
in the babies and set off to Victoria Park.[5] Elsie M.'s ten-year-old elder sister led expeditions to Victoria Park or London Fields, equipped with jam
sandwiches and bottles of lemonade made from powder. (They 'led the
poor girl a dance, no wonder she never married, I reckon she had enough
of kids to last her a lifetime'.)[6] Indoors and close to home babies were
lugged around by their elders. 'I never seemed to have a baby out of my
arms after I was six', recalled an eldest girl.[7] Girls of nine or ten, according
to district nurse M. Loane in 1909, would 'often nurse a fifteen-pound baby
for more hours than a strong man would like to hold an equal weight with
similar care'.[8] Sometimes, too, the little nurse took her baby to be suckled
during the working mother's dinner break.[9]

Unless school was really close, children over three were taken and
fetched, morning and afternoon.[10] John Ezard's escort, in Battersea in the
1900s, was his sister Muriel. She would drag him:

> away over the Dogs' Home Bridge, through the school gates and
> into the cloakroom to deposit cap, and, in winter, overcoat and
> long wool muffler as well, before giving me a push into my class-
> room....At the end of the school day Muriel would meet me in the
> passage and steer me home.[11]

Sometimes neighbours' children were added on. A child in Chelsea,
besides her own brothers, took 'other children for mothers that couldn't
take them': she delivered them to their classrooms then fetched them
home later, and 'hardly ever went out without at least five children'.[12] Out
of school they had to be kept from straying or from mishap. Such responsibilities were constant for all older girls and often for boys too; sometimes,
as we have seen, they took priority over school. Like younger precursors of
previous decades, nursemaids who entered employment straight from
school had already served their apprenticeship.

Much children's work took the form of daily chores. In most families

there were regular jobs—always for girls, and sometimes for boys. Alice
Lewis recalled this:

> We all had our share of work: we did our bedrooms, one would
> sweep, one would clean the brass door handles, we'd help wash up.
> We girls did some of the ironing....We had nothing to grumble at.
> We thoroughly enjoyed ourselves.[13]

The everyday work was fitted in around school. At lunch time 'we all had
our jobs...one of us would do potatoes or washing up, or get the...baby to
bed'.[14] 'After dinner and before we returned to school, one had to clear
the table, one to wash up, another to dry, and another to sweep the
floor.'[15] After school it was the same. 'We had to go straight from school,
go in, get your errands, do what work was allocated to you and God help
you if you didn't do it.'[16] Clothes had to be kept in repair: one mother
made a daily check when the children came in, and rips, sagging hems or
missing buttons had to be dealt with at once.[17] There were always woollen
stockings to darn or knit: in the evening 'mother would say, "Got some
knitting for you", you'd just sit there and knit these stockings'.[18]

Cleaning took a good deal of domestic time. Smoke-laden London air
left soot on every surface, and in bad weather mud and slush were carried
in on each pair of boots as well as splashed on clothes. With no detergents
or domestic machinery for the endless sweeping, dusting, scrubbing and
washing, mothers used children to supplement their own elbow grease.
Crowded tenement rooms did not help: 'they are filled with furniture, and
require, if they are to be clean, unceasing labour (much of which falls on
the girls)...'[19] And standards were often high. M. Loane, a district nurse who
observed and recorded the daily life of those she visited, wrote in 1905 that
'in nearly all poor people's houses, however dirty they may seem, an excessive amount of scrubbing is done'.[20] In a house-proud home doorsteps were
whitened, grates black-leaded, chimney breasts and the casing of coppers
hearthstoned (a dirty copper was a disgrace), windows cleaned, all floors
regularly scrubbed and furniture and surfaces dusted.[21] In blocks of model
dwellings communal stairs and landings were swept, scrubbed and hearthstoned by women in regular turn.[22] Paradoxically, improved standards of
housing in this period meant more work: the family who were no longer
hugger-mugger in one room had more space, more windows, more furniture and more ornaments, all of which meant more scrubbing, dusting,
sweeping and polishing, besides curtains and bed linen to wash and probably (with more storage) a larger stock of clothes to keep clean and mended.

Children helped prepare meals. They cleaned potatoes and other vegetables or fruit. When Dot S., in 1900s Hackney, was detailed with her
brother to top and tail gooseberries ('for afters on Sunday'), their mother
told them 'Sing while you work, then I know you're not eating them'.[23]

They cleared up, too. A child in a Toynbee Hall production of 'The
Old Woman who Lived in a Shoe' was kept away by her mother as punish-

ment 'for neglecting or refusing to wash up the tea things on the previous
night', having presumably rushed off to rehearsal instead.[24] Washing-up
was slow work. Even if water did not have to be fetched (and slops later
removed), it had to be heated on fire or stove and poured into a bowl.
Boiling water and soda or hard soap were the only solvents of grease: there
were none of today's scouring pads or cloths; light was often poor, and
space cramped. Knives were not stainless steel, and got rusty and stained
unless rubbed with an abrasive like brick dust. Cutlery used for fish needed special treatment:

> Dad would say 'take them forks into the garden and clean them in
> the earth'. That way they didn't smell of fish, see. Then they'd get
> a good wash in soda water.[25]

The weekly cycle of work included getting clothes washed, mangled, dried
and ironed. On washing-day children's help was ancillary: generally the
mother did the actual washing unless she was incapacitated.[26] They were
nevertheless useful enough to be often kept from school on wash-day.[27]
They stoked the copper fire for successive stages of the wash: 'either me or
my brother used to have to sit in front of the copper hole and feed it with
the shavings and wood till the water boiled';[28] they fetched and emptied
water; they helped wring out and hang clothes to dry. They also looked
after any babies and toddlers, and kept them out of the way. This was a
responsible task. In Rotherhithe in 1911 Frederick Beamish, aged one, fell
to his death on wash-day. His mother had been doing washing in the first-
floor back room, and went down to hang it out in the yard, leaving him to
play soap bubbles with six-year-old Florrie. Florrie climbed on to the dress-
er 'to cut bread and butter' (for him perhaps), and while she was busy with
that he scrambled on to a chair at the window and fell out.[29] Mangling,
though hard work, was a job children did; and older girls did ironing, too,
once the clothes were dry enough: 'there was no ironing boards then, we
used the tables; we'd hot up the old flat iron on top of the stove, put it
inside an old sock and iron away'.[30]

Once a week was cleaning-day, when 'the house was turned inside out
and everybody used to have their own special jobs, even the boys'.[31] Eliza
H. recalled the scrubbing:

> Saturday morning, no school. Right. Everything was wood. We had
> the table and on the shelf there was the salt box, the knife box and
> the boot box. They all had to be scrubbed. Outside the back yard,
> where the sink was—scrub 'em. There was...a bench where moth-
> er used to have her tub on to do her washing. That had to be
> scrubbed. The toilet was wood—that had to be scrubbed....The
> copper lid—that had to be scrubbed. And then you got brick dust
> and a board and you sprinkle the brick dust on there and you got
> to do the knives. Knives and the forks and spoons—all had to be
> done. That was only in your morning's work.[32]

In Gladys B.'s family, in Hackney in the 1900s, cleaning-day was Friday, and the tasks rotated:

> One would one week clean the boots and the shoes for us all, another would do the knives and forks, another would clean the stove and emery the steel round it. And hearthstone the copper. And hearthstone the steps. That was a child's job.[33]

Saturday, though a holiday from school, was 'anything but a holiday to most London children', according to T.E. Harvey of Toynbee Hall in a 1906 pamphlet discussion of school-children's essays. London teachers (in response to a request from Toynbee Hall's Enquirers' Club) had sent in hundreds of essays on 'What I did last Saturday'. Harvey's discussion drew mainly on eighty-four boys' essays from one Finsbury school (where he was a manager). The essays by girls he found 'naturally somewhat less interesting', since 'all but a few, and those chiefly younger girls, give a large part of their Saturdays to work at home, preparation and purchase of food also forming part of the task for many'.[34] Twelve boys' essays were reproduced, and though the boys, like Harvey, may have thought chores less interesting, or a less appropriate activity to report, all mention domestic tasks. One woke and washed his two little sisters; one (whose family moved that day) helped to pack and looked after the baby; one went to get wood 'for my mother's fire'; another took his baby brother out for the morning; and several went on errands.[35] Another describes domestic preliminaries to the real day. Here is the first third of his essay:

> Last Saturday I rose at twenty minutes to six, I had my breakfast, and started doing my mother's work. When I had done it, I went out and tried to get some wood. When I had obtained some, I took it home, and I washed myself and went to Sidney Street to see my aunt, over money affairs between her and my mother. When I had arrived home, and told my mother what my aunt said, I went to work.[36]

Harvey mentions two boys who were 'chiefly occupied in minding babies'—one referred to 'my baby', a common phrase in the girls' essays. Younger boys, he noted, were responsible for cleaning the knives and forks, while preparing breakfast was 'only attempted by their seniors'.[37] A 'very large number' of the boys started the day 'by lighting the fire or doing housework', and some made breakfast. But 'very few', he insisted, had 'anything like the monotonous round of housework and scrubbing which falls to the lot of the girls...'[38] A table based on the essays classified about ninety-four of the girl essayists from three schools as having spent 'most of the day' on housework, apparent support for his generalization.[39]

But these girls did not all spend most of the day in his 'weary succession of scrubbing, washing and polishing'. One of their tasks was minding the baby, which was, as Harvey remarked, 'although an absorbing task...often evidently a pleasant one, too'.[40] It could be combined with games like those mentioned in their essays: 'swinging, hopscotch, skipping, egg-cap, dolls, "gobs", "boncer", "fivestones", "mothers and fathers", "school", and "higher and higher"'. Nor was the content of 'housework' uniform. Girls from 'comfortable artisan homes' wrote of watering the flower-pots, sweeping rugs and mats, and cleaning the silver ware, which suggested 'a very different milieu from St Luke's', the Finsbury parish he knew.[41] To make his contrast between boys and girls, he played down differences within each group.

Children's load always increased in poverty and crisis. As we have seen, throughout the working class almost all family groups were at times under pressure, threatened or actual, from unemployment, drink, illness, old age and death. If a wage-earner was ill or unemployed, children either tried to earn, or replaced a mother or older sister who then took paid work. If an ageing grandparent or sickly child needed nursing and company, or when anyone was ill, children shared in the extra caring and took on more domestic responsibility to release others.

It bore hardest on elder girls, especially if the mother was out of action. Worn-out mothers, weakened by years of hard work, poor diet, many pregnancies and minimal medical care, struggled against increasing illness, or succumbed to it, and daughters took up their burden. Grace Foakes, third of four children in a Wapping tenement in the 1900s, but eldest girl, recalled her mother's illness when she was ten:

> My mother would give me instructions from her bed and I would clean and dust and make dinner for my father, my brothers and my sister.

Upon leaving school at fourteen she worked as a waitress, but her mother's health deteriorated and she had to stop earning and take over at home. She did the weekly wash, cooked, shopped, and looked after father, sister and three brothers, and received 1s. 6d. pocket money from her father.[42] When mothers died, gave up, walked out or turned to drink, a daughter (or a new wife) was critical to the family's survival. In a family observed by Booth when he lodged in the same house, a thirteen-year-old drudge did all the work of the household, for both parents and a seven-year-old sister, because the mother 'drank, and...never did a thing'.[43]

Errands and Foraging

'Errands', like housework, was a recurring label for children's work and covered many tasks. All involved leaving the house, and saved adult time. Children were handy for any sort of message—to run round and tell any news or need to friends, relatives, neighbours, workmates, employers, shop-keepers, and even teachers. They went for midwife, doctor, or policeman, and for minister, priest or rabbi. Teachers sent children out on errands, especially to find absentees. They were trusted with money, to make purchases, to redeem pawned pledges,[44] or in transactions concerning rent or club money, loans or gifts. They took tools to be sharpened, boots to be mended, parcels to pawn, and rabbit skins, bottles or rags to sell.

Most shopping was done as errands by children. Many households bought in small quantities and for immediate use, to control consumption, and because cash and storage space were always short; and children made the endless trips. ('Run round the shop and get this—run round the shop and get that.')[45] Before school they were sent to get bread, milk or the materials for dinner—ham bones or 'pieces' from the butcher, 'pot-herbs' (carrots and onions) and potatoes. After morning or afternoon school they went to nearby shops for 'ha'p'orths and penn'orths of daily necessities':[46] paraffin for the lamp, or pickles; or fetched for tea 'a pennyworth of tea, a halfpenny-worth of sugar, twopence-halfpenny-worth of tinned milk, a pennyworth of jam, and a loaf of bread'.[47] They were familiar with prices, quantities and values, and knew 'how much a farthing will fetch in tea or sugar' at 'what seems to the mothers of gently nurtured children an impossibly early age'.[48] Soon they were trusted with shopping for more substantial purchases in the street market, which required more skill. The market-shopper had to compare the value offered at each stall, to avoid being given underweight or substandard goods, and to time purchases so as to profit by the reductions made as it got late, without delaying till nothing was worth buying. Gissing admiringly described such child shoppers at Lambeth Walk on a Saturday night:

> Little girls of nine or ten were going from stall to stall, making purchases with the confidence and acumen of old housekeepers; slight fear that they would fail to get their money's worth.[49]

Shopkeepers recognized children's responsibility for family purchases and courted their custom: bakers would give children something sweet as makeweight (added if the loaf was underweight) rather than just bread—a bun or a slice of bread pudding which hardly ever reached home; other shopkeepers offered sweets. Sometimes, of course, there was no choice of shop: you went where you had a 'trust book' and the shopkeeper (after coaxing) would give you tick. Or economy was the determinant and you went where bargains could be had. Some bargains required an early start. In a 'raggle-taggle band' lined up each morning in 1890s Anerley for twopennorth of stale bread, early birds got 'a glorious lucky dip of rolls, milk loaves and enough bread to last for days'.[50] In Alice Lewis's Chelsea family,[51]

> two of us would get up around five in the morning, we'd take turns, to walk to Harrods. For sixpence you got three loaves. Then we'd run across the road to the fish shop, carrying our pillowcase to put things in, to get sixpence worth of fish. Then we'd go to the

butcher's for sixpence worth of odd meat, that's the leftovers, and
it gave enough dinner for the nine of us.

Lilian Westall queued at a Mortlake butcher's at seven every morning for
'threepennorth of pieces' (about two pounds of scraps from trimmed
meat) which would make the family dinner.[52]

Stocking up fuel, especially on wash-days, was another morning job.
Mrs B., in 1890s Poplar, regularly went for her mother to the local sawmill,
with 'a great big bit of sacking' to fill with 'twopennorth of waste wood'.[53]
In Hackney, with its furniture industry, children collected offcuts. Elsie
M.'s mother woke her about seven, gave her a cup of tea and a piece of
toast, and sent her off to queue for waste wood from the cigar-box makers.
She had to be among the first, even if it was an hour till the door opened:

> ...the manager would point to the first, second and third...and
> would let us in the factory where we would put our piece of canvas
> on the floor and he would put as much wood as would go on the
> canvas and tie it up and we used to get that for a penny. Mind you,
> no-one could have a pennyworth more than twice a week and
> sometimes one had to go every morning for a whole week before
> being lucky enough to get some.[54]

Another early errand on wash-day might be fetching a pennyworth of gun-
powder to start a reluctant copper fire.[55] Some morning errands
overlapped into school hours. One school-board man waited near the
pawnshop on Monday mornings:

> Used to be a pawnshop down where we lived and the kiddies used
> to go—their mothers used to say 'Go and take this parcel and if
> you see Mrs So-and-so ask her to take it in'. Well he'd stand oppo-
> site there. Yes. And if he see a child there he'd go over and say
> 'What are you doing?'—'I've got to take this parcel'—'Take that
> parcel home! School!'[56]

Shopping was done by girls when there was a choice. They were likely to be
within call, especially if minding little ones, and perhaps were held more
competent, or needing more to learn competence. Descriptions of street
and market scenes more often mention girl shoppers, though not to the
exclusion of boys. The child-study theorist, Earl Barnes, assumed that girls
did more shopping. Reporting on a questionnaire investigating the ideals
and ambitions of London Board-school children he commented that the
girls in the sample seemed 'more drawn towards money than the boys', and
explained that 'the girl is constantly running back and forth for little supplies to the shops, and so comes to have a sense of money as desirable'.[57]
Since girls had less access to money of their own than boys they no doubt
did regard it as 'desirable'; but they were also probably closer than their
brothers to the mother's budgetary struggle, and concerned with it for that
reason.

On Sunday mornings many children were sent to a local baker's with a dish containing the Sunday dinner, which would be ticketed and left in his oven to cook, then fetched several hours later. The charge was a penny— less than the cost of heating an oven at home, which few had anyway. The practice (which continued at least till the 1930s) is often mentioned in autobiographies and many old people recall it. Thomas Burke, for instance, wrote of Camberwell in the 1890s that 'a regular Sunday morning spectacle was the procession of children carrying the joints and pies to be cooked at the local baker's at a fee of one penny a dish'.[58] Descriptive accounts of London life from Vallès in the 1870s to Sims in the 1900s include similar vignettes.[59] In poor Jewish districts, too, bakers' ovens were used for the Sabbath meal, and after school on Fridays children were sent with pans of 'cholent' to cook slowly overnight and be collected next day.[60]

Taking weekday dinners to a working father, brother or sister was another child's errand. If home was near it saved money to send 'a basin of something hot—soup or a meat pudding usually—tied up in a handker- chief'.[61] Sometimes, too, a child was employed by workpeople to fetch their dinners from nearby food shops. This was a regular job for Mary P., born in Haggerston in 1903. She went in her dinner hour to the coat factory where her mother worked, took orders and money from the work girls, then ran out for hot saveloys, fried fish and potatoes, pease pudding, and so on. After school she went back to wash their dishes.[62] (This example serves to remind us how children's work eluded the record: factory inspec- tors looking for children illegally employed in production would not notice such a job; neither employer's books nor business histories would record it; nor would school records, since she missed no school.)

Another errand was fetching beer to wash down supper or Sunday din- ner.[63] The Communard exile and journalist, Jules Vallès, described in the 1870s how after opening time on Sunday (one o'clock) London pavements would fill with little girls going for jugs of stout or six-ale.

> Il faut les voir se dresser sur la pointe des pieds pour se hausser jusqu'au comptoir, puis retourner à la maison en essayant de ne rien verser, surveillant la bière qui danse, se cognant avec les autres en route.

> [You should see them, on tiptoes to reach the counter, then trying to get home without spilling any, watching over the beer as it slops, jogged by passers-by on the way.][64]

The practice was opposed by temperance campaigners. They denounced publicans for encouraging the children with sweets;[65] protested that pubs were full of bad language and not fit places for children; and worried that children sipped the beer as they carried it back.[66] No doubt they did, to stop it slopping, but without taking much for fear of trouble. An East London parish nurse told Booth:

They sip the beer, but only on the general principle that they take
a little of everything they are sent to fetch; and if it were milk they
would take a great deal more of it. Children of the rough class fetch
the beer from the public bar because they are often given a penny
by some of the men there; children of the better class go into the
jug and bottle entrance, get their beer, and go away at once.[67]

Fetching beer was definitely a job. The pavement outside pubs was much
used for play (particularly in the evenings, when it was well lit), but the
child on business would have no time to linger: 'it was constant come and
go, one moment to go in and get the jug filled, and out again the next;
none of the children waited to talk or play with one another, but at once
hurried home'.[68]

Some children's errands were for provisions not obtained by shopping:
wherever free food was to be had there were children in crowds, waiting on
their own account, or for something to feed their little charges or to take
home. Whitechapel children lined up for surplus dripping from the
London Hospital kitchens: tuppence-worth filled a jug.[69] At Sweeting's, 'the
great fish salesman's in Cheapside', there was a great crowd of boys and
girls 'any evening at half past eight, waiting for fish cuttings to be given
away', wrote a journalist in 1886.[70] Nearly twenty years later 'a daily distribution of...stale food, customers' leavings and other waste' was made every
morning by Sweeting's, as by other firms. The first children were waiting
outside at 5.30 a.m.; by seven o'clock, when the door opened, there might
be fifty or sixty. They were each then given 'a parcel of bread and pieces'
by a shopman with a basket:[71]

> whereupon the children instantly separate and scamper away. And
> how often does their haste suggest that the family breakfast is
> impossible till they reach home.

Children were major clients of the soup kitchens set up in winter. Some fed
them on the spot, but many served take-away helpings. When the Costers'
Mission in Finsbury served free Irish stew weekly in the early 1870s, 300 or
so children came for it, some singly, some 'brought by their sisters and
brothers', and 'of all ages, from the sturdy street boy of ten to the tiny six-
months-old baby in arms'.[72] In Haggerston, the Priory sisters dispensed
soup to children who queued with pitchers and their all-purpose tonics to
those who brought medicine bottles.[73] Walter Southgate used to join 'a
long queue of adults and children' outside the Russia Lane Mission, 'carrying a varied assortment of utensils for carrying home this wholesome
food...scrags of meat, lentils, pea flour, carrots, celery and stock from
butchers' bones'.[74] Hymie Fagan soon learnt from other boys at the
Spitalfields Soup Kitchen for the Jewish Poor to hold back instead of pushing forwards, so as to get the richer mixture lower in the boiler.[75]

Children, again, collected free food given out by individuals. For many years Mrs Kelly, stall-keeper outside the Britannia Theatre, Hoxton, filled children's jugs with free broth from her big pan of sheep's heads, as well as sending her daughter to deliver left-over food where she knew it was most needed.[76] In Walthamstow in the 1900s the landlady of the Chequers Inn organized contributions from local traders and made a boiler full of soup ('like a big copper') which she ladled into the children's jugs.[77] Handouts of another kind were collected by children one Edwardian Christmas, when 'hundreds' of Christmas dinners were given away by the flamboyant Horatio Bottomley, Hackney's popular Member of Parliament.[78]

Children getting handouts probably spared adults embarrassment as well as saving them time. This was likely too, with their foraging. Two 1904 photographs, 'Waiting for the scrap pail' and 'Race for the scraps', show first a mother and three children peering round a corner, then the three boys grabbing a bucket which a girl has just put outside the shop door.[79] Children also picked up 'specked' fruit and ageing vegetables discarded by market stall-holders, coal dropped in unloading, and anything else of possible use.

Markets offered other opportunities, and there a child's eye might be caught by items which had not in fact been jettisoned. Or depredations might be planned. Arthur Harding and his friends worked as a team:

> There was plenty of fruit stalls there where you could get an apple or something like that. We used to go in twos and threes—not more because people would notice you....One would go in front and ask, 'how much is oranges?' while the others would get round the back and pinch them. Or we'd pick up fruit when the stalls had packed up.[80]

Two eleven-year-olds were charged at Clerkenwell Court in 1891 with picking pockets at Caledonian Cattle Market. (On Fridays there, instead of cattle, there was a very popular 'miscellaneous fair' with food and clothing stalls.) Annie Holt and Annie Bennett were 'picking up refuse' there one Friday when one was seen by a constable running off with a purse in her hand. According to the police, she said she had taken it from a lady's pocket, and that they had been taught to thieve by an older girl who kept a share of their takings. The rest they spent on 'ice-creams and other eatables'.[81]

Thieving was certainly a common part of many children's culture.[82] In rough neighbourhoods they mostly took for granted that anything left unguarded was fair game, and some went further. Dockland children watched for unguarded wagons to raid from behind: Mr N. recalled how he and his friends in Wapping in the 1900s would wait near the Morocco wharf for a chance to break open a case of oranges, 'pinch a few oranges and dive down the side turning'.[83] Some preyed on other children, and stole money, boots from their feet, loads they were delivering, even their brass buttons.[84] Or there were near professionals like the 'little girl' who in 1875 was 'committed for very artful street robberies': she would go up to a girl in the street, tell her she had a smut on her face, then steal her purse while she was wiping it off;[85] or the eleven and twelve-year-old girls who in 1887 (with 'a male desperado of ten') 'were charged with breaking into five or six houses and carrying off some ten pounds worth of property'.[86]

Theft could feed the family as well as the individual. Celia R., born in Lambeth in 1899, one of thirteen, used to be sent to the street market to try her luck; and on her return would be asked 'What did you get, Cis? Oh, we'll have that for dinner'.[87] But not all families acknowledged or condoned it, as Minnie Bowles's brother learnt:

> [He] came frantically banging on the door saying, 'Quick, mum, open the door, I've got an apple I pinched for you', with the green-grocer hot on his tail. Mum just opened the door and said to my brother 'Give the man back his apple—now apologize and say you will never do it again'.[88]

Children also brought home fuel. They scavenged or filched anything combustible—broken boxes from markets, floorboards and other wood from derelict buildings, lumps of coal fallen from passing carts, even coconut shells from Blackheath Fair.[89] Some went looking for driftwood from river or canal. A few were mudlarks, and at low tide, 'with their petticoats kilted or their trousers tucked up', searched the muddy edges of the Thames wherever it was not yet embanked, to 'pounce upon little knobs of coal...lovingly coil up limp lengths of sodden rope...[and] make prizes of bits of wood...')[90] Roads were fruitful, too. Whenever the surface of tar-soaked wooden blocks was taken up, you could see:

> ragged children—it is generally a little girl who carries the biggest burden—staggering along bravely with a sack-load or an apron-load of wood saved from the debris of the repairing operations.[91]

From gasworks children collected cinders and coke, from sawmills the off-cuts left from stacks of timber as they were sawn into planks.[92] They worked hard at picking up the fuel, filled sacks or homemade carts, carried or pushed it home, then hawked any surplus round neighbouring streets.

Fetching water was a job which took much time and effort. In the 1870s many London houses had no constant supply of water, though some districts were better supplied than others. (It depended on the particular water company, and on local administration.) In the 1870s and 1880s the 'intermittent principle' prevailed in poor districts. Water was turned on daily for a short time, perhaps not even an hour,[93] during which water butts and 'every receptacle—tub, pail, can, mug' were filled.[94] In many houses, according to George Sims in 1883, more water came through the roof than through a pipe, and a single outdoor butt furnished dozens of families.[95] When constant supply was more generally established, during the 1890s, it was still to ground floor or landing rather than to every household; and unreliable. The tall new blocks of model dwellings caused pressure problems; and frosts brought trouble. Shared sources and limited or interrupted supplies meant queues, whether at pump, butt, or tap, or at the emergency standpipe or vestry cart, and of course children's time could best be spared. A mother who ran short would send a child to borrow from a neighbour. Even when supplies improved, water frequently had to be brought in pails to where it was needed, perhaps up long flights of stairs, and the heavy task 'too often fell on children'.[96]

It was the general character of errands that any payment was discretionary, in the nature of a reward rather than a wage. Errands done for the family were taken for granted, or perhaps rewarded with thanks or an extra slice of bread. Errands done for a neighbour (usually someone elderly or incapacitated or hard-pressed for time) were mostly done either on the mother's instruction or at least with her permission. Any payment might also be under her control, to claim for the general purse, as Eliza H.'s mother sometimes did, or to forbid altogether, like Grace S.'s mother, or to allow as pocket money.[97] Within the family the adult's right to the child's time was unquestioned, and although in good times the children might well be given a copper for some particular effort, it would never be a prerogative. Grace Foakes, in Wapping in the 1900s, worked hard to help her father sell surplus dripping which he bought from the cooks on the 'Leith boats'.

> when they berthed he would buy a large enamel bowl of dripping from them. He would bring it home and send me all around the tenements and surrounding streets asking if anyone wanted any. I was given a great many basins to bring home. Father first weighed the basin then put into it a half-pound of dripping. I had to return those basins one at a time so that I did not get them muddled up....This took me a long time and meant a lot of running up and down the tenement stairs. The profit he made paid for our own dripping. We had the best of it, for there was always lovely gravy at the bottom of the bowl. I thought it well worth the trouble of coming and going, for nothing tasted as good as that gravy spread on our morning toast. Besides, it was free—and that made it all the nicer![98]

In accounting their share of the dripping 'free', she of course discounted the value of her own time and labour, which in fact made the difference between the price her father paid for the big bowl of dripping, and the sum of all the neighbours' tuppences for the little basins she delivered. The value of errands, as often of domestic work in general, and of much children's work, was invisible.

Domestic Enterprises

Some families lived through joint work by some or all members in a common enterprise. This took many shapes, from the prospering stall or shop to sweated homework. Children's help was in every case significant.

Directly or indirectly, whether they joined in the work or saved adult time on errands or in domestic labour such as child care, they increased production and saved the cost of employed assistance.

Laundry, especially in the poor fringes of middle-class areas, was frequently a cottage business 'based on the labour of many family members'.[99] The children of 'small laundry people' were considered by Mrs Nickless, a Notting Dale headmistress, to be among the hardest worked in her very poor school.[100] As in the family wash, but with far more to be done, they helped with mangling, ironing and delivery. Mangling was the heaviest job: you forced round a big handle while feeding the wet clothes and sheets through the rollers which squeezed out the water, putting them through repeatedly until they were flat and damp. This was time-consuming and heavy, rather than skilled, and was sometimes done by women who did not do other stages of laundry.[101] A writer described in 1904 his dilettante attempts, during a sojourn in the East End, to help his landlady, who 'added to her income by mangling':

> for amusement and the experience of the thing I often relieved her at the grindstone. The tariff was 'twelve articles for one penny', and if one did the work conscientiously and as one would like to see it done it was difficult to earn more than three pence an hour...at the end of an hour I felt that I had done an excellent day's work.[102]

Ella Holme, from South London, thought mangling the worst work done by girls, and described how an eleven-year-old who did twenty-four hours a week at the mangle (for 1s. 6d.—less than a third of the landlady's rate above) was left 'absolutely unfitted for school'.[103] In Cambridge Heath in the 1890s young Eric Dear operated an enormous mangle for his washerwoman mother, and 'hated the job as much as he hated school'.[104] Eliza H., in Poplar, helped her mother with it. 'As soon as I came in from school..." There's three dozen mangling—out there and do it".'[105] Sometimes she delivered the finished work, too. There was no question of her being paid: it was help and taken for granted. Her mother received the rate for the job, low as that was, whether she or her daughter who had done the work.

The smoking of fish—salmon, cod, sprats, and above all haddock—was a backyard speciality in Stepney and often a family enterprise. Mothers and daughters cleaned the fish and dipped them in salt water; men and boys hung the fish in drying cupboards and later carried them in hampers to market.[106]

Woodchopping, too, was often organized on a family basis, with significant help from the children. Sometimes it was done in big wood-yards, for a master, apparently on the old system where an adult worker was paid for all the work done, and could hire assistance or bring in relatives. (The earnings of wife and children were thus subsumed in his.) A woodchopper who was prosecuted in 1875 for failing to send his son to school was one of 'over 100 hands, many of whom brought their children to help them', who worked for a Mr Groom, of Camberwell. He was said to be 'in full work with his wife and could earn £3 a week'.[107] The case was reported in February, and the boy had not been to school since November: as this was winter work, when there was a chance to pay off debts incurred during slacker times, the family were probably trying to earn all they could.

Other families chopped wood on their own account and sold bundles to shopkeepers or local entrepreneurs (like Groom), or hawked them round the streets. A poor South London family described in 1885 subsisted by chopping wood in their one room. It was a small room with little furniture; its ceiling was crumbling, its walls damp, and there was no fire in the grate. 'Father, mother, and three little ones' were:

> all busily employed wood chopping, an occupation extensively carried on in this particular district. The father saws up the logs, the wife chops away with her hatchet, and the eldest 'piles', or makes the sticks up into bundles ready for sale. By hard work, this family are enabled to earn 12/– or 15/– per week.[108]

Mrs Nickless told the 1902 committee on children's work of a similar family in Notting Dale, which she called typical: four sisters of twelve, ten, nine and eight, worked some fifty hours a week chopping and bundling the wood, the eldest starting as soon as she was up. In a Hackney family, parents, a son of thirty and a schoolgirl of thirteen all worked at wood-chopping in a shed rented for three shillings a week.[109]

Woodchopping also kept down costs when cash was hard to come by. Eliza H.'s father used to collect driftwood from a stretch of Thames shore. Back at home he sawed it up; 'we'd all have to sit and chop it up into sticks'; then they bundled and stacked it. When money was tight her mother would sneak some of the bundles and sell them ('for a couple of coppers'), whereupon 'he'd miss them and grumble'.[110]

In shops children helped in many ways, and if no related child was available one was employed. Retailing involved much work besides selling. Almost everything had to be weighed out and packaged in the shop, in advance or on the spot, and many more individual purchases were made than today. Shops had heavy shutters to take down in the morning and put up at night. Counters and shelves had to be kept clean and tidy, and floors swept or scrubbed out at the end of the day.[111] Elaborate displays in front of the shop were mounted and packed away daily. Children helped with all this, and with serving. They also guarded pavement displays. Even those too young to serve could still mind the shop at slack times, and call through to the kitchen when a customer came.[112] In small shops children were now and then left in charge altogether.[113]

On stalls, too, children helped with plenty of jobs besides serving the customers. Stalls were set up and filled first thing; during the day they had to be constantly restocked and the wares guarded; then eventually stall and remaining stock were packed away again, often very late.[114] Like shops, they often had a child look-out, and in busy times a 'barker' (sometimes youthful) to shout out the prices and merits of their goods. Some children 'established quite a trade' in feeding the costermongers' oil lamps.[115]

The hours of selling were very long: till eleven or twelve on Friday and Saturday, the busiest nights. Children took over altogether (on stalls especially) when things were slack, or helped serve and restock when there was a rush. The 1902 committee heard many examples of children's long hours at stalls. A ten-year-old Hackney girl, for instance, stood fifty hours a week at her mother's vegetable stall. (She minded it an hour at dinner-time, every night till late, all day on Saturday, and a good part of Sunday. Her mother was a widow with six children, two older and three younger than her.)[116] According to Spencer, of the LCC's Public Control Department, London street stalls at this time employed an enormous number of children, between 12,000 and 20,000: 'on Friday from six till midnight, and on Saturday from nine a.m. till past midnight'. Their pay was 'usually a fixed sum, from 6d to 2s'. Although it was illegal for boys under fourteen and girls under sixteen to be out selling after nine p.m., this restriction was 'practically inoperative' in London.[117] The large margin between Spencer's figures (12,000 to 20,000!) probably arose from uncertainty about how many children worked on family stalls and how many for employers. In any case, the obvious element of guess-work again reminds us to be cautious with statistics on children's work.

Homework

Homework was often a family enterprise, especially where there was no regular adult wage coming in and homework earnings supplied rent and food. To live by homework, of almost any kind, required long hours of monotonous work. Children's participation took two forms, doing related errands, and joining in the work itself.

Children went to buy necessities for the process, like glue or thread. They also made trips to the employing firm (not always local), fetching materials and returning the finished work. They walked where possible, one way at least, to save the fares. The journey between home in East or South London and a warehouse or workshop in the City or the West End was often several miles. William N., whose mother made ship's fend-offs from hessian stuffed with cork dust and covered with canvas or rope, would go by train from Poplar to Fenchurch Street, buy fifty-six pounds of rope in the Minories and somehow ('often with the help of passers by') get it back to the train and home. When enough of the heavy fend-offs were finished, he and his mother lugged them to Fenchurch Street. (She carried four, two on each shoulder, and he two, and it took two train journeys.)[118]

Employers, or their foremen, had considerable power over the outworkers. They set standards, deadlines, and rates of pay; they could give or withhold work which was desperately needed, and approve or reject what was already done. They checked finished work for faults before paying for it, often with 'ruthless waste of a worker's time'.[119] The diarist, A.J. Munby, noticed at his Savile Row tailor's in 1861 how women and girls returning finished trousers had to wait till the gentleman customer had gone: 'always when I am there I see several pale, poorly clad girls slowly open the door, and either wait humbly within or slink out again on seeing a customer'. Once such a girl was waiting, with a 'large black bundle of trousers', while he discussed the 'deep and difficult' matter of the cut of a new coat. After ten minutes they noticed her:

> still standing there, on the mat by the door, meek and silent, hold-
> ing the bundle in her thin arms. I stopped. 'You had better go',
> said the fashionable young tailor in his lordly but not unkind way.
> I heard her say 'Yes sir', very low; and the door was opened just a
> little, and with another curtsy she glided silently away.[120]

The gentleman customer was ill at ease, so she must go. But more was involved. Contemptuous disregard for the convenience or needs of the homeworker was an integral part of the way in which the exploitative relationship was maintained. She had always to be reminded of her individual insignificance, to recognize that it was a favour to be given the work which so many sought, to be fearful of giving offence. This is the link between the 'lordly' young West End tailor and the 'hardfaced' manager of an East End match factory whom Mrs Layton observed when a child in the 1860s:

> There seemed to be a good many women and children waiting for
> some more work to be given out and their paltry earnings paid to
> them. Some were getting into trouble because they had only
> brought part of their work back. The girl I was with was one of the
> unfortunate ones. They all made reasonable excuses, but what was
> quite clear to my childish mind was that they all wanted the money
> for the work they had done to buy food for their dinners. Some
> had to plead very hard for their pay, and it was given with a rough
> word of warning that if the rest of their work was not done and
> brought in that night there would be no more work for them the
> next day, and that if they could not do the work there were plenty
> who could.[121]

Delays and bullying were as common in the clothing industry of the East End. A waistcoat maker in Whitechapel in the 1880s, for instance, 'worked for a small exporter in Cable Street, about ten minutes walk away, but it sometimes took two hours or more, taking back work and getting more in'.[122] The Select Committee on the Sweating System in 1888 was told that homeworkers generally lost 'one and a half days per week' this way. Checking work permitted the display of power.

> They lose a good deal of time in getting the work examined, and
> they have frequently to stand for three or four hours at a time: it is
> the invariable rule that no seats are provided....If the examiner finds
> the first two or three pairs of trousers faulty, he will not go through
> the whole work, but throws them at her and tells her to alter
> them....The sweater generally gives the work out in the morning,
> to be returned in the evening, or in the afternoon, to be returned
> the following morning. Little children are often employed in going
> for the work, or taking back work in the afternoon...[123]

Sending a child with finished work was the homeworker's chance to
reduce the financial loss incurred by the inevitable wait. Children's earning power was unlikely to match the mother's. If it was their time lost
walking to and from the putter-out, and waiting once there, the mother
could continue sewing, pasting or folding, or put the time to other use.

So in every district where homework was done children ferried bundles or sacks of finished work, for their mothers or for neighbours: brushes
and rabbit skins in Southwark; artificial flowers and fancy boxes in Finsbury
and Hoxton; sacks in St George's-in-the-East; matchboxes and paper bags
in Shoreditch; boots and shoes in Hackney; trousers and shirts in
Whitechapel; tennis balls in Woolwich; or in Bethnal Green, matchboxes,
belts and bead trimmings. The loads could be heavy. Edith Hogg was
shocked by the weights carried by Southwark children taking brushes 'to
the shears' for the bunched bristles, glued by their mothers into holes in
the wooden backs, to be cut to an even length.

> It is one of the melancholy features of the neighbourhood to see
> sickly children hardly more than infants staggering along in the
> wind and rain, splashed from hand to foot by the black greasy
> mud, panting for breath, and with every muscle of their rickety lit-
> tle bodies strained beneath the load, upon which the chance of
> next day's dinner depends.[124]

The strain was not always so severe. Sometimes a soap-box cart was available
to take the weight; and some loads, like the eight gross of matchboxes
which Harriet Harding used regularly to deliver,[125] were more cumbersome
than weighty. The children were not always so sickly and small. Nor was
every putter-out an ogre. Mrs. C., one of fourteen in a Hackney family in
the 1900s, did not fear the tailor for whom her mother worked.

> I've seen my mother have 40 pairs of trousers in the corner—
> sixpence halfpenny a pair: permanent turn-up, the buttons round
> the top, buttons down the fly, put the band linings on...and the pock-
> ets, and make the holes in the front...and buckles, they used to have
> on, and all for about tuppence three farthings a pair. And me, I used
> to have to—sometimes in my dinner time—put them on an old cart,
> rush them up to where they'd got to go...Russia Lane, that was where

the tailor man was then, and often there used to be a button off, and I used to say 'Well put it on yourself, I ain't got no time, I've got to run home for a bit of bread and jam'—have me dinner and go to school.[126]

In many kinds of homework (though less so in tailoring or shirt-making) children also joined in the actual work. Low rates of pay meant that if a family depended on homework earnings, the children's help was indispensable. This was argued and illustrated in Frank Hird's impassioned attack on child labour in homework, *The Cry of the Children* (1898). Often there was a domestic production line. In paper-bag making, for instance, the mother cut out the bags, one child folded them, another pasted, while another counted them into dozens and strung them together. Working all day (in dread of a visit from the School Board man), mother and children could earn seven shillings and sixpence a week, of which half-a-crown at least (one third) went on rent for their single room. The mother alone could not finish enough. When the children went to school, Hird was told, 'they don't get no dinner an' no tea....If the kids don't work there isn't the money to buy it'. Hird was convinced: 'these women', he admitted, 'tell a truth that is painfully obvious: if the children do not work, the children suffer'.[127] Some (those who did go to school, perhaps) worked late into the night. 'Children working with their parents are frequently kept at their sewing or pasting until ten or eleven at night', reported Nettie Adler.[128] Other investigators found the same. Edith Hogg, addressing the 1900 Conference of Ladies on Domestic Hygiene, on 'The National Evil of Child Labour', told them: 'It is unfortunately true that homework almost invariably means child labour—chiefly girl labour—at all hours of the day, and often far on into the night'. She had found:

> case after case of little match box makers working habitually from the time that school closes till eleven, or even midnight; of little artificial flower makers beginning to twist green paper round the wire stems at five a.m., and toiling through the long weary day in a small filthy attic.[129]

And even when children did not stay up to help, they slept in the room where work had gone on all day and might still continue.

Sewing work did not produce as oppressive an atmosphere as fur-pulling or anything which required glue, except where irons (heated by gas or on the fire) were needed for pressing. Handwork could be taken outside, and done in company. Women attending a Spitalfields Mothers' Meeting in the 1870s would 'bring their trade work with them—such as hair-net making, fancy-box making, etc.'.[130] Sewing the covers on umbrellas was a homework task often done sociably outside: on hot summer evenings, Hird reported, it was 'no uncommon thing to find the backyards of some of the houses filled with women and children sewing at umbrella frames most industriously, two little ones perhaps working on one umbrella'.[131]

The riverside industries of sack and sail-making were also outdoor, though hardly in fresh air. (Uncovered and overflowing dustbins produced 'an insupportable stench of decaying fish and vegetables' in one alley where Hird watched such work.)[132] Outside almost every house in the squalid courts of St George's-in-the-East and Wapping, children after school were busy 'binding the edges of the sacks together with coarse twine, which they push through the rough jute with a thick needle'. Special hooks in the wall held one end fixed to keep the material taut. In the same way, ropes strung along a wall kept 'enormous lengths of sail cloth' stretched flat for the women and children to hem, for sails, tarpaulins and covers for barges or hayricks.[133]

Homework was never well paid. Matchboxes in 1871 were made for tuppence-halfpenny a gross. The employer provided the thin sheets of wood (to be folded and pasted into outer and inner box), the 'glass paper' (to be cut into strips and pasted on as the striking surface), and the labels. He did not furnish glue, nor hemp for bundling each completed gross. 'It's hard work having to find your own paste', a writer for the *East London Observer* in 1871 was told,

> and the hemp comes dreadfully expensive considering what we are paid. A penn'orth of hemp won't tie up more than one and twenty gross of boxes; and it takes five farthings' worth of flour to make enough paste for seven gross.[134]

So for every twenty-one gross (3,024 boxes), this woman was paid four shillings and fourpence-halfpenny, but spent fourpence-three-farthings. By 1889 the rate was down to twopence-farthing a gross; a fast worker who rose at five in the morning and worked till nine at night earned only 1s. 6d. for eight gross, and spent twopence-halfpenny a day on flour and hemp. (She had good relations with the factory and was not kept waiting; she also lived alone and gave all her time to the boxmaking.)[135] Worship Street court, which served Shoreditch, Bethnal Green and Hackney, heard 'many cases of match-box makers in distress'. The magistrate there deplored the long hours of matchbox-makers' children, 'set to work with knife and palate the moment they return from the Board School'.[136] Hird described such a family, where a mother and two children (of seven and nine) earned tuppence-three-farthings a gross, 'the ordinary price': working from seven a.m. till 11.30 p.m. (the children probably broke for school), they made just one shilling and threepence-three-farthings a day.[137] The rate was still only tuppence-farthing in 1908, when Mrs Todd, in Bethnal Green, was interviewed for the *Methodist Times*. After fifty-five years making matchboxes, since she was four, she was very fast, making seven gross in a fourteen- or fifteen-hour day, without help, earning eight shillings a week if work was available.[138]

Children's involvement in homework was blamed for low rates of pay, in the 1900s campaigns against their employment. According to Hird, for instance:

Whatever trade a woman may follow in her home [if] compelled to call in the services of her children to augment the weekly wage, she is practically an agent in lowering the prices paid for her own handiwork—prices that have fallen in ever-increasing ratio during the last few years, almost entirely owing to the general employment of children by their parents.[139]

In box production, he said, child labour had 'reduced the former price of twopence-halfpenny for half a dozen corset or boot boxes to the same price for a dozen'.[140] There is little statistical material by which to judge such assertions, but homework rates clearly did not rise. Comparing results from investigations into homework by the Women's Industrial Council made in 1897 and 1907, Clementina Black remarked that since the first report conditions had not improved and rents had risen, whereas wage differences were 'only downwards'.[141] But it is unclear how far children's work was responsible, and how far all the other factors. Homeworkers were women who needed to earn but had to do it at home, usually because of small children or other dependents who needed care, sometimes because of physical handicap. Their lack of choice, their numbers and their relative isolation as workers minimized their power to resist reductions; while rising unemployment in the 1900s and changes in the organization of many London trades (brushmaking, for instance, emigrated to provincial factories) increased pressure on production of this kind.

In any case a vicious circle existed. Homework was in certain trades very advantageous to the capitalist. As Edith Simcox pointed out in 1879, contrasting these trades with ones which required costly machinery:

in the primitive art of sewing, and in all those simple industries in which the fingers of women and children form the chief or only machinery employed, no saving can be effected by massing the required labour; on the contrary, it is found cheaper to let it house itself, and save the employer any expenditure on factories.[142]

The homeworker using children's help to increase her earnings produced for a single piecework wage work which could not be done by one worker alone, thus setting a standard of production which the employer was happy not only to accept but to require. The demand for his goods, and therefore the supply of work to be put out, was often fluctuating and seasonal. Turning this irregularity to advantage, he could insist on larger and larger stints from each worker in busy times, with the threat that otherwise they would not get work when things were slack. As work grew scarce he could use the same threat to keep rates down or even to reduce them. An excessive supply of work could only be dealt with by the homeworker who found help, just as a low rate of pay mattered less if more hands were available to do the work in a shorter time, and if some of those hands were unpaid children's. So the employer benefitted by the product of the unpaid (or

partially and indirectly paid) labour of the 'helpers', by an elastic work-
force and by the elimination of many overhead costs.

Homework was sometimes available seasonally even in trades which
moved into the factory. Hird described how, when work was plentiful in
East End belt-making, women employees would bring work home at night.
One girl of fifteen did her ten hours at the factory, then came home
around 6.30 p.m. with twelve dozen more belts to do. Buckle, clasp and
slide had to be attached to each belt (by sewing if they were ribbon or elastic, or with punched eyelets if they were leather), at the price of a
penny-farthing a dozen. She lived with her mother and a nine-year-old sister in a four-roomed house shared with three other families; on her return
a child from each family came to help, and the five children worked all
evening. Though of school age, they had also been working already—one
at matchboxes, one having 'had the charge of several younger brothers and
sisters in the intervals of going to school', one 'helping her mother to sew
trousers' and carrying them to the tailor's shop. For their four hours on
belts they would earn 1s. 3d., or three farthings each per hour.[143]

Children were also employed by neighbours. Homeworkers without
children of the right age, or needing more, would call in those of relatives
or neighbours, paying them little so as to maximize earnings. An 1860s
inspector's East End report described a pattern, which though modified by
School Board demands, did not disappear:

> At home children of eight and seven help their mothers to hem
> shirts, to stitch cloth caps and neckties, to sew tapes on crinoline
> skirts; one began to make boot linings at six years old, another
> made fringe trimmings at four; children of five and six work on
> belts and braces, at seven on chenille nets and boys' buckram caps.
> This, though home work, is not mere family work; the child of a
> neighbour is constantly had in to help; some will hire two or three
> such, and usually keep them for the twelve hours at work.[144]

Generally, though, 'where more than four or five are employed, it is rare
for any child under nine to be found, and few are under ten'. Many children were employed on silk trimmings, 'usually three or four together,
some, if not all, being members of the family of the woman for whom they
work'. It was 'by no means uncommon for girls of eight years old to work
at home or for a neighbour', because, as Mrs Wright of Hope Street put it,
'it is only by employing children that we can make any profit'.[145] The out-
worker was paid piecework rates by the putter-out, and when work was
plentiful took on children to help and paid them by the week, with deduc-
tions for any time missed.[146]

Well after the establishment of compulsory schooling homeworkers
still employed children. Clara Collet, reporting for Booth in the 1890s,
found that in the Bethnal Green manufacture of upholstery trimmings:

Child labour is exploited in this industry by women who take as much work as they can get from the various factories, and pay young persons 2s. a week, or perhaps as much as 4s., 5s., or 6s., to do simple parts of the work. These women escape the notice of the factory inspector, and it is to be feared, when they have enough work, keep the children at it extremely long hours, beginning perhaps at eight in the morning and going on till 9.30, or even sometimes, as I have heard, till eleven at night....

In such work as beaded drops or corded ornaments, in which parts can be made separately and put together afterwards, there is great scope for farming. Children can be set to bead over the wooden balls or do other parts of the beadwork, and as there is no factory rate for these parts, the sub-contractor can make her own terms, and the more sensitive the parents are as to their social position the lower the rate at which they will allow their children to work for 'a friend at her own home'.[147]

The similar trade of making ornamental beadwork for bonnets and dress trimmings, in nearby De Beauvoir Town and Stoke Newington (parts of Hackney), was in the hands of 'a growing number of small occupiers' who employed a large number of children: 70 per cent of persons employed in such local outwork there in 1895 were under fourteen, and it is likely that they too were engaged in twos and threes.[148]

Joint enterprises whose scale ranged from laundries and market stalls to the one-room production line making matchboxes were well suited to the working-class domestic economy, in which pooled labour and earnings produced a joint (if not always equally apportioned) subsistence. Their implications for children varied with the nature and scale of the enterprise and the level of subsistence achieved. In homeworking households children were an essential part of the domestic labour force, whether participating directly or indirectly in the piecework. Because homework was the resort of impoverished women with few alternatives, themselves exploited by their employers, the children in homeworking households shared with their mothers the experience of hunger, cold, insecurity of health and housing, and other results of poverty. But where the joint family enterprise had a more secure base, in property as well as labour, the children's labour could be less central. In some cases enough surplus would be generated for their labour to be dispensed with, especially if older siblings were already in place. This explains why the children of shopkeepers were more likely to stay on at school and train as pupil teachers. It also illustrates the more general tendency for children's work to be marginalized with rising living standards, and to seen more as merely 'help'.

15. *Union Jacks often hung in classrooms and assembly halls. They also figured on special occasions, notably Empire Day, which was already celebrated in some schools from 1908, though more important later.*

11
Children, National Identity and the State

◄◆►

Aliens and Little Britons

OF 500,000 OR MORE children of school age in London in the 1870s, probably at least 30,000 were Irish.[1] Thousands of these attended Catholic
schools; but still more went to the Board schools for part or even all of their
schooling, whether for convenience, from religious indifference, or because
there was no Catholic school.[2] Many Jewish children also attended Board
schools, as they grew too numerous for such long-established schools as the
Jewish Free School, Stepney Jewish School or Commercial Street Infants
School for Jews.[3] In 1888 there were over 10,000 Jewish children in London
elementary schools, almost all of them in East London, and only about a
quarter of them born abroad.[4] The majority attended Board schools.

School records presented children generally as a mass. Where categorization was attempted it was likely to concern the class and morality of
their parents ('poor, but in regular work', 'irregular work...idle and dissolute': see Chapter 6), rather than the divisions which might interest us
today. In particular, there was little direct reference to the many children
whose immediate origin or cultural identity was not English. The general
term 'children' denied difference. Just as it often only meant boys (as in
discussions of attendance, for example), so also it often meant only those
schoolchildren who were English, at least nominally Christian (preferably
Protestant) and white. Others, though present in Board schools, were subsumed into the majority.

At the peak of Irish immigration, in the middle decades of the nineteenth century, there were substantial Irish communities in Holborn (St
Giles and the Strand), Stepney, Poplar, Walworth and Rotherhithe; the generations which followed both maintained earlier settlements and spread
more widely.[5] Towards the end of the century tens of thousands of Jews,
refugees from discrimination and pogroms in Russia, Poland, Galicia and
Romania, found haven of sorts in the inner East End; Whitechapel became
predominantly Jewish; and some of the surrounding neighbourhoods partly so.[6] There were also settlements of Germans (in Whitechapel and further

out around Canning Town) and Italians (around Saffron Hill, in Finsbury, where the School Board employed an Italian-speaking attendance officer three days a week.[7] In a mixed neighbourhood like cosmopolitan Soho children spoke a variety of first languages and none predominated.

Local concentration meant that although the proportion of minority children might be tiny in relation to overall figures, particular schools and neighbourhoods could be largely Irish, Jewish, Italian, German or whatever.[8] The records tell us little about the children in such neighbourhoods who were new arrivals from abroad or belonged to 'foreign' communities, and even less about those scattered more widely across London.

Poor Jewish and Irish children lived in much the same conditions as other local children, as doubtless did children from smaller or less concentrated minorities. At the same time they were different, on the one hand in their sense of identity, created in home, community, and perhaps religion; and on the other in being perceived and treated as different by some of their peers and by the school. So their experience both overlapped with and differed from that of other poor children.

In school, English was enforced and assimilation encouraged. 'Foreign' parents and children were not put at their ease. When Mark Gertler first went to school his Yiddish-speaking mother, in her anxiety, picked him up as they stood in the queue, though he was seven and heavy:

> At last our turn came to approach the desk, at which a man was sitting, very stern and angry—making us feel from the start that we were in the wrong, and that he jolly well meant to 'let us have it'. 'Put that boy down *at once*. He is not a babe!—Name of Gertler I see, what's his *Christian* name?' Of course my mother could make nothing of it at all, until some woman at the back came to the rescue. 'Mux', she said. 'Mux!' said the man. 'Never heard such a name—no such name in *this* country—we'll call him *Mark* Gertler', and nodding to a woman near by and pointing his pen at me he said, 'Next!'[9]

On starting school many children had to learn English, and become bilingual. (Ena Abrahams remembered the local cinema to which Yiddish-speaking grandmothers and mothers took children in the 1920s as 'terribly noisy, because we all used to do simultaneous translation'.)[10] Some succumbed to school influences as their English improved (especially if there were no grandparents around) and gave up on their first language. Ruth Adler's teacher in 1920s Stepney said: 'If you want to learn English, you must speak English, read English and *dream* in English'. Her father 'roared with laughter' on hearing this, but she stopped speaking Yiddish nevertheless. Her parents for a time answered her English with Yiddish but eventually they too spoke English. As she observes, this was 'a very common story, not only among Jews'.[11] Irish children did not all come from Irish-speaking areas: those who did might not retain their knowledge of the language; and those born in London might never learn it.[12] In retrospect adults often regret not having maintained their mother tongue: 'if you're made to feel that your language is second-rate it does something to your self-image, which it probably takes you the better part of your lifetime to recover from'.[13]

Hebrew teaching was provided in some boys' schools with a strong Jewish presence, but only after heavy lobbying. In Scawfell Street school, Haggerston, in 1894, a request for Hebrew lessons was refused when the school managers said there were only thirty-three 'Hebrew' children at the school, not between 100 and 150, as the petitioner claimed. This suggests both reluctance to make provision and also uncertainty about how to determine Jewish identity: Jewish children born in England presumably did not count.[14] At Orange Street school, in Waterloo, a request for a girl to be excused school during an unspecified fast—probably Jewish—was approved by Mrs Burgwin, the head, but subsequently disallowed by the inspector.[15] If Jewish religion and scholarly language might thus sometimes win recognition, however limited and problematic, this was not the case for their vernacular, Yiddish, nor for the language and culture of any other group. There was no question of Irish, Welsh or Scottish Gaelic being recognized. Irish children even in Catholic schools might receive ambivalent messages about their heritage: insistence on the separate religious identity did not rule out hints that Ireland was backward or the poor Irish uncivilized;[16] and Irish was not taught.[17]

The last decades of the nineteenth century were characterized by imperialist, militarist and jingo fervour, especially in the increasingly important popular press. The term 'alien', which basically meant Jew, was used to focus xenophobia in a vociferous campaign for the restriction of immigration which resulted in the 1905 Aliens Act.[18] Even writers who opposed immigration control assumed that there was a problem to which anglicization was the answer, and might lapse into using stereotypes.[19] Children were exposed to such ideas both in the general culture and in their specific experiences.[20]

In London Board schools most teachers had been through training colleges where admission was conditional on being a practising Christian.[21] They had generally been raised to believe in British superiority, though some resisted attempts at the turn of the century to bring imperialist politics into the classroom.[22] Not all teachers were as venomous as one ('so patriotic that she wore a Union Jack apron') at the predominantly Jewish Commercial Street school in 1905, two years after the Kishenev pogroms but in the year of the Anti-Aliens Act, who told the class:

'Now all you foreigners who come from Russia—you should all go back to your own country!' And a girl sitting in the front—her name was Yetta Solomons—she was so incensed about that...she took out this inkwell and flung it at her, and she smashed her glasses...and all the ink ran down her. I'll always remember that.[23]

Text books and teachers' books regularly presented anglocentric images and information. They took for granted that Britons (or Anglo-Saxons, as they were increasingly often called) deserved their Empire:

> It was assumed that all the subject peoples welcomed the peace and order of British rule and that it was the duty rather than the pleasure of the British people to carry out the task of maintaining the Empire.[24]

The relative standing of each subordinate country depended on its usefulness to Britain; agricultural production, transport and industry all happened magically with no mention of labour unless in terms of native indolence and inefficiency. Following the 'pseudo-scientific racism' developed over the previous century, the peoples of the Empire were ranked in a hierarchy of race based mainly on skin colour. (The original inhabitants of India, for example, were 'a dark-skinned race, who had to give way to a people of fairer type and superior intellect and knowledge'.)[25] In the popular application of Darwin's theories, 'white skin and '"Anglo-Saxon civilization" were seen as the culmination of the evolutionary process'.[26]

The cumulative effect of lessons and stories which celebrated England's past could be powerful, according to the Jewish writer, Israel Zangwill. In his *Children of the Ghetto* (1892), a partly autobiographical novel set in the Jewish East End, eleven-year-old Esther Ansell spoke Yiddish at home. But she 'led a double life, just as she spoke two tongues'.

> The knowledge that she was a Jewish child, whose people had a special history, was always at the back of her consciousness; sometimes it was brought to the front by the scoffing rhymes of English children, who informed her that they had stuck a piece of pork upon a fork and given it to a member of her race.

> But far more vividly did she realize that she was an English girl; far keener than her pride in Judas Maccabaeus was her pride in Nelson and Wellington; she rejoiced to find that her ancestors had always beaten the French, from the days of Crécy and Poitiers to the day of Waterloo; that Alfred the Great was the wisest of kings, and that Englishmen dominated the world and had planted colonies in every corner of it; that the English language was the noblest in the world, and men speaking it had invented railway trains, steamships, telegraphs and everything worth inventing. Esther absorbed these ideas from the school text-books.[27]

The Empire Day movement of the 1900s encouraged schools to celebrate Britain's imperial achievements. Miniature Union Jacks were distributed; there were displays of drill by the boys; the pupils joined in tableaux and processions in which the countries of the Empire were represented by costumed pupils; national songs were sung; and finally the whole school and watching parents joined in singing:

> What is the meaning of Empire?
> Why does the cannon roar?
> Why does the cry 'God Save the King'
> Echo from shore to shore?

The Britannia who presided over the scene was played by a tall child, probably fair-skinned, and different countries were represented by contingents of children, of appropriate costume and, if possible, looks.[28]

Lightweight educational material—suggestions for children's recitations and performances for instance—often presented the happy child-like negro (Sambo, Aunt Eliza, Darkies, etc.).[29] Ostensibly sympathetic, they implied white and British superiority by trivializing and patronizing other peoples. Racist stereotypes abounded in children's comics and books (burgeoning in this period), with fair-skinned heroes endlessly defeating 'ruffians of every shade of colour'. Black people were 'just like children', according to a character in an 1884 novel by the best-selling G.A. Henty:

> They are always either laughing or quarrelling. They are good-natured and passionate, indolent but will work hard for a time; clever up to a certain point, densely stupid beyond. The intelligence of an average negro is about equal to that of a European child of ten years old....[30]

Savages were childlike; Britons the wise adults.

The xenophobic classifications prevalent in the popular culture of the late nineteenth and early twentieth century are identified by Peter Fryer as follows:

> Uneducated whites divided people into three 'races'. There were white people born in England, Wales and Scotland: 'us'. There were white people born elsewhere: Irish people and foreigners. And there were non-Europeans: 'niggers'. This word was applied...to anyone whose complexion showed that he or she had not been born into the master race.[31]

(Jews were presumably counted as foreigners.) The extent to which such attitudes were held by different sections of the population, and in particular by the working class, is subject to historical debate. It is not clear, for instance, how far anti-semitism as such was prevalent in the East End, though in Irish neighbourhoods it may have been fostered by the accusatory myths in Catholic tradition of infant slaughter by Jews. Certainly people were wary of the 'outlandish' foreigners with strange clothes and customs and a foreign tongue, and concern over pressure on housing and jobs caused hostility to the obvious scapegoats.[32] H.S. Lewis, Cambridge graduate and Jew who lived for many years in the Toynbee Hall settlement, argued that 'external differences' mattered more to 'the general run of man' than those which depended on doctrine or ritual.

> Mere dissimilarity of appearance, language, ideas in itself pro-
> duces antagonism. Even the townsman and the countryman are in
> imperfect sympathy with each other, and where differences are
> more essential distrust will be correspondingly greater.[33]

The term 'alien', so prevalent at the time, suggests the tendency to define
self (or community or society or nation) against 'other': those who fit and
belong as opposed to those who do not. At the same time, the notion that
external appearance evoked antipathy clearly contributed to the emphasis
by the Jewish establishment ('Anglo-Jewry') on urgent 'anglicisation' of the
newcomers.

The repertoire of xenophobic stereotypes, virulent or not, provided
easy scapegoats and a vocabulary of insult. They obstructed understanding
between locals and newcomers and could affect children's experience in
school. The supposition that all Irish were stupid, for instance, impeded
progress at school for some Irish children.[34] Jewish children, however, who
were perceived as 'sharper and more intelligent than the English', and
indeed won more prizes and scholarships[35] were resented or mocked.

Autobiographical material (from London and elsewhere) suggests that
newcomers were often seen and treated as different both at school and in
the neighbourhood, especially of course if they were few, and if culture and
language reinforced difference. The exact character of the neighbourhood
mattered—whether one group predominated, how much of a mix or what
particular mix there was, and the rate of turnover. In a very mixed neighbourhood a degree of tolerance was probably necessary. People in 1920s
Shadwell, for instance, lived in a complex combination of race and religion, but 'prejudice never led to physical violence'; everyone ('except
possibly the Nonconformists'), celebrated St Patrick's Day and the young
Louis Heren, though Protestant, wore shamrock to school:

> The native-born Cockneys were certainly a minority, and the
> majority were immigrants, mainly Irish Catholics and Polish Jews.
> Some African and West Indian seamen had married local women
> and settled down. One of the ropes, or lodging houses, was home
> for Indian pedlars, Sikhs who hawked garish scarves and
> shawls....There was no racial violence, but religious prejudice was
> intense throughout the neighbourhood. I suppose we were all
> anti-Semitic because we knew that the Jews had killed Jesus. Many
> of our Jewish neighbours spoke only Polish and Yiddish. The
> beards and the side-curls of the Orthodox were absolutely for-
> eign....Apart from the Jews, the mutual antipathies of the Catholics
> and Protestants were constant, and the Nonconformists hardly
> ever spoke to anyone....Yet we all lived peacefully alongside each
> other if not together. We were all poor....[36]

Political and economic context interacted with stereotypes to produce a
specific local impact. When a particular group was perceived as flooding in

and affecting wage-rates, rents and conditions, hostility was intense. Anti-Irish sentiment (though it also fluctuated with the level of Fenian activity) was therefore strongest in the middle decades of the nineteenth century.[37] Young Tom Barclay in 1860s Leicester found that children echoed their parents' animosity, jeering at the newcomers' speech and generally abusing them:

> 'Hurroo, Mick!'
> 'Ye Awrish Paddywhack!'
> 'Arrah, bad luck to the ships that brought ye over.'
>
> These were the salutes from the happy English child: we were battered, threatened, elbowed, pressed back to the door of our kennel amid boos and jeers and showers of small missiles.[38]

By the 1890s, especially in London, antagonism was directed at newer arrivals.[39] Walter Southgate recalled of his Hackney childhood then how he and his friends made an 'old Jewish gentleman' in prosperous Gore Road their butt.

> Why I don't know, but no boy could pass this old man's house without kicking on his door, ringing his bell, throwing stones at his gate and occasionally breaking his windows....It had become a ritual. There was no rhyme or reason for it except he was a Jew and they had invaded the East End as had other races in the past and were exploited by their compatriots, cheapening their labour products to the detriment of the East End English cabinet makers.[40]

In each case current fears and prejudice provided substance for taunts and identified victims both for ordinary mischief and for more serious bullying and aggression.

Differences of religion or origin clearly were for some children (especially boys) an excuse for gang rivalry and territoriality. Barclay noted dispassionately that local boys' hostility was not only against the Irish: 'Sassenach kids fought among themselves; street fought street and district district without the slightest cause'. In mid-century Clerkenwell 'small boys and lads' of 'the Catholic Irish and the "patriot" Italians' fought in endless scrimmages for Garibaldi or the Pope;[41] in South Hackney in the 1890s boys from Sidney Street Board school fought boys from the free Catholic school down the road, to the dismay of an eleven-year-old girl whose route home lay through the battlefield ('And if you can show me any more horrible little roughs than Irish Roman Catholics...');[42] and it is likely that the sons of the Wapping Irish saw Whitechapel Jewish boys as the enemy.[43] Of course the victims of predatory or bullying behaviour were not always of another background, but such difference was one possible 'justification'. Whatever the pretext, many individual children, girls and boys, were picked on by street bullies, as was Rose Kerrigan in Glasgow before the First World War.

We were waylaid quite often coming home from *cheder* [Hebrew school], especially on winter nights. My mother hid in a doorway one night when we were coming home. We'd come home crying 'cos these boys had hit us. We were running from them and my mother came out with an umbrella and gave them such a fright that they never came back.[44]

Adults as well as children might be the butt of taunts or worse because appearance marked them out. Just as jeers and perhaps stones might greet an obvious 'nob', a missionary, or a School Board officer, so too an obvious identity as Jewish (especially newly arrived), Irish or generally 'foreign' might trigger hostility. A black Bermudan merchant in 1873 won his case for assault after such taunts resulted in a brawl: as someone of less substance would not have brought the case it is hard to judge the typicality of the incident but it is unlikely to have been exceptional.[45]

Children's own sense of difference would stem both from internal sources (how their household lived, its history, its religion, its consciousness) and from external ones (neighbourhood and school responses). Tom Barclay, under attack in Leicester, combined contempt and hatred for 'the Sassenach' with awareness of historical context and a certain pride in being Irish. As his mother said, 'Ah well, sure, what better could one expect of the breed of King Harry?'; and when he and his younger siblings were literally besieged in their hovel, he thought of the Siege of Limerick. Zangwill's Esther Ansell, as we have seen, knew herself as Jewish but 'still more vividly' realized that she was 'an English girl'.[46]

Children from smaller and less numerous minority groups probably had an especially difficult time. Difference of appearance and language was still against them; and they might not have the support of a local community. In some cases, notably with children of African, Caribbean, Indian or Chinese origin, they had also to contend with images which, as we have seen, denigrated them as savage, dirty, uncivilized and childlike, or devious, cunning and artful. Names based on race or national origin and alleged attributes (Chink, for example) were used by other children to taunt and tease, just as cries of 'Jew' or 'Paddy' were commonplace; or if a girl had her hair done in one long plait, 'the boys [would] come and try to have a swing on it and then shout out "There goes a Chinaman"'.[47] (Here boys' obsession with pulling girls' plaits is combined with the racist taunt.) Where one parent was English there might be further stigma.

In the London school records I covered (not all those available, however) I came upon no reference to children wholly or partly of African, Caribbean, Indian or Chinese origin. They certainly existed throughout London, as descendants of slaves or migrants; and in East-End dock areas as the offspring of traders or sailors, 'men of all colours and races' who had settled there, often with local women.[48]

Children of marriages between Chinese men and English women in the well-established Limehouse Chinese colony were described by a journalist in 1903 as 'dark-haired, black-eyed boys and girls', who looked 'healthy and well dressed' and were 'real little pictures'.[49] Children of 'Asiatic' or mixed parentage figure fleetingly in the memoirs of Joseph Salter, a missionary employed in connection with the Strangers' Home for Asiatics, Africans and South Sea Islanders, opened in Limehouse in 1857.[50] In nearby Shadwell in the 1860s, he recalled, some of the sailors' boarding houses were run by Chinese, Malayan or Indian proprietors, each 'assisted by an English mistress' known by such names as 'Mrs Mohammed, Mrs Peeroo, Mrs Janoo...Chinese Emma, Calcutta Louisa, and Lascar Sally'.[51] Theirs were perhaps the children to whom he referred patronizingly as 'degraded children claiming parentage with the foreign world' who had 'learnt the song of redeeming love' at the local Ragged School.[52] He also described the lively Sabbath scene in Bluegate Fields, Shadwell, with 'Asiatics' in every direction, some with 'the coloured offspring of their companions in their arms, dressed out, and giving them sweets and fruit'.[53] On the older children he commented:[54]

> Such a group! presenting so many nationalities in one view as perhaps could be gathered nowhere else. These innocent children have often been looked on with anxiety and pity, having so distinctively the evidence of their parentage. The dark little face with the woolly hair of Africa curling above the smiling eyes, or the features, perhaps not quite so dark, with the luxuriant flowing hair of Hindoostan. Others, too, were observed, whose little prattling lips unconsciously utter the abominations learnt at their own depraved homes, whose eyes and face link them with unmistakable accuracy to the empire of the Celestials.

Salter's main interest was in adults (especially newly-arrived or in workhouse, court or prison); his fragmentary references tell us little about children beyond that they existed, before 1873 and by inference later, not only in Shadwell but also in Westminster.[55]

But his writing illustrates the ingrained race bias of even the most passing mention.[56] As a missionary, he saw the unconverted as 'degraded' and uncivilized. He could observe the customs of other peoples, learn their languages, and differentiate between the places and cultures they came from; he was at ease with members of the suite of a wealthy Nawab who settled in Paddington for a time; and he disapproved of the blatant racism of a workhouse keeper who was against treating the 'troublesome darkies' too kindly'.[57] Nevertheless, non-Christian religious beliefs were 'abominations', and children of mixed parentage (their exact origin inferred from physical features) were to be pitied. The general impression he gives is undoubtedly that superiority belonged more naturally to the white and British Christian.

There can be no doubt that East-End children whose physical appearance suggested foreign parentage were sometimes made to feel different or even inferior, whether (at best) by being patronized, or by being ridiculed, teased, insulted and bullied; that this could happen in school as well as out; and that it could come from adults—teachers included—as well as from children.

State, Child and Parent

The changes in childhood experience outlined in the chapters above developed from and continued a process begun much earlier. From the late eighteenth century the continuing advance of the middle class (economic, social, political and in numbers) had been characterized by greater separation of gender and age roles, of production and consumption, of public and private; and by a dominant ideology where one type of family unit and one set of age and gender relations were increasingly presented as 'natural' and so universally appropriate and desirable.[58]

As the state came to play a significant role in shaping and reinforcing the transformation of childhood, in the nineteenth and twentieth centuries, these dominant ideas about childhood and the family were reflected in parliamentary decisions as well as rhetoric. They were complemented by the assumption that different customs in the working class implied the inadequacy (or worse) of working-class parents and therefore justified an intervention in family life which might otherwise appear contradictory. Compulsory school and protective legislation imposed the 'proper' experience of childhood—school, economic dependence and submission to adult (and class) authority—and steadily prolonged its duration. And where children did not fit the new requirements (school attendance, full economic dependence, subordination to adults, keeping up with rising standards of physical and mental fitness and of appearance) the parents could be labelled as inadequate or bad, and might even have to hand over responsibility for their children to the state.

So a significant part of the changes in childhood over this period was the transformation of the balance between parent, child and state.[59] With compulsory education, labour restrictions and protective legislation, the theoretical authority of parent over child ceased to be absolute and the child's potential for any degree of independence was reduced, while new definitions and obligations were established, for parenthood as well as childhood. In the prevailing mood of dismay at the scale of social problems and the inadequacy of voluntary resources, and with 'national efficiency' the watchword,[60] it was increasingly accepted that as children were 'a national asset' the state should take an interest in their health and upbringing. As Margaret Alden, a doctor writing in 1908, put the argument:

> The nation that first recognizes the importance of scientifically rearing and training the children of the commonwealth will be the

nation that will survive. Unless due attention is paid to the young life which will one day govern and maintain an empire, we shall speedily fall behind in the competitive struggle. Few people will be inclined to admit that England is on the down grade, and yet other mighty empires have perished in the past. The question as to whether we are degenerating as a race is still *sub judice*, and perhaps the most hopeful sign of the times is the increased interest in every problem that affects the life of the child...what is wanted is that far more serious attention should be given to child problems on the part of the State as a whole...[61]

The social worker Reginald Bray went further:

The rearing of children must be regarded as a co-operative undertaking, in which there are three parties—the father, the mother and the State.[62]

But for all the allusions to 'the nation's children' or 'the children of the state', opinion was divided and confused over what and how much the state should provide, and what risks were entailed.

These divisions are easily seen in the debates of the 1900s about whether the state should provide free meals for needy schoolchildren.[63] This had been a socialist demand from the mid-1880s, put forward by Social Democratic Federation (SDF) candidates in the School Board elections and proposed by socialists on the London School Board.[64] It was raised with increasing urgency in following years, especially by teachers and others much in contact with poor children, who saw the inadequacy of even extensive voluntary effort.[65] Attempts to assess the extent of undernourishment produced varying figures, but it was clear that thousands of London schoolchildren did not get enough to eat.[66] Stoked by the findings of the Physical Deterioration Committee (1904) and of the Medical Inspection and Feeding of School Children Committee (1905), the debate grew hotter. Discussion focussed on how to balance the needs of children with the relative responsibilities of parents and state.

Those who supported school meals cited humanitarian grounds ('children are not fed; they require to be fed'),[67] or the national interest,[68] or both. They divided, however, on whether it should be 'all children, destitute or not',[69] who should be fed at public expense, or only 'all children who need feeding'. And the issue was further complicated by the Social Democratic Federation argument that all children should be not only fed but altogether maintained at state expense: this was in the national interest as the only way to resolve the social problems which were producing 'national deterioration'. For Ramsay MacDonald and most of the Labour Party this was excessive.[70] MacDonald argued that children went hungry because families were being disabled by poverty, the result of capitalism. Socialism would bring state support for the family but must not supplant it. School meals, meanwhile, were desirable. At local level considerable

Labour effort went into the campaign for school meals, especially from the Women's Labour League and the Co-operative Women's Guild.[71]

Those who opposed free meals insisted that parents must be responsible for their children and that this responsibility must not be undermined by injudicious subsidy, or parental authority and the family itself would be put at risk. Like Helen Bosanquet and the Charity Organization Society,[72] they held that poverty was mostly the result of improvidence or worse, and that malnourished children were the victims of 'injudicious feeding and neglect' from their earliest years. If schools provided meals, mothers would became 'slack', girls would not learn domestic skills,[73] and fathers would have no incentive to 'exertion and self-restraint'.[74] In the interests of the community, Bosanquet wrote, it was better:

> to allow in such cases the sins of the parents to be visited upon their children than to impair the solidarity of the family and run the risk of permanently demoralizing large numbers of the population by the offer of free meals to their children.[75]

Some opponents claimed that the supporters of state responsibility thought 'that the children are more the property of the State than the property of their parents...and that the State is the best parent'.[76]

One typical response was that parental responsibility was important, but so too was 'our responsibility as members of the big family of the State, for the feeding of all our children'.[77] Margaret McMillan, who defended the school meal on educational as well as health grounds and as 'radical in [its] bearing on the future of the race, also suggested that communal kitchens, far from threatening family and home, would allow mothers to extend 'the office of motherhood and homemaking'.[78]

Sir John Gorst, a prominent if unorthodox Conservative, combined the positions. He supported school meals even though he believed 'that the duty of bringing up children [rested] in the first instance with their parents', and was against early schooling.[79] In his book, *The Children of the Nation* (1906), he argued that the state had duties too. 'The nation's children' were 'the future British people', on whose 'condition and capacity' would depend 'not only the happiness of our own country but also the influence of our Empire in the world'.[80] So hungry children should be fed, (and there should be free medical aid for those who needed it), whatever the moral obligation of the parents. It would be 'the height of bad economy' that 'children should be left to starve in order to coerce their parents into feeding them', and put children at risk 'for the remote possibility of mending the parent'.[81] The socialist proposal to feed all children at the public expense, however, went too far, and would undermine parental responsibility.

> [It] would take the children still more than now out of the hands of their parents, and make them still more than now children of the

State....[It] would be a boon to those now on the edge of the poverty line; it would lift some of those now under the line above it. But
it would tend, as free education has tended, to lessen parental
interest and parental co-operation in the upbringing of children.[82]

Margaret Alden, though she saw the socialists as anti-family and though
confident that 'nothing which permanently saps or undermines parental
responsibility is likely to benefit the community in the long run', favoured
state action (in conjunction with voluntary effort) to educate ignorant
working-class parents in their duties. She argued that:

many of the measures which have been adopted to safeguard the
life and health and well-being of children, so far from lightening
the duty of the parents, have made that duty imperatively binding.[83]

For her, 'the fresh conception of "State parenthood" was an exciting step
forward'.

All these views, crossing and complicating party lines, belonged to the
tide of concern over poverty and its consequences which in the 1900s was
carrying most Liberals and some Conservatives towards more interven-
tionist policies.[84] It swept the Liberals into government, and licensed their
attempts to tackle the causes of poverty as well as alleviating its effects. But
although the range of state action was extended there was inevitably much
compromise, and certainly no socialist transformation of the economic
order. With one of the Liberals' first measures, for instance, the Education
(Provision of Meals) Act of 1906, local authorities were empowered but not
obliged to provide meals for needy children. (Need was to be assessed by
local Children's Care Committees; despite intense Labour lobbying local
provision developed slowly and unevenly.) Or again, medical inspection of
schoolchildren was made legal (1907), but until 1914 treatment was left to
the parents.

Despite rearguard insistence on parental duties and compromise over
the degree of provision, some degree of state intervention on behalf of
children had wide support. In the debates preceding passage of the
Children Act of 1908 the Lord Advocate noted how much opinion had
changed.

There was a time in the history of this House when a Bill of this
kind would have been treated as a most revolutionary measure;
and, half a century ago, if such a measure had been introduced it
would have been said that the British Constitution was being
undermined. Now a Bill of this kind finds itself in smooth water
from the outset. This measure is not the development of the political ideas of one party, but the gradual development of a
quickened sense on the part of the community at large of the duty
it owes to the Children.[85]

With this Act, children's separate identity and needs were fully recognized. Previous protective measures were consolidated and strengthened,
with more rigorous supervision of fostered and boarded-out children and
further offences of negligence added to those of cruelty. The authorities
were given more power to remove children from their home, temporarily
or permanently; they were authorized to assume control of them up to the
age of sixteen and even to organize their emigration. It was made illegal to
sell or give tobacco to anyone under sixteen, or to allow children to be on
licensed premises during opening hours. The separate position under the
law of children (under fourteen) and young persons (fourteen to sixteen)
was codified. Separate courts were established for juvenile offenders; parents were to be required to attend throughout legal proceedings; the role
of probation officers (introduced in 1907) was reinforced and the system
of reformatory and industrial schools reorganized.[86]

The Act was dubbed the 'Children's Charter', with echoes of Magna
Carta and a triumphal sense of progress. But although it did reflect a new
consensus on childhood, it was not in fact a 'charter' for children.
(Twentieth-century charters seldom give what they seem to promise.) The
rights it gave them were the rights of those without power, all passive—
rights to protection and support, rights not to be abused or exploited. The
State '[took] upon itself the duty of over-parent',[87] and if parents failed in
providing properly for them, it would step in to provide substitutes.

'The true strength of a nation', wrote Nettie Adler (later of the LCC
Education Committee) in 1902, 'lies in securing happy and healthy lives for
the young children of the State, in giving them that which is their rightful
possession—their childhood'.[88] The Children Act could not in fact, any
more than other reform legislation of the period, give children 'a happy
and healthy childhood'.[89] But it did bring into law and into state practices
the view of childhood which had come to prevail in much public discussion
as well as in middle-class practice and creed.

The new provisions consolidated and fixed the reality of dependence
underlying the current rhetoric of joyous and carefree childhood. It was
for adults to define and organize childhood, and children (up to sixteen)
were to be dependent and without autonomy. The family was the ideal and
proper context for childhood, provided it functioned in the approved way.
At the same time the balance between parents and the state was altered,
with the domestic authority of parents ultimately subordinate to the overriding power of the state. Parents as well as children were being regulated.[90]

This had class implications, of course. The legal endorsement of a largely middle-class consensus gave it increased potency. The appraisals and
decisions involved in the exercise of 'securing a happy childhood' were to
be made by people of overwhelmingly middle-class background, and the parents most likely to come into conflict with the state were poor and working
class. The professionals dealing with children and the family—teachers,
health visitors, school doctors, probation officers and so on—could put their

views on childrearing across as dogma rather than suggestion, with sanctions in reserve for those who clung to other notions. Their judgements of what was generally proper for children and young people were apt to prevail whatever the particular situation and character.

One result of increased official interest in children as future citizens was that more children ended up in institutions. Protective legislation between 1889 and 1891 established children's right to reasonable treatment, and the authorities' right to remove them into institutional care if they saw fit (see Chapter 9). Physical and mental handicap (one often assumed to imply the other) alike disqualified children from ordinary life. As medical inspection revealed the extent of children's ill-health and handicap, more specialized schools, Homes and hospitals were set up, both by voluntary associations and local authorities, and by the 1920s there were over 500 institutions catering for children with physical disabilities, including seventy-seven for the blind, fifty for the deaf and seventy-eight for the so-called 'physical defectives'. In such institutions visits by relatives were restricted and regimes were often harsh.[91] Institutional children were expected to work, as well, especially girls, even though the rhetoric of sheltering children from work permeated both the rhetoric of rescue and the critique of the working-class family.[92]

Following the Mental Deficiency Act of 1913 new asylums and 'colonies' were set up, and children and young people defined as 'idiot', 'imbecile', 'feeble-minded' or 'moral defective' could also be removed into institutional care. Failure in school would contribute to the first three of these assessments: they covered children who at seven were deemed incapable of benefitting from education in special school or class, or who before they reached sixteen were discharged from special school as ineducable. On leaving special school young people could be detained if they were not considered capable of managing for themselves; or if they were held to combine mental defectiveness 'with strong vicious or criminal propensities' such that they needed 'care, supervision and control for the protection of others'. Prescriptive views of gender and sexuality along with eugenic influence put girls who got pregnant 'too soon' at risk under this clause, and probably also young homosexuals. The medical model of homosexuality, influenced by eugenics, was gaining influence.[93] As a medical officer of health wrote in 1906:

> The tendency of the girls to nurse dolls or of the boys to play soldiers is absolutely natural. The failure to exhibit these normal tastes may be held to indicate mental defect, and often that defect is elusive in being shown only by perverted moral traits.[94]

Similarly, common prejudice and eugenic logic decreed that young women who were sexually active outside marriage were surely 'promiscuous' and society must be protected from the burden of their producing degenerate progeny.[95] So if their families rejected them, they ran a real risk of long-term incarceration (and had no chance of keeping the baby). 'Elizabeth', institutionalized at eighteen after bearing an illegitimate child, spent over sixty-one years in a 'colony for mental defectives' opened in 1920.[96]

Thus the new definitions and reality of childhood and of state responsibility had wide repercussions. They set new standards of childhood, of parenthood and indeed of adulthood. Where parents failed in their duty to provide children with a proper childhood, the state as over-parent could punish them and remove their children. Where adults did not conform to standards of self-sufficiency or sexual codes, they could be detained by the authorities. Because of eugenic concern with the proliferation of the unfit they were not only to be excluded from citizenship and kept indefinitely dependent and childlike, but also segregated from the other sex.

Schooling the Nation

In redefining childhood, as in the construction of national identity, the school played a central part. The introduction of compulsory school made it possible to monitor children in large numbers and to establish standards of what was normal and abnormal in child development, achievement and behaviour. Within and between schools this facilitated grading and social stratification. Children who fell below the standards (often on arbitrary and flimsy grounds) could then be defined as defective and might as they grew older be denied adult rights—political, social, economic and sexual.

Compulsory school attendance was more effective than labour legislation in limiting children's work, unwaged as well as waged. At the same time, it provided a wedge with which to open up the privacy of the working-class family. The discipline of the school, as we have seen, extended into the home as new domestic routines developed to ensure that requirements for punctuality and appearance were met. Visits by attendance officers to check on absentees, then by all the later representatives of authority, permitted reconnaissance into working-class domestic life. And where the results of such observation were deemed unsatisfactory, intervention might follow.

The idea of the state as over-parent was part of a wider rhetorical convention, in which state authority and power were likened to the authority of the parent or perhaps teacher.[97] If government and its officers (whether imperial, national or local) were 'paternal' and took over parental responsibilities, and if England was the 'Mother' of Empire, the governed, on the other hand, were children, helpless and incapable, perhaps wayward; their 'need' was for direction and control rather than rights and powers. This was used at home to justify structures of government which minimized both participation and accountability, along with denial of political rights to those deemed eugenically unfit. It was also the rhetorical justification for

Empire, since natives were childlike and would regress into savagery without the firm adult hand to guide and control them.

Yet again, the school had its part to play. The 'future British people' needed to learn their place in the nation and the world, in a complex interplay of class, gender and culture. We have seen already how class and gender structured education in this period, and how (despite minority voices) racist and imperialist ideology permeated the culture both of school and the larger society. The acknowledged object of the school was integrative: to 'civilize' the children of the poor and to anglicize foreign children—to ensure that the next generation met the needs of the modern nation-state. 'The newly-arrived Russo-Jewish immigrant is, in all essentials, a mediaeval product', but 'his children grow up into something like the type of modern Englishmen', wrote Charles Russell in 1900.[98] The Jewish Free School was praised by a reporter in 1895 as a 'factory of English citizens', and he recounted his amazement on finding that of the hundred or so teachers engaged in 'turning these little foreigners into English folk', only one—not all, as he had supposed—was 'English and presumably Christian'.[99]

The young writer, Israel Zangwill, was more critical of the process of integration. In *The Children of the Ghetto*, he wrote of the children of every country and kind who came 'from the reeking courts and alleys, from the garrets and the cellars' to be anglicized, 'all hastening at the inexorable clang of the big school-bell to be ground in the same great, blind, inexorable Governmental machine'.[100] Zangwill refused to identify with the perception, common to the Anglo-Jewish establishment and the liberal middle class, that anglicization was necessary. As he saw, the school in this period played a central part in the consolidation of modern national identity. Although there were some who learnt their lesson imperfectly, or who rejected it, or were themselves rejected as misfits, Board-school children were being taught to be British.

Nor was national identity the only preoccupation in the not-so-hidden curriculum of school, which often, as we have seen, seemed more important than the regular curriculum. Children were also supposed to be learning social, political and economic lessons. They were to learn that boys and girls had different 'natural' characteristics and abilities, and therefore different expectations. They were offered models of family life (often far from their own) in which mothers stayed at home, fathers never drank, and children were always good. Thrift, hard work, hygiene and temperance were constantly promoted; and they were taught that employers (like teachers and authority in general) had their best interests at heart, that passivity was the best political policy. In short, as the next generation they were to furnish a model working class.

Of course the history of labour struggles (over housing as well as workplace issues) in the decades which followed suggests that this attempt to tame the working class through school was not wholly successful. 'The poor', and the working class in general, were neither passive nor indeed homogeneous in their response to pressure and change. On the other hand, the chief contribution of school in preparing working-class pupils for their future lives, according to the Tyneside writer Jack Common, was to teach them to endure being bored, and this may have been more successful.

> We learn reading and boredom, writing and boredom, arithmetic and boredom, and so on according to curriculum, till in the end it is quite certain you can put us to the most boring job there is and we'll endure it.[101]

In much adult employment this training did prove necessary.

For London children the 'civilizing' influence of the school was in constant competition with life in the outside world, which most children found infinitely more interesting and convincing. For most children, sympathetic teachers were few and far between; and the gulf was too great for even these to be seen as models, whether for future employment, outlook, or comportment.[102] 'Civilizing' views and values probably had most purchase where (as with gender difference and, for some at least, models of family life) there was a certain overlap with existing patterns. The ideal of 'home' being presented, with its offer of both maternal love and material comforts, must have been very alluring, and was certainly widely sought after as twentieth-century economic and demographic changes made it seem more attainable.

Conclusion

If the remaking of the working class through its children remained incomplete, what of the transformation of childhood? Here change was certainly underway and pressures from above, whether through school or legislation, were only one factor. Rising living standards over the first fifty years of compulsory school were of great importance. At the same time the spreading influence of working-class respectability, reinforced by the tendency for more settled patterns of life both in household and neighbourhood, meant growing constraints on children's behaviour (especially for girls).

Almost all working-class children in 1900s London spent nine years at school, while the poorest often started earlier and had an extra two years. Fewer children than in the 1860s went hungry or were barefoot in winter (though some still did). The autonomous young street arab of fifty years before was now a rarity: children lived in homes or Homes. More of them, too, grew up in households whose main wage-earners were adult: father alone or with teenagers, mother only when necessary. They were dependent.

As living standards improved and there was some lessening of insecurity, daily life in many families was probably less stressful. Housing standards were beginning to improve. Families were less often crammed into one room. Many had more space, more windows, more furniture and more ornaments, even if this meant more scrubbing, dusting, sweeping, and polishing, along with curtains to be washed, bedlinen to be changed, more clothes to be kept clean and neat, even sometimes a copper and a front doorstep to be kept white. In most such homes food was prepared in a proper kitchen, on a stove regularly blackleaded, and was eaten formally at set meals.

Working-class respectability, reinforced by rising living standards and the tendency for more settled patterns of life both in household and neighbourhood, also meant growing constraints on children's behaviour. Children had to be scrubbed and tidy, for school and Sunday school at least. The appearance and behaviour of the girls was especially significant as a testimony to familial respectability and the mother's competence.

But poor children, respectable and rough, were still numerous, and poverty still significantly shaped their lives. Their levels of nutrition and health were inferior to those of better-off working-class children, let alone those of the middle class; and their life choices and chances were more limited. Although now dependent for longer, poor children, girls especially, still bore much responsibility: the older family economy had been modified rather than abolished. They had more and earlier knowledge of 'adult' preserves, including budgetting, insecurity and bereavement. Their range of social contact and understanding was wider than that of more sheltered children. They knew that dependence was finite and they would soon be supporting themselves.

Rough or respectable, comfortable or poor, boys meanwhile were freer than girls. Their obligations as to work had been lightened, but they retained the street boy's freedom to play and to roam, and sanctioned by the indulgent axiom, 'boys will be boys', they made the most of it; they had more access to money and more freedom in spending it. Girls' load by contrast, always more domestic, may even have grown heavier. Rising living standards, as we have seen, meant more housework; expectations of neatness were also rising; child care was becoming more demanding; and protective legislation did not dent the expectations of domestic help from girls. They were increasingly restricted by conventions as to what was proper; and their horizons, present and future, were narrowed by the demands of child care and family. The 'poor' and the 'comfortable' girl might learn somewhat different skills (from bartering with the pawn-shop man to setting the table), and the 'little mother' was more likely to be poor, but girls generally were domestic apprentices from their earliest years.

If working-class childhood was being transformed, then, how it was experienced by particular children depended as much on their sex as on class, education, respectability or any other factor.

Notes

————◆————

Introduction

In the later stages of this book two books appeared which are highly relevant: Ellen Ross, *Love and Toil: Motherhood in Outcast London* and Hugh Cunningham, *Children of the Poor: Representations of Childhood since the Seventeenth Century.* I have made extensive reference to the articles by Ross which preceded the book; her work and mine deal with many of the same sources and issues, but from the differing standpoints of the child and the mother. Hugh Cunningham's book, too, takes up some of the same questions as mine, but with a larger canvas and with an emphasis on representation where mine attempts to explore experience.

1. C.f. Mayhew, *London Labour* 1, p.468; *Oxford English Dictionary* (by mid-century as 'a young person of either sex below the age of puberty'); Sykes, 'Hygiene and Sanitation', p.26. The 1871 census (*Report*, p.xii) gave the 'stages of life' as children (five to ten), boys and girls (ten to fifteen), and youths and maidens (fifteen to twenty); its tables often make twenty a watershed. Puberty by 1883 was said to occur for boys between fourteen and sixteen; for girls between thirteen and sixteen: Crichton Browne, 'Education and the Nervous System', p.322.
2. For chronology (mainly boys) see Waugh, *Queen's Reign*, pp.89–104; c.f. Atkinson, 'Law and Infant Life'; Pinchbeck and Hewitt, *Children*, chap.16; Spalding, *School Board*, pp.137–46; May, 'Innocence'. The age of criminal responsibility was raised to eight in 1933 and to ten in 1963. The issue is still under debate.
3. Livius, *Father Furniss*, pp.137–8.
4. Gorham, 'Maiden Tribute'; Weeks, *Sex, Politics and Society*, chap.5; Mort, *Dangerous Sexualities*, part 3; Davin, 'When is a Child'.
5. Ragged schools began in the 1840s, peaked in the 1860s, declined with school-board competition in the 1870s, picked up in the 1880s through extending their mission and charitable operations, and slumped in the 1890s with the abolition (in London) of school fees. The last one closed in 1906: see Clark, 'Ragged Schools'; 'Ragged School Union'. There is a Ragged School Museum in London.
6. For the last, see Samuel Butler, *The Way of All Flesh*, 1903, chap.22.
7. This is illustrated in Frances Hodgson Burnett's *The Little Princess* (1902): 'I am only a little girl like you', says wealthy Sara to Becky, little drudge at Sara's boarding school, who is fourteen but looks twelve. But according to Miss Minchin, the headmistress, 'Scullery maids are not little girls' (pp.52, 67).
8. Mrs W. (b. Finsbury, 1896), transcript, p.8.

1 Indulgence and Insecurity

1. C.f. Greenwood, *Seven Curses*, part 1; Smith, 'Destitute Children' (1885); Dendy, 'Children of Working London', p.40; Booth, *Poverty* 1, p.246; [Watt Smyth], 'School Children out of School', *BMJ*, 16 Jan. 1904, p.140. (Flora Tristan, earlier, even referred to children as 'birds of prey': *Promenades dans Londres*, p.70.) See also Davin, 'When is a Child not a Child?'.
2. Gissing, *Nether World*, pp.129–30.

3. The phrase is from Newsholme and Stevenson, 'Decline in human fertility', 1906, p.66.

4. For birth control see McLaren, *Birth Control*; Levine, *Reproducing Families*. On women's experience of pregnancy and childbirth see Davies (ed.), *Maternity* (1915), especially figures pp.194–5 on miscarriages, still-births, and children dead under one year.

5. Jane W. (b. Limehouse, 1896), transcript p.4. C.f. 'Thomas Morgan' (born Blackfriars, 1892) in Thompson, *Edwardian Childhoods*, p.24: 'I was the last one of thirteen. I don't know nothing about those that died. I don't know nothing about one sister, Ada, she died about twenty-five.'

6. The eldest brother of Mr N. (b. 1899) lived 'well away on the other side of the water' (in Rotherhithe), and after mother and daughter-in-law quarrelled the family in Wapping 'never saw him': transcript, p.46.

7. Eliza H. (b. Isle of Dogs, 1900), transcript tape 2, side 1, p.1; and Phyllis H. (born Kings Cross, 1908), in SE1 People's History Group discussion, 10 June 1980.

8. Alf Slater (b. 1927), in Peckham People's History Group, *The Times of our Lives*, p.40.

9. Minnie Brittain (b. Richmond, 1907), ms. memoir, p.5.

10. Bessie C. (b. Bermondsey, 1893), transcript p.34.

11. For demography of British childhood in this period see Hair, 'Children in Society, 1850–1980'. For infant mortality, see Wohl, *Endangered Lives*, chap.2.

12. Newman, *Health of the State*, p.111.

13. *MOH London, Report* 1892, p.10; c.f. J. Priestley, 'High Death Rates in Lambeth', *Public Health*, Oct. 1898, p.58. See also table on infant mortality by district in Booth, *Final Vol.*, p.27; and tables pp.16–20.

14. Newsholme, *Vital Statistics*, p.127. Rowntree found a still greater range in York, between 247 and 94 per thousand: *Poverty*, p.206.

15. Newman, *Health of the State*, p.111.

16. *R.C. Alien Immigration*, 1903, evidence q.3,963; Newman, *Infant Mortality*, pp.225–6. See also Sponza, *Italian Immigrants*, pp.226–7.

17. *MOH London, Report*, 1895, p.24. Diphtheria rates in London in the 1880s and 1890s were higher than in comparable cities at the time: see *MOH London, Report* 1893, p.27; F.W. Alexander, *Report on the Causes of Diphtheria* to Sanitary Committee of Board of Works for Poplar, 1894.

18. Logbook, Gainsborough Road: 9 Oct. and 20 Nov. 1875; 15 Jan., 17 June, 27 Oct., 8 Dec. 1876; 29 Jan., 5 Oct. 1877; 7 Jan. 1878; 5 May, 3 Feb., 17 Feb. 1892. C.f. Rubinstein, *School Attendance in London*, pp.76–81; Hurt, *Elementary Schooling*.

19. McLaren, *Birth Control*, chaps 12 and 13; Brookes, *Abortion*; Phillips, *Abortion*, p.106; Lewis, *Politics of Motherhood*, pp.199–200; Chamberlain, *Old Wives' Tales*, pp.115–23; Hackney WEA, *Threepenny Doctor*, 1983 edn, pp.4–5, 9, 22.

20. Woodward, *Jipping Street*, p.7. See also Carolyn Steedman's introduction (1983).

21. Peel, *Life's Enchanted Cup*, p.83: the author's sister, helping at a birth in Notting Dale, had asked the girl if she wanted to see the new baby.

22. Celia R. (b. Waterloo before 1900), interviewed by Anna Davin at SE1 People's History Group 29 Jan. 1979.

23. Booth, *Final Volume*, p.42; see also vol.1, pp.159–60.

24. Berdoe, 'Slum Mothers and Death Clubs' (1891), p.562. See also Hilton, *Marie Hilton*, p.91: after twenty-five years' crèche work in Stepney Mrs Hilton maintained that 'the women of the East End loved their children as fondly as did the women of the classes', and the poor had been 'grossly libelled' on this count. C.f. *S.C. Children's Life Insurance Bill*, 1890, evidence of Will Crooks, especially q.2,273; Martin, 'Mother and Social Reform', *Nineteenth Century and After*, 73, 1913, esp. p. 1, 236–7.

25. Foakes, *Walls*, p.69; Sharp, 'Kit's Hair', *Macmillan's Story Readers*, Book 5, 1903, p.113. For general discussion, see Evans, *Mouths of Men*, pp.86–104.

26. Rolph, *London Particulars*, p.7.

27. Ruth Lamb, 'How to Nurse', *Girl's Own Paper* 2, 1881, p.700.

28. *Women and Children in Public Houses*, 1908, p.8.

29. From 1893 the Public Control Committee of the LCC regularly listed fatal accidents caused by oil lamps, with addresses. Some lamps had clearly been burning all night.

30. Anna Wickham (b. 1884) recalled her mother's stories of a lodger who on Sunday mornings 'always threw his farthings out of his bedroom window into the yard below', for the children to find and spend: Smith, *Anna Wickham*, p.68. See also [Wright], *Great Unwashed*, pp.204–5; Booth, *Poverty* I, pp.183–4; Bosanquet, *Rich and Poor*, pp.68–9.

31. Bunting, *School for Mothers*, pp.48, 75.
32. Greenwood, *Seven Curses*, 1869, p.7. He proposed a book on 'The Haunts and Homes of the British Baby'.
33. *Physical Deterioration Committee, Report*, 1904, p.56; c.f. Newman, *Infant Mortality*, p.247, and Bunting, *School for Mothers*, p.70. Health visitor Emilia Kanthack wanted dummies forbidden by law: see her *Preservation of Infant Life*, p.51. For 'maternal ignorance' see Davin, 'Imperialism and Motherhood'; Dyhouse, 'Working-class Mothers'; Lewis, *Politics of Motherhood*, chap.2.
34. F.G. Haworth, letter *BMJ*, 26 March 1904, p.763. C.f. Pritchard, *Infant Education*, pp.44–5; Maynard, *Baby*, p.19; Bunting, *School for Mothers*, pp.49, 69.
35. They were challenged by M. Pember Reeves and Anna Martin; c.f. also defence of parents by Dr F.J. Waldo in a discussion of overlaying, *BMJ*, 24 Sept. 1904, p.755.
36. Scharlieb, *Mother's Guide*, p.13.
37. Bray, 'Children of the Town' (1901), p.121.
38. Questionnaire on child street-sellers circulated in 1883 by Edwin Chadwick: answers to question 7 from M Division of the Metropolitan Police, Chadwick Papers 99, University College Library, London.
39. *Physical Deterioration Committee*, 1904, p.476, evidence Dr Lewis Hawkes, qq.13,013 to 13,017. C.f. Dr Louis Queston at 1912 International Eugenics Congress, quoted by Martin, 'Mother and Social Reform', p.1,060.
40. Booth, *Final Vol.*, p.42; see also *Poverty* 3, p.213 (Tabor, 'Education'); Booth, *Industry* 5, p.332; Paterson, *Across the Bridges*, p.56 ('little cruelty, perhaps too much kindness').
41. Booth, *Poverty* I, pp.159–60. C.f. P. Thompson, *The Edwardians*, p.62–9.
42. Booth, *Poverty* 3, p.213 (Tabor, 'Education').
43. Reeves, *Round About a Pound a Week*, pp.178–9.
44. Bray, 'Children of the Town' (1901), p.121.
45. Booth, *Poverty* 1, p.26. His metaphor of the photograph is based on the contemporary understanding that it combined realistic immediacy with scientific accuracy.
46. Descriptions of the categories are taken from Booth, *Poverty* 1, p.33. For critique see Stedman Jones, *Outcast London*, pp.54–6. Booth acknowledged that the teachers whose information he used might well have 'drawn lines of demarcation somewhat above the levels we have attempted to maintain', and that 'a very little change in this would be enough to throw large numbers down from E to D and C, or from C to B': *Poverty* 3, p. 200. He had also, however, tried to 'avoid understating': *Poverty* 1, pp. 5, 165, 173.
47. East London figures (*Poverty* 1, chap.2. pp.33–51) show greater extremes. Classes A and B are more numerous: together 12.50 per cent of the total population (1.25 and 11.25) rather than 8.4; C and D together are 20.8 rather than 22.3; E and F together 55 9, rather than 51.
48. Booth, *Poverty* 1, p.131.
49. Stedman Jones, *Outcast London*, p.56.
50. Members of the 'aristocracy of labour', whose composition, identity and numbers have been much disputed, would fall within this stratum. See Hobsbawm, 'Labour Aristocracy', 'Working-Class Culture', 'Making of the Working Class'; 'Debating Labour Aristocracy'; 'Aristocracy Reconsidered', and 'Artisans and Labour Aristocrats?'; Crossick, Artisan Elite, and 'Emergence of the Lower Middle Class'; Gray, *Labour Aristocracy*; Ross, 'Not the Sort', McClelland, 'Masculinity and the "Representative Artisan"'.
51. C.f. Johnson, *Saving and Spending*, p.2. Several households described in the early 1890s for the Economic Club show how poor health and irregular employment produced poverty and insecurity: Economic Club, *Family Budgets*, pp.18–19, 22, 24.
52. Note a railwayman who disguised his white hair for fear of being laid off: Thompson, *Edwardians*, p.53.
53. Stedman Jones, *Outcast London*, chaps. 1–7; Hobsbawm, 'Nineteenth-century Labour Market'. The economic crises of 1866–72 and 1883–8 caused unemployment and bankruptcy even among artisans and traders: c.f. Stedman Jones, 'Working-class Culture and Working-class Politics', pp.190–1.
54. Booth, *Poverty* 1, p.161.
55. For drinking practices of East London coopers and dockers, see Gilding, *Journeymen Coopers*. For comparative discussion of working-class drinking: *Movimento Operaio e Socialista* 8:1, 1985; Rosenzweig, *Eight Hours*, chap.2.
56. Booth, *Poverty* 3, p.200. C.f. also Jasper, *Hoxton Childhood*.

57. See for example zinc-caster father of Daisy Buckle, in Shoreditch in the 1890s, who took to drink and ill-used her and the children: Tottenham History Workshop, *How Things Were*, p.14. Settlement worker Anna Martin saw male alcoholism and related violence as a central problem ('Mother and Social Reform'; 'Working Women and Drink').
58. Booth, *Poverty* 1, p.161.
59. Quoted from Barnardo case records by Wagner, *Children of Empire*, pp.121–2.
60. Stanley, *Five Dials*, p.136.
61. Haw, *Workhouse to Westminster*, pp.1–10; 45–9.
62. Examples from *SBL Minutes*: 19 Nov. 1873, p.1,218 (Greenwich, Richard Betty); 7 Jan. 1874, p.78 (Hackney, Henry Leath); 18 March 1874, p.416 (Lambeth, James Henry Buckley); 15 April 1874, p.486 (Hackney, Charles Farey, blacksmith eight weeks out of work); 13 May 1874, p.620 (Finsbury, Elizabeth Hoy, chandler's widow); 6 Jan. 1875, p.143 (Greenwich, Eliza Harris, widow of coffee-house keeper); 24 Feb. 1875. p.769 (Southwark, David Crammond, boilermaker, ill and out of work nine weeks); 9 June 1875, p.769 (Southwark, Charles Dowd); 21 July 1875, p. 1,000 (Hackney, William Johns).
63. Crossick, *Artisan Elite*, p.174; see also table 6:3 p.112. He suggests that the gap between artisans and the rest may have been widening over these decades: such improvement would have meant greater security (through insurance especially) as well as better wages. See pp.108–9 (also his 'Emergence'); and on the insecurities of the shopkeeper and the salaried white-collar worker: pp.23–4. According to Arnold White ('Nomad Poor', pp.716–7), 'a large and growing class of temperate and would-be industrious folk', including artisans, were homeless and slept in London's casual wards.
64. Rowntree, *Poverty*, p.136; and see pp.52–85; *Human Needs*, p.34. This model has been widely used, e.g. by Anderson (*Family Structure*, esp. chaps 5 and 11); Foster (*Class Struggle*, pp.96–9); Tilly and Scott (*Women, Work, and the Family*, chap.6); and Parr (*Labouring Children*). It has also been challenged, extended and supplemented: c.f. Hareven (ed.), *Transitions*.
65. C.f. Paterson on this phase in woman's 'burdened life': *Across the Bridges*, pp.29–34; Reeves, *Pound a Week*, chap.11.
66. References to women's 'self-denial "for the sake of the kids"' (Free, *On the Wall*, p.143) are numerous. C.f. Martin, 'Mother and Social Reform'; Loane, *Englishman's Castle*, pp.182–9; Reeves, *Pound a Week*, and Davies, *Maternity*. Helen Bosanquet (née Dendy) drily recommended 'man's fortunate selfishness' for keeping him 'an efficient worker' (*Standard of Life*, pp.19–20); like Dora Bunting, medical officer at the St Pancras School for Mothers, she thought women should consider their own health (*School for Mothers*, p.39). For more recent discussion, see Oren, 'Welfare of Women', Tilly and Scott, *Women, Work and the Family*, pp. 138–40; Ross, 'Fierce Questions and Taunts', pp. 584–7; and on 'maternal altruism', Whitehead, '"I'm hungry, Mum"', especially pp. 102–11.
67. Davies, *Maternity*, p.5. Women were thought to need less food than men: see for example Bennett, 'Food and its Uses in Health', 1883, p.161. Newsholme (*Elementary Hygiene*, 1893, p.57) saw 'no reason why women should not require as much food as men, assuming that their frames are as large, and their work as laborious', but added that in more normal circumstances, women needed one tenth less food. Booth assumed that a woman's consumption would be 0.75 of a man's (*Poverty* 1, pp.132–6).
68. Roebuck and Slaughter, 'Ladies and Pensioners', p.108. The Test Census is printed as Appendix II to the *Report on the Aged Deserving Poor*, 1899. See also Thane, 'Women and the Poor Law', esp. pp.33–5.
69. See summary of return in the amount of aged pauperism in the Report, *R.C. Aged Poor*, 1895, p.xii.
70. *R.C. Poor Laws*, 1909, evidence Alderman Macdougal (Manchester), q.36,513, point 17.
71. Spender, *State and Pensions*, p.44.
72. From return in *R.C. Aged Poor*, 1895, p.xii. Wandsworth Guardians Workhouse Subcommittee in 1911 were 'much struck with the number of married men, especially over sixty, whose wives had left them, or were remaining outside and earning their livelihood': *Streatham News*, 4 Nov. 1911.
73. Booth, *Pensions*, p.4; c.f. *R.C. Aged Poor*, 1895, p.cvi; his evidence, q.10,863.
74. On older men's difficulty in getting work see for example Spender, *State and Pensions*, chap.2; *R.C. Aged Poor* 1895, evidence of George Lansbury q.13,905; of A.R. Jephcott (Birmingham engineer) qq.14,573–5; and of Henry Allen (Birmingham carpenter) q.16,679 ('a woman can struggle on by charring and other simple work, find a living

where a man cannot, where a man can starve'). Booth noted that men's effective working life was ten years shorter in towns, not only because of worse health but because they were 'accounted incapable sooner still': *Pensions*, p.321.

75. C.f. Quadagno, *Aging*, pp.152–3 (using 1901 census): most older women with a recorded occupation worked past sixty-five; their rates of retirement were lower than men's; and high rates of retirement happened only after seventy-five. See also pp.158–62 and table 6:6, on occupations.

76. C.f. Tebbutt, *Making Ends Meet*, pp.35–6.

77. Booth, *Pensions*, p.326. Anderson (*Family*, pp.140–7) notes the link between grandmothers (or substitutes), child care and working mothers. (His figures do not show more mothers taken in than fathers.)

78. Dolling, *Ten Years*, p.123.

79. C.f. Quadagno, *Aging*, p.144: 'many examples can be found of grateful children supporting aged mothers in their declining years'.

80. In Arthur Harding's memoir (Samuel, *East End Underworld*), both parents survive into old age, and he lives with his mother and sister till marriage then next door to them (he stayed in Bethnal Green 'longer than I should have done' because of 'me mother, me sister and me brothers'), but his father fades out of household and narrative.

81. Booth, *Industry* vol. 4, p.323. See also Thompson, *Childhoods*, p.23, where the child Tommy Morgan is sent by his father to an adult sister, Lily, to borrow money, and she says ' "What? Not me...If I had a mint of money...I wouldn't let him have it to get in the pub." '

82. *R.C. Aged Poor* 1895 xiv, evidence Sir Hugh Owen (Permanent Secretary to the Local Government Board) q.206.

83. Booth, *Pensions*, p.6 and see pp.325–7. Also Spender, *State and Pensions*, chap.1; Meacham, *Life Apart*, pp.57–8.

84. Frank S. (b. 1884) used to accompany his cabinet-maker father from Battersea to Hoxton, to visit the grandmother and take her something (transcript, p.38); Mrs C. (b. Bermondsey, 1893) took sixpence from her father to her granny 'not too far away' every Sunday morning (transcript p.37). Rose Wheeler (b. 1896) made Sunday visits to her grandparents 'taking cakes baked by her mother and bringing back washing for her mother to do on Monday': Tottenham, *How Things Were*, p.100. Grace Foakes (b. Wapping, 1903) recalled how her mother's eighty-year-old aunt, after visits when she 'borrowed' a shilling, would 'keep away for a week or two' till Grace was sent to ask why she hadn't been round: *Between High Walls*, p.21.

85. Booth, *Pensions*, pp.7–8.

86. Redfern, *Story of the CWS*, p.216.

87. Rowntree, *Poverty*, pp.441–5.

88. Rowntree, *Poverty*, pp.441–5, table of proportions of the population in poverty in different age groups. C.f. Bowley and Hurst, *Livelihood*, p.47; and Foster, *Class Struggle*, p.96.

2 Where the Poor Lived

1. Sims, *How the Poor Live*, p.13.
2. Stedman Jones, *Outcast London*, p.208; and for a comprehensive account, part 2, 'Housing and the Casual Poor'.
3. Reeves, *Pound a Week*, p.39.
4. C.f. Acorn, *Multitude*, p.130, for a man from Enfield working in Bethnal Green who 'took home a week's groceries in a sack, and often tramped to work and back when short of the twopenny railway fare'.
5. By 1908 the London County Council claimed that with low rents on their suburban estates and low fares on their trams it was cheaper to move out of central London (Barker and Robbins, *London Transport* 2, p.98); but the new estates could not accommodate everybody nor were they to everyone's taste. C.f. (after WW1) Jasper, *Hoxton Childhood*, pp.108–11; Ron Barnes, *Coronation Cups*, p.46; and see Dyos, 'Slums of Victorian London', for Camberwell's growth through centrifugal migration.
6. Booth, *Poverty* 1, p.277 (on South London).
7. Lees, *Exiles of Erin*, p.60; Sponza, *Italian Immigrants*, p.19; Fishman, *East End Jewish Radicals*, chap.2.
8. Lees, *Exiles of Erin*, p.63.

9. SBL *Minutes School Management Committee*, 13 July 1888, p.1,199.
10. Booth, *Poverty* 1, pp.26–7; also *Poverty* 3, pp.61, 278. Less credibly, an organizer for the Metropolitan Association for Befriending Young Servants wrote (E.S., 'Women Who Ought to Work', *Eastward Ho* 3, May-Oct. 1885, p.49) that their registers showed families so nomadic that they moved: 'almost from day to day, and in the course of a month or two, make a cheerful trip from Stepney Green via Whitechapel to Shoreditch, and then after a few pleasant days at Bethnal Green and a peep at Mile End, back again, via Shadwell and Wapping to Stepney as before'.
11. SBL *Committee on Capricious Migration of Children*, 1878–9; see also Rubinstein, *Attendance*, pp.64–5. C.f. SBL *Minutes* 7 Dec. 1893, p.11; 1 Feb. 1894, p.389; 19 April 1894.
12. White, 'Nomad Poor'; Kline, 'Truancy [and]...the Migratory Instinct' (1898); and for the Irish poor as 'rolling stones', see Lees, *Exiles of Erin*, p.58.
13. Simpkinson, *South London Parish*, p.244.
14. Chance, *Welfare and Protection*, p.20.
15. But note the 'immobility' of casual labour, especially in the docks: Stedman Jones, *Outcast London*, esp. pp.81–6; Hobsbawm, 'London Labour Market'. Women's and children's work opportunities were also localized.
16. Logbook, Gainsborough Road, 21 Aug. 1875. It had opened the previous week.
17. Church (b. 1893), *Over the Bridge*, pp.14–21.
18. See Allen, 'Education in Battersea' (1870); Balfour on Battersea, Booth, *Poverty* 1, part 4, chap.2; Stedman Jones, *Outcast London*, pp.40, 55, 208; Roebuck, *Urban Development*, chap.7; Pudney, *Crossing London's River*; Creighton, 'Battersea and New Unionism'; and for the twentieth century, Stanley and Griffiths, *For Love and Shillings*.
19. Roebuck, *Urban Development*, p.128; Booth, *Poverty* 1, p.278.
20. People's Autobiography, *The Island*, pp.9–10; Booth, *Religious Influences* 3, p.101. See also Meacham on successive phases of neighbourhoods (*Life Apart*, pp.45–52): he adds to Roberts' label (*Classic Slum*) those of 'heroic' and 'post-classic'.
21. White, *Worst Street*, pp.11–23.
22. For migratory habits and seasonal migrations, see Samuel, 'Comers and Goers', esp. from p.131. Stedman Jones, *Outcast London*, pp.88–92, distinguishes casual from vagrant labour, but the two groups were perhaps less separate in people's experience than in historical analysis: there was overlap and movement between them.
23. Logbook, Coleraine Park, 27 Oct. 1882; see also 25 Nov. 1881; 8 Sept. 1882; 19 Oct. 1883. (My thanks for access to Christine Protz of Tottenham History Workshop.)
24. Booth, *Poverty* 1, p.257 (Argyle).
25. O'Neill, *Pull No More Bines*, especially chap.10.
26. See 1880s exposés such as Sims, *How the Poor Live*; Mearns, *Bitter Cry* (which draws on Sims); William Booth, *In Darkest London*; and evidence to *R.C. Housing of the Working Classes*, PP 1884–5.
27. *East End News*, 17 July 1869. See also Vallès, *Rue à Londres*, p.36; *Social Notes* 2, 9 Nov. 1878, p.567; Meacham, *Life Apart*, p.31. For smells in Bermondsey during his boyhood, see G. Sadler (b. 1908) in Peckham, *Times*, pp.21–2.
28. Paterson, *Bridges*, p.10.
29. C.f. Reeves, *Pound a Week*, especially chap.3. Incidence of infant mortality was higher in top-floor households in Kensington in 1897 (15 cases out of 43; 10 lived on first floor, six on ground, and six in basement): *MOH London, Report*, 1897, p.45.
30. In the 'worst streets' of Battersea moves were often made within three streets, and in a year or two the exiles might be back 'within a few doors of one of their many forsaken homes': Booth, *Poverty* 1, p.296 (Balfour on Battersea).
31. For neighbourhood networks, Meacham, *Life Apart*, chap.2, esp. pp.44–9; for women's mutual aid, Ross, 'Survival Networks'. For men's networks and work, Hobsbawm, 'London Labour Market'; also Lees, *Exiles of Erin*, pp.88–92.
32. C.f. Tebbutt, *Making Ends Meet*, pp.20–1.
33. In Maugham's novel, *Of Human Bondage* (which drew on his own experience in Lambeth in the 1890s), the medical student attending a birth where the woman died asked the husband if anyone in the house would put him up (so he needn't sleep with the corpse), but the midwife explained that they had just moved in and didn't know anyone yet (pp.564–6). C.f. Reeves, *Pound a Week*, pp.39–41.
34. John Bellamy (b. 1884) had 'twenty-one different abodes' in his first fourteen years (mostly in Hoxton): 'We just could not pay the rent': 'Looking Back', p.2. See also Booth,

Poverty 1, p.296 (Balfour on Battersea): in the 'worst streets' moving was 'closely connected with arrears of rent'; and Meacham, *Life Apart*, pp.42–3.

35. Rolph, *Particulars*, p.11. In Shoreditch around 1917 costers' barrows were for hire by the
hour, day or week; the rate for a day was tuppence: Jack Welch (b. Shoreditch, 1903), ms.
memoir, p.32. The horse and van used by the Jaspers in 1914 cost 1s. 3d. an hour ('We
must have thought we was the aristocracy after previous moves with a barrow'): *Hoxton
Childhood*, p.56.

36. Lewis, ms. memoir, p.3.

37. Thompson, *Childhoods*, 1981, pp.13–4.

38. Linton, *Not Expecting Miracles*, p.2.

39. Chaplin, *Autobiography*, p.33.

40. Pritchett, *Cab at the Door*, pp.26, 30.

41. Booth, *Poverty* 1, p.296 (Balfour, 'Battersea'); c.f. Booth, *Final Vol.*, p.177.

42. C.f. McLeod, *Class and Religion*, p.5; he quotes Booth, *Poverty* 3, part iv, p.166: 'Southwark
is moving to Walworth, Walworth to North Brixton and Stockwell, while the servant-keep-
ers of Outer London go to Croydon and other places.'

43. Booth, *Final Vol.*, pp.170–1. C.f. White, *Worst Street*, pp.12–14.

44. C.f. Paterson, *Bridges*, p.19; Reeves, *Pound a Week*, p.32 (shared access), p.33 (washing
arrangements). Eliza Henman remembered that to buy hot pies from a late street seller
without disturbing the landlady ('a bit of a misery'): 'we lowered a pail on a string out of
the window and he'd put two pies in': Richman, *Fly a Flag*, p.50.

45. Booth, *Poverty* 1, p.159.

46. Jephson, *My Work*, p.15.

47. Richman, *Fly a Flag*, p.22.

48. Greenwood, *Little Ragamuffin*, pp.185–6.

49. For a neighbour who called the police on being woken by the sounds of a child being
kicked and beaten by his father (1876): Wagner, *Children of Empire*, p.126.

50. NSPCC *Annual Reports* show many cases were reported by neighbours, whether to police
or to the society (29 per cent and 71 per cent respectively of 955 London cases in
1889–90): my thanks to Susan Magarey for sharing research on this. C.f. Conan Doyle,
'Copper Beeches', 1892: 'There is no lane so vile that the scream of a tortured child, or
the thud of a drunkard's blow, does not beget sympathy and indignation among the
neighbours, and then the whole machinery of justice is so close that a word of complaint
can set it going'; and Ross, 'Labour and Love', p.83.

51. Mrs B. (b. Southend before 1914) attributed frequent moves during her childhood to her
mother's fear that the neighbours would call in the NSPCC. (Comment during pensioners' class at the Lee Centre, Lewisham, 1980.)

52. Southgate, *That's the Way it Was*, p.33.

53. *Eastern Post*, 19 Oct. 1901, reported in Bermant, *London's East End*, p.147. C.f. Arkell,
'Notes on the Map', p.xxxix.

54. Florence S. (b. Deptford, 1904), transcript p.44.

55. Jasper, *Hoxton Childhood*, p.49; People's Autobiography, *The Island*, p.25; *Hoxton Childhood*,
p.61.

56. Elsie M. (b. Hackney, 1905), transcript pp.C4–5. (In the same passage she presents the
urge as hereditary: 'my sister takes after her, she likes to move a lot'.) See also pp.1–4.

57. C.f. (earlier) Dickens' Betty Higden: *Our Mutual Friend*, 1864–5, esp. chap.16; see also
Booth, *Pensions*, pp.16–19; Digby, *Pauper Palaces*, chap.12. Dying in the workhouse was
dreaded, not least because the 1832 Anatomy Act allowed dissection in anatomy schools
of 'unclaimed' corpses of workhouse and hospital dead: Richardson, *Death, Dissection and
the Destitute*.

58. For 1870s opposition to out-relief to widows because it helped them survive on impossibly low earnings and so undercut the wages of other female workers: see *Local Government
Board, Report*, 1873–4, Appendix B (Henry Longley, Poor Law Administration in London),
pp.179–82; *Poor Law Schools Committee*, PP 1896, especially discussion between witness Miss
Baker (Holborn Guardian), Mrs Barnett, and Sir John Gorst (qq.2,564–71) about giving
widowed mothers the amount paid when children were boarded out; for figures on out-
relief and indoor relief to widows with small children, see *R.C. Poor Law, Report*, 1909, part
II, p. 35, paras 83–9. See also Thane, 'Women and the Poor Law', pp. 41–4.

59. *Brixton and Lambeth Gazette*, 3 March 1911, p.5.

60. White, *Rothschild Buildings*, p.159.

61. *Crèche Annual, 2nd year,* 1872–3, p.19; see also SBL *Minutes* 24 Sept. 1873, p.957, Hackney: Amelia Fletcher and Mary Ashton; and 19 Nov. 1873, p.1,218, Hackney: Esther Scott, charwoman with three children whose father is in lunatic asylum, 'an ailing woman...struggling hard to keep the children and herself out of the workhouse'.

62. *Crèche Annual, 18th year,* 1888–9, p.12.

63. Sims, *How the Poor Live,* p.54. He also cites a Mrs B. who had added to her own children 'a little girl whose father had gone off tramping in search of work'. William Nn applied the saying 'It's the Poor that Helps the Poor when Poverty Knocks at your Door' to his father's adoption. C.f. Barnes, *Coronation Cups and Jam Jars,* pp.37–8: his grandmother in the 1930s despite her ill-health took on four children because their parents were in hospital, and on the parents' death tried to keep them but was thwarted by her concerned relatives.

64. Kimmins, *Polly of Parker's Rents,* p.94.

65. The orphaned mother of Florence S. (b. Deptford, 1904) spent her childhood with older sisters each in turn: transcript, p.13. For other adoptions by relatives see Rogers, *Labour, Life and Literature,* p.19; Alice Lewis, ms. autobiography, p.3: 'when my aunt Aggie died, mum took in one of her three children, Florrie, for seven years'; Black, *Married Women's Work,* pp.87, 95, 113. See also *Crèche Annual, 21st year,* 1891–2, p.12; Greenwood, *Prisoner in the Dock,* p.58; *Bulletin East London History Society* 30, Sept. 1974, p.2 (reference in accounts book of the Black Eagle Brewery, Spitalfields, to pension for an 86-year-old woman who 'after Drayman Bright's death took charge of his children and brought them up'); Rolph, *Particulars,* pp.76–7, 110; Ezard, *Battersea Boy,* p.28: a park-keeper's wife who took in five children when their mother died so that the father could continue his work as a late-night waiter. C.f. Vincent, *Bread,* p.66; Anderson, *Family,* pp.148–9.

66. SBL *Minutes,* 26 March 1873, pp.326–7, Greenwich; 4 Feb. 1874, p.258, Greenwich; 14 April 1875, p.532, Westminster; 30 June 1875, pp.901–5, Finsbury. For applications on behalf of children apparently not related, see SBL *Minutes,* 28 April 1875, p.581, Greenwich; 30 June 1875, p.905, Southwark; 4 Aug. 1875, p.1,105, Finsbury.

67. The coroner Edwin Lankester gave evidence in 1871 that he held 'a good many' inquests on illegitimate children brought up by grandparents, 'but very few where the mother is taking care of them; the mother, as a rule, does not take care of an illegitimate child'. Of course when she was able to do so and to breast-feed it, the child had a much better chance of survival. *S.C. Protection of Infant Life,* PP 1871, evidence q.3,085. In the same enquiry, Daniel Cooper, secretary of the Children's Rescue Society, defended the families who took in such babies against charges of avarice and wilful neglect, and agreed that it was 'the kindliness that exists among the poorer classes in these matters in an immense proportion, and not the payment of money' that led to the children being taken in: evidence qq.2,597–604, 2,668.

68. See for instance SBL *Minutes,* 23 July 1873, p.817, Hackney: a shoemaker dying of consumption with three children at home and 'the two eldest...away with relations'.

69. The ship's carpenter father of Amelia K. (born Poplar, 1878) was away in Argentina for eight years; her mother had a live-in dressmaking job, and her parents-in-law took the eldest girl while her parents had the two boys (Amelia and three others were born after his return): transcript pp.1–6. C.f. SBL *Minutes,* 9 July 1873, p.683, Southwark: an unmarried woman hawker with two children and a third 'under the care of an uncle' ('the father has deserted them').

70. Rose U. (b. Bow, 1897), eight when her parents split up, often stayed with grandparents when there were 'problems at home', especially later when her mother lived with a man she hated: transcript pp.5, 18–19.

71. C.f. Ada Bennett (b. Walworth, 1901): her mother died when she was three; a ten-month-old sister was brought up by friends 'as their own' (they did not meet for seventeen years); while she and her five-year-old brother went first to her father's aunt (who had ten children of her own), then 'ended up in the workhouse off and on for the next eight years', till her father's remarriage: Peckham, *Times,* p.85.

72. C.f. Mr White (b. Hoxton, 1896): old people often lived alone 'but there was always someone round'. His grandmother in Southend used to have his sister down there, and on her marriage wanted him, 'but Mother said no': Richman, *Fly a Flag,* p.36.

73. Newton, *Years of Change,* p.7. (His father was also angry because the uncle took him to hear socialist speakers in Victoria Park.)

74. R. Burr Litchfield suggests that extra household members (kin or lodgers) were more

likely where there were young children: 'Family and the Mill', p.192.

75. After her death, in the interim before the widowed father moved to Fulham and remarried, twelve-year-old Harold spent the summer term with relatives in Hounslow, and nine-year-old Cecil was 'for part of the time billetted on our Grandma Speed...and for part of it on Aunt Carrie', who lived close to each other in Fulham: Rolph, *Particulars*, pp.82, 68, 72, 69.

76. MacDonald, *Women in the Printing Trades*, p.103.

77. C.f. Miss N. (b. Shadwell, 1895), whose mother's mother looked after six grandchildren while her daughter went out cleaning: transcript, pp.1–6; and Mrs K. (b. Battersea, 1897), whose mother worked in a laundry while the grandmother looked after them (though she may have lived nearby rather than with them): transcript, p.4.

78. For an important general discussion of lodging, including the confusion in the census between 'visitor' and 'lodger' and 'boarder', see Davidoff, 'Separation of Home and Work?'. The extent and character of 'lodging' in London in this period still needs extensive census research. Lees suggests (*Exiles of Erin*, pp.133–5) that Irish households in London were more likely than English to have lodgers: 'only 4.8 per cent of all London households included lodgers', but 18.5 per cent of Irish households and with unskilled Irish 32 per cent. Her discussion relates to 1851 and 1861, a period of influx when the numerous arrivals would stay for a time in existing households before setting up their own. When the flow diminished, later, so possibly did proportions of lodgers. But the gap between her 4.8 and 18.5 or 21 per cents is one of class as well as nationality and figures for lodgers within the working class generally may not have been so different. In Preston in 1851, for instance, 23 per cent of households had lodgers. They were concentrated amongst the poor: the figure for households headed by women was 33 per cent, by handloom weavers 38 per cent, and so on. See Anderson, *Family*, pp. 45–8 and Table 10. Armstrong gives 15 per cent for mid–nineteenth-century York, 17.5 per cent (quoting Drake and Pearce) for Ashford, and 21.8 per cent (quoting R.J. Smith) for Nottingham: 'A Note', pp. 210–12.

79. C.f. Black, *Married Women's Work*, p.63: Mrs W., a boot and shoe maker, whose husband earned 'a small regular wage', had five children, an old father (nearly blind), and mother and widowed sister 'for whom she did what she could'. She let out one room, but the investigator 'had her doubts' whether the lodger 'paid his 4s. with any regularity', and 'strongly suspected' that, when he was not in work, he shared their food.

80. Wright, *Some Habits*, pp.210, 215. Comparable relationships between landlady and lodger occur in Dickens' novels, e.g. Copperfield's with Mrs Micawber. See also Willis, *101 Jubilee Road*, p.103 (young craftsman in South London lodgings in the 1890s); and Jacobs, *Out of the Ghetto*, p.19: Leah Goldstein, to whom his family let one of their rooms in the 1920s, became an 'intimate member of my family'. For a servant closely integrated with the family (though finally left behind) see Rolph, *Particulars*, pp. 14–15, 111–12.

81. 'One of his beds was the old Blackwall Stairs....He used to tear large posters off the wall to cover himself and keep warm': William Nn, ms. autobiography, p.15.

82. William Nn, ms. autobiography, p.10.

83. Jasper, *Hoxton Childhood*, p.8.

84. William Nn, ms. autobiography, pp.16, 7, 9.

85. Sims, 'Evicted London', p.207. See also Anon, *Narrow Waters*, pp.105–6: when a demolition project in East London in 1905 meant the eviction of several households, 'before the day was out, every one of the twenty or so inhabitants had been taken in by neighbours as poor and crowded as themselves'.

86. Mary H. (born Canning Town, 1895): transcript, p.26.

87 *Crèche Annual, 17th year*, 1887–8, p.9 (also quoted in Hilton, *Marie Hilton*, p.101): Mrs Hilton's comment: 'It is touching to note the admirable way in which many poor women live. Although their own lives are one long sacrifice, they will cheerfully undertake any service for one who appears to be in greater suffering.'

88. Newton, *Years of Change*, p.45.

89. Anderson (*Family*, p.150) notes how depression in mid-century Lancashire led to 'huddling' ('more and more houses became empty, and more and more had two families sharing the rent and fuel and pooling their resources'), and suggests that 'wherever possible' (but not always) the sharers were kin.

90. SBL Minutes, 4 Aug. 1875, p.1,106: Elizabeth Peneton aged sixty with her daughter earned 12s. washing by which they supported themselves and the daughter's nine-year-

old; see also 12 March 1873, p.261, Louisa Beynon. C.f. Bedford Institute, 5th Annual Report, 1871, p.63, for an elderly widow and daughter working together at folding envelopes; PRO file ED/14/19 4 May 1883 (Shoreditch cases) for French polishing by widow working with her mother, which earned 11s a week for a family of seven; [Harkness], *Toilers*, chap. 2: mother-in-law and daughter-in-law, living together and jointly making matchboxes (Shoreditch); households 1,3 and 28 in sample case-notes for a very poor street, Booth, *Poverty* 1, pp.7–11; and Malcolmson, 'Laundresses', pp.454–5.

91. SBL *Minutes*, 7 May 1873, p.425; 29 April 1874, p.543. C.f. Anderson, *Family*, p.144–6.
92. SBL *Minutes*, 26 March 1873, p.327, Greenwich: the Melliship household. ('Man and wife appear to be hardworking people, but the children are constantly running the streets and are badly behaved.')
93. SBL *Minutes*, 4 Aug. 1875, p.1,104.
94. C.f. Mrs Finch and fourteen-year-old Jane, in COS case cited Fido, 'Charity Organization Society', p.225–6.
95. See for instance details reported in inquest in the *Beehive* 7, Jan. 1871, p.7; c.f. SBL *Minutes*, 10 July 1872, p.496, Greenwich: Mrs Mary Ann Heritage, trying to support three children (no word from husband who had left for Australia), living rent-free with her brother; *Annual Report on the Health of Kensington*, 1876, p.30: a house hit by smallpox was shared by two families headed by brothers (as well as another family and a single man occupying the kitchen). *MOH London, Report*, 1895, p.38 (a typhus case where two sisters and the child of one share a back room in Whitechapel); two spinster sisters who earned a joint living by washing and mangling, remembered by Newton, *Years of Change*, p.6; Black and Meyer (eds), *Makers of our Clothes*, cases 51, 287, 339.
96. Bowley and Hurst, *Livelihood and Poverty*, pp.62–3 (Northampton), and pp.25–7 (general discussion).
97. C.f. Mrs Layton (b. Bethnal Green, 1866), in Davies, *Life as we have Known it*, pp.15–19.

3 Close Quarters

1. According to Llewellyn Smith's *New Survey* (p.147), rents rose between 1880 and 1890 by 33.3 per cent in Stepney and 26.7 per cent in Bethnal Green; the mean increase for twenty London boroughs was 13 per cent.
2. Booth, *Poverty* 1, pp.29–32.
3. Reactions were mixed. Lord Salisbury quoted his assertions in proposing the Royal Commission on the Housing of the Working Classes: *Hansard 3rd series* (Lords), vol. 284 (22 Feb. 1884), col. 1690. An Education Department minute had called Williams's first allegations of 'overpressure' 'a conceited and insolent attack', and him 'a flippant young gentleman'; and another referred to 'those superfluous officers the Board Inspectors' (as opposed to Department ones): PRO ED/14/19. (C.f. Gautrey, *Lux Mihi Laus*, p.120; and Sneyd-Kynnersley, *HMI*, p.138.) The School Board in 1889 called for legislation to reduce overcrowding: Rubinstein, *Attendance*, p.57.
4. Williams, *Overpressure*, reprinted from letters to *The Times* in 1884.
5. Williams, *Overpressure*, p.13.
6. See table in Booth, *Final Volume*, p.4; Lawrence, 'Housing Problem' (1901), esp. pp.64–8; and Burnett, *Housing*, p.156.
7. Booth, *Poverty* 3, pp.199–200.
8. Williams, *Overpressure*, p.13.
9. Lawrence, 'Housing problem', p.64. C.f. the artisan Thomas Wright's descriptions of living in a crowded court because of housing shortage, in [Wright], *Great Unwashed*, 1868.
10. Booth, *Final Volume*, pp.4–5; and for standards and definitions of overcrowding, Llewellyn Smith, *New Survey*, 1930, pp.150–3.
11. For these questions in national context see Meacham, *Life Apart*, chap.2.
12. C.f. 1930s Battersea mother with five surviving children, quoted in Rice, *Working Class Wives*, p.129: 'I expect some people think living in two rooms one didn't have much work to do. I would rather clean a house down than clean my two rooms every day'.
13. Paterson, *Bridges*, p.10; see also *LCC Public Control Committee, Report*, 1904, Appendix: 'Smoke Nuisance in London'.
14. For flies, see *MOH London, Report*, 1907, Appendix 2: 'Nuisance from Flies' (Dr Hamer), pp.5–7.

15. C.f. Jacobs, *Out of the Ghetto*, p.15: 'Monday to Friday, day and half the night, was one long "wash-day" '. We were never free of masses of sheets, pillow slips and various items of clothing in different stages of attention. I remember well the awful smell which was always with us'.

16. Economic Club, *Family Budgets*, p.23. Still more crowded was a widow in Spitalfields in 1871, supporting herself and her little boy by mangling: her one small room was 'nearly filled with the bedstead and mangle': *Bedford Institute, 5th Annual Report*, 1871, p.62.

17. Thompson, *Thomas*, p.302, referring to Southwark in the 1890s.

18. See Arlidge, *Hygiene*; Oliver, *Dangerous Trades*. C.f. 1879 inquest on a St Pancras home-worker aged forty-eight, who 'became blind through the colours used in her trade', flower-making: *Women's Union Journal*, Sept. 1879, p.7.

19. See PRO HO 45 10116/B12393N for file on inquiry into work where anthrax cases occurred, including hair-sorting and brush-making; also Oliver, *Dangerous Trades*, p.660.

20. On homework, see Women's Industrial Council, *Home Industries* (1897), and *Home Industries* (1908); Mudie-Smith, *Sweated Industries*; S.C. *Home Work*, PP 1907 vi and 1908 viii; Black, *Sweated Industry*; White, *Rothschild Buildings*, pp.235–9; and Chapter 10 below.

21. Samuel, *Underworld*, pp.22–3.

22. Paterson, *Bridges*, pp.52–3.

23. Ethel V., transcript, side 1, p.27.

24. C.f. Bibby, *Pudding Lady*, p.73: a wife whose compositor husband was on night work was 'in a rather nervous state and worries if the slightest noise is made', and tried to have the two children out all morning.

25. Vallès noted that people in poor quarters, English and French alike, preferred to stay out of the wretched homes, without light or air or space. A poor London woman went out on the doorstep to breathe and to talk with the woman next door, suckling her own baby or the other's; the street was 'le salon des misérables,...boudoir des mères, jardin des mômes' (*Rue à Londres*, p.37).

26. Reeves, *Pound a Week*, p.52.

27. S.C. *(Lords) Means of Divine Worship*, PP 1857–8, evidence Rev. J. Colbourne (St Matthew's, Bethnal Green), q.644. Hannah Cullwick, as a servant in Margate in 1867, slept on an 'old turn-up straw bed in the kitchen': Stanley, *Cullwick*, pp.59, 61.

28. Gompers, *Seventy Years*, p.2. He and four brothers shared such a bed in a one-room Spitalfields home in the 1850s.

29. Alice Lewis (b. Fulham, 1898) recalled straw mattresses as 'very hard'; her mother bought flock ones as an improvement: 'They was always lumpy and...mum would 'ave one down, unpick it and we girls would sit there smoothing out the lumps. Then we'd stuff it back and sew up the mattress': ms. memoir, p.4. These stuffings (horsehair especially) shed much dust.

30. In Ridge's novel, *Mord Em'ly*, the servant heroine, Maud Emily, loses place and therefore bed, and a friendly police sergeant and his wife put her up on a 'chair bedstead' in their attic (p.239). C.f. Gissing, *Odd Women*, p.70; Acorn, *Multitude*, pp.192–3 (one which kept collapsing), pp.276–7 (one 'absolutely without temperament'); Bibby, *Pudding Lady*, pp.46, 52.

31. Samuel, *Underworld*, p.63.

32. Lewis, ms. memoir, pp.3–4 (her brother-in-law's family). See also White, *Rothschild Buildings*, pp.50–1. In the 1900s a servant's fold-away press bedstead cost three guineas from Heal's: Laski, 'Domestic Life', p.146.

33. Gamble, *Chelsea Child*, pp.14–16. Nasaw, *Children of the City*, p.8 (from Ravage, *American in the Making*, 1917), cites a new arrival in New York amazed to see his relatives' apartment transformed into a camp where slept two families and assorted relations and boarders.

34. For two-bedroomed flats in an East-End model block, see White, *Rothschild Buildings*, pp.44–53. When old working-class housing is modernized it is common to merge two rooms or even two flats into one: expectations of space today are higher in all classes.

35. Reeves, *Pound a Week*, pp.46–7.

36. The earliest memory of Alice Linton (b. Shoreditch, 1908) was 'of sitting up in bed with my mother and watching our local midwife bathing my new baby brother....Mother was sitting up in bed trying to put a clean vest on me, but I struggled, not wanting to miss anything': *Not Expecting Miracles*, p.1.

37. Burnett, *Useful Toil*, p.215.

38. Paterson, *Bridges*, p.15.

39. The mother of Ada S. (b. Spitalfields, 1884) had a little front room 'like the holy of holies', used only on Sundays: transcript, side 1, p.46. Parlours in North Street, Cambridge Heath, were used for sleeping but by day reverted to sanctity: Southgate, *The Way it Was*, pp.18, 23, 67.

40. Head, 'The Church and the People', p.264.

41. Rolph, *Particulars*, p.42.

42. There is little on such questions in the conventional documentary evidence; and no oral material for the earlier part of my period. Segregation and taboos may have been gaining importance, possibly in part because of middle-class influence, e.g. at school.

43. Reeves, *Pound a Week*, pp.55–6; White, *Rothschild Buildings*, p.48.

44. C.f. *MOH London, Report*, 1906, Appendix 3 ('Tenement Houses'), pp.1–3, for homes where 'many thousands of foot-tons of work per annum need to be performed merely on carrying water upstairs' and bringing down slops.

45. C.f. Willis, *Jubilee Road*, p.105: 'nights are reserved, one for the boys, another for the girls, and the last, usually very late Friday, for Tom and his wife'.

46. White, *Rothschild Buildings*, pp.48–9. In winter the fear of catching cold on the way home might discourage baths out: c.f. Lilian Blore (b. 1905) in Peckham, *Times*, p.66 (and for public baths recalled by Stan Hall (b. 1910), see p.65). See also Allin and Wesker, *Say Goodbye*, p.[25].

47. Goulston Street Baths, Whitechapel ('possibly the best in London') had sixty-eight baths for men and only twenty-one for women. Jewish women also used the Mikveh (communal baths) for ritual cleansing after menstruation and before marriage: White, *Rothschild Buildings*, pp.48, 49.

48. Loane, *Simple Sanitation*, p.67. C.f. Reeves, *Pound a Week*, pp.55–6.

49. Elsie M. (b. Hackney, 1905), transcript, p.B27.

50. Samuel, *Underworld*, pp.55, 54.

51. Mrs T. (age not known) in class at London City Lit, 7 Dec. 1976. A Stoke Newington child orphaned and sent to a Home in 1906 was outraged when slapped on the bare bottom: at three she already knew 'that part of my anatomy was not supposed to be exposed to anyone's gaze': Wheway, *Edna's Story*, p.9.

52. Mr M. (b. Islington, 1870) was one of six children who slept in two rooms 'boys and girls separate'; his mother 'watched that. Mm. Separate, not mixed. Pretty good woman': transcript, pp.49, 59.

53. Foakes, *Walls*, p.4; my notes from Hackney People's Autobiography group, 31 Jan. 1973. Note also defence of his overcrowded Clerkenwell parishioners' morals by Rev. B.O. Sharp, *R.C. Housing*, PP 1884–5, evidence, qq.1,297–9, 1,375–7.

54. Thompson, *Childhoods*, p.13.

55. Peckham, *Times*, p.33.

56. While mother-daughter and father-son sharing was acceptable, father-daughter was not, and mother-son not always: when Edward Humphries, aged thirteen, got a live-in job as a page-boy, his mother was relieved because of hints that it was not proper for her to share with such a big boy: Burnett, *Useful Toil*, p.210. See also White, *Rothschild Buildings*, p.50–2.

57. See for instance Bessie C. (b. 1893), whose mother made boxes from 8.0 a.m. to 8.0 p.m.: transcript, pp.5–6, 9–10; and Mrs K. (b. Battersea, 1897), whose mother worked the same hours in a laundry: transcript, pp.4–5. Because of women's long hours many crèches were open till eight, some till nine, and one in a poor laundry district (Blechynden Street) 'till 10 if necessary'. See Howgrave, 'Public Nurseries' (1872), p.147; 'Infant Nurseries in West London', *Women and Work*, 1874, p.18; 'Latymer Road Mission: Our Work', *Light and Shade*, 1882, p.18, March 1882, pp.38, 54; Chadwick Papers, 99, police answers to questionnaire (1884), M division (Southwark); McCulloch, *Open Church for the Unchurched* (West London Mission crèche founded in Soho in 1887); *LCC Public Control Committee, Report*, 1904, report on crèches.

58. This employment grew from the turn of the century. William E. (b. Wapping, 1897), youngest of seven, spent lonely evenings waiting for his office-cleaning mother to get back, around 10.30 or 11.00. His father was usually in the pub. They sometimes met her from work, and the parents had a drink while he waited outside: transcript, pp.8, 26.

59. *Mary Ward Centre, Report*, 1909, p.7: amongst 100 poor Deptford children, sixty-seven, a third under seven, 'were found to be locked out of their homes after school hours till seven, eight or even nine o'clock at night'. Some were given tea by neighbours.

60. London, *People of the Abyss*, p.49.
61. Ten-year-old Arthur Harding, with his younger sister Mary, helped on the market stalls run by their mother and older sister (then fourteen), and on Saturday nights 'would finish about 12.30 to 1 o'clock': Samuel, *Underworld*, p.61. See also *Employment of Schoolchildren Committee*, PP 1902, qq.896–9; Anon, *Children and the Labour Question*, pp.34–5; Cunynghame, *Street Trading*, p.4.
62. Even there, an eleven-year-old's birthday party could last till nine o'clock: Burke, *Son of London*, p.108.
63. Charles C. (b. Bromley-by-Bow, 1891), transcript, side 2, pp.7–8.
64. C.f. Tottenham, *How Things Were*, p.51.
65. Thomas Wright's 'well-to-do mechanic's son' had to go to bed at eight o'clock, but sometimes on Saturday was allowed to stay up as a treat: *Habits*, pp.14, 17, 200. Mrs Bartle (b. Poplar, 1882) also had a set bedtime; she recalled with delight when her older brother took her in the evening to see the frozen lake in Victoria Park in spite of her mother's objection: transcript, p.37.
66. Edith H. (b. Paddington, 1894), transcript, pp.5,7 (eight o'clock bedtime 'right up to the time we went out to service'); Mrs W. (b. Finsbury, 1896), transcript, p.9 (seven o'clock); Mr N. (b. 1899), transcript, p.36 (put himself to bed by nine, 'no pansy stuff there, you do for yourself'). See also Meacham, *Life Apart*, p.161 (he argues, however, that bedtime was 'almost universally' early); and Thompson, *Edwardians*, p.58 (a sheet-metal worker's wife getting her children to bed before he came in).
67. *Employment of Schoolchildren Committee*, PP 1902, evidence Miss Adler, qq.3,344, 3,384; Miss Neville (School Manager in Notting Dale), q.2,581. C.f. 'Physical Degeneration', part 8: 'School Children out of School', *BMJ*, 16 Jan. 1904, p.140 (twelve or one).
68. Booth, *Poverty* 3, p.210 (Tabor, 'Elementary Education'). C.f. Harkness, *Captain Lobe*, pp.54–6.
69. Sherwell, *West London*, p.129.
70. Harvey, *London Boy's Saturday*. Several hundred essays were collected from different London schools; Harvey's selection and discussion focussed on those from one boys' school near Toynbee Hall, where he was Deputy Warden. Of a group identified as from 'more comfortable' homes in nearby model dwellings, the four who gave times of going to bed went at 10.45, 11.00, and (two) after 10.30.
71. In the 'Saturday' essays (see above), four boys went to the music hall (one leaving only at 11.45); and seven had been selling in street or market. Albert M. (b. Shoreditch, 1894) 'used to stop up to about eleven' on Saturdays ('they didn't use to come home from the pub...till about twelve'), but during the week was called in by ten o'clock: transcript, pp.B40–1.
72. Baillie, *Paradise*, p.14. Another middle-class child first saw stars only when she was five, having never been out after dark: White, *As Once in May*, p.287.
73. C.f. Thompson, *Dear Girl*, p.75, Ruth Slate's diary, 12 Jan. 1906: 'Though it was so late, the street seemed full of children, some barefooted, looking as though they had no thought of going home, and the sight made one shudder...I had no idea there were places quite so bad in Manor Park.'
74. Sturge, 'Claims of Childhood' (1899), pp.94–5.
75. C.f. Peter Wilby, 'And So Not to Bed', *Sunday Times*, 2 June 1985.
76. Malcolmson, 'Laundresses', p.457. See also Jane W. (b. Limehouse, 1896), transcript, p.5, whose mother would be 'up all night doing washing' (and saying 'we're going to have different pictures tonight' would drape the clothes over all the pictures); and Mary H. (b. Canning Town, 1895), transcript, pp.12–13. Domestic washing was also sometimes done at night, c.f. *Friends' Home Mission 8th Annual Report*, 1874, p.41 (Myra Cumber on East End women): 'they wash at night and then things dry and they put them on in the morning.'
77. See Crichton Browne, *Overpressure*, 1884, p.27: in conducting a census of headaches among London schoolchildren he also asked them about fatigue, and found:

> a great deal of sleeplessness amongst the children attending elementary schools in London...many of the children belonged to families inhabiting one-room houses, and...it was the domestic turmoil that kept them awake. The baby has much to answer for in...juvenile insomnia, and so has the light, and the tramcars, and 'the cabs in our yard,' and 'mother's mangle,' and other noisy adjuncts of modern civilization.

78. [Wright], *Great Unwashed*, p.148. Jack Welch (b. Shoreditch, 1903) used to lie awake listening to the singing of 'lone revellers staggering home in the dark': memoir, p.36.
79. Jack Welch (b. Shoreditch, 1903), ms. memoir, p.35.
80. Marie Welch (b. Hoxton, 1904), ms. memoir, pp.3–4.
81. Jack Welch (b. Shoreditch, 1903), ms. memoir, pp.6–7 describes his family's precautions.
82. Albert and Elsie M. (b. 1897 and 1905), transcript, p.B6; Miss H. (b. 1900), quoted White, *Rothschild Buildings*, p.42, in a vivid discussion of the problem (pp.42–3). Jim Allen (b. 1915), recalls being six in a bed during his Peckham childhood:

> Those in the middle
> Had no respite;
> It was shove, push and fiddle
> For most of the night.
>
> Those next to the wall
> Had to fight to get free
> To get past the rest
> When they wanted to wee.
>
> The ones on the outside
> Would start to complain
> When those close to the wall
> Had to crawl back again.
>
> There was moans and groans
> And cries of 'Oh no!'
> Then twelve little ears
> Heard a voice from below
>   'Get to sleep!'
>
> Six little heads
> Settled down in the gloom,
> Three up, three down,
> And quiet was the night
>   Till the bugs came out!

    See Peckham, *Times*, p.48; also Booth, *Poverty* 2, p.47; Jacobs, *Ghetto*, p.21.
83. Jones in Cohen, *Memories*, p.62; Jack Welch (b. Shoreditch, 1903) also describes periodic fumigation: ms. memoir, p.6.
84. Fred Davey (b. Waterloo, 1916), SE1 People's History Group, June 1980. See also White, *Rothschild Buildings*, pp.41–3.
85. Many children did domestic chores before breakfast: c.f. Harvey, *Saturday*, pp.6–7. Some also helped prepare shops and stalls for the day; others, mainly boys, did paper rounds; while on Saturdays some girls went cleaning steps.
86. Paterson, *Bridges*, p.2.
87. Newman, *Health of the State*, p.141.
88. Ravenhill, 'Hours of Sleep' (1909).
89. Anon, *On Marriage—Address to Mothers*, p.10.
90. Bray, 'Children of the Town', p.123.
91. C.f. Miss H. (b. 1900), quoted in White, *Rothschild Buildings*, p.51: 'We slept two, three in a bed like nothing. We never had a hot water bottle or extra blankets—we didn't need it. You all warmed one another.'
92. See Freeman, *Religious and Social Work*, p.63, for a factory girl sent on a country holiday who cried herself to sleep: 'it was so awful having a bed to myself, not having mother and Jemima in it'.
93. C.f. Loane (*Castle*, p.175): poor children when sick preferred the living room, being 'so unaccustomed to solitude that they cannot endure to remain for ten minutes alone'.
94. C.f. Head, 'Church and People', p.265: if 'the necessarily prevailing principle of family life as conducted in three rooms is "Go out", not "Stay in",' in a one-room home it was inevitable.
95. Bray, 'Children of the Town', pp.123–4.
96. Bray, *Town Child*, p.29.
97. This point is also made and discussed by Ellen Ross in 'Survival 'Networks'.
98. Chase, *Tenant Friends*, p.70; Ryan, 'Tenement to Mansion', p.314.

99. Mary F. (b. Bermondsey, 1895), transcript, p.4. Mrs Bartle emphasized that in Poplar, in spite of 'all those roughs and drunkards', 'you never heard of assaults on children—that was when you got to the more respectable neighbourhoods': transcript, p.3.
100. C.f. Fagan in Cohen, *Memories*, p.13: shrieks from women in the street below alerted his mother when he met a dare to hang by his knees over a fourth-floor railing.
101. See for example Jack Welch, ms. memoir, pp.13–14; Haw, *Lad of London*, p.83, 88; Southgate, *The Way it Was*, p.88; Tottenham, *How Things Were*, p.57; Peckham, *Times*, p.10; Jasper, *Hoxton Childhood*, p.24. Mrs Muckell (b. Leather Lane, 1907) remembered how the girls kept watch from the bridge, and how the boys had to turn on their backs and respond to the order 'cocks afloat': family tradition, Christine Holloway, March 1983.
102. Mr N., (b. Aldgate, 1899), transcript, p.8.
103. Mrs Bartle, transcript, p.6.
104. Foakes, *High Walls*, pp.6, 7.
105. Amelia K. (b. Poplar, 1878) married in 1902 and lived next door to her mother, who had bad legs, because 'of course somebody had to do her work', then later took the mother into her household (transcript, p.4). C.f. Mrs W. (b. Finsbury, 1896): grandma next door, transcript, p.12; Alice Lewis (b. Fulham, 1898): mother and aunt both married Fulham men and 'lived near each other for years', ms. memoir; 'Case 15' in Bibby, *Pudding Lady* (p.66) had 'very few cooking utensils' but borrowed from mother-in-law in same house. Mary Jasper (*Hoxton Childhood*) after marriage lived sometimes with her mother's household and sometimes separate but nearby; if she was alone her young brother went and slept with her.
106. Ross, 'Survival Networks', p.9.
107. McLeod quotes a 1902 diary entry from Poplar: 'Funeral of Mrs Spooner this afternoon—a patriarchal [sic] old lady who lived in Willis Street, which is (apparently) chiefly inhabited by her thirty-four grandchildren and forty-two great-grand-children': *Class and Religion*, p.10.
108. Lees, *Exiles of Erin*, p.83; c.f. Anderson, *Family*, pp.148, 152–61.
109. More prosperous relatives were not always generous: c.f. Jasper, *Hoxton Childhood*, pp.39, 58; Cohen, *Memories*, p.30.
110. *Local Government Board, Report*, 1873–4 (Appendix B, report 14, Henry Longley on Poor Law Administration in London), p.186. On workplace collections for widows: Crossick, *Artisan Elite*, pp.175, 179. For neighbours taking in children, see Chapters 5 and 6.
111. Jephson, *My Work*, p.21 (on 1880s Waterloo).
112. Hunt, *Reminiscences*, p.78.
113. Newton, *Years of Change*, p.7.
114. Ross ('Survival Networks', p.8) cites a magistrate's estimate that 'neighbours and credit could sustain a deserted woman with children for about two weeks'.
115. Parr, *Labouring Children*, p.64.
116. Thea Thompson, asking why the family of Tommy Morgan was 'so poor, drunken and disorganized', notes that the parents were 'newcomers to London, not born and bred there'; Mrs Morgan had no London relatives to 'help her with her hardships and big family in a day-to-day way', and Mr Morgan's relations lived in Greenwich, 'too far away to be of immediate use and inclined to drink also': *Childhoods*, p.11. The frequency with which they moved house must also have weakened links with neighbours.
117. *Crèche Annual*, 1883.
118. C.f. *Child's Guardian* 1, Oct. 1887, pp.73–4: the three older children of a book-folder at work all day were being fed by the proprietress of a nearby fish-and-chip shop who sent them up scraps of fish; and SBL *Minutes*, 4 Feb. 1874, pp.257–8, 15 July 1874, p.875, and 28 April 1875, pp.580–1 (Chelsea: Amelia Tongue); 25 Nov. 1874, p.1, 267 (Chelsea: Elizabeth Bowles); 6 Jan. 1875, p.144 (Lambeth, Henry Lamb).
119. Loane, *Castle*, p.108.
120. C.f. Southgate, *That's the Way*, p.38. He also tells of a gin-drunk neighbour who 'sought refuge in our cottage until she sobered up before facing her infuriated husband' (p.24).
121. William Nn (b. Poplar, 1896), ms. memoir, p.54. Evidence is too sparse to gauge how often this happened.
122. *Child's Guardian* 4, Nov. 1890, p.132. The case was taken up by the NSPCC (probably contacted by the neighbour) after the baby's death at five months, and the mother was charged with murder. C.f. discussion in previous chapter.
123. Mary P. (b. Hackney, 1903), transcript, side 6, p.6.

124. Mrs Bartle, transcript, p.5.
125. Quinlan, *Devil's Alley*, pp.24–5, 120–1, 163–4.
126. Mrs C. (b. Hackney, 1903), recorded 1973 by members of the People's Autobiography of Hackney group; my notes from a group hearing of the tape, p.1.
127. C.f. Mr L. (b. Hackney, 1882), 'people kept fowls, and if anybody was ill and they heard, they'd give you a couple of eggs': notes from Hackney People's Autobiography meeting, 8 Nov. 1973; Mrs C. (b. Bermondsey, 1893), 'that time my mother was very ill—the woman [neighbour] came in and collected up every bit of washing. Took it out and done it and brought it back': transcript, p.36; Mrs K. (b. Battersea, 1897), transcript, pp.35–6; Ezard (b. 1900), *Battersea Boy*, p.27; Newton (b. Hackney, 1902), *Years of Change*, pp.7–8: 'sent by my Aunt up the street to some neighbour: "Take this bowl of soup to Mrs Beasley, and ask if she feels any better. Oh and ask her if you can get her any errands while you're there. Don't drop the basin. Look where you're going." '
128. C.f. Hake, *Suffering London*, p.10; Kimmins, *Polly of Parker's Rents*, p.94. For more examples and discussion see Ross, 'Survival Networks', throughout.

4 Beyond Four Walls

1. Mrs Langley (b. Stepney, early 1890s), in Richman, *Fly a Flag*, p.34.
2. Reeves, *Pound a Week*, p.192.
3. C.f. *MOH London, Report*, 1893, p.20 (friends from adjoining houses in the Portobello Road visited a child with smallpox and some sixty-four further cases resulted); ditto 1899, p.31: children visiting and playing together blamed for the spread of a diphtheria epidemic in North Woolwich.
4. Henry Brooker ('a London artist'), 'Oranges and Lemons', Geffrye Museum, Bethnal Green. They are probably his own children; and look very clean and healthy.
5. See Gomme, *Games* 1, p.149.
6. Fulljames (b. 1910), in Peckham, *Times*, pp.32–3. The more crowded the home, the less chance of such refuges.
7. C.f. 'One of the Crowd', *Toilers*, p.64 ('the awfully dirty passage served as a playground for half a dozen...little children'); and Ryan, 'Tenement to Mansion', p.312 (children playing marbles on a tenement landing) and p.314 (on balconies of a model dwelling).
8. Morten, *Nurse's Notebook*, p.128.
9. Mrs C. (b. Bermondsey, 1893), transcript, p.34.
10. Dendy, 'Children', pp.39–40; c.f. *Cross Commission, 2nd Report*, PP 1887, evidence Mrs Burgwin q.17,418; Booth, *Poverty* 3, p.210 (Tabor, 'Education'); Chase, *Tenant Friends* (on the 1890s), p.70.
11. C.f. Low, 'Street Games', pp.518–20; Pugh, 'Street Amusements', pp.266–271; Douglass, *Street Games*.
12. Rolph, *Particulars*, p.58.
13. C.f. Bray, *Town Child*, p.50: 'a swarm of maidens quarrelling for the possession of a rope that has fallen from a cart'.
14. Twisting games were fun but dangerous: see J.B., 'Our Lodgers', in *Children* 2, April 1897, for casualties brought to the Hackney Children's Hospital when the string broke. See also Ridge, *Storyteller*, p.199; Southgate, *The Way it Was*, p.25; and Sims, *Living London* 3, p.270. For nostalgic letter recalling the importance of the lamp-post in a 1930s childhood, *Daily Mirror*, 6 July 1978.
15. This pleasure was forbidden but not stopped by the Metropolitan Police Act of 1839. Boys used to make a slide behind Buxton Street, Spitalfields, and when 'the old ladies wanted to go to get their supper beer...the boys and girls would hold their arm and see they didn't slide': Ada S. (b. Spitalfields, 1884), transcript, side 1 p.14.
16. Douglass, *Street Games*, pp.107–8. An 1880s advocate of technical education commented on how 'mechanical energies' and 'creative powers' amongst poor children were wasted, being devoted only to 'the making of tipcats and catapults and...the construction of mud pies and oyster-shell grottoes': Cunynghame, 'Technical Education', p.87.
17. Rolph, *Particulars*, p.57, of Finsbury Park neighbourhood between 1906 to 1910. See also Baillie, *Paradise*, p.158; and for 1919 Poplar photo: Richman, *Fly a Flag*, p.39.
18. Bray, *Town Child*, p.50.
19. Foakes, *High Walls*, p.66; Eliza H. (b. Isle of Dogs, 1900), transcript, side 1 p.17.

20. Baillie, *Paradise*, p.181. C.f. Ridge, *Mord Em'ly*, pp.60–5 for a fallen horse, 'followed instantly (for Walworth is a place where something is always happening)' by a fight, then a fire engine.
21. Jack Welch (b. Shoreditch, 1903), ms. memoir, pp.19–20; c.f. Jobson, *Creeping Hours*, p.52.
22. Southgate, *The Way it Was*, p.25.
23. Ridge, *Mord Em'ly*, pp.64–5.
24. Frank S. (b. Hoxton, 1884) lived in Battersea one street away from two families who were always having 'a damned good scrap in the middle of the road': transcript, p.61; see also Mr N. (b. 1899), transcript, p.37.
25. Mrs Bartle (b. Poplar, 1882), transcript, p.42; see also Miss A. (b. Penton Rise, Islington, 1896), who 'used to be right up the front' when drunks were arrested—'it was an excitement for us children': transcript, p.44.
26. Southgate, *The Way it Was*, p.52.
27. Baillie, *Paradise*, p.14. In memories, spoken or written, there is none of the drab monotony of the street in Morrison's introduction to *Mean Streets*.
28. Greenwood, 'Neglected Children', *Seven Curses*, pp.8–9.
29. William Nn (b. Poplar, 1896), ms. memoir, p.55.
30. Paterson, *Bridges*, p.60. The nature of rubbish was not constant: the oyster shells used for poor children's play in mid-century had given way by this time to cans.
31. Greenwood, *Seven Curses*, p.8.
32. Bray, *Town Child*, p.55. It was the aimlessness which worried him: 'no particular destination to be reached, no special street to be crossed, no definite task to be worked through, and no final goal of all desire to be reached'.
33. C.f. Rogers, *Labour, Life and Literature*, p.4 (mid-century); Southgate, *The Way it Was*, p.46; and Tottenham, *How Things Were*, esp. pp. 52–5, 96.
34. See Hill, annual *Letters*, e.g. 1871, p.9, 1877, pp.11–12, 1879, pp.10–12; Findlater, *Lilian Baylis*, p.32; Barnett, *Canon Barnett*, 1, pp.141–3.
35. *Lancet*, 24 Sept. 1870, p.449. This appeal probably went unheard: in 1879 Octavia Hill wrote that the Kyrle Society was ready 'to find money for due supervision of Lincolns Inn Fields and St Anne's Churchyard, Soho, if the Trustees of the one, and the Vicar of the other, will but allow them to be opened to the public': *Letter*, 1879, p.10.
36. Churchyard playgrounds still exist in central London.
37. 'Archbishop Benson's Friends', *Church Monthly* 6, 1893, p.191.
38. Bray, 'Children of the Town', p.101. West and North London still have more parks, despite efforts to redress the balance with Victoria Park, Finsbury Park, Southwark Park, and now also Burgess Park (Southwark) and many small 'patch parks'.
39. White, *Rothschild Buildings*, p.185; Bill Jones in Cohen, *Memories*, p.63. C.f. Mrs Layton (b. Bethnal Green, 1866) in Davies, *Life*, p.4; Ethel V. (b. Whitechapel, 1895), transcript, side 2, p.23.
40. Mrs Bartle (b. Poplar, 1882), transcript, p.39; Poulsen, *Victoria Park*.
41. Foakes, *High Walls*, pp.12–13, 23.
42. Lord Brabazon, chair of the Metropolitan Gardens Association, recommended separation, but it may not have been usual, except in school playgrounds: 'Public Playgrounds' (1893), pp.268–70.
43. Brabazon, 'Public Playgrounds', pp.267–71.
44. SBL *Minutes*, 25 Jan. 1894, p.295.
45. Douglass, *Street Games*, p.61.
46. Charlie Connor (b. about 1899), letter 1972. My thanks for the late Bob Gilding's permission to quote.
47. *Times*, 15 Oct. 1870, p.9 col. 5.
48. Southgate, *That's the Way*, p.72.
49. *MOH London, Report*, 1898, p.37.
50. Grant, *Farthing Bundles*, p.133. Arthur Harding used to accompany his sister and her friend in going through empty houses both for fun and in case they found anything they could use or sell: Samuel, *Underworld*, p.30. C.f. Jasper, *Hoxton Childhood*, p.94.
51. Tennant, *Street Arabs*, p.6.
52. Booth, *Final Volume*, p.66. C.f. Mrs T., comment in City Lit class 1976, 'the lamp-post was our parliament'.
53. Ethel V. (b. Whitechapel, 1895), transcript, side 1, pp.3, 27–8. For model dwellings, c.f.

Jerry White, *Rothschild Buildings.*

54. LCC, *Outdoor Memorials*, 1910, p.8.

55. *South London Press*, 18 Aug. 1911, p.3; 25 Aug., p.3; *Times*, 24 Aug. 1911, p.6 col. 5.

56. Manning (b. Hackney, 1886), *Life for Education*, p.21. Joe Jacobs (b. Whitechapel, 1913) followed a demonstration in about 1925 and forgot to go home for dinner: *Out of the Ghetto*, p.22.

57. C.f. Ezard, *Battersea Boy*, pp.28–9; Richman, *Fly a Flag*, p.22.

58. C.f. Meacham, *Life Apart*, pp.45–52, and Chapter 2 above; also Bailey, 'Bill Banks', p.340.

59. C.f. Southgate, *That's the Way*, p.23. Possible tensions are sensitively discussed in McLeod, *Class and Religion*, pp.102–3.

60. Mrs Jones (b. Poplar 1903), Richman, *Fly a Flag*, p.38. C.f. Ross, 'Respectability', p.50: mothers' 'close regulation of girls' play and dress stemmed from a special anxiety for their safety and sexual reputations'.

61. C.f. Thompson, *Childhoods*, p.3.

62. For debates on the aristocracy of labour, one source for this discussion of respectability, see Hobsbawm ('Labour Aristocracy', 1964; and later articles collected in *Worlds of Labour*); Stedman Jones (*Outcast London* and 'Working-class Culture'); Crossick (*Artisan Elite* and 'Emergence'); Gray ('Styles of Life'; *Labour Aristocracy*); Meacham (*Life Apart*, chap.1); Bailey ('Bill Banks'). Ross ('Respectability') puts gender at the centre of her discussion; c.f. also Roberts, 'Family'.

63. Stedman Jones ('Working-class Culture', pp.182–3) traces the 'emergence of a new working-class culture in London' at this time, 'staunchly impervious to middle-class attempts to guide it'; c.f. Bailey, 'Bill Banks'. Ross ('Respectability') focusses on neighbourhood respectability and notes (p.45) 'working-class culture's capacity for reorganizing and transforming concepts from the dominant culture'.

64. The title rough was sometimes claimed cheerfully and proudly, however (rather as feminists took 'virago' and 'shrew' in the 1970s): c.f. Mag Ayling (b. Deptford, 1909), about following the water-cart and hanging on behind carts: 'some girls wouldn't, but we were rough' (notes from Goldsmiths' College class, 2 March 1983).

65. C.f. interesting exchange reported by Maude Stanley (*Clubs*, p.174): a lady who asked 'Should you call yourself a good specimen of a working girl?' was answered: 'I think you would find us as many differences amongst us as you would find amongst ladies'.

66. Bailey, 'Bill Banks' (discussing Wright, 'Bill Banks's Day Out'); Martin, 'Working Women and Drink', quoted by Ross, 'Respectability', p.46.

67. Tebbutt, *Making Ends Meet*, p.22, quoting *Pawnbrokers' Gazette*, 4 Aug. 1894; on working-class shame and use of intermediaries ('poppers'), see pp.43–5; Johnson, *Saving and Spending*, pp.184–5.

68. Tebbutt, *Making Ends Meet*, p.19; Johnson, *Saving and Spending*, pp.176–9. Pawning was more difficult and probably more shaming in the suburbs: Tebbutt, *Making Ends Meet*, p.59. One of the few occasions when Jack Welch (b. Shoreditch, 1903) got his ears boxed was when he 'put an end to a couple of our assets' by breaking the 'fancy vases which had made so many trips to the pawnshop': ms. memoir, p.18.

69. C.f. Ross, 'Respectability', esp. pp.40–2.

70. C.f. workplace struggles over 'cabbage' and 'work for the queen': the use of employers' materials and time on the worker's own projects, which were part of artisan culture. (See Linebaugh, *London Hanged*, for earlier conflict.)

71. Arthur Harding soon learnt (Samuel, *Underworld*, pp.24–5) the use of being seen as deserving: 'They were always asking whether we was good children or not, and whether we were clean, and whether we went to Sunday School'; 'The clothes you wore had to be something that didn't fit—so that they would give you some...for your Sunday best'; 'There was always a few bob to be got from them, provided you was well-behaved'. C.f. Ross, 'Respectability', pp.40–2; Bailey, 'Bill Banks', pp.340–3.

72. Bailey, 'Bill Banks', p.347. C.f. his argument that the historian's 'reconstructed world of working-class respectability' is 'an artificial composite'; and that it is dangerous to infer 'a continuity in casting where there may only have been a continuity in performance' (p.339); donning a Sunday suit did not prevent the 'customary resort to the pub', nor the pawning of the suit next day (p.342).

73. Booth made the apt point (*Poverty* 1, p.54) that although both higher-class labourers and foremen fell within his 'class F' (income 30s. up to 45s. or 50s.), 'the foreman of ordinary labour generally sees things from the employer's point of view, while the skilled

artisan sees them from the point of view of the employed'. Artisan respectability might be rougher.

74. These had much less hold in London than in the north; 'the great majority of London workers were neither Christian, provident, chaste nor temperate': Stedman Jones 'Working-class Culture', pp.196–8. Wright ('Composition', pp.521–3) identified three working-class groups, each with their own pride and identity, using attitudes to class and education as his touchstone. All are in some sense respectable.

75. Meacham, *Life Apart*, p.27.

76. Chaplin, *Autobiography*, p.50.

77. Ross, 'Respectability', p.39; c.f. pp.47–51. Respectability was assessed by 'their dress, public conduct, language, housekeeping, child-rearing methods, spending habits, and, of course, sexual behaviour'.

78. C.f. Martin, *Married Working Woman*, p.30: 'The feeling that she is the indispensable centre of her small world is, indeed, the joy and consolation of her life'.

79. The ban on Sunday play was widely enforced, even by parents who attended no services, like those of North Street, Cambridge Heath: Southgate, *That's the Way*, p.76. In 1890s Crouch End a widowed dairy-keeper was not on speaking terms with the people who kept a sweet shop next door, because she let her daughter play the piano on Sundays: *Hornsey Historical Society* Bulletin 21, 1980.

80. Jobson, *Creeping Hours*, p.82; c.f. p.15. Their 'respectability' was undeniable, but they lived in a street 'with a bad reputation' (p.94) and a huge gin palace at one end (p.24); he used to queue for stale bread (p.55); his mother 'kept open house' for her sisters in service and various friends; and his father, too, had 'sundry old men' who came to talk (pp.37–9).

81. Ada S. (b. Spitalfields, 1884), transcript, side 1 p.29. A cat-o-nine-tails on the table reminded children not to speak or to put food on another's plate in the strict childhood of Mary H. (b. Canning Town, 1895): transcript, p.15. Her mother bore nineteen children (only seven reached adulthood), and took in washing; her unreliable docker father drank and was eventually incapacitated by an accident. They were always tidy and clean; said prayers before bed; and could not visit friends or play out in the evening (pp.31, 15, 34). C.f. Thompson, *Edwardians*, p.65. Rose R., born in Walworth in 1923 and brought up by grandparents, recalled a cane on the table and enforced silence at mealtimes: conversation, 1975.

82. Mrs W. (b. Finsbury, 1896), whose father was a piano mover and whose mother cleaned offices, was discouraged from some friends 'especially if they swore': transcript, p.29; c.f. John T. (b. Bow, 1879), transcript, p.10. Dot S. (b. Hackney, 1899) never heard her parents swear, and was clouted by her deaf mother for saying 'bother': ms. memoir. Mr N. (b. Aldgate, 1899) recalled that swearing was not allowed in the house, though 'Course it was natural in the East End...a sort of everyday language': transcript, p.49. C.f. Southgate (*That's the Way*, p.22): adults often used swear words, but children must not.

83. The memories of Eliza Henman are rich in examples of close control: see recording by Samuel, transcript, A27–30, 33, 36; and Richman, *Fly a Flag*, p.50 (where she describes having to be in by 9.30 even at twenty-one and right up till marriage).

84. Mrs C. (b. Bermondsey, 1891), transcript, p.34.

85. C.f. Frank S., (b. Hoxton, 1884), transcript, p.57.

86. Mr C. (b. Bromley-by-Bow, 1891) led a fairly independent daytime life, but his sisters had to help in the house: transcript, side 2, p.11. Indoor discipline was strict (pp.26, 31, 34).

87. Mrs Bartle (b. Poplar, 1882), transcript, pp.1, 14.

88. Mrs Bartle, transcript, p.17.

89. Mrs Bartle, transcript, pp.5–7.

90. Mrs Bartle, transcript, p.2. C.f. Booth, *Poverty* 1, pp.159–60: 'in class E they have for playground the back yard, in class D the even greater delights of the street'.

91. Mrs Bartle, transcript, pp.3–4; 42–3.

92. Mrs Bartle, transcript, p.39.

93. Children's mockery overlapped with organized opposition between 1878 and 1885, c.f. Bailey, 'Salvation Army Riots'.

94. Mrs Bartle, transcript, pp.40–3.

95. Eliza H. (b. Isle of Dogs, 1900) was only allowed to go a couple of streets away, and word was sure to get back if she went further, which meant 'another bashing': transcript, side 1 p.33.

96. The following discussion is based on the transcript of an interview by Raphael Samuel. My thanks for access.
97. Foakes, *High Walls*, p.38.
98. C.f. Baillie, *Shabby Paradise*, p.106: the daughter of a Poplar vicar, after a sailing holiday she foreswore 'dolls, party frocks and lessons in embroidery as deplorably effeminate', 'attempted to pursue a vaguely nautical curriculum', 'insisted on wearing boys' boots' and 'refused categorically to endure the detestable bonnets tied under the chin with satin bows, which were then the accepted headgear for little girls'.
99. Foakes, *High Walls*, pp.41, 31, 13.
100. Eliza H. (b. Poplar, 1900), transcript, side 1, pp.31–2.
101. In the school primers rags, or even careless dress, went with moral failings, and the good child was always neat even though her garments might be faded and much patched: Davin, 'Do as you are told'.
102. Grace Smith, notes of conversation, 29 Dec. 1975.
103. Bray, 'Children', p.118. C.f. Meacham, *Life Apart*, p.27. Bray had strong views on the street: it was 'the abode of irrelevant, disconnected and casual change', producing 'a confused torrent of chaotic perceptions' instead of a sense of the order of things (pp.28–9). He also argued (p.53) that being 'always one of a multitude' had a bad effect on character: such children 'find the routine existence of the individual insipid and distasteful; they become more noisy and uncontrolled in their ways, less tolerant of any restraint, less capable of finding any zest in pleasures of tranquil enjoyment'.
104. Rolph, *Particulars*, pp.1–2, 13.
105. In a memoir of 1930s Liverpool a suddenly penniless middle-class family learn about parish relief and discover that 43s. a week relief has to support two parents and seven children (Forrester, *Tuppence*, pp.30, 38), and take a room without checking the gas meter, set by the landlord so as to extract a profit (p.47); while men in the dole queue give the father tips for survival (p.75). Those who grew up in poverty learnt such lessons early.
106. C.f. Warner, 'Results', p.76; and *Report on Children in Receipt of Poor Relief*, 1910–11, p.32 (quoted Meacham, *Life Apart*, p.27): the respectable working woman, to prevent contact with 'undesirable associates', would 'sacrifice not only money, but health itself...by keeping her children within stuffy little rooms rather than let them play in the streets'.
107. *MOH London, Report*, 1906, Appendix 2 (Report of Medical Officer (Education)), pp.6–7. (Dr Niall had visited 14 infant schools 'varying from slum areas of Vauxhall and North Lambeth, through artisan areas of Lambeth and Kennington to the vastly different districts of Brixton and Norwood'.) C.f. Warner, 'Results'; and *MOH London, Report*, 1905, Appendix 2, pp.20–1.
108. C.f. *MOH London, Report*, 1908, pp.8, 15, 57; and *MOH London, Reports*, e.g. 1904, Appendix 3, p.12; 1908, Appendix 5. C.f. *R.C. Physical Training*, PP 1903, Dr Kerr's evidence qq.7,197; 7,205; 6,059.
109. *MOH London, Report*, 1908, Appendix 5, p.8. C.f. Scharlieb, 'Recreational Activities', p.12. The girls were too young for menstruation to be the cause. According to M. E. Loane (*Simple...Midwifery*, p.25) 'English girls' started menstruation between eleven and seventeen, usually around fifteen; c.f. Glasson, *Motherhood*, p.8 (thirteen to sixteen). Neither was specific about class, but as inferior nutrition delays menarche working-class girls probably started late rather than early.
110. Ross, 'Respectability', p.52; Tebbutt, *Making Ends Meet*, pp.57–8.
111. Martin, 'Social Reform', p.1,074. The indomitable mother in Jasper, *Hoxton Childhood*, managed to teach her son 'manners' acceptable in a superior family (p.76), and to observe important occasions with everyone appropriately dressed, despite her drunken and irresponsible menfolk, and although she too drank, worked for money, and at times fought (her husband).
112. David Pugh, from 'the upper end of Scawfell Street...the upper ten', was ostracized, because 'all the "herbs" thought he was a snob': Jasper, *Hoxton Childhood*, p.76.
113. William Nn (b. Poplar, 1896), ms. memoir, p.12; c.f. Ross, 'Respectability', p.45.
114. The following discussion is based on the early chapters of Foakes, *High Walls*.
115. Mrs Bartle, transcript, p.13.
116. Ada S. (b. Spitalfields, 1884), transcript, pp.A31–4.
117. Ada S., transcript, p.A34.
118. 'Mother Kate', *Old Soho Days*, p.35.

119. Fagan, in Cohen, *Memories*, p.24.
120. Armstrong, *Her Own Way*, p.8. (My copy was 'awarded to Olive Lucas for Punctual Attendance' at Bridge Road school, West Ham, in 1894.)
121. Mrs Bartle, transcript, p.13.
122. Mrs M., (b. Hoxton, 1896), notes of tape played at Hackney People's Autobiography meeting, 1974.
123. Conversely, when upper-middle-class Naomi Haldane started to menstruate, at twelve, her mother at once removed her from the boys' preparatory school she had been attending and set up lessons under a governess with 'four of those strange beings, girls of my own age': Mitchison, *All Change Here* (the chapter is headed 'Boy into Girl').

5 Caretakers or Schoolchildren?

1. C.f. Parr, *Labouring Children*, pp.16–20: 'caretaker' is her term. See also Chapter 6.
2. London servants preferred jobs within reach of their families; c.f. Jermy, *Memories*, p.72. Regular contact is implied by the frequent changes of family address for servants registered with MABYS (Metropolitan Association for Befriending Young Servants): E.S., 'Women Who Ought to Work', *Eastward Ho* 3, May–Oct. 1885, p.49. According to Butler (*Domestic Service*, 1916, p.70): 'Almost every servant that I ever knew has had someone dependent on her' was the refrain of 'many mistresses and maids'.
3. C.f. Parr, *Labouring Children*, pp.21–3. Overcrowding and mutual dependence could also have an explosive effect, with young wage-earners moving out because of conflict, or the family breaking up. Or if parents moved older children might choose to stay put.
4. Paterson, *Bridges*, p.58.
5. Local boards set the age and conditions for leaving school. London's leaving age was always among the highest. For successive London regulations, see Rubinstein, *Attendance*, pp.35–8.
6. See Lewis, 'School Fees and the School Board', throughout.
7. Rubinstein, *Attendance*, pp.2–4, 30–1, 91–8; Lewis, 'School Fees and the School Board', pp.292, 300; and for right-wing individualist opposition, Pomeroy, *Education Tyranny*. For mill-owners' increasing support for schooling (as labour discipline) from the 1830s, see Carson, 'Early Factory Crime', pp.45–6.
8. C.f. cases in Pomeroy, *Education Tyranny*.
9. C.f. Rubinstein, *Attendance*, and Hurt, *Schooling*.
10. For examples see SBL *Byelaws Committee, Uniform Enforcement*, 1874; and PRO HO45 9813, file 25043A. An 1884 letter from the Education Department noted that in certain courts the magistrates' views made it hard to get cases heard (SBL *Minutes* 7 Feb. 1884). C.f. Rubinstein, *Attendance*, pp.98–109.
11. For details, see Rubinstein, *Attendance*, pp.42–53.
12. PRO HO45 9813, file 25043A/6.
13. PRO HO45 9813, file 25043A/7.
14. *School Attendance Gazette*, Jan. 1901, p.163. See also Spalding, *School Board*, pp.130–1; Reeves, *Recollections*, pp.11–12, 16.
15. Rubinstein (*Attendance*, p.49) and Crossick (*Artisan Elite*, pp.268–9) suggest that 'Riverside Visitor' was Thomas Wright, who wrote as 'Journeyman Engineer'; an identification accepted by the British Library. For Wright, see Reid, 'Intelligent Artisans'.
16. Anon, 'School Board Work', *Good Words*, 1872, p.652. C.f. his voluntary help serving free dinners: 'Riverside Visitor', *Pinch of Poverty*, pp.183, 286–8.
17. This perspective was less important in London, where children were not employed by big manufacturers, than in textile areas.
18. R.C. *Factory and Workshop Acts, Report*, PP 1876, p.44. He also favoured extending 'the glorious benefits of the half-time system': *Factory Inspectors' Reports*, PP 1871, p.10.
19. This was a recurrent comparison: the coster both stood for sturdy independence, and demonstrated that education was not essential to success as a trader.
20. PRO HO45 9813, files 25043A/24 and 25. The time lost by repeatedly attending court would indeed deter parents.
21. *Light and Shade*, Dec. 1881, p.10. (He refused to hear their case against a boy who had 'made a serious disturbance in the Boys' Shelter' and had squared up to the manager when asked to leave.)

22. Letter from Thomas J. Barstow and John Hosack, 13 Jan. 1879 (PRO HO45 9813, file 25043A/16). In 1880 Hosack again complained, adding, 'I can testify...from the scenes I continually witness in Court, that the spirit of antagonism between the poor of this district and the School Board officers does not diminish' (25043/29).
23. Rubinstein, *Attendance*, p.109.
24. Vallès, *Rue à Londres*, p.37.
25. Sims, 'At the Front Door', p.31.
26. Dendy, 'Children of Working London', p.37.
27. Farmilow, 'Aggie's Baby', *Chapel Street Children*, p.14.
28. UCL Chadwick Papers 99 (police responses to questionnaire on boys and girls working as street sellers, 1883), answer from M Division (Southwark) to question 7.
29. Paterson, *Bridges*, p.54.
30. Wragge, *London I Loved*, p.25.
31. Page, 'No Green Pastures', part 1, p.35.
32. Lamb, 'How to Wash and Dress the Baby', p.475.
33. Davies, *Life*, p.4.
34. Samuel, *Underworld*, p.30.
35. J.B., 'Our Lodgers', *Children* 2, p.54, April 1897.
36. Lamb, 'How to Wash and Dress the Baby', p.474.
37. Williams, *Round London*, pp.85–7.
38. SBL *School Accommodation and Attendance Committee, Report*, 1892–3, Appendix 8, pp.207, 209. John Bellamy (b. Shoreditch, 1884) used to join 'a pal of mine who often stayed away from school to mind the kids and make the porridge, which I enjoyed with him': 'Looking Back' p.2.
39. C.f. 'Pearl Fisher', *Harvest of the City*, pp.51, 118, 119 (report on St Giles in the mid-1880s) for a boy nurse in charge of siblings; and two others (one only six, the other fourteen) each caring for sick parents in rooms which they kept beautifully clean and neat.
40. *Light and Shade*, Nov. 1881, p.86.
41. Jack Welch (b. Shoreditch, 1903), transcript, pp.5–6.
42. LCC *MOH London, Reports*, 1895, p.48; 1900, p.27.
43. LCC *Public Control Committee, Minutes* 1899–1900, List of Lamp Accidents.
44. 'Brenda', *Froggy's Little Brother*.
45. C.f. Bratton, *Impact*, chaps 4 and 5; Drotner, *Children's Magazines*, shows a similar trend.
46. For chronology and details of compulsion: Rubinstein, *Attendance*, chap.3; Smith, *Education*, chap.9.
47. Howgrave, 'Nurseries', p.147.
48. See Hilton, *Hilton*, and the fund-raising *Crèche Annual*; also For a smaller Mile End crèche, see PRO ED 14/1.
49. One at Nassau Street in Marylebone may have started as early as 1850 (*Social Notes* 2nd series: 1, 21 Aug. 1880, p.48). For greater detail see Davin, 'Work and School' (thesis), Chapter 4.
50. Gorst, *Children of the Nation*, p.40.
51. Major, 'Educational Appliances', pp.xviii and 48–9; see also *Lancet*, 11 June 1870, p.852; and Allen, 'Education in Battersea' (1870), p.vi, para 35. (C.f. LCC *Report on Crèches*, 1904, p.45.)
52. Howgrave, 'Nurseries'.
53. PRO ED 14/18, correspondence with Rev. W. Tyler in June 1872 (includes details on how the crèche was run); c.f. SBL *Minutes*, 29 May 1872.
54. PRO ED 14/1, correspondence between School Board and Education Department, Nov. 1873. Baby Room was an alternative term for crèche, used already by Matthew Arnold in his *General Report* for 1858 (*Reports*, p.76). The provision of crèches in poor districts was suggested by London Divisional Superintendents when consulted by the SBL Byelaws Committee in 1874 on how to improve attendance.
55. *Cross Commission, Second Report*, PP 1887, evidence Mrs Burgwin, q.17,188. (The LCC *Report on Crèches*, 1904, Appendix 1, says the Orange Street crèche opened in 1889.)
56. PRO ED 14/1, SBL to Education Department 16 Oct. 1879. They included ones at Anglers Gardens, Popham Street and Gifford Street, in Islington; Bath Street, Finsbury; Bell Street and Haverstock Street, Marylebone; Chaucer Street, Orange Street and Westcott Street, Southwark; and Pooles Park, Finsbury.
57. PRO ED 14/1, SBL to Education Department, 11 Oct. 1877; Auditor's disallowance 16

Oct. 1879; upheld by Local Government Board 12 Oct. 1880. Other school boards still set up Baby Rooms, however: Newport Road school, Leytonstone, opened with classroom space for 240 boys, 180 girls (an interesting difference) and 116 infants, and a Baby Room for thirty-eight 'to meet the difficulty of the elder girls being kept at home to look after the babies': *Leytonstone Express and Independent*, 9 June 1883.

58. 'Mother Kate' [Warburton], *Old Soho Days*, p.67.

59. Her pay was even less enviable than her responsibility: probably only 12s. a week (SBL *Minutes*, 6 Dec. 1883, p.13).

60. Sims, *How the Poor Live*, p.32.

61. PRO ED 14/1, 28 Feb. 1881; *Cross Commission, 3rd Report*, PP 1887, Mark Wilks (Chair of SBL School Management Committee) questioned by Canon Gregory, q.49,123. R.B. Williams, superintendent of Visitors for East Lambeth was another advocate: q.40 and qq.805–80. The *Crèche Annual* countered similar opposition: 1876–7, p.7; 1893–4, p.9.

62. PRO ED 14/1, 16 Dec. 1880; Sims, *How the Poor Live*, p.32. See also SBL *Medical Officer, Report*, 1902, p.23, for comment on 'half a dozen' still in existence.

63. *Eastward Ho* 4, Dec. 1885, p.169. C.f. *Women and Work*, 24 Oct. 1874, p.5. Police responses to Chadwick's 1884 inquiries about street children and institutional provision noted few crèches (two or three in most divisions, none in some), though their information may have been incomplete: UCL Chadwick Papers, item 99 (answers to question 5).

64. The 1904 LCC list names eight established in the 1870s; eighteen in the 1880s; fourteen in the 1890s; and eight from 1900 to 1904. Eight had failed (two through 'lack of funds'). It omits ten named in Howgrave's 1872 COS report, and several identifiable from other sources: some may have gone under; but one in Wellclose Square was going strong in 1899, when 'over 4,000 children were sheltered and fed' (Oesterley, *Walks in Jewry*, p.57).

65. McCulloch, *Open Church*, p.83; c.f. LCC *Report on Crèches*, 1904, Appendix 1; Kozak, 'Nursery at Wesley House', p.9.

66. *Eastward Ho* 4, 1885, p.169.

67. LCC *Report on Crèches*, 1904, p.4–6.

68. C.f. Kimmins, *Polly*, pp.210–12.

69. This problem was sometimes acknowledged. 'In some localities women may be enabled to bring their children cleaner than in others. Many of our children are very clean; but if only one in ten were objectionable, it would be necessary to change all': *Crèche Annual 1872–3*, p.29. Any stigma for using a crèche would be amplified by such procedures.

70. LCC *Report on Crèches*, 1904, p.6. Another advantage with a neighbour, if she lived in the same house or close enough for them to be bundled up and carried round, was that the children need not be woken before being handed over: c.f. Chew, 'All in the Day's Work: Mrs Bolt', *Life and Writings*, p.162.

71. LCC *Report on Crèches*, 1904, p.6. Irregular need was another factor. Laundry work (women's main local employment) was seasonal: c.f. Latymer Road mission report that 'the nursery is a little slack owing to the scarcity of work in the neighbourhood'; *Light and Shade*, Sept. 1881, p.62.

72. *R.C. Poor Laws, Minority Report*, PP 1909, p.772.

73. *Light and Shade*, March 1881. Publicity for the crèche stresses saving infant lives rather than souls, though.

74. Hilton, *Hilton*, p.228. He adds that 'a training home for servants soon became associated with the crèche'.

75. Much depended on the individuals. Mrs Hilton's crèche apparently commanded local support: when she was very ill, local people arranged a procession, with music and banners, and collected about £16: *Crèche Annual, 1895–6*, p.12. By 1901 Mrs Hilton's crèche had passed to the National Association for the Reclamation of Destitute Waif Children, 'which owes its existence to Dr Barnardo': Woolmer, 'Caring for London's Children', p.372.

76. One friend, Miss Georgina Hogarth, 'never failed to send an annual donation' and 'the cash, somehow or other, invariably arrived': Ridge, *Storyteller*, pp.111 and 37.

77. Howgrave, 'Nurseries', p.147.

78. Parr, *Labouring Children*, p.17.

79. One account implies an unlikely autonomy: 'If the child is well-grown he may secure admittance at two years and three quarters': Iselin, 'Childhood of the Poor', p.472.

80. *Cross Commission, 2nd Report*, PP 1887, evidence, q.15,663, Miss Whittenbury, Sidney Road Infants School, Homerton. C.f. boy admitted at two and a half to ensure sister's atten-

dance because mother ill: Miss H. (b. Kensington, 1902), transcript, p.12.

81. SBL *Byelaws Committee and School Accommodation and Attendance Committee, Reports*. Between 1889 and 1901 the numbers of children under three recorded as in school dropped from 876 to 286.

82. Amelia Wheeler (b. 1872), Tottenham, *How Things Were*, p.88.

83. Grant, *From Me to We*, p.42. For heads trying to obtain birth certificates, see Logbooks, Walnut Tree Walk, 11 Jan. 1878; Flint Street, 13 Feb., 4 June 1878; Coleraine Park (Boys), 21 Nov. 1881. Birth certificates themselves were not always accurate: c.f. Lewis, ms. memoir, p.1 (hers gave a birth date eight weeks late, because her mother could not afford it at first); and *Daily Mirror*, 23 Feb. 1979, letter about an 1870s mother who from poverty did not register the death of a baby son or the birth of her next (born the following year) who grew up with the birth certificate of the one who had died.

84. SBL *Special Sub-Committee, Saffron Hill School, Report*, 1889. She also noted that other parents avoided sending children at five by pretending they were younger ('sometimes they run the street until they are over six, nearly seven'), and then after a while would start asking 'why is so-and-so not put up, as he or she is seven'. Jewish parents of children born abroad were accused of using uncertainty about their ages to get them out of school and to work: SBL *Minutes*, 19 April 1894, pp.1,047–9.

85. SBL *Special Sub-Committee, Mrs Mansfield, Minutes*, 1881.

86. Grace Smith (b. Kentish Town, 1905), interview notes, 29 Dec. 1975.

87. Kennedy, 'Board School London', p.90.

6 Needed at Home

1. Information on this is scanty, but c.f. Black, *Married Women's Work*, p.23 (laundry-worker's consumptive husband tended the two youngest and cooked dinner for all five children), p.29 (seasonally unemployed husband looked after the children; wife working as a paper-sorter), and p.90; also Toogood, 'Role of the Crèche', p.81. The father of Miss H. (born Kensington, 1902), a restaurant manager, cared for the children during the day when the mother was very ill: transcript, p.12.

2. George Lansbury told the 1895 *R.C. Aged Poor* (qq.13,824–5) that in Bow and Bromley many old people on outdoor relief minded the children of their daughters 'who go to work for Bryant and May's, and also shirt stitch, and that kind of work'. C.f. Black, *Married Women's Work*, p.19; and numerous examples: e.g. McCleary, *Infant Milk Depots*, p.35, case 12; Miss N. (born Shadwell, 1895), transcript, p.5, and Mrs K. (born Battersea, 1897), transcript, p.4.

3. [Harkness], *Toilers*, 1889, pp.21–3.

4. When Frank S. (born Hoxton, 1884) was out of work his wife did laundry-packing and he walked the pram from Battersea to Chelsea and back each day so that her sister could have the children: transcript, p.80.

5. Christian Social Union *Report*, quoted Malcolmson, 'Laundresses', p.457.

6. Davies, *Life*, pp.20–2 (and p.3 her elder sister); c.f. Bosanquet, *Rich and Poor*, p.834. Arlidge noted in 1892 (*Diseases*, p.557) that with 'the almost universal adoption of the perambulator', young nurses suffered less often from 'lateral curvature of the spine and general one-sidedness produced by 'carrying children on one arm'.

7. An Acton laundress supporting two children on her own paid the landlady 1s. a week to look after the baby, and 2s. 6d. a week rent; she earned about 12s. 6d. a week: *R.C. Labour*, PP 1893–4, 'Employment of Women', p.22, Witness 139.

8. A Poor Law Inspector reported that it was 'very common' for 'old women in receipt of relief [to]...mind their neighbour's child during the day while they are getting work'. As Poor Law Unions refused relief in such cases, it is not surprising that they could not confirm this: *S.C. Protection Infant Life*, PP 1871, evidence q.3,884 and Appendix 4. Behlmer (*Child Abuse*, p.40) cites an 1877 report of numerous unlicensed nurseries run in cramped Clerkenwell homes by widows and spinsters.

9. Coate, 'Some Phases of Poor Life'. Rates varied (and rose) from 2s. 6d. a week in 1858 (*Times*, 7 Jan., police reports, Eleanor Emmerson); to 3s. to 4s. 6d. a week or 3d. to 6d. a day in 1871 (*S.C. Protection Infant Life*, 1871, Appendix 4); to 6s. or 7s. in 1873 (SBL *Minutes*, 28 May, pp.552, 1,105); to 4d. to 8d. a day in the 1890s (*Crèche Annual*, 1893–4, pp.14–15 and *R.C. Labour*, PP 1893–4, 'Employment of Women', pp.22–3); while rates

quoted in 1915 range from 6d. to 1s. 2d. a day, with one minder earning from 11s. to 14s. a week (Black, *Married Women's Work*, p.19; see also p.62; pp.111–2). Crèches never paid their way, but they were always too dear for some mothers (see previous chapter).

10. Black, *Married Women's Work*, p.19.
11. Bosanquet, *Rich and Poor*, p.83.
12. For northern half-timers, see Hicks, 'Education of the Half-Timer'; Robson, *Education of Children in Industry*; Frow, *Half-Time*; and Silver, 'Ideology and the Factory Child'.
13. SBL *Final Report*, p.196.
14. *R.C. Factory Acts*, PP 1876, evidence, Buxton and Croad (London School Board), q.3,112.
15. For a girl half-timer in domestic box-making in Shoreditch in 1883, see PRO, ED 14/19, 4 May 1883; and for one in a pipe-making workshop in Tabard Street (Borough), see GLRO A/RNY/86, ms. letter E. Beard to Mrs H. Selfe Leonard, 24 Nov. 1887.
16. C.f. *School Board Chronicle*, 13 March 1880, p.246; SBL *Minutes*, 20 March 1884, p.862.
17. Here my concern is with reasons for the difference between boys' and girls' attendance patterns—sickness and lack of shoes were common to both.
18. See SBL *School Accommodation and Attendance Committee, Reports*, Table D.
19. Samuel, *Underworld*, p.31.
20. Mrs M. (born Hoxton, 1896), my notes of tape played at Hackney People's Autobiography meeting 4 April 1974, p.1. C.f. William Nn (born Poplar, 1896), ms. memoir, pp.17, 42: when his father was missing work through ill-health, he stopped going to afternoon school to help his mother make rope or canvas fendoffs [fenders] for a nautical dealer. From eleven till fourteen, he was an unofficial half-timer; and he was not allowed to sit the scholarship exam for secondary school.
21. SBL *Byelaws Committee, Reports*, e.g. 1889–90; *School Accommodation and Attendance Committee, Reports*, 1894–1900, Appendix 5. See also Rubinstein, *Attendance*, pp.36–7.
22. LCC *Education Committee, Minutes*, 26 Oct. 1902, pp.1, 182.
23. *The Times*, 23 Sept. 1891, p.8.
24. *Daily Chronicle*, 13 Oct. 1902, p.9.
25. C.f. cartoon Irishwoman registering for the new old-age pension, who cannot give her date of birth and says 'Faith, yer honour, there was no such thing as dates when I was born': *Punch*, 28 Oct. 1908, reproduced in Quadagno, *Aging*. Booth thought labourers often did not know their exact age: *R.C. Aged Poor*, PP 1895, evidence, q.10,967.
26. *H.M. Inspector's Report*, 1893, copied into Logbook, Maidstone Street, 28 Aug. 1893.
27. Logbook, Maidstone Street, 6 Sept. 1895, 3 March 1896, 12 March 1898, 31 Oct. 1899, 9 May 1900. C.f. also NUT *Report on School Attendance*, Oct. 1891, p.3 (PRO ED 10/11); and Macnamara's 1900 claim that some 25,000 of the 755,940 children on the school rolls in London were so often away that 'practically the only education they get [is]...their names on the school rolls': 'Progressivism', p.795.
28. For average ages per standard, see Logbook, Maidstone Street, 19 Sept. 1902. On greater irregularity of older children, c.f. SBL *School Management Committee, Minutes*, 14 Dec. 1888 (on Morris Road school, Tower Hamlets).
29. SBL *School Accommodation and Attendance Committee, Report*, 1892, Appendix 8, pp.266–8.
30. The logbook for Bell Street school has similar entries, but without age or standard: see 8 and 15 Oct. 1894; 29 March, 3 May, 24 Aug., 29 Nov. 1895; 31 July 1896; 3 Feb. 1897. In slum schools 'a full fourth of the children on the rolls are seldom seen in school', according to Tabor ('Education', p.501).
31. Attendance at Brunswick Road school, Hackney, was 'little over 70 per cent and many of the boys are confirmed truants...away from school for weeks together. In the girls' school the percentage is equally low but there is no truancy': SBL *Minutes*, 13 July 1888, p.1,220 (School Management Committee Report).
32. Quoted in Spalding, *School Board*, p.136.
33. If domestic arrangements allowed, infants were more often kept at home in bad weather or for minor illness; they also succumbed in greater numbers to the infectious diseases which regularly swept through schools.
34. This return was quoted by Macnamara at the School Attendance Officers' national conference in 1900 to show that one-fifth of the children on the rolls made half-time or less. Both in this speech (*School Attendance Officers' Gazette*, Jan. 1901, p.162), and in 'Progressivism' (1900), he ignored the differences between boys, girls and infants, and his definitions and comments relate entirely to boys.
35. Logbook, Cottenham Road, 17 Feb. 1873, 10 July 1873.

36. Logbook, Gainsborough Road, 12 June 1885.
37. See examples in Rubinstein, *Attendance*, pp.60–1. Outwork is discussed more fully below.
38. C.f. Logbooks, Bell Street, 14 Dec. 1894, 18 Jan. 1889, 17 May 1897; Garratt Lane, 23 Nov. 1894, 19 April 1897, 18 April 1898; Gainsborough Road, 14 May 1897, 6 May 1898; Anglers Gardens, 27 Nov. 1885; Randall Place, 4 March 1892.
39. *Crèche Annual, 1880–1*, p.10.
40. Letter from Southwark Divisional Inspector, 15 April 1872 (PRO ED 14/1). Only 4,772 girls were on the rolls, to 7,647 boys; and 5,531 infants between three and five were reported not at school.
41. Hodson, *Letters*, pp.38–40. C.f. Mrs Layton (quoted previous chapter), who like other local children always stayed away on washing day: Davies, *Life*, p.4.
42. Logbook, Anglers' Gardens, 30 Jan. 1888, 17 Sept. 1890.
43. It was claimed in 1890 that 'on Mondays children were often kept away from school because the mother had not been "to pawn"' and had no money yet for the fee: SBL *Special Subcommittee, Administration of Byelaws, Report*, p.82.
44. Logbook, Cottenham Road, 18 Sept. 1874; 10 May 1875; similar references abound in other logbooks.
45. See Spalding, *School Board*, p.186; SBL *School Management Committee, Report*, 1889–90, p.lxxv; Logbooks, Bell Street, 5 Dec. 1895, 24 Jan. 1896; Anglers Gardens, 17 March 1893; Randall Place, 9 Feb. 1900, 10 May 1895.
46. Memorial from SBL to Education Dept, 28 Feb. 1881, asking for help over Baby Rooms (PRO ED 14/1).
47. C.f. Rubinstein, *Attendance*, p.64: 'helping mother', along with working in theatres and fields, 'enjoyed a tolerated position in the eyes of the Board and the Government, if only because it seemed impossible to stop'.
48. SBL Byelaws Committee on...uniform enforcement, 1874, evidence, qq.587–8.
49. Florence H. (born Bethnal Green, 1892), transcript, pp.11–12.
50. Ernest Gray in House of Commons debate on Education Estimates, 17 June 1897, reported *Schoolmaster*, 26 June 1897, p.1,129. C.f. Rubinstein, *Attendance*, p.63.
51. Quoted *Education Report, 1899*, PP 1900, p.297.
52. C.f. Rubinstein, *Attendance*, p.47: before 1901 prosecution was unlikely unless attendance fell below seven out of ten.
53. Mag Ayling, on her aunt (born 1891, Deptford), recorded in class at Goldsmiths' College, 15 June 1983.
54. SBL *School Management Committee, Report*, 1887–8, p.xlv.
55. For one head's punctuality campaign, see Logbook, Flint Street, 1877, 12 July (several sent home), 23 Aug. (over 20 turned away), 6 Sept., 13 Sept. (a great number sent home), 'next week I shall punish them with the cane'), 18 Sept., 19 Sept. ('I have punished the late children, but it seems to do little good'), 27 Sept. (more punctual), 9 Oct. ('again lost their mark through coming late'), 10 Oct. (kept in), 18 Oct. (sent home), 24 Oct. (more punctual, none sent home).
56. The logbooks show so many causes of lateness (as of absence) that it seems unnecessary to look beyond ill-health, inadequate clothing, domestic and other responsibilities and the rest. But defensive entries by heads do often blame the parents' lack of interest in education.
57. SBL *Minutes*, 20 Dec. 1883, pp.184–6. Inspector McWilliam's district was north Lambeth and north Southwark (Neckinger to Kennington Oval, Thames to Camberwell Green) but for this report he included nine other schools, mainly East End.
58. The system was later criticized for improving only the punctuality of those already punctual: it made the regular child 'one who sacrifices everything for the sake of perfect punctuality', and offered no incentive to the child whose chance was already lost: Memo from chairman, SBL Subcommittee, Medal System, SBL *Minutes*, 30 March 1900.
59. C.f. SBL Chairman's lament in 1880 that unpunctuality interfered with scripture instruction: Reed, 'Ten Years', pp.674–5; and SBL *Management Committee Reports*, 1887–8, p.xlvi, and 1888–9, p.xiii (worse still, 'this loss occurs principally in those cases where there is least probability that home or Sunday school teaching will compensate').
60. *Cross Commission, 2nd Report* 1887, evidence HMI Nickal, qq.39,874–9.
61. SBL *School Management Committee Reports*, School Returns, 1887–8 to 1893–4.
62. *Employment of Schoolchildren*, PP 1902, evidence Hetherington (Hackney), q.956; Bevan (Hackney), qq.2,691–8; Eves, Appendix 18.

63. *Crèche Annual, 1895–6*, pp.8–9.
64. Celia R. (born Waterloo, 1899) was regularly caned for being late because her mother sent her on last minute errands: notes from SE1 People's History Group, 4 Aug. 1981.
65. C.f. discussion in Rubinstein, *Attendance*, (pp.98–103, esp. p.102) of a ruling in 1884 that a twelve-year-old nursemaid was 'discharging the honourable duty of helping her parents': 'a reasonable excuse for her non-attendance at school'; and Lewis, 'School Fees and the School Board', p.292.
66. *Hansard* 1 March 1899, cols 962–3 and 972.
67. Memo from chairman, SBL *Subcommittee, Medal System*, 1900.
68. See, for instance, SBL *Minutes*, 8 Feb. 1884: in the Board's reply to an Education Department enquiry on obstacles to improved attendance all four points concern enforcement.
69. *Cross Commission, 2nd Report*, PP 1887, evidence Mrs Burgwin (head Orange Street, Southwark), qq.17,064–5. For extended discussion of social causes of poor attendance, and of attempts to deal with them, see Hurt, *Schooling*, chaps 5–8.
70. For example SBL *School Management Committee, Report 1887–8*, p.xliv (Inspectors' Reports); or Memorial from Metropolitan Board Teachers Association, 1889 (PRO ED/10 10). Lewis ('School Fees and the School Board') argues convincingly that arguments based on moral categorization were becoming less tenable.
71. SBL *Inspectors' Reports*, PP 1878, p.8.
72. SBL *Inspectors' Reports*, PP 1878, p.31.
73. SBL *Minutes*, 20 Dec. 1883, p.186.
74. Albert M. (born Hoxton, 1894), transcript, pp.A36–41.
75. SBL *Special Committee, Administration Byelaws*, 1890, Report, p.68.
76. As previous note, p.142.
77. The managers' moralizing reminds us that such questions occasioned continuing political struggle within the Board and school administration more generally: c.f. Lewis, 'School Fees and the School Board'.
78. C.f. Marsden, 'Residential Segregation'; 'Education and Urbanization', pp.88–90.
79. Only two other Board Schools in Tower Hamlets charged as much: SBL *School Management Committee, Report*, 1886–7, Table R, School Returns, Tower Hamlets.
80. Mrs Bartle, transcript, pp.16–17. The school's superiority was attested in inspectors' reports, which praised its achievements in examinations and also in drill.
81. The rates were 91.3 per cent for boys, 89 per cent for girls, and 80 per cent for infants at Thomas Street; 71.1 per cent, 75.8 per cent, and 71.7 per cent at Sydney Road: SBL *School Management Committee, Report*, 1886–7, Table R, School Returns, Tower Hamlets and Hackney.
82. See SBL *School Management Committee, Report*, 1886–7, School Returns, London. The few mixed schools are not included here; and calculations are made on the basic fee only (it was reduced for the brothers and sisters of a child already attending the school). Infants' fees were lower, but still preserved differences.
83. C.f. SBL *Special Subcommittee, Administration Byelaws, Minutes*, 24 Oct. 1889: heads' responses to the question, 'Do you have many cases of truancy among your scholars?' record from five to ten times as many truant boys as girls, despite a reverse ratio in attendance figures.
84. *Employment of Schoolchildren*, PP 1902, p.9 (report of H.M. Inspector King).
85. In 1871 339 cases of boys and seventy of girls were dealt with by the School Board Industrial Schools Officers: most boys were remanded or sent to Industrial (i.e. Truant) Schools, and under half of the girls (SBL *Minutes*, 13 Dec. 1871, p.25). Subsequent reports suggest a similar pattern.
86. SBL *School Accommodation and Attendance Committee, Report*, 1892–3, Appendix xviii, gives details concerning nineteen boys and seven girls in Finsbury in 1892: four boys were sent to Truant Schools, and no girls; fines were higher for the boys. Spalding (*School Board*, pp.143–5), in 1900, records 740 boys in the SBL's five residential Industrial Schools, and fifty girls. London children could be sent elsewhere, but the national sex ratio was similar: in 1895 there were 13,133 boys in such institutions to 4,241 girls: *H.M. Inspectors' Report*, 1895.
87. SBL *Special Committee, Administration Byelaws*, 1890, p.91.
88. *Social Notes* 1, 11 Sept. 1880, p.96.
89. SBL *Special Committee, Administration Byelaws*, 1890, p.91.

90. *Board of Education Report*, PP 1899, p.295 (Mr King's General Report on schools of the Metropolis). Boys' average attendance for 1898 was 85.3 per cent and for 1899 85.8 per cent; girls' was 81. 1 per cent (1898) and 81. 6 per cent (1899); infants' 78.2 per cent and 71.1 per cent.
91. Spalding, *School Board*, pp.136–7.

7 A Centre of Humanizing Influence

1. See Davin, 'Reading Books'.
2. The term standard was in general use from 1862, with One as the lowest.
3. Tabor, 'Elementary Education', p.213.
4. LCC *MOH London, Report*, 1904–5, pp.14, 25.
5. William Nn, ms. memoir, p.40.
6. Rolph, *Particulars*, pp.26–7.
7. SBL *School Management Committee, Report*, 1892–3, p.xviii. C.f. *School Board Chronicle*, 24 July 1880, p.78.
8. Arnold, *Reports* (1853), p.24.
9. Gardner, *Lost Schools*, p.158; he contrasts this rigid order with the flexible clustering of the working-class private school: pp.156–9.
10. Whitbread, *Nursery-Infant School*, p.41; Bartley, *Schools for the People*.
11. 'For economy, I suppose, the younger boys used slates which they cleaned with expectoration and the sleeves of their jackets, a process that dried out the operator's throat and wore out his coat sleeves': Willis, *Jubilee Road*, p.75.
12. Ezard, *Battersea Boy*, p.40. C.f. *Cross Commission, 2nd Report*, PP 1887, evidence Miss Whittenbury, qq.15,621–5.
13. Logbook, Flint Street, 23 May 1878.
14. Church, *Bridge*, p.72. C.f. Ashby, *Ashby*, p.19: 'How dull school was!' (of a village National school in the 1860s).
15. Wigram, *Elementary Arithmetic*, pp.25, 40. (Later Bishop of Rochester.) C.f. Birchenough (*Education*, pp.253–5) for mid-century examples of scripture-based instruction in geography and arithmetic. For the alternation of morals and mystery in Bible teaching see Ashby, *Ashby*, pp.22–3.
16. Spalding, *School Board*, p.161, on the 1882 Education Code.
17. C.f. Digby and Searby, *Children, School and Society*, pp.34, 36; documents pp.159–63; Lowndes, *Silent Revolution*, pp.35–6 (note photograph of teacher with stuffed dog).
18. Green Street School, Rotherhithe, Logbook, 8 Feb. 1886. (Thanks to 1981 Vicar of St Mary's, Rotherhithe, for access to old logbooks.)
19. Ashby, *Ashby*, p.19.
20. Logbook, Walnut Tree Walk, 20 Nov. 1896.
21. Gardiner, *Games*, p.44; c.f. p.28.
22. Logbook, Flint Street, 8 Feb. 1876: visit from the Inspector, Mrs Floyer; Logbook, Green Street, Rotherhithe, 25 May 1887. See also Miss Loch, 'Needlework', in Spalding, *School Board*, p.235.
23. Miss Christiansen, SBL *School Management Committee, Report*, 1891–2, p.xxiii ('This seems a very successful arrangement'); *Instructions to Inspectors*, PP 1902, Appendix 1.
24. Logbook, Flint Street, 3 Oct. 1884.
25. Earlier Froebel influence was blighted by the 1862 *Revised Code*; but in 1874 the Board appointed a Froebelian to lecture to Infant teachers: Birchenough, *Education*, pp.275–6; Whitbread, *Nursery-Infant School*, p.47; Salmon and Hindshaw, *Infant Schools*, pp.89–91, 117–21.
26. Cit. Birchenough, *Education*, p.308. C.f. Whitbread, *Nursery-Infant School*, p.49.
27. For progressive US 'kindergartners' from the 1890s, like Dewey, emphasizing community and peer group as source of moral values and sanctions rather than family, c.f. Cavallo, 'Politics of Latency', pp.169–73.
28. C.f. Mary H. Hart (sec. Froebel Society), *Children of the Street*, pp.40–3: 'the child is but too often unduly crammed so that it may pass the first standard at the age of seven'. She wanted the Baby Rooms made more joyous, to counter the degrading effects of 'the atmosphere of ignorance and sin' in which children grew up.
29. Bray, *School Organization*, p.141.

30. These discussions can be followed in *Child Study*, the *Paidologist*, and *Pedagogical Seminary*; and see Wroe, *Public Infants Schools*; and *Children under...Five*, PP 1908. C.f. Steedman, 'Mother Made Conscious', 'Prisonhouses' and *Childhood, Culture and Class*; Davin, 'Imperialism and Motherhood'; and (US) Cavallo, 'Politics of Latency'.

31. *Report on School Children under Five*, PP 1906, pp.28–9.

32. C.f. Bray, *Town Child*, p.104.

33. See Sykes, 'Hygiene and Sanitation' (no school before five or even seven), and ensuing discussion (including Rev. Fairclough: children better off at school); also *Paidologist* 7, Nov. 1905, p.183; vol. 8, July 1906, p.117; vol. 9, March 1907, pp.11–18 (Kate Palmer); and Margaret McMillan's writings throughout.

34. *School Children under Five*, PP 1906, pp.46, 58–60. (The Chief Inspector cut some of her report as 'not entirely reliable': too impassioned, perhaps.)

35. See Gardner, *Lost Schools*, esp. chaps 3, 4.

36. *Education Code*, PP 1905, Article 53; *School Children under Five*, PP 1906, p.58; Gorst, *Children of the Nation*, p.176; see also *Children below...Five*, PP 1908, pp.15–16; Whitbread, *Infant-Nursery School*, pp.64–6.

37. Their conclusions were not fully endorsed by the President of the Board of Education: c.f. speech announcing reduction in the grant payable for children under five: PRO LCC EO/PS/1/16 (Day Schools Sub Committee); *Hansard, Commons Debates*, 16 July 1909.

38. *School Children below...Five*, PP 1908; and Memo from LCC MOH Education [James Kerr] to LCC Day Schools Sub Committee, 2 Nov. 1908 (PRO LCC EO/PS/1/16).

39. See PRO LCC/EO/PS/1/16, 1908–10, for debate on what such women should be paid and whether motherliness or training was more important.

40. Holmes, *What Is*, pp.116, 104, 87. C.f. Salmon and Hindshaw, *Infant Schools*, p.292. For Holmes, see Gordon, 'Holmes: Reassessment and Bibliography'; Simon, *Education and the Labour Movement*, pp.116–19.

41. Seaborne, *English School*, p.200. He suggests (pp.107, 142) that the eighteenth-century trend of more provision for girls but more segregation was intensified under the monitorial system. The National Society in 1835 favoured dividing the sexes (p.141).

42. Nancy Ball notes Scottish influence on the Wesleyans and Evangelicals: *Educating the People*, p.105.

43. Arnold, *Reports*, for 1852, pp.14–15; for 1853, p.24. C.f. *Education Report*, PP 1870, pp.141–2 (pro), and 282–3 (anti).

44. Stevenson, *Virginibus Puerisque*, pp.28–9.

45. SBL *Minutes*, 21 June 1871, p.164. (Motion put by Huxley, as chairman of the Education Committee.)

46. Rider Haggard claimed that single-sex education threatened the survival of empire: girls were too delicately nurtured for a colonial life and 'The flag of Britain in too many places is flying over a generation of bachelors': 'Co-Education', p.568.

47. The headmaster of Fleet Road, W.B. Adams, strongly favoured mixed schools: *Cross Commission, 2nd Report*, PP 1887, qq.14,994–7, 15,001–6. (On Fleet Road see also Morley, 'Eton for Nothing'.) See also Grey and Tylee, *Co-Education*; and Bray, *School Organization*, pp.148–51.

48. Twenty-five per cent opposed the change; many were indifferent; only 5'+'p-,,'per cent removed their children: Jephson, *My Work*, p.107.

49. 'Una', 'Mixed schools and separate playgrounds', *Woman's Gazette* 3, July 1878, p.107.

50. Similarly, the roof-top playground at Michael Faraday school was assigned to the girls, according to the newspaper report of the opening in 1897, because the School Board 'knew that the death roll of Walworth would be greatly increased if the boys...were allowed to play on the roof': quoted *Walworth in Print* 73, Dec. 1985—Jan. 1986.

51. William Nn (b. 1896), ms. memoir, p.40. Jack Common, as a five-year-old new boy, went confidently to the boys' entrance of his Tyneside school and was seen off by the caretaker with 'a sort of contemptuous relish': *Kiddar's Luck*, p.38.

52. Logbook, Cottenham Road, 12 Feb. 1897. C.f. SBL *Minutes*, 25 Jan. 1894: continuance of a temporary school (Knee-Hill, Greenwich) approved, but 'if boys over eight years old were retained in the School separate approaches must be provided for the sexes'.

53. SBL *Minutes*, 24 Jan. 1872, approval of plans for Essex Street school.

54. Logbook, Coleraine Park, 10 Feb. 1882.

55. Pritchett, *Cab*, p.64.

56. William Nn, ms. memoir, p.43. (They were chased off daily by the local policeman.) The SBL recommended one urinal place for every twenty boys and one closet for every twenty-five; for girls and infants one closet for every fifteen: Porter, *School Hygiene*, p.293. That standard was not always achieved: c.f. Conway, *Peckham Park Schools*, p.12.

57. C.f. Brockway, *Bermondsey Story*, cit. Laski, 'Domestic Life', p.156: 1900s court with one lavatory for twenty-five households: 'queues lined up outside that water closet, men, women and children, every morning before they went to work'.

58. Willis, *Jubilee Road*, p.50.

59. Willis, *Jubilee Road*, pp.50, 84. (C.f. Sharp, *Schoolgirl*, for middle-class boy's similar code.) Willis likens the school's separate entrances and departments to those of a factory.

60. Ridge, *Storyteller*, pp.114–15. (He made the boy a six-year-old, probably in the interests of heightening the story: it could only be a guess.)

61. Foakes, *Walls*, p.69.

62. C.f. Rolph, *Particulars*, pp.26–7: on first day at school he saw a sobbing little girl who turned out to be a boy, and several others 'in this epicene state'. Breeching was a 'domestic crisis, with neighbours popping in to admire the emancipated victim and the new clothes'. Years later, he learned that 'little boys at that time wore dresses not because their mothers were grieving that they hadn't turned out to be little girls, but because no-one had yet invented plastic or otherwise disposable nappies'.

63. Church, *Bridge*, p.142. His invocation in this passage of Jehovah as the patriarchal model of the human male echoes Holmes on authoritarian education (*What Is*, pp.42–59), e.g. (p.47): 'What [Man] has suffered at the hands of his Schoolmaster—the God of Israel (and of Christendom)—he has taken good care to inflict on his pupil, the child.'

64. Jobson (b. Anerley, 1889), *Creeping Hours*, pp.95–6.

65. Rubinstein, *Attendance*, p.25.

66. Conway, *Peckham Park Schools*, p.9; Gittings and Manton, *Second Mrs Hardy*, p.16.

67. Stanley, 'Religion at the London School Board', pp.741–2; Jones, *Stanley*, pp.25–30; and c.f. G.L. Bruce's *Report* to his Tower Hamlets constituents, 1893.

68. Holmes, *What Is*, p.47. C.f. *School Children under Five*, PP 1906, Chief Inspector Cyril Jackson's Introductory Memorandum, p.ii: 'The child in the large class is drilled to a listless quiet under the order "Sit still while teacher talks".' In monitorial schools or where several classes met in one hall it was worse: c.f. Ashby's memories of his 1860s village National school (Ashby, *Ashby*, pp.16–17).

69. SBL *School Management Committee, Report*, 1888–9, p.xvii.

70. *Chambers National Reading Books* (1873), National Primer, Step Two. In fact, of course, girls, too, played with tops in London streets: see Ridge, *Storyteller*, p.200; Foakes, *Walls*, p.41.

71. Holmes, *What Is*, p.125. For teachers' memories of the examination procedure c.f. Lowndes, *Silent Revolution*, pp.12–14.

72. Pritchett, *Cab*, p.62. This was at 'a rough Church of England school' (St Matthews) in Camberwell, in about 1908. Such arrangements were less common in Board Schools by then.

73. Macdonald, *Board School Laryngitis*, p.4.

74. Macdonald, *Reminiscences*, pp.248–9.

75. Payne, *Primary Instruction*, pp.6–7; Birchenough, *Education*, p.282; *Education Report, 1887*, PP 1888, p.7 (Stokes on Southwark in Metropolitan Report); LCC *MOH London, Report*, 1904–5, p.43. C.f. William Nn (ms. memoir, p.47), each year 'automatically placed in the higher class leaving all the "duffers" behind'. When he left from the top standard, X7, some of his classmates were still in Standard Four.

76. Field, 'Ear and Hearing', p.798; and Dr Kerr estimated that at least 5 per cent of schoolchildren had serious problems of hearing: LCC *MOH London, Report*, 1904–5.

77. Fifteen girls out of forty in Standard One at Orange Street school could not see the blackboard from the back row: *Cross Commission, 2nd Report*, PP 1887, evidence Mrs Burgwin q.17,097. SBL *Committee of Representative Managers, Report on Defective Eyesight*, pp.107–8; Warner, 'Results', p.76; LCC *MOH London, Report*, Appendix 2 (Kerr), pp.37–8.

78. Church recorded the dramatic impact (on his reading especially) of his first spectacles, obtained after a school medical inspection found him to be short-sighted: *Bridge*, pp.82–6, 92–7.

79. HMI's report, Logbook, Gainsborough Street, 8 Nov. 1893.

80. Bessie C. (b. Bermondsey, 1893), transcript, p.49.

81. Elsie M. (b. 1905), transcript, p.32. 'It was a terrible disgrace to get a hander' (p.47).

82. Logbooks, Garratt Lane, 28 Jan. 1884; Walnut Tree Walk, 1 Nov. 1886.

83. See Logbook, Garratt Lane, 1883–4, for a succession of teachers (and three heads), and constant canings and punishments for disorderly behaviour etc. The inspector's report (9 May 1884) attributed low standards of order and work to the turnover of staff.

84. *Bilton's Reading Books*, 1869, Book 4 part 2 (For Girls). Approved for use in London schools: SBL *Minutes*, 21 Feb. 1872.

85. *School Managers' Series*, 1871–2, Standard One, p.43, Dialogue 6.

86. *Marshall's Universal Readers*, 1875–7, Book 1, p.55; p.91.

87. *SBL Inspectors' Reports, 1875*, PP 1878 (Mr Noble) p.5. See also Hurt, 'Drill'.

88. C.f. Fletcher, *Women First*; Atkinson, 'Fitness, Feminism and Schooling'; and May, *Madame Bergman-Osterberg*.

89. Board of Education, *Syllabus of Physical Exercises*, 1909, pp.2–5.

90. SBL *School Management Committee, Report*, 1887–8, p.liii.

91. SBL *Special Sub-Committee, Corporal Punishment*, 1902, Witness 21.

92. C.f. Common, *Kiddar's Luck*, p.118 (Tyneside, 1914).

93. SBL *Special Sub-Committee, Corporal Punishment*, 1902, Witness 15, on standing in the corner. A headmistress in 1880 criticized a candidate teacher who continually sent children out: 'This mode of punishment to be discontinued throughout the school.' Logbook, Anglers Gardens, 14 July 1880.

94. Bessie C. (b. 1893, Bermondsey) recalled a double sanction: 'if we got the cane the names went down in the punishment book, that was worse than having the cane really': transcript, p.49. C.f. SBL *Special Sub-Committee, Corporal Punishment*, 1902, Witness 20.

95. From headmistress's evidence to the 1898 Pupil Teacher Commission, cit. Widdowson, *Next Class*, p.70.

96. Personal communication in class, Morley College, 1977.

97. Mannin (b. 1900), *Confessions*, p.39.

98. Willis, *Jubilee Road*, p.75.

99. Logbooks, Anglers Gardens, 1 Dec. 1876; Nichol Street, 10 Oct. 1884; Randall Place, 11 Oct. 1889. Village children's reward after inspection took a paternalist form: in Tysoe, oranges from 'a hamper of great, golden rare fruit' sent by the Marquis of Northampton (Ashby, *Ashby*, p.18).

100. George A. (b. 1904), communication in class, Morley College, 1977.

101. SBL *Circular*, 31 July 1891.

102. Bray, 'Ordinary Day School', in Spalding, *London School Board*, p.184.

103. Logbook, Flint Street, 16 May 1878 (a father dragged out a boy 'kept in by my orders'); 22 July 1881 (two girls fetched out by their mothers); *Times*, 8 Sept. 1891, p.11, col. 2 (a builder attacked a teacher who had kept his son in at dinner time for making mistakes in a dictation exercise: fined £5). In another case, during a mass detention after a third of the children were late, three mothers came to protest, but they were talked round: Logbook, Anglers Gardens, 9 Sept. 1880.

104. SBL *School Management Committee, Minutes*, 27 July 1888, p.1,328, and 3 Aug. 1888, p.1,380. A child who escaped through the window of the Mistress's room at Randall Place School, Greenwich, was luckier, though she was suspended and her case taken to the School Managers: Logbook, 17 May 1882.

105. SBL *Special Sub Committee, Corporal Punishment*, 1902, Witness 29. Another head (Witness 17) said her teachers wanted power to slap for offences 'too slight for caning', and that parents also wanted their little ones slapped.

106. Pugh, *City*, p.189.

107. Mannin, *Confessions*, p.39.

108. At Cottenham Road Girls school in 1877, the inspector found discipline seriously defective; 'corporal punishments, though not individually severe, are administered with excessive frequency; more than twice as frequently as in the Boys' school, and altogether out of proportion to...other girls' schools in the district'. The grant was withheld (Logbook, June 1877).

109. Lowndes, *Silent Revolution*, p.17.

110. Pritchett, *Cab*, p.92. 'To talk in class was a crime, to leave one's desk inconceivable.' This was Rosendale Road school, Herne Hill, whose pupils were 'a mixture of working class and lower middles, with a few foreigners and colonials'. Pritchett came under a teacher

who was being allowed to try other methods (p.93): 'by some magnetism, he could silence a class almost without a word. He never used a cane....His one punishment took the form of an additional and excruciating lesson in [manners]....He would make us a write a formal letter of apology...it often took us a whole day and giving up all the pleasant lessons the rest were doing, to work out the phrasing of these letters of shame.'

111. Logbook, Garratt Lane, 14 Dec. 1883. The previous head left after a build-up of 'insolence' and punishment; this one (perhaps a temporary appointment) stayed only a month.

112. See for instance *SBL Inspectors' Reports, 1877*, PP 1878 (Williams on Tower Hamlets) p.54: caning was 'practically abandoned in a considerable number of girls' and infants' schools, and in one or two boys' schools'. In Tysoe's National School 'the master never caned a girl, no matter how maddening she might be', though for boys 'it was so easy to get a beating': Ashby, *Ashby*, p.19. In middle-class girls' schools 'caning was out of the question' (Hughes, *London Girl*, p.36).

113. Gautrey, *Lux*, p.116. See also Turnbull, 'So extremely like Parliament', pp.128–9.

114. In 1880 corporal punishment was reported as 'excluded from the discipline of one boys' school, fourteen girls' schools, and fifteen infants' schools, and in the great majority...the order and discipline are as faultless as ever': *School Board Chronicle*, 3 Jan. 1880. Three years later Inspector McWilliam reported that his territory included thirteen girls' schools doing without it, and four infants' schools: SBL *Minutes*, 20 Dec. 1883, p.193.

115. Booth Coll. B68 f.94.

116. SBL *Special Sub Committee, Corporal Punishment*, 1902, Witness 17.

117. Logbook, Anglers Gardens, 25 Feb. 1880. (On first joining the school the teacher concerned had 'unfortunately' struck the recently broken arm of a girl). C.f. Walnut Tree Walk, 19 June, 3 July, 11 Sept., and 22 Oct. 1885, for conflict over punishment between head and ('insubordinate'!) assistant.

118. *Revised Instructions to Inspectors*, PP 1887, article 58. From 1902: 'punishment which causes bodily pain' was banned in infants' schools; while with older children, 'corporal punishment should be discouraged as an ordinary expedient in boys' schools and altogether in girls' schools': *Revised Instructions*, PP 1902, p.8.

119. SBL regulations in 1871 made the head responsible for all corporal punishment, and banned its use by pupil teachers. In 1874 it was also forbidden to assistant teachers. Later they were allowed to cane under supervision.

120. C.f. petition in 1886 signed by 5,000 assistants and 900 heads: Gautrey, *Lux*, p.116.

121. Mrs F. (b. Portobello Rd, 1891), quoted Humphries, *Hooligans*, p.78.

122. 'I once officially investigated a case...in which a dozen girls had absented themselves on a Monday to take part in a Wesleyan Sunday School treat, with the knowledge and presumed approbation of the headmistress. They were all caned on the Tuesday morning for omitting the formality of bringing notes from their parents to account for and excuse their absence': Gorst, *Children of the Nation*, pp.180–3.

123. Ben Thomas and his brother were caned by the head of their Catholic school in Limehouse for going to the Salvation Army children's night (Thomas, *Ben's Limehouse*).

124. Margaret A. (b. Pentonville, 1896), transcript, p.47.

125. Mannin, *Confessions*, p.37. (The teacher's aspirin and sense of martyrdom are presumably retrospective colour.) For other cases of lost control, see *Daily Chronicle*, 13 Oct. 1902, p.9, col. 4; Logbook, Flint Street (Infants), 9 July 1877.

126. Logbook, Bell Street, 30 Sept. 1893.

127. Logbooks, Walnut Tree Walk, 30 Sept. 1878; Randall Place, 25 Aug. 1891.

128. Humphries (*Hooligans*, pp.77–8) suggests this was easier for girls, whose resistance to authority often took more devious or verbal form than the direct confrontations of some boys.

129. C.f. SBL *Minutes*, 15 Feb. 1894: Mr C. Waters (of Verbena Gardens, Hammersmith) complained that his child, Maude 'was caned by the Head Teacher to an extent that he would not tolerate'. Humphries found in Bristol that parents protested more often about unfair punishment for girls: 'Hurrah for England', pp.195–6.

130. Humphries quotes richly from memories (mainly Bristol) of conflicts over caning: *Hooligans*, pp.70–89. Stedman Jones (*Languages of Class*, p.222) argues that 'one of the main working-class objections to the Board Schools' concerned discipline.

131. C.f. Logbook, Maidstone Street, 27 Sept. 1889. The *Child's Guardian* (organ of the SPCC), 31 July 1889, appealed to teachers to report excessive punishment; and claimed

to have intervened in the conduct of some seventy teachers.

132. *Schoolmaster*, 12 Feb. 1898, p.275. C.f. *Schoolmaster*, 23 April 1898, p.764; 16 July 1898, p.97.

133. C.f. complaint about 'trifling fines', leaving the offender with 'a comforting conviction [of]...the secret sympathy of the bench': *Schoolmaster*, 24 July 1897, p.139.

134. Mrs Leopard was fined £2 with £1. 3s. costs: *Schoolmaster*, 23 April 1898, p.764 (Reddins Road school, Peckham); Mrs Pierpoint was fined 20s. with 23s. costs: *Daily Chronicle*, 13 Oct. 1902, p.9 col. 4 (St Matthias National School, Bethnal Green).

135. *Globe*, 17 July 1897, quoted *Schoolmaster*, 24 July 1897, p.139. C.f. Salt, 'Corporal Punishment', pp.18, 19.

136. *Daily Chronicle*, 13 Oct. 1902, p.9 col. 4. Ommanney (*House in the Park*, pp.36–8), weekly boarder in a private school, secretly and desperately prayed after his first mild caning that his mother should not hear of offence or punishment, and was deeply grateful to his teacher for her silence. C.f. Hurt, *Schooling*, pp.162–5.

137. SBL *Special Sub Committee, Corporal Punishment*, 1902, witnesses 27, 26. C.f. 1860s Leeds: 'Parents did not accept that teachers (and especially pupil teachers) had the right to punish their children' (Frith, 'Elementary Education in Leeds' (thesis), pp.85–7).

138. This was also a time when the working-class private schools were being squeezed out. Until the mid-1870s they provided a real alternative to Board or voluntary school education: a fifth of working-class children in Leeds in 1869 attended them; in 1870, 30 per cent in Portsmouth and 11 per cent in Southampton; and in 1871, 44,000 London children, or about 9 per cent of possible elementary pupils. See Field, 'Private Schools', p.13; Frith, 'Elementary Education in Leeds' (thesis), p.87; Gardner, *Lost Schools*, chap.6. In 1874 13,415 notices were served warning parents that the schools their children attended were classified as 'inefficient', and Board school intake increased by 12,345: SBL *Minutes*, 31 March 1874 (report of Bye Laws Committee). Mission and Ragged schools were among those condemned as inefficient.

139. For comparative developments, see De Coninck Smith, 'Copenhagen Children'.

140. C.f. Booth Coll. B68, facing f.135, on Risinghill Street school, Pentonville: 'Rows between parents and teachers over the flogging of children have given it a bad name.'

141. C.f. *School Attendance Gazette*, Dec. 1902. Police escort for teachers was occasionally needed in such cases: c.f. Hurt, *Schooling*, p.163.

142. Humphries, *Hooligans*, p.87.

143. *The Times*, 7 Oct. 1891, p.14, col. 2: the £2 fine and £121 costs bankrupted him.

8 Beacons of Civilization

1. Weylland, *These Fifty Years*, pp.95–100.

2. Vere, *Father Cuthbert's Curiosity Case*, p.108.

3. For teachers' background, see Widdowson, *Next Class*; Copelman, 'Classroom Struggle' (thesis). Social insecurity could increase the need to differentiate themselves: Marsden, 'Education and Urbanization', pp.94–5; Gardner, *Lost Schools*, chap.4.

4. *Schoolmaster*, 6 March 1897, p.419.

5. *School Attendance Gazette*, Oct. 1903; *Jewish Chronicle*, 17 Nov. 1911 (fire at Rutland Street school); and White, *Rothschild Buildings*, p.178 (invasion of Commercial Street school by excited parents after nearby zeppelin landing).

6. Marsden, 'Residential Segregation', p.140: teachers at poor schools often preferred to commute in from more salubrious areas, such as Fulham, Lewisham, Hackney, Greenwich, Wandsworth and Camberwell.

7. Masterman, 'Realities at Home', p.16; Tabor, 'Education', p.204; Wilson, *Rebel Daughter*, p.82. C.f. Kelsall ('Board Schools', p.15); Girouard (*Sweetness and Light*, p.64); for educational ideology and Board-school architecture, see Copelman, 'Classroom Struggle' (thesis), pp.86–92; Weiner, 'Architectural Form' (thesis).

8. Dendy, 'Children', pp.33, 41.

9. *School Board Chronicle*, 3 Oct. 1874, p.320.

10. HMI King in 1875 thought private adventure schools were useless, 'not only because the children learn nothing, but also because discipline, order, cleanliness and decency are unknown' (Gardner, *Lost Schools*, p.96).

11. Willis, *Jubilee Road*, p.53.

12. An 1880s textbook enjoined student teachers to 'regard regular washing, combing and dusting as essential to a pupil's admission to school': Currie, *Principles*, p.149. C.f. Gautrey, *Lux*, p.91.

13. Martin, 'Mother and Social Reform', p.1,240. C.f. Logbook, Walnut Tree Walk, 14 Dec. 1877 (two children sent home to wash and get clean aprons, who 'have not returned'); 5 Oct. 1883 (mother 'gave trouble' after child sent home, her clothes 'too dirty for her to sit beside any child').

14. C.f. Logbook, Anglers Gardens, 9 Dec. 1881, 24 Oct. 1888, 23 April 1890.

15. *Education Report, 1875–6*, PP 1876, p.cxlvi, cit. Spalding, *School Board*, p.161n. From 1882 a 'merit grant' was tied to assessment of the school's organization and discipline.

16. *Education Report*, PP 1886, p.299; Philpott, *London at School*, p.298. C.f. Kennedy, 'Board School London', p.90: 'Female costume is more manageable; you can do more with scraps to make a girl presentable. Besides, a girl thinks more of "looking nice" than a boy does'.

17. Bray, 'Day School', p.179. Pinafores proved respectability in the working class; but a scholarship girl at a superior Nottingham school in the 1900s encountered a snobbish rule against them: Annie Wilson (b. 1898), in Thompson, *Edwardian Childhoods*, pp.92–3.

18. Mrs C. (born Hackney, 1902), transcript, p.6.

19. *SBL Inspectors' Reports*, PP 1876 (John Noble), p.2.

20. Willis, *London General*, p.12.

21. C.f. William Nn (b. Poplar, 1896), ms. memoir, pp.11–12; Benson, *Streets and Lanes*, p.174; Alice Lewis (b. Fulham, 1898), ms. memoir, p.6.

22. She had grown up 'in the needy streets of Kentish Town, Finsbury Park and off the Seven Sisters Road', married a promising young shop-walker of strict Yorkshire background (later a rather precarious Managing Director), and in her penurious and slapdash housekeeping never reconciled the two traditions. Pritchett recalled of his first day at Rosendale Road school that: 'wearing my father's classy cut-downs I knew the distinction of our family and its awkward difference from the families of all the other children': *Cab*, pp.17–21; 90–1.

23. C.f. Lewis, ms. memoir, p.6; Edith Hall (b. 1908): 'the black wool of the seams worked into my chilblains and it was very painful' (*Canary Girls*, p.6); C.H. Rolph's friends ended up with a 'frightful bootful of sock' (*Particulars*, p.50); and William Nn would be 'standing in hobnail boots all day with a thick seam of wool under each foot' (ms. memoir, p.11).

24. Marie Welch (b. Hoxton, 1904), ms. memoir, p.29. For a home business based on recycled wool (1920s Birmingham), see Dayus: *Life*, p.57.

25. 'Riverside Visitor', 'Education and Boots'.

26. *Encyclopaedia of Retail Trading*, 1910: boys' school boots 4s. to 4s. 11d. new. Mrs W. (b. Finsbury, 1896) recalled a Bath Street shop which sold odd shoes cheap: transcript, p.6.

27. 'The best boys' saw to their own soles and heels; and 'home-mended boots and patches were not signs of poverty, quite the reverse': Willis, *London General*, pp.13–14. Iron 'feet' for such repairs can still be found. 'Blakeys' were little metal plates nailed on to protect the leather sole.

28. Miss Kingston, P.E. teacher, thought East End children would do better with no boots than the worn-out ones they wore: *R.C. Physical Training (Scotland)*, PP 1903, q.3,864. If bare feet were becoming stigmatic, shoes, however broken-down, would assert respectability.

29. Rolph, *Particulars*, pp.47, 50; Wallie Easey (b. 1907), notes of conversation, 19 Dec. 1978. C.f. Mrs Bartle (b. Poplar, 1882), transcript, p.6. Bare feet can also be seen in photographs from poorer schools, e.g. East Street (Walworth), 1900, held by Southwark Record Office.

30. C.f. Baillie, *Paradise*, p.25.

31. SBL *Minutes*, 14 Dec. 1893, p.128.

32. PRO file ED 14/18, 5 Dec. 1878, 28 Jan. 1879.

33. SBL Minutes, School Management Committee, 9 Nov. 1888, p.1,773 (Marner Street Infant school, Tower Hamlets); 3 Aug. 1888, p.1,374 (East Lane school, Southwark).

34. Gautrey, *Lux*, p.91. Logbooks often refer to children sent home, 'head in an objectionable state', and sometimes to parents' protests. At Anglers Gardens in 1882, for instance, a father bringing back a girl who had been sent home 'caused a disturbance, rendering

the assistance of a constable necessary'. The headmistress 'still refused to take her back until the head had been cleaned'. The child returned in the afternoon after this had been done; and next day the father was called and apologized: Logbook, 15–16 May 1882.

35. Ethel Mannin (*Confessions*, p.36) recalled indignantly the use even by teachers of the term 'the dirty girls', in her Board school between 1908 and 1914.

36. Health Education Council leaflet, *What to do about Head Lice*, n.d. [1983].

37. Pritchett, *Cab*, p.63.

38. Gautrey, *Lux*, pp.91–2. His version of these 'specimens of notes sent to headmistresses by indignant mothers' cannot be wholly reliable unless he had actual documents, as he was eighty-five by then.

39. Porter (*School Hygiene*, p.154) said teachers would find such notices 'exceedingly useful', and gave a sample text. Cards were also available in Yiddish (LCC *MOH London, Report*, 1904, Appendix 3, p.17).

40. Mannin, *Confessions*, p.36 (Clapham Board school in 1908).

41. By 1915 6,000 children had had their hair cropped in the cleansing stations: Hurt, *Schooling*, p.134.

42. With 'dreadful snobbery...a parent of one of the better-off children would occasionally write and request that her precious darling be not sat next to some poor child whose hair smelled of the solution of quassia chips advised by the nurse': Mannin, *Confessions*, p.36. Quassia (sometimes called 'squashy') was a South American bark.

43. Foakes, *Walls*, p.12. Porter (*School Hygiene*, p.148) advised that 'girls should have their hair cut short like boys'; while girls who did have long hair should wear it in a pigtail, or otherwise tied back, 'to prevent infection'.

44. C.f. Alexander, 'Becoming a Woman', pp.259–60 (interwar London).

45. Foakes, *Walls*, p.12.

46. It was also important that the better-class parents should not fear their children might 'catch things' at Board schools.

47. *SBL Inspectors' Reports*, PP 1878, p.5 (John Noble).

48. Ridge, *Storyteller*, p.202.

49. Of course deployment of these assumptions was not just manipulative: they were part of contemporary middle-class ideology.

50. *School Managers' Series*, 1871–2, Standard Five, p.45.

51. Widdowson, *Next Class*, p.67 (she grew up to be a teacher).

52. Conway, Peckham Park Schools, p.59, from 1908–14 school memories of Elizabeth Bird. The father's comment was pertinent since his fastidious daughter had herself lived with a grandmother (short-sighted perhaps) for a while after her mother's death.

53. *Cross Commission, 2nd Report*, 1887, evidence, qq.17,298, 17,310–11. Rubinstein ('Socialization') and Marsden ('Residential Segregation', p.141) quote similar claims.

54. Sims, *How the Poor Live*, p.32. Sims was acquainted with Mrs Burgwin (they worked together for the provision of cheap dinners for school children), but such ideas were too commonplace then to be ascribed to one person's influence. C.f. Stedman Jones on Booth, in 'Working-class Culture', *Languages of Class*, p.208.

55. Mann, *Census Report*, 1851, p.xxxvii.

56. *Education Census*, PP 1852–3, Summary Table pp.8–9; and see *Report*, p.xxxiii.

57. As previous note; and c.f. *Newcastle Commission, 3rd Report*, PP 1861, p.481 (Dr W.B. Hodgson's report). For the working-class private school, see Gardner, *Lost Schools*. The 100 or so dame schools in Battersea in 1870 contained more girls than boys (1,064 as against 769): Allen, 'Education in Battersea', pp.ii-iii.

58. Okey, *Memories*, pp.16, 24–5. C.f. *Education Census*, PP 1852–3, p.xxxvii.

59. *Newcastle Commission, 1st Report*, PP 1861, p.123. The Commissioners approved, and suggested (p.134) that male students should be instructed in 'similar subjects': they were of the greatest practical importance, would exercise the mental faculties, and were likely to interest children.

60. Arnold, *Reports*, p.25 (1853). C.f. Yoxall, *Domestic Economy*, pp.7–8; c.f. Silver and Silver, *Education*, pp.48, 110, 102–3.

61. *Code*, PP 1862 (and subsequently), clause 51 (c). Other essential conditions were that the buildings be adequate, the head teacher certificated, the registers properly kept, and three persons designated to receive the grant: none concerned the content of teaching.

62. *Code*, PP 1862, clause 89.

63. *Code*, PP 1868, Clause 188, Table, p.13; pp.16–17. This was also true under the School Board. Henrietta Muller and Helen Taylor's attempt to equalize the salaries of boy and girl pupil teachers was lost, as was a motion to bring girls' pay up to three-quarters: SBL *Minutes*, 6 Dec. 1883, p.31; 13 Dec. 1883, p.83.

64. SBL *Minutes*, 28 June 1871, p.48. C.f. PRO file ED 10/42, for scale of marks for student teachers' scholarship examination in 1886: the minimum required for a needlework pass was higher than for any other subject.

65. *Codes for 1873–8*, PP 1878; *Code*, PP 1884, Schedule V, p.26. At the end of their third year girls reached the stage expected of boys after their first year.

66. See *Education Report, 1885*, PP 1886, pp.xxvi-ix. C.f. *Education Report, 1899*, PP 1900, for similar differences, though women now did some Euclid. A student at Stockwell Training College in 1898 learnt to teach how to cut out and make a boy's shirt, and during her holidays practised buttonholes, gussets and gathers, and cut out patterns: Wilson, *Rebel Daughter*, p.84.

67. Jones, *Stanley*, p.43, quoting from his Presidential Address to the Education Section, Social Science Congress, Manchester 1879.

68. Women members of the Board often demanded equal treatment for both sexes in scholarships or pay and employment (Turnbull, 'So extremely like Parliament', pp.130–1). But most favoured domestic instruction despite the resulting curriculum differences.

69. SBL *Minutes*, 28 June 1871, p.48.

70. C.f. Inspector T.M. Williams on the : 'only a very insignificant proportion' of children in East End Board schools did 'any subject beyond the three Rs and the rudiments of English grammar and geography': *SBL Inspectors' Reports*, PP 1878, p.48.

71. Men in the family had first claim on protein: Loane, *Castle*, p.134; Newman, 'Death Rate', p.112; Ross, 'Fierce Questions and Taunts', pp.585–7; Meacham, *Life Apart*, pp.81–2; Oddy, 'Working-class Diet', pp.320–1. Girls also had less access to money and less chance to supplement home provisions.

72. SBL *School Management Committee, Report*, 1886–7, p.7.

73. *SBL Inspectors' Reports*, PP 1876, p.9; c.f. *Education Report, 1900*, PP 1901, Appendix A to General Report for Metropolitan Division, p.313; *Education Report, 1901*, PP 1902, p.17; SBL *Minutes*, 14 Feb. 1884, p.557; and SBL *School Management Committee, Reports*.

74. SBL *School Management Committee, Report*, 1889–90, p.lxxxiii. More practice in mental arithmetic was advised. Inspector McWilliam justified it as useful in their future lives, 'in all kinds of positions' and 'when they become wives and mothers': SBL *Minutes*, 20 Dec. 1883, p.192.

75. Inspector Noble blamed 'inefficient pupil teachers and candidates who do not take the trouble to think for themselves', but said nothing of the inferior training of pupils and their teachers before them: SBL *Inspectors' Reports*, PP 1876, p.9.

76. *SBL Inspectors' Reports*, PP 1878, p.23 (Williams on Hackney and Tower Hamlets 1875–6); SBL *School Management Committee, Report*, 1889–90, Report on Examination for Scholarships, p.lxxxiv; and c.f. following years.

77. PP 1887 *Cross Commission, 2nd Report*, qq.17,088–9, evidence Mrs Burgwin.

78. C.f. *Minute Explaining Article 7(b) of the Code of 1878*, PP 1878, p.5; and Codes from 1879 (e.g. 1884 recommendation that girls' arithmetic be judged more leniently, and 'the sums set will be easier': *Code*, PP 1884, Schedule 1, p.20).

79. C.f. SBL *Minutes*, 28 Jan. 1871, p.169.

80. SBL *Minutes*, 15 Jan. 1873, p.91 (School Management Committee Report). Secular instruction comprised three periods in the morning (9.45–10.30, 10.40–11.20, 11.20–12.00), and three of about forty minutes in the afternoon: Spalding, *School Board*, pp.184–5. From a total of twenty hours forty-five minutes, five hours spent on needlework would take nearly a quarter. In 1884 the limit was cut to four hours.

81. PRO file ED 14/18: SBL to Education Department, 17 Nov. 1873.

82. C.f. SBL *Minutes*, 26 May 1884, pp.82–3; 17 July p.258; and Logbook, Mantua Street, 3 Sept. 1884.

83. Arnold, *Reports*, p.167 (1876).

84. *SBL Inspectors' Reports*, PP 1878, p.49 (Inspector Williams, Hackney and Tower Hamlets). English Literature or Recitation was taken by 2,487 boys and 1,400 girls; Animal Physiology by 1,753 boys and no girls; Physical Geography by 1,233 boys and 101 girls; French by 160 boys and no girls; Botany by no boys and 38 girls; Mechanics by 74 boys and no girls; Mathematics by 213 boys and no girls; Domestic Economy by no boys and 1,680 girls.

85. SBL *School Management Committee, Report*, 1889–90, p.xiv; 1892–3, p.vii. An early proposal to make Domestic Economy an 'essential' subject for senior girls (supported by Emily Davies and Elizabeth Garrett Anderson), was defeated by nine votes: SBL *Minutes*, 28 June 1871, p.169.

86. SBL *Annual Report*, 1886–7, p.37. Such lessons might mean 'little more...than the ruling of interminable squares with their diagonals at the top of the slate and the laborious copying of the resultant figure in freehand below': Lowndes, *Silent Revolution*, p.33.

87. SBL *School Management Committee, Reports*, 1890–1, p.xxvii (Report of Drawing Instructor); 1887–8, pp.xxvix, lvi; 1889–90, p.xviii; and subsequently, esp. 1892–3, p.xxiv, where an improvement is suggested.

88. SBL *School Management Committee, Reports*, 1886–7, p.20; 1887–8, p.viii, Tables VI and VII, p.xxix. See also Spalding, *School Board*, p.214.

89. SBL *School Management Committee, Report*, 1890–1, p.xxvii (Report of Drawing Instructor); also Instructions to Inspectors, PP 1902, Appendix 1: 'In all schools...boys should learn to draw and girls to sew.' Pritchett, at a Herne Hill Board school before WWI, blossomed in the classroom of an experimental teacher, but next year a conventional one rejected his (impressionist) painting of London Bridge as 'a mess' and set him to study volume and shading. 'Imagine: a whole hour drawing a pudding basin in pencil and then shading it': *Cab*, pp.93–4, 110.

90. *Cross Commission, 2nd Report*, PP 1887, evidence q.17,197–8.

91. SBL *School Management Committee, Report*, 1890–1, p.xxvii (Drawing Instructors' Reports).

92. SBL *School Management Committee, Report*, 1892–3, p.xxiv (Drawing Instructors' Reports).

93. C.f. Waring, 'To Make the Mind Strong'.

94. SBL *School Management Committee, Reports*, 1887–8 to 1893–4: in 1891–2 it was taught in 81 boys' schools and 27 girls'; in 1892–3 in 111 boys' schools and 39 girls'; in 1893–4 in 121 boys' schools and 55 girls'.

95. SBL *School Management Committee, Report*, 1889–90, p.lxxv (Science Lecturer in Girls' Departments, Report). The object was to improve Friday afternoon attendance, which 'shows a decided tendency to fall off' (Spalding, *School Board*, p.186). Several of the schools selected were of 'special difficulty'.

96. SBL *School Management Committee, Report*, 1893–4 (Science Lecturer in Girls' Departments, Report).

97. Spalding, *School Board*, pp.211–12.

98. *Special Reports*, PP 1897, p.157 (Pillow, 'Domestic Economy Teaching').

99. *SBL Inspectors' Reports*, PP 1878, p.43 (Ricks). C.f. *Education Minute* (16 Jan. 1878), PP 1878, p.4, reminding inspectors to encourage teaching 'likely to promote habits of thrift'.

100. See for example PRO ED 14/19, Memorial from SBL to Education Department, 21 July 1880.

101. *Code*, PP 1878, pp.24–5 (Third Schedule); c.f. Sneyd-Kynnersley, *Passages*, p.317. He once inspected household articles made at 'a school maintained by a bountiful Earl', which included items (hemmed and seamed by the third class and coronetted by the first) too embarrassing to identify (p.316).

102. C.f. Gautrey, *Lux*, p.121; and SBL *Minutes*, 24 Jan. 1884, p.357; SBL *Minutes*, 24 Jan. 1884, pp.309, 357 and 13 March, pp.730, 735. For new provisions, see *Revised Instructions*, PP 1884, p.10, article 42, and p.20.

103. SBL *Minutes*, 20 Dec. 1883, p.197; 31 Jan. 1884, pp.619–20 (cutters-out and assistants appointed); 13 March 1884, p.735; 3 April 1884, p.964.

104. *Code*, PP 1884, p.20 (Schedule 1). Of course girls who were already competent may have found this restrictive.

105. SBL *School Management Committee, Reports*, 1892–3, pp.xxi-ii; 1893–4, p.xli; Yoxall, *Domestic Economy*, pp.20–1.

106. Eliza H. (b. Poplar, 1900) did mending for her teacher at Harbinger Road British School: transcript, pp.24–6; Elizabeth Bird in 1914 made smocked winceyette nightdresses for a much-loved teacher, wishing she would have 'some nice lace' on them instead: Conway, *Peckham Park Schools*, p.59.

107. Four experimental centres were set up in 1889 with help from the Drapers' Company; then the Education Department made laundry instruction eligible for grant under the 1890 Code, and expanded the programme: SBL *School Management Committee, Reports*, 1889–90, p.lxxx; 1890–1, p.xlii; 1891–2, p.xli.

108. Old Camden residents interviewed in 1983 recalled asking from door to door if anyone wanted laundry done for three pence, then taking it to class: 'Interaction' display at Exploring Living Memory Exhibition, Festival Hall, London 1981.

109. SBL *School Management Committee, Report*, 1890–1, p.xlii.

110. *Education Report*, PP 1886, p.xx.

111. Logbook, Mantua Street, 19 Feb. 1885. What subject the extra hour was taken from was not reported.

112. PRO file ED 14/37: School Board to Education Department, 30 Nov. 1875. See also Yoxall, *Domestic Economy*, p.14.

113. PRO file ED 14/37: Return, 15 Feb. 1882; SBL *Report*, 1886–7, p.39.

114. SBL *Minutes*, 27 March 1884, p.897. Boards outside London were more cautious, because of the cost of kitchens and equipment (Yoxall, *Domestic Economy*, p.15), and maybe because 'the social problem' weighed less heavily on them.

115. SBL *School Management Committee, Reports*.

116. *Education Inspectors' Reports, 1902*, PP 1903, pp.211, 216 (Report of Miss Deane, Cookery Inspectress).

117. Calder, 'Cookery', pp.134. The extension of cookery instruction also provided jobs for her students.

118. C.f. Lord Reay (later chairman of the Board), opening the Edinburgh School of Cookery and Domestic Economy in 1891: 'the great thing a good cook could do was to make something out of nothing': *Times*, 6 Oct. 1891, p.7.

119. May Parsons, from Melvin Road school, Penge, quoted by Stewart Headlam, *Church Reformer*, May 1894, pp.107–8.

120. 'Physical Deterioration and the Teaching of Cookery', pp.88–9, *Contemporary Review*, 1904.

121. Pike, *Children Reclaimed*, p.157: 'Immense service will be rendered to the community if female street wanderers can be transformed into well-trained domestic servants. Unattractive as they are, these girls will be the life-companions of men in a coming generation, and if their husbands are expected to appreciate home, home will need to be something different from what the girls themselves have known.'

122. *Education Report*, PP 1900, vol. 2, p.329.

123. Brabazon, *Reforms*, p.50.

124. Headdon, 'Industrial Training', p.130; *Cross Commission, 3rd Report*, PP 1887, evidence, q.50,368. C.f. J.H.O., 'A morning in the "kitchen garden" ', *Light and Shade*, Oct. 1881, p.71, for praise of course (with miniature equipment and songs and marching): 'the little girls do admirably, and make one long for the time when they will be old enough to go out to service'.

125. *Cross Commission, 3rd Report*, PP 1887, evidence, q.50,417–19.

126. With other choices they preferred daily employment in factory, workshop, laundry, tea-rooms, shop or pub; they were also in less demand as servants than country girls, who were supposed to be cleaner and more tractable.

127. *Special Reports*, PP 1897, p.186 (Pillow, 'Domestic Economy Teaching').

128. PRO file ED 14/37: SBL Circular, 9 March 1883. This was not always the case: c.f. Lowndes, *Silent Revolution*, p.32. Even in the 1930s, gas stoves might be first encountered in service: c.f. Foley, *Child in the Forest*, p.164.

129. SBL *School Management Committee, Report*, 1891–2, p.xxxiv.

130. *Education Inspectors' Reports*, PP 1902, p.36. C.f. Lord, 'Domestic Economy'.

131. *Special Reports*, PP 1897, p.169 (Pillow, 'Domestic Economy Teaching').

132. Morley, *Studies*, pp.135–41.

133. Mrs Lord, 'Domestic Economy', p.228. (She was SBL Domestic Economy Superintendent, and very dedicated.)

134. C.f. Miss Deane's annual reports, e.g. in PP 1903, pp.211, 217; *Physical Deterioration Committee, Report*, PP 1904, pp.42–3 and throughout; *British Medical Journal*, 2 Jan. 1904, p.37; also Davin, 'Imperialism and Motherhood', esp. p.27.

135. Board of Education, *Teaching of Infant Care and Management*, Circular 758, 1910, p.5, para ii (Campbell).

136. Board of Education, *Teaching of Infant Care and Management*, Circular 758, 1910, prefatory note (Morant). See PRO file ED/1 1/51 for the preparation of the circular.

9 Children, Work and Independence

1. *Newcastle Commission*, PP 1861, Part 3, Josiah Wilkinson's Report, p.354; *Children's Employment Commission, 2nd Report*, PP 1864, p.lxiii. In 1876 HMI Redgrave noted that few eight-year-old children were employed in London: *Factory and Workshops Acts Commission*, PP 1876, q.339.
2. *Children's Employment, 2nd Report*, PP 1864; *5th report*, PP 1866, pp.77, 204. C.f. Bevan, *Industrial Classes*, p.87, for East End girls' employment in silk, 'at the machines, threading beads, arranging tassels, braid or buttons'.
3. For the relation between child and interlocutor in Mayhew's interviews: Steedman, *Tidy House*, chap.5. For Mayhew: Thompson, 'Mayhew and the Morning Chronicle' and Yeo, 'Mayhew as Social Investigator'; Bradley, introduction to Mayhew, *Selections*; Humpherys, *Poor Man's Country*.
4. Mayhew, *London Labour* 1, pp.151–2.
5. Mayhew noted this of coster-girls (*London Labour* 1, p.43), but it had wider application.
6. Mayhew, *London Labour* 2, p.572.
7. Davies, *Life*, p.20; c.f. Anon, 'School Board Work', p.652. Nursemaids in England and Wales increased by 110 per cent between 1851 and 1871 (almost twice the total increase in female domestic servants): Burnett, *Useful Toil*, p.138. But these were older live-in nursemaids and nannies, rather than the local child coming in daily.
8. Davies, *Life*, p.20–1.
9. *Ragged School Union* 20, Sept. 1868, pp.200–1. After 1870 this street was frequently checked by school attendance officers: c.f. Reeves, *Recollections*, p.27; then mentions of it cease. Such regular hiring places usually served specific trades with irregular needs: building workers, musicians and diamond workers all had street labour markets.
10. C.f. 'Louey', who at 'barely thirteen' spent her time from eight in the morning till eight at night 'absolutely alone in charge of a baby of six months' whose parents both went out to work: Benson, *Streets and Lanes*, p.207. (This novel drew from the author's experience 'visiting' in the slums before her early death in 1890.)
11. Burnett, *Useful Toil*, pp.137, 216.
12. A rhyme found pencilled on the attic wall in a Norfolk vicarage no doubt applied to much London employment, too:

> The pay is small
> The food is bad
> I wonder why
> I don't go mad.

(Quoted Ryder, *Cavell*, pp.6–7: the vicarage was built 1867–9 by Edith Cavell's father.)
13. McBride's census samples ('As the Twig is Bent', p.45) suggest a rural or Irish origin for three-quarters of London servants in this period.
14. Mr N. (b. 1899), transcript, p.56.
15. The opportunities should not be overestimated: districts with most servants were also those with fewest London-born adult females: c.f. Horn, *Victorian Servant*, p.28.
16. C.f. Barnardo tract, *My Cottage*, by 'a late Holiday Mother' (*c.* 1885), for account of training in domestic work followed by job in service.
17. [Margaret Harkness], *Toilers*, p.79 (chap.6, 'Slaveys'). According to this writer the Metropolitan Association for Befriending Young Servants had some 8,000 slaveys on its books; and total numbers were incalculable. Skivvy and general were other terms used.
18. Hubbard, *Few Words*, p.3. C.f. 'GMZ' (letter, *Labour News*, 20 Feb. 1875) on 'poor little drudges who go out as maids-of-all-work to small tradespeople': 'negro slavery would be better'.
19. C.f. Coveney, *Image of Childhood*, pp.82–4; and May, 'Innocence and Experience', p.16.
20. Mayhew, *London Labour* 1, pp.151–2.
21. Cold was an acute problem. Mayhew's description of the early-morning wholesale market in November and his quotations from an old seller stress the plight of 'poor little things there without shoes and stockings, and their feet quite blue with the cold': *London Labour* 1, pp.145–50.
22. The passage reads (p.152): 'I always gives mother my money, she's so very good to me. She don't often beat me, but when she do, she don't play with me. She's very poor, and goes out cleaning rooms sometimes now she don't work at the fur.' Then she talked about

her stepfather (also 'very good' to her, though 'No, I don't mean by that he says kind things to me, for he never hardly speaks'). Then, 'When I gets home, after selling creases, I stops at home. I puts the room to rights: mother don't make me do it, I does it myself. I cleans the chairs, though there's only two to clean. I takes a tub and scrubbing brush and flannel, and scrubs the floor—that's what I do three or four times a week.'

23. More, *Coelebs*, p.252. C.f. Gillis (*Youth and History*, p.103) on middle-class boys: by the middle of the century 'neither parents nor schoolmasters were interested any longer in pushing boys in the manner common earlier. Precocity was in disrepute, associated with street urchins rather than respectable schoolboys'; Musgrove, *Youth*, pp.51–7; Davin 'When is a Child'.

24. C.f. Parr, *Labouring Children*, p.37; Gorham, 'Maiden Tribute', p.374. For Shaftesbury 'the early independence of children' engendered 'moral pestilence': quoted Tremenheere, *I Was There*, p.73.

25. C.f. an orphan group Mayhew talked to in a Drury Lane lodging house: flower-seller sisters of fifteen and eleven, and their brother (thirteen), a coster's boy: *London Labour* 1, pp.135–6; or a boy and girl supporting siblings of five and two, and aiming 'to keep everything right and 'pectable till mother comes back again' (she'd 'hooked it at the hopping time', i.e. taken off for the hop harvest): 'One of the Crowd', *Toilers*, pp.88–9.

26. Elson (*Climbing Boys*) from the age of seven set off periodically to fend for himself, always keeping touch with his mother. Some of Mayhew's informants ran away from brutal or exploitative parents (c.f. *London Labour* 1, pp.468–9); others left on more trivial occasion. Barnardo (*City Waif*) describes Bridget, a twelve-year-old who had fled her mother because of ill-usage and lived by selling papers. (Although 'Irish by blood', having been 'born in Whitechapel' she could be claimed as 'really a Cockney'; she was 'a blithe little lass' and 'a general favourite': p.8.)

27. C.f. Stretton, *Little Meg's Children*; 'Brenda', *Froggy's Little Brother*; and discussion (especially on Stretton) in Bratton, *Impact*, chap.4. Also Davin, 'Waif Novels', forthcoming in Norma Clarke and Adam Lively (eds), *In the Shadow of the Classics*. The journalist, George Sims, wrote similar vignettes: c.f. *How the Poor Live*, p.23.

28. C.f. the boys in *Oliver Twist*, but not Jo in *Bleak House*.

29. Shaftesbury, 'Emigration and Ragged Schools', House of Commons, 6 June 1848: *Speeches*, p.228. Numbers are hard to estimate, whether in mid-century or later. Greenwood claimed in 1869 that 100,000 London children lived outside families or institutions, scratching a living by odd jobs and scavenging, sleeping rough or in cheap lodgings, 'destitute of proper guardianship, food, clothing, or employment' (*Seven Curses*, p.6). Parr (*Labouring Children*, p.37) posits 30,000 'neglected children on the streets' (a rather broad definition) in London around 1876. Perhaps their symbolic importance grew as their numbers declined.

30. Sources for their lives are fragmentary. Besides Mayhew's reports (especially *London Labour* 1, pp.468–85) and the writings of 'child-savers' (e.g. Carpenter, *Ragged Schools and Reformatory Schools*; Pike, *Children Reclaimed*), see S.C. *Destitute Children*, PP 1861. Court reports are informative, also police answers to Chadwick's 1883 questionnaire on poor children. The most convincing fictional account is Greenwood's *True History of a Little Ragamuffin* (1866); c.f. his *In Strange Company* (1873), chap.1; and Augustus Mayhew, *Paved with Gold* (1858). In 'waif novels' daily details of survival are sentimentalized and sketchy, even when titles promise more: c.f. Sargent, *Street Arab*, or Crockett, *Cleg Kelly, Arab of the City*.

31. According to Mayhew, boys had more street opportunities than girls: 'The female child can do little but sell (when a livelihood is to be gained without recourse to immorality); the boy can not only sell, but work': *London Labour* 1, p.471. C.f. Pike, *Children Reclaimed*, p.155.

32. At mid-century English or Irish coster-girls started to sell in the streets when about seven; Jewish children (mainly boys) at about ten: Mayhew, *London Labour* 1, pp.46–7, 524–38; vol.2, pp.133–8.

33. For mudlarks ('crowds of boys and little girls, some old men, and many old women'): Mayhew, *London Labour* 2, pp.173–6; and see below for later reference. On dust-yard work (and its family character): Mayhew, *London Labour* 2, pp.187–201.

34. They were also the principal customers of the Irishwomen who sold 'refuse'—damaged fruit and vegetables: Mayhew, *London Labour* 1, p.117.

35. Boys in Mary Carpenter's Bristol ragged school were ill-clad, slept rough, and lived 'by

petty depredations', but 'all appear better fed than the children of the decent poor', quoted Saywell, *Carpenter*, p.4.

36. For testimonies, see Mayhew, *London Labour* 1, pp.418–23. C.f. Springhall, *Coming of Age*, pp.158–63. C.f. also Barnardo, *Young Thief*.

37. Children employed by costers sometimes lived with them, and according to Mayhew, were 'generally treated with great kindness by the costers' wives or concubines': *London Labour* 1, p.470; c.f. p.34.

38. Greenwood, *Little Ragamuffin*, chaps 13–15.

39. *OED*'s first examples for street arab are from the Ragged School Movement in 1848. 'Urchin' was common from the 1780s, and 'guttersnipe' (in this sense rather than meaning rag-picker) was first noted in 1882. May ('Innocence and Experience', p.19) cites use of 'Hottentot' and 'English Kaffir'. Se also Cunningham, *Childhood*, chap.5.

40. Mayhew, *London Labour* 1, p.413.

41. C.f. Barnardo, *Young Thief*. Barnardo took Shaftesbury and other interested gentlemen on philanthropic hunts wherever sleeping boys might be unearthed (Bready, *Barnardo*, pp.81–6); other rescue agencies adopted the same tactic: Behlmer, *Child Abuse*, p.58.

42. Samuel, *Underworld*, p.62; Chaplin, *My Autobiography*, p.39. For NSPCC, see note 49 below.

43. C.f. Barnardo, *City Waif*.

44. C.f. Fredur, *Sketches*, p.105: a throng of urchins in a labyrinthine back street 'scampers off and vanishes in every direction' on hearing 'Nix! the chunk!'. ('Chunk' he explains as cockney for a board, and thus the Board-school officer.)

45. Samuel, *Underworld*, p.48.

46. Booth, *Poverty* 1, pp.38–9. The trend from the 1870s was for larger Homes and larger organizations: the National Children's Home (1869) soon set up branch homes; the Church of England Waifs and Strays Society (1881) had 2,000 children in sixty-five Homes and with foster parents by 1895 (Rudolf, *First Forty Years*; and see Heasman, *Evangelicals*, p.89). State provision was also expanding.

47. C.f. May, 'Innocence and Experience'; Behlmer, *Child Abuse*, p.11.

48. McLeod ('Social Policy', p.111) quotes an enraged reaction by *The Times* to this attack on the privacy of the home.

49. C.f. Behlmer, *Child Abuse*. Local Societies for the Prevention of Cruelty to Children were set up from 1883; the London one (1884) was renamed National in 1889. Hesba Stretton, waif novelist, was a prominent campaigner: Bratton, *Impact*, pp.83–7. For US parallel, c.f. Gordon, *Heroes*, chap.2.

50. Behlmer, *Child Abuse*, p.11.

51. Industrial Schools Amendment Act, 1880; Criminal Law Amendment Act, 1885. Walkowitz (*Prostitution*, p.211) notes as result more stigmatization of prostitutes, and more separation from the rest of the working-class community.

52. C.f. Mr Roffey (Willis, *Jubilee Road*, p.105): aristocrat of labour 'quite content to relax in his armchair while [his wife] is everlastingly on the go'; the children 'invaluable assistants' each with their 'own duty to perform'.

53. Newton, *Years of Change*, p.8. His widowed grandmother made two pairs of court shoes for a special order ('she made them completely: shaped them, lasted them, sewed them, turned them, put them back on the last—second lasting, we called it—and one of her sons finished them for her'): this suggests that the division of labour was not always strictly followed, since she could do the man's tasks although a woman.

54. *Employment of Schoolchildren*, PP 1902, evidence Miss Ella Holme (School Manager in Southwark and Bermondsey), Appendix 19 and q.2,268; c.f. Miss Bevan, q.2,718; Miss Adler, q.3,377.

55. Willis, *London General*, p.15. For a doctor's son's opinion of 'surgery boys' c.f. Bligh, *Tooting Corner*, p.113.

56. Hogg, 'Schoolchildren as Wage Earners', p.242.

57. Arthur Harding's mother taught her children that the clean and well-behaved got more money when West End ladies came to school or mission: Samuel, *Underworld*, p.24.

58. Hogg, 'Schoolchildren as Wage Earners', p.242.

59. Hogg, 'Schoolchildren as Wage Earners', pp.235–8 and throughout.

60. PRO file ED 10/12: Catherine Webb (for Women's Industrial Council) to Board of Education, Nov. 1898; SBL *Minutes*, 10 Feb. 1898, pp.670–1, c.f. 3 March 1898, pp.807, 927.

61. SBL *Minutes*, 7 July 1898; 13 Oct. 1898; Adler, *Wage-Earning Children.*
62. *Hansard*, 17–18 June 1898, 28 April 1899; also Gorst, 'Children as Wage Earners', pp.11–12.
63. *Children Working*, PP 1899; and *Employment of Schoolchildren*, PP 1902, evidence Sir Charles Elliott, Appendix 4. That his figures for an especially poor borough, Tower Hamlets (boys 6.3 per cent, girls 4.2 per cent; 5.3 per cent overall), fall below rather than above the average, confirms doubts about these statistics.
64. Hogg, 'Schoolchildren as Wage Earners', p.235.
65. SBL *School Returns, 1886–7*: average attendance for Regent Street girls' school, 68.5 per cent (boys 61.1 per cent). Attendance rates for thirty-five Greenwich Board schools averaged 79.6 per cent for girls (boys 83 per cent). Maidstone Street girls averaged 72.3 (boys 75.2 per cent); the averages for forty-five Hackney schools were 76 per cent (girls) and 81 per cent (boys).
66. LCC *MOH London, Report*, 1904, pp.72–3. The much larger borough of Hackney reported 403 lists from employers, and 3,125 workers' addresses. C.f. *Report on the Sanitary Condition of Hackney* (Alice Teebay), 1900, p.34, for inadequacies of employers' lists and migratory habits of outworkers.
67. C.G. Perkins, letter to *Daily Mirror*, 19 June 1980. His mother took in washing and he did all her fetching and carrying (recording by Rosemary Skinner, Goldsmiths' College class, May 1981, my notes). C.f. letters from Mrs Nella Harryman (on late 1920s) and Mrs V. Wainman, *Daily Mirror*, 1 July 1980.
68. C.f. Dickens, *Bleak House*, chap.21 for the scrimping employer, Judy Smallweed.
69. Walter P. (b. Spitalfields, 1903), notes of conversation, 9 June 1975.
70. C.f. Davin, 'Imperialism and Motherhood'.
71. *Employment of Schoolchildren*, PP 1902, evidence Ella Holme, Appendix 19 and qq.2,171–80.
72. Anon, *Children and the Labour Question*, pp.17–18.
73. Eliza H. (b. Poplar, 1900), transcript, p.A8.
74. *Employment of Schoolchildren*, PP 1902, evidence Ella Holme, Appendix 19. (The entry 'information refused' occurs more often in her case notes than in those of other witnesses; this suggests either more awkwardness in approaching people, or more honesty in admitting failures.)
75. *Employment of Schoolchildren*, PP 1902, evidence Miss Bevan (head of Gainsborough Road school), Appendix 22.
76. *Employment of Schoolchildren*, PP 1902, Report, p.8.
77. *Employment of Schoolchildren*, PP 1902, evidence Rev. A. Chandler, qq.3,500–6; Mr Thompson (head, Hermit Road school, West Ham), qq.2,395–9.
78. *Employment of Schoolchildren*, PP 1902, evidence Miss Holme, q.2,208 and Appendix 19.
79. *Employment of Schoolchildren*, PP 1902, evidence Miss Neville, qq.2,646–7; Mrs Desprelles, qq.1,786–91.
80. *Employment of Schoolchildren*, PP 1902, evidence Sir Charles Elliott, q.16.
81. SBL *Minutes*, 10 Feb. 1898: Edith Hogg (on behalf of the Women's Industrial Council), letter to London School Board about their investigation, 30 Jan. 1898.
82. *Employment of Schoolchildren*, PP 1902, Appendix 48, p.467.
83. Hogg, 'Schoolchildren as Wage Earners', p.242, p.239.
84. *Employment of Schoolchildren*, PP 1902, Appendix 29, Miss Bannatyne (head of Belvedere Place school).
85. A.D. Innes, *Women's Industrial News*, April 1896, on preliminary findings of investigation by the Education Committee of the Women's Industrial Council.

10 Patterns of Children's Work After 1870

1. Florence C. (b. Hackney, 1902), my notes, p.10.
2. C.f. Edith H. (b. Paddington, 1894, one of eleven children), transcript, pp.5–7. Mrs W. (b. Finsbury, 1896) as eldest girl of six had to get the others washed and dressed, prepare them for school and then get herself ready, by which time her mother would arrive home from her office cleaning job: transcript, p.4.
3. Eliza H. (b. Poplar, 1900), transcript, pp.B15–22.
4. Mrs Bartle (b. Poplar, 1882), transcript, p.10. C.f. *Crèche Annual, 1895–6*, pp.8–9: the gift of an old pram relieved a child who made two trips daily before school carrying first a

baby then a toddler to the crèche.

5. Mrs Layton (b. Bethnal Green, 1866), in Davies, *Life*, p.4.

6. Elsie M. (b. Hoxton, 1905), ms. memoir, pp.4–5.

7. Phyllis H. (b. Kings Cross, 1908, eldest of eight): my notes from SE1 People's History Group, 13 May 1980.

8. Loane, *Castle*, p.116; c.f. PP 1902, *Children's Employment*, evidence Miss Neville (Manchester Street school, St Pancras), q.2,595.

9. PP 1893–4, 'Employment of Women', *R.C. Labour*, witness 155, p.23: for an Acton girl paid three shillings a week to look after a baby and bring it to the laundress mother at work.

10. C.f. Bessie C. in 1890s Bermondsey: transcript, pp.9–10, 47 (she herself went alone to school at five). Note also Logbook, Flint Street, 29 Oct. 1877: 'A child was lost going home from school this morning.'

11. Ezard, *Battersea Boy*, p.37.

12. Miss H. (b. Kensington, 1902), transcript, p.61.

13. Lewis (b. Fulham, 1898), ms. memoir, p.11.

14. Edith H. (b. Paddington, 1894), transcript, p.6.

15. Minnie Bowles (b. 1903), in Cohen, *Memories*, p.7 (Clapham).

16. Bessie C. (Bermondsey, b. 1893), transcript, p.6. C.f. 'when a girl came home from school, she took off her coat, put on an old dress, and started helping mother': Mary P. (b. Hackney, 1903), tape side 1.

17. Eliza H. (b. Poplar, 1900), transcript, p.A27.

18. Eliza H. (b. Poplar, 1900), transcript, p.B2.

19. Bray, 'Children of the Town', p.123.

20. Loane, *Simple Sanitation*, p.51.

21. Ross, 'Not the Sort', esp. p.48.

22. In a Peabody block in Wapping there was a five-week rota: William E. (b. Wapping, 1897), transcript, p.39.

23. Dot Starn, ms. memoir.

24. *Toynbee Record*, Feb. 1894, p.80. The mother perhaps resented her daughter's pleasure, and even the settlement itself, especially if she felt the choice of play implied criticism.

25. Lewis (b. Fulham, 1898), ms. memoir, p.8.

26. There were exceptions to this. Jane W. (b. Limehouse, 1896), remembered being stood on a box and taught how to scrub: transcript, p.8.

27. See Chapter 5 above. In SBL *School Management Committee, Report*, 1891–2, p.xiii, inspectors puzzle (drily or obtusely) over 'the curious effect on the attendance caused by a very fine day—notably a fine Monday'.

28. Elsie M. (b. Hoxton, 1905), ms. memoir, p.8; c.f. Minnie Bowles (b. Kennington, 1903), in Cohen, *Memories*, p.5.

29. *South London Press*, 11 Aug. 1911, p.2.

30. Lewis (b. Fulham, 1898), ms. memoir, p.111.

31. Elsie M. (b. Hoxton, 1903), ms. memoir, p.17; c.f. PP 1902, *Children's Employment*, evidence Mr Gardner, qq.3,048–9.

32. Eliza H. (b. Poplar, 1900), transcript, p.B13.

33. Gladys B. (b. Hackney, 1904), transcript, p.A28. C.f. White, *Rothschild Buildings*, p.156, for girls' work 'shared on a rota basis'.

34. Harvey, *Saturday*, p.16.

35. Harvey, *Saturday*, pp.9–16.

36. Harvey, *Saturday*, p.12.

37. Harvey, *Saturday*, pp.8, 6.

38. Harvey, *Saturday*, p.7. London was perhaps more relaxed about domestic work by boys: a Tyneside father called his helpful son 'a Jessie fussing about the hoose': Common, *Kiddar's Luck*, p.101.

39. Harvey, *Saturday*, p.17. Older girl essayists (Standards five to seven) did 'housework for most of the day' in 96 per cent, 100 per cent, and 90 per cent of cases at the three schools; younger girls (Standard four) in 87 per cent, 95 per cent, and 97 per cent. The table only compares girls' time spent in housework with boys' time spent in paid work outside the home. It shows all-day employment of older boys in 32 per cent, 15 per cent and 5 per cent of cases (younger: 12 per cent, 5 per cent, and 7 per cent); while more were employed for part of the day only: 56 per cent, 83 per cent and 45 per cent of older

boys and 75 per cent, 85 per cent and 60 per cent of younger. (His comment: 'the best summary of such essays as these is hardly to be found in statistics, but lovers of these deceptive symbols may care to have the following table'.)

40. Harvey, *Saturday*, p.12.
41. Harvey, *Saturday*, p.18. Such girls also mentioned reading, piano lessons and expeditions with parents.
42. Foakes, *Walls*, pp.25, 72–3. Her wage-earning sister later added a weekly shilling for her.
43. Booth, *Poverty* 1, p.158. The girl twice ran away after beatings; eventually the landlady administered a 'rebuke, dignified, well-timed, and as it appeared, efficacious, of the father's drunken ways' and spoke to the mother.
44. Hymie Fagan's job on Fridays was 'to redeem the four brass candlesticks and the table-cloth, which had been pawned on Monday morning': Cohen, *Memories*, p.22; c.f. White, *Buildings*, p.161.
45. Charles C. (b. Bromley-by-Bow, 1891), transcript, p.A25. C.f. grocer's advertisement in a Southwark school magazine: 'What to do with our girls and boys—Send them for the Tea, Coffee, Cocoa, Sugar etc.': *The Monnow*, Feb. 1909, p.12.
46. Bosanquet, *Rich and Poor*, p.126. C.f. Paterson, *Bridges*, p.36. According to a Loughborough Junction mother in 1891, shopkeepers reluctant to sell really small quantities would relent for a child purchaser, and might also 'give him the benefit of the doubt' when there was 'no definite measure for a ha'p'orth': Economic Club, *Budgets*, p.20.
47. Ethel V. (b. Whitechapel, 1895), transcript, p.B8; Paterson, *Bridges*, p.36.
48. 'Teaching Cookery in a Board School' (*Cassells Magazine*, May 1891), p.184. C.f. Morrison's 'quaint little women with big baskets' who 'regard the price of bacon as chief among human considerations': *Mean Streets*, p.17. Elderly women (sometimes men too) recall in minute detail what they would buy and the prices.
49. Gissing, *Thyrza*, p.38.
50. Jobson, *Hours*, p.55. He also bought 'a pennyworth of specked apples or oranges' from the greengrocer, and 'sixpennorth of pieces' from the butcher. C.f. eight-year-old regularly sent before 7 a.m. to buy stale loaves: Economic Club, *Budgets*, p.21.
51. Lewis (b. Fulham, 1898), ms. memoir, p.7.
52. Lilian Westall (from ms. memoir), in Burnett, *Useful Toil*, p.215. C.f. William Nn, ms. memoir, p.7.
53. Mrs Bartle. (b. Poplar, 1882), p.3.
54. Elsie M. (b. Hoxton, 1903), transcript, p.3.
55. C.G. Perkins (b. Plumstead, 1899), my notes from tape, May 1981.
56. Eliza H. (b. Poplar, 1900), transcript, p.A22; and c.f. pp.A3–4.
57. Barnes, 'Children's Ideals', p.8. It is unclear whether the explanation is based on preconceptions about gender roles, or on observation, direct or second-hand.
58. Burke, *Son of London*, p.36.
59. Vallès, *Rue à Londres*, p.81; Sims, 'Sunday Morning East and West' (*Living London* 1), p.285.
60. Blacker, 'Memoirs of the Mittel East'. Stricter observance would require that it be cooked and fetched before sunset on Friday, but then the bakers' ovens would not be free.
61. Okey, *Memories*, pp.26, 33.
62. Mary P. (b. Hackney, 1903), transcript, p.F2 (c.f. p.A1: 'I was the envy of the school').
63. When two London pubs were watched for two hours one Sunday in 1897, 547 of the 2,246 persons counted entering were supposed under thirteen. There were 158 girls and 125 boys with jugs or bottles; and thirty-four babies were counted: Johnson, *Children and Public Houses*, p.4 (from memorial to Newington magistrates, 20 Sept. 1897).
64. Vallès, 'Un Dimanche Anglais', *Rue à Londres*, p.81.
65. C.f. Cummins, *Landlord Cometh*, p.9.
66. See for example Johnson, *Children and Public Houses*, p.3.
67. Booth, *Final Volume*, pp.67, 65.
68. Booth, *Final Volume*, p.67 (from notes on dinner hour in a poor South London quarter).
69. Walter P. (b. Spitalfields, 1903), conversation Whitechapel, 9 June 1975.
70. *Toby*, 17 July 1886, p.6.
71. Young, 'Charitable and Benevolent London', p.204, and photograph p.203.
72. Greenwood, *Strange Company*, p.21.

73. Elsie M. (b. Hoxton, 1903), ms. memoir, p.6.
74. Southgate (b. Bethnal Green, 1890), *That's the Way*, pp.41–2.
75. Fagan (b. Stepney, 1903), in Cohen, *Memories*, p.26. C.f. White, *Rothschild Buildings*, p.160. 'Soup Kitchen for the Jewish Poor' can still be seen inscribed in stone on a Brune Street façade.
76. Marie Welch (b. Hoxton, 1904), ms. memoir, pp.19–24.
77. Waltham Forest Oral History Workshop display, 'Exploring Living Memory' exhibition, 1986: photograph (line of children with jugs, and landlady giving them loaves) dated '*c.* 1904', and accompanying extract from unidentified transcript.
78. Dick O. (b. Hackney), 'half a leg of lamb, vegetables...tea, sugar and different stuffs— meat, mince pies and that...': transcript, p.10. C.f. Southgate, *That's the Way*, chap.23, on Bottomley's election largesse.
79. British Library Prints and Photographs, Malby 3492–3; from Poplar series.
80. Samuel, *Underworld*, p.35.
81. *Times*, 21 Sept. 1891, p.3.
82. Humphries argues (*Hooligans*, chap.6, on 'social crime and family survival') that steady criminalization of children's street activities in the twentieth century increased petty crime by urban children trying 'to compensate for their dispossessed earnings' (p.167).
83. Mr N. (b. 1899), transcript, p.27.
84. Greenwood, *Prisoner*, pp.42–6 (children who stole boots from three small boys just given them at school, 6d. from a little girl, and a load of boots being delivered by a twelve-year-old); Manning, *Life*, pp.23–4; William Nn (b. Poplar, 1896), ms. memoir, p.12.
85. *Women and Work*, 28 Aug. 1875.
86. *Globe*, 15 Aug. 1887, p.2. (The magistrate let them off with a warning; then they burgled another house and stole a canary, a silver watch and a purse.)
87. SE1 People's History Group meeting, 21 July 1981, my notes.
88. Cohen, *Memories*, p.7. (Minnie Bowles (b. 1903) was raised in Vauxhall and Clapham.) The lesson was sometimes harsher: c.f. Foakes, *Walls*, pp.28–9. Elderly people mostly describe others stealing, or the times when they learnt they must not steal. Harding (Samuel, *Underworld*) is unusually frank.
89. Chase, *Tenant Friends*, p.46.
90. Rowe, *Picked Up in the Streets*, pp.285–7. Such opportunities declined when the river was embanked.
91. Sims, 'London "Up" ', p.187. Sims saw road surfaces taken up and relaid constantly, for drains, gas, electricity, or just new surfaces.
92. Southgate (b. Bethnal Green, 1890), *That's the Way*, p.87.
93. *Sanitary Condition of Bethnal Green in 1895* (Bate), p.30. See also LCC *Public Control Committee, Annual Reports*.
94. Mansion House *Council on the Dwellings of the People, Report*, 1885, p.28. So water was left standing 'as long as it lasted, to catch every pollution which their surroundings afford'. C.f. Laski, 'Domestic Life', pp.156–7.
95. Sims, *How the Poor Live*, p.39.
96. Loane, *Simple Sanitation*, p.13: husbands, 'unwilling to make an everyday business of it', might be 'prevailed on to carry a considerable amount once or twice a week', for washing and cleaning.
97. Eliza H. (b. Poplar, 1900), in Richman, *Fly a Flag*, p.50 (and c.f. transcript); Grace S. (b. Kentish Town, about 1900), notes of interview, 29 Dec. 1975.
98. Foakes, *Walls*, pp.7–9.
99. C.f. Malcolmson, 'Laundresses', esp. pp.453–62.
100. *Children's Employment*, PP 1902, evidence Mrs Nickless (St Clements school), Appendix 11, p.330.
101. A common form of charitable aid was to buy a mangle for a poor woman to permit her to earn.
102. Sherard, *Child Slaves*, pp.49–51.
103. *Children's Employment*, PP 1902, evidence Miss Holme, qq.2,208, 2,184, 2,198–9, and Appendix 19.
104. Southgate, *That's the Way*, p.65.
105. Eliza H. (b. Poplar, 1900), transcript, pp.B33–4.
106. [Harkness], *Toilers*, pp.64–7.
107. *Labour News*, 27 Feb. 1875.

108. Coate, 'Phases of Poor Life', pp.126–7.
109. *Children's Employment*, PP 1902, evidence Mrs Nickless (St Clements school), qq.1,317–26; Miss Bevan (Gainsborough Road school), Appendix 22, pp.366–9.
110. Eliza H. (b. Poplar, 1900), transcript, pp.B33–4.
111. Ten-year-old Tom Richards (b. Walworth, 1905, third of sixteen children) had two regular Saturday night jobs. He scrubbed out a butcher's shop, and received meat 'pieces' to take home besides consuming cocoa and dripping there. Around 12.30 he went to scrub a baker's floor and lay fresh sawdust, and got home to bed around two o'clock: notes of conversation, 1 Nov. 1975.
112. Molly Baird (née Gonley, Otautau, 1907), my aunt, minded her mother's shop in a small New Zealand town when only three: note of conversation, September 1984.
113. A medical officer investigating scarlet fever in Limehouse found a sweet shop in the charge of three children: LCC *MOH London, Report*, 1897, p.29.
114. Arthur Harding at nine or ten helped his sister on her stall in Roman Road, and on Saturday nights they finished about 12.30 or 1 o'clock: Samuel, *Underworld*, p.61.
115. *Children's Employment*, PP 1902, evidence Spencer (LCC Public Control Department), q.4,143.
116. *Children's Employment*, PP 1902, evidence Edwards (Head, Cranbrook Road school, Hackney), qq.896–9.
117. *Children's Employment*, PP 1902, evidence Spencer, qq.4,139–48, 4,184. The estimated number of market stalls (excluding isolated street stalls) in 1901 was 7,055: LCC *Public Control Committee, Report on Street Markets*.
118. William Nn, ms. autobiography, pp.17–18.
119. Black, *Makers of Our Clothes*, p.59.
120. Munby diaries vol. 9, p.74, 30 July 1861.
121. Davies, *Life*, pp.12–14.
122. *Board of Trade, Sweating System in East London, Report*, PP 1887, p.16.
123. *S.C. Sweating System*, PP 1888, p.139, evidence the Rev. J. Munro, q.147.
124. Mrs Hogg, 'Brushmaking', posthumously published in Mudie-Smith (ed.), *Sweated Industries*, pp.92–5.
125. Samuel, *Underworld*, p.31.
126. Mrs C. (b. Hackney, 1902), transcript, p.4.
127. Hird, *Cry*, pp.38–40.
128. Adler, 'Juvenile Wage-Earners', p.208.
129. Hogg, 'Child Labour', p.171.
130. Bedford Institute, *Fifth Annual Report*, 1871, p.42.
131. Hird, *Cry*, p.29.
132. Hird, *Cry*, p.42.
133. Hird, *Cry*, pp.40–3.
134. *East London Observer*, 29 April 1871.
135. [Harkness], *Toilers*, pp.34–7.
136. Williams, *Round London*, p.14; c.f. [Harkness], *Toilers*, p.39.
137. Hird, *Cry*, p.35.
138. *Methodist Times*, 27 Aug. 1908 (cutting, Gertrude Tuckwell collection, Trades Union Congress Library, Box 1 file 216i).
139. Hird, *Cry*, p.35.
140. Hird, *Cry*, p.18.
141. Women's Industrial Council, *Report on Homework*, introduction; c.f. WIC, *Home Industries of Women*.
142. Simcox, 'Industrial Employment', p.247.
143. Hird, *Cry*, p.23.
144. *Children's Employment, 2nd Report*, PP 1864, p.84 (HMI Mr Lord); c.f. pp.86–7.
145. *Children's Employment Commission, 5th Report*, PP 1866, Mr Lord's report (Silk Manufacture), p.73 and evidence, witness 14, pp.77–8.
146. *Children's Employment Commission, 5th Report*, PP 1866, Mr Lord's report (Silk Manufacture), p.73; evidence, witness 13, Fairall (officer from Shoreditch Police Court), p.77; evidence, Ann Lee (domestic workshop owner), p.78.
147. Collet, 'Women's Work', p.267 (Booth, *Poverty* 4).
148. *Factory Inspectors' Report 1895*, PP 1895, (Mr Goddard), p.57.

11 Children, National Identity and the State

1. C.f. Cardinal Manning's 1865 appeal for funds to add 20,000 Catholic school-places in London to the 11,500 existing: Bermant, *East End*, p.66.
2. Kirk, *Reminiscences*, pp.30–52; p.49 (1898 appeal on behalf of the large number of Catholic children 'forced to attend non-Catholic schools in Kensal'). C.f. McLeod, *Class and Religion*, p.78.
3. The Jewish Free School in Bell Lane, established in 1817 and under government inspection from 1853, had 1,068 boys and 700 girls in 1859; the Whitechapel school, the result of an amalgamation of two Bishopsgate schools, in 1859 held about 650 children: *Newcastle Commission*, PP 1861, 3rd Report, pp.478, 486.
4. *S.C. Sweating System*, PP 1889–90, 1st report, Appendix C; c.f. Smith, 'Influx of Population', pp.105–7; Tabor, 'Elementary Education', p.206 (both in Booth, *Poverty* 3).
5. Denvir, *Irish in Britain*, pp.392, 398; Lees, *Exiles*, pp.66–7; Hutton, 'Irish in London', esp. p.119.
6. C.f. map of Jewish settlement by Arkell in Russell and Lewis, *Jew in London* (1900), based on house-to-house records of school visitors; and Jacobs, *Out of the Ghetto*, p.11 for list of such schools in about 1920.
7. Rubinstein, *School Attendance*, p.48.
8. For overview and case studies, see Merriman, *Peopling*.
9. Gertler, 'First memories', in his *Selected Letters*, p.24. (His mother had already been berated by the attendance officer for not sending him to school—she had not realized she was supposed to: pp.23–4.) C.f. Jewish Women in London, *Memories*, Ena Abrahams, p.79; Jacobs, *Out of the Ghetto*, p.12.
10. Jewish Women in London, *Memories*, pp.85–6.
11. Jewish Women in London, *Memories*, Ruth Adler, p.31.
12. C.f. Kirk, *Reminiscences*, p.36; Lees, *Exiles*, pp.189–90; Samuel, 'Irish Religion', p.102.
13. Jewish Women in London, *Memories*, Ena Abrahams, p.86.
14. SBL *Minutes* 1 Feb. 1894, p.412. C.f. Booth, *Poverty* 3, pp.105–7 on defining and counting Jews in London. The problems of deciding who was Irish were at least as great; but separate statistics are rare since they were included in 'from the rest of the British Isles'.
15. *Cross Commission, 2nd Report*, PP 1887, q.17,068, evidence Mrs Burgwin.
16. C.f. Livius, *Father Furniss*: decades of mission work 'visibly transformed' Irish children 'rude, unmanageable and uncivilized in all their habits', who became quiet, docile, obedient and really pious (p.84 etc).
17. For Catholic education generally and the impact of the 1870 Act, see Hickman, 'Incorporation of the Irish in Britain' (thesis) esp. chap.5.
18. Fishman, *1888*, pp.144–76; Feldman, 'There was' and 'Jews in London'.
19. C.f. Canon Barnett's introduction to Russell and Lewis, *Jew in London*; Russell's own essay; and Lewis's critical comments on his co-author's unthinking use of stereotype.
20. It is interesting that Booth and his informants found adult Irish to be all pro-Boer, while Irish children 'identified themselves with the British cause': McLeod, *Class and Religion*, p.76 and n.155.
21. C.f. PRO ED 14/19 (1880): of twenty-three women's training colleges only Chichester accepted women who were not communicants and did not take a Scripture test. An applicant to Homerton College in 1880 was refused because her father was a freethinker. For a (fictional) Jewish teacher with an unsympathetic Christian headmistress, see Zangwill, *Children of the Ghetto*, p.94.
22. Copelman, 'Elementary Schoolteachers', pp.157–8, citing *Board Teacher*, Feb. 1897, p.32, May 1901, p.103, Nov. 1905, p.280, June 1907, p.135.
23. White, *Rothschild Buildings*, p.168. (Mrs A., born Galicia, 1895, in Rothschild Buildings 1897–1915.)
24. Chancellor, *History for their Masters*, p.128. See also MacKenzie, *Propaganda and Empire*, chap.7.
25. Pitman's New Era Geography Reader, *Our Imperial Heritage*, c. 1910, p.24. C.f. for geography teaching Marsden, 'Politicization'; and for imperial history of geography, MacKenzie, 'Geography and Imperialism'.
26. Fryer, *Staying Power*, p.179; and chap.7 for the rise of English racism (which 'is to race prejudice as dogma is to superstition': p.134).
27. Zangwill, *Children of the Ghetto*, p.83. The tension between traditional culture and angli-

cization of the younger generation is a central theme in the novel, with the need for a new but still Jewish identity. C.f. also chap.14, 'The Hope of the Family', where Benjamin visits from the Orphan School where he is a scholarship boy.

28. C.f. Grace Kimmins, *Book of Festival and Dance* for Bermondsey celebration, including songs and descriptions of costumes and dances; and MacKenzie, *Propaganda and Empire*, chap.9 for the Empire Day movement.

29. Marsden, 'Politicization', p.47.

30. Quoted Fryer, *Staying Power*, p.189; see also MacKenzie, *Propaganda and Empire*, chap.8.

31. Fryer, *Staying Power*, pp.188–9.

32. C.f. Barnett's introduction and Russell's essay in *The Jew in London*; but Arkell (p.xliii) implies otherwise.

33. H.S. Lewis, 'Another View', *Jew in London*, p.198.

34. For discussion of stereotypes and racism (here in relation to East End Jews), see Lee, 'Working-class Response', esp. p.108.

35. Russell, 'Jewish Question', p.30. In one Glasgow class Rose Kerrigan and the only other Jewish pupil always came top, despite an anti-semitic teacher: Jewish Women in London, *Memories*, p.55.

36. Heren, *Growing Up*, pp.10–11.

37. C.f. references to popular hostility to Irish and Catholics in Livius, *Father Furniss*, p.97 (1850s-1860s); Kerr, *Memoir of a Sister of Charity*, pp.29–30. C.f. Kerr, *Edith Fielding*, pp.24–5.

38. Barclay, *Memoirs and Medleys*, p.5.

39. C.f. Russell, 'Jewish Question'; Lewis, 'Another View'.

40. Southgate, *That's the Way*, p.34. He explains anti-semitism in terms of both economic threat and anti-alien agitation.

41. T.A. Jackson, *Solo Trumpet*, p.54, quoted in Samuel, 'Irish Religion', p.101.

42. Mrs Bartle (b. 1882), transcript, p.18.

43. For Irish antagonism to Jews, see Arkell, 'Notes on Map', in Russell and Lewis, *Jew in London*, p.xliii.

44. Jewish Women in London, *Memories*, Rose Kerrigan (b. 1903), p.55. C.f. Adler, *Family of Shopkeepers*.

45. *The Times*, 17 Oct. 1873, p.9 col. 5. C.f. Fishman, *1888*, pp.142, 157–8 and *Jewish Radicals*, p.90 for taunts ('bloody Jew', 'Jew bastard') and attacks.

46. Zangwill, *Children of the Ghetto*, p.83.

47. *Daily Express*, 2 Oct. 1906: in cuttings scrap-book of St Anne's Church, Westminster Archive. My thanks to Judith Walkowitz for alerting me to this source.

48. De Banke, *Hand over Hand*, p.56.

49. Armfelt, 'Oriental London', p.84.

50. Salter, *Asiatic in England*, pp.10–14. Salter claimed to have taught himself 'Hindoostanee', 'Oordoo', and 'other oriental languages': Arabic and some Chinese (p.42 etc).

51. Salter, *Asiatic in England*, p.26. Some women used 'the oriental vernacular' and acted as interpreters at the police-courts. For more on 'the orientals' vicious associates', Lascar Sally, Calcutta Louisa, Sally Abdoolah and Chinese Emma (an editorial note warns 'the sketch of this woman is too gross for publication'), see report of the Missionary to Asiatics in London in *London City Mission Magazine*, Nov. 1858, p.288. C.f. Lascar Loo in Kipling's story, 'Badalia Herodsfoot'.

52. Salter, *Asiatic in England*, pp.33–4.

53. Salter, *Asiatic in England*, p.199.

54. Salter, *Asiatic in England*, p.203.

55. Salter, *Asiatic in England*, pp.69–70, 182, and see above. His books and magazine articles purvey stereotypes about opium dens, unprincipled lodging-house keepers preying on their countrymen and wily oriental huxters and beggars.

56. Such bias was all too common in writing about the East End: c.f. Williams, *Round London*, esp. chaps 6 and 9.

57. Salter, *Asiatic in England*, pp.71–3.

58. Davidoff and Hall, *Family Fortunes*.

59. C.f. Gorst, *Children of the Nation* (1906); de Montmorency, *National Education and National Life* (1906); Heath, *Infant, Parent, State* (1907); McMillan, *Child and State* (1911); Pepler, *Care Committee, Child and Parent* (1912); Dyer, *Education and National Life*, 1912.

60. Searle, *National Efficiency*; Davin, 'Imperialism'.
61. Alden, *Child Life*, pp.1–2.
62. Bray, *Town Child*, p.116.
63. See Hurt, *Schooling*, chap.5; and Bulkley, *Feeding*.
64. See Amie Hicks, *Justice*, 29 Nov. 1884, p.7; 3 Oct. 1885, p.1. C.f. SBL *Minutes*, 6 March 1884, p.680: unsuccessful proposal by George Mitchell and Edward Aveling; and SBL *Subcommittee...Administration of the Byelaws*, 1891: unseconded proposal by Stewart Headlam. See also McMillan, *Child and State*, pp.41–7 (success of Bradford measures).
65. Charitable effort failed to feed even half: SBL Subcommittee...Meals, *Minutes*, 1889, p.48. (For auditors' challenge to expenditure on this enquiry: PRO file ED 14/24, 7 Aug. 1890.) See also Bulkley, *Feeding*, pp.16–19.
66. Estimates included 43,843, or 12.8 per cent of those on the rolls (SBL Subcommittee...Meals, *Minutes*, 1889); 55,050, or 10 per cent of average attendance (SBL General Purposes Committee, 'Underfed Children Attending School', *Minutes*, 1898–9); 122,000, or 16 per cent of elementary schoolchildren (*Physical Deterioration Committee*, PP 1904, pp.25–6, Evidence of Dr Eicholz).
67. School doctor, L. Haden Guest, in Hecht (ed.), *Rearing an Imperial Race*, p.35. C.f. McMillan, *Child and State*, pp.41–7.
68. C.f. E. Gwynn, 'The Medical Officer of Health as a Public Teacher', *Public Health*, Nov. 1898, p.79; *Physical Deterioration Committee*, PP 1904, Report, p.15, para 6; Macnamara, 'In Corpore Sano', p.238; *School Children under Five*, PP 1906, pp.9–10; Bulkley, *Feeding*, pp.27–35. Also: Selleck, *New Education*, pp.161–5; Davin, 'Imperialism', pp.9–18; and Hurt, *Schooling*, pp.104–5.
69. Anon [Hubert Bland?], *After Bread, Education*, p.9. This demand was backed by socialists (with exceptions, like Blatchford and Chew); but also won wider support.
70. C.f. Stewart, 'Ramsay MacDonald, the Labour Party and Child Welfare'.
71. Collette, *For Labour and for Women*, pp.120–8.
72. C.f. Fido, 'Charity Organization Society', p.214.
73. Bosanquet, 'Physical Degeneration', pp.72, 74.
74. Bosanquet, *Standard of Life*, p.168. (The proper incentive was 'the spectacle of [their] children's hunger'.)
75. Bosanquet, *Standard of Life*, p.225. Margaret McMillan's riposte: *Child and State*, p.44.
76. Miss Elliott, Hon. Sec. of Southwark Health Society and chair of a local Care Committee, in Hecht (ed.), *Rearing an Imperial Race*, p.47; and see pp.35, 71–2, 77–8, 86–7.
77. Haden Guest, in Hecht (ed.), *Rearing an Imperial Race*, p.35.
78. McMillan, *Child and State*, pp.44–45; 182–3.
79. Gorst, *Children of the Nation*, p.1. Gorst (1835–1916) had a distinguished and varied career, largely in law and politics; he was his own man, always interested in education and committed to social reform; and left the Conservative party in 1909 over free trade. He dedicated the book to 'the Labour members of the House of Commons in token of my belief that they are animated by a genuine desire to ameliorate the condition of the people'.
80. Gorst, *Children of the Nation*, p.1.
81. Gorst, *Children of the Nation*, p.71.
82. Gorst, *Children of the Nation*, pp.73–5.
83. Alden, *Child Life*, pp.166–7.
84. Lloyd George, according to Bruce (*Welfare State*, p.24), 'felt himself, as he put it in 1911, "carried forward on a tide of social pity that was only waiting for a chance of expression".' C.f. (p.16) the influence of the increase over 150 years both of social consciousness and concern and also of a margin of national wealth permitting wider rediffusion.
85. Quoted in Pinchbeck and Hewitt, *Children*, vol. 2, p.612.
86. Alden, *Child Life*, chap.10 gives a useful summary.
87. Alden, *Child Life*, p.163.
88. Adler, *Wage-Earning Children*, p.7.
89. As Margaret Alden pointed out, other problems like housing had also to be tackled: *Child Life*, p.171.
90. Clause 25 of the Children Act allowed a parent convicted of cruelty to a child and proved to be a habitual drunkard to be sentenced to detention for two years in a Home for

Inebriates.

91. C.f. Humphries and Gordon, *Out of Sight*, pp.66, 88 and throughout.
92. C.f. Davin, 'When is A Child', pp.53–6.
93. C.f. Weeks, 'Discourse, Desire and Sexual Deviance'.
94. *MOH, London, Report*, 1906 , p.29.
95. C.f. Potts and Fido, *'Fit Person to be Removed'*, pp.13–14.
96. Potts and Fido, *'Fit Person to be Removed'*, pp.13–14, 146.
97. Parental rhetoric (extended maternal responsibility) was also used in this period to justify women's activities in the public sphere, over issues relating to women, children and the family. C.f. most recently Koven, 'Borderlands'; Thane, 'Women in the British Labour Party'; Lewis 'Gender, the Family and Women's Agency'.
98. Russell, 'Jewish Question', p.139.
99. *Daily Graphic*, 22 Oct. 1895. In the drawing which accompanied the article the boys are nevertheless depicted as 'alien', with orientalized features.
100. Zangwill, *Children of the Ghetto*, p.30.
101. Common, *Kiddar's Luck*, p.40.
102. But see Copelman, 'Elementary Schoolteachers', p.177, on children who went on to become teachers.

Bibliography

This bibliography is arranged in the following sections: Archival Material; Parliamentary Papers; School Readers; Theses; Oral Material; Memoirs (published and unpublished); Books; Articles. The place of publication is London, unless otherwise stated.

Archival Material

Booth Coll.: Booth manuscripts, held at the London School of Economics and Political Science.

LCC: London County Council. Committee Minutes and Reports are held at the Greater London Record Office; printed records also in the British Library. For the Report on Crèches, see LCC Public Control Committee, Report, 1904.

Munby diaries: Diaries of Arthur J. Munby, held in library of Trinity College, Cambridge.

PRO HO45: Public Record Office, Home Office papers.

PRO ED: Public Record Office, Education Department papers.

PRO LCC: Public Record Office, London County Council papers.

SBL: School Board of London. The Board's manuscript records (including committee reports and school logbooks) are held in the Greater London Record Office; printed reports and minutes may also be consulted in the British Library; some are also printed in Parliamentary Papers.

UCL (University College, London) Chadwick Collection, 31: Helen Taylor correspondence.

UCL (University College, London) Chadwick Collection, 99: police responses to questionnaire on boys and girls working as street sellers, and institutional provision for them, 1883.

Parliamentary Papers

1851 xliii (1399) Census of Great Britain, Tables.

1852–3 xc (1692) Census Tables relating to Schools ('Education Census').

1857–8 ix (387) Select Committee (Lords) on Deficiency of Means of Spiritual Instruction and Places of Divine Worship in the Metropolis, Report.

1861 vii (460) Select Committee on the Education of Destitute Children.

1861 Royal Commission on the State of Popular Education in England ('Newcastle Commission'):
Part 1, xxi.i (2794–i)
Part 2, xxi.ii (2794–ii)
Part 3, xxi.iii (2794–iii).

1862 xli (2924) Minute of Privy Council on Education establishing a Revised Code of Regulations.

1863–6 Royal Commission on Children's Employment:
1st Report, 1863 xviii (3170)
2nd Report, 1864 xxii (3414)
3rd Report, 1864 xxii (3414–1)
5th Report, 1866 xxiv (3678).

1868–9 xlvii (4115) Revised Education Code.

268

1871 vii (372) Select Committee on the Protection of Infant Life.
1871 xiv (348) and (446) Factory and Workshops Inspector's Report.
1874 xxv (1071) Local Government Board, Third Annual Report, 1873–4.
1876 Royal Commission on Factory and Workshop Acts:
    Report, xxix (1443)
    Evidence, xxx (1443–1).
1878 lx (236), School Board of London, Inspectors' Reports for 1876, 1877.
1878 lx (158) Education Code, 1878, with modifications since 1873.
1878 lx (2069) Committee of Council on Education, Minute explaining Article 7(b) of the Code of 1878. [Schools' eligibility for annual grant.]
1884 lxi (293) Board of Education, Report of Dr Crichton Browne upon Alleged Over-Pressure of Work in the Public Elementary Schools, Memorandum; also Mr Fitch's memorandum thereon.
1884–5 Royal Commission on the Housing of the Working Classes:
    1st Report xxx (4402)
    Evidence (4402–1).
1886 xxiv (4849–1) Education Report, 1885–6.
1886–8 Royal Commission on the Working of the Elementary Education Acts in England and Wales ('Cross Commission'):
    1st Report 1886 xxv (4863)
    2nd Report (and evidence) 1887 xxix (5056)
    3rd Report (and evidence) 1887 xxx (5158)
    Final Report 1888 (5485) xxxv.
1887 lxxxix (331) Sweating System in East End of London, Board of Trade Report.
1888–90 House of Lords Select Committee on the Sweating System:
    1st Report (and evidence) 1888 (361) xx, xxi.
1890 xi (344) Select Committee (Lords) on the Children's Life Insurance Bill.
1893–94 xxxvii (6894) Royal Commission on Labour: 'Reports on the Employment of Women' by Eliza Orme, Clara Collet etc.
1895 Royal Commission on the Aged Poor:
    Report, xiv (7684)
    Evidence etc., xiv (7684–1), xv (7684–2).
1895 xxviii (7814) HM Inspectors of Schools, Divisional Reports, 1894.
1896 xliii Local Government Board, Departmental Committee on existing systems for the maintenance and education of children under the charge of Managers of District Schools and Boards of Guardians in the Metropolis ('Poor Law Schools Committee'):
    Report xliii (8027)
    Evidence and Appendix, 1896 xliii (8032) and (8033).
1897 xxv (8447) Education Department, Special Reports on Educational Subjects, vol. 1 (including Margaret Eleanor Pillow, 'Domestic Economy Teaching').
1899 viii (296) Select Committee Aged Deserving Poor, Report.
1899 xx (9400) Education Report, 1898–9.
1899 lxxv (205) Elementary Schools, Children Working for Wages, Return for England and Wales.
1900 xix (328) Education Report, 1899.
1902 Employment of Schoolchildren, Interdepartmental Committee:
    Report xxv (849)
    Evidence xxv (895).
1903 Royal Commission on Alien Immigration:
    Report and Evidence, ix (1741)
    Evidence, ix (1741–1, 1742, 1743).
1903 Royal Commission on Physical Training (Scotland):
    Report, xxx (1507)
    Evidence, xxx (1508).
1904 xxxii Interdepartmental Committee on Physical Deterioration:
    Report, xxxii (2175)
    Evidence and appendices, xxxii (2186, 2210).
1906 Interdepartmental Committee on Medical Inspection and Feeding of Children Attending Elementary Schools:
    Report, xlvii (2779)

Evidence, (2784).

1906 xc (2726) Report on Children under Five years of Age in Public and Elementary Schools by Women Inspectors of the Board of Education.

1907–8, Select Committee on Home Work:
  1st Report, 1907 vi (290)
  2nd Report and Evidence, 1908 viii (246).

1908 lxxxii (4259) Attendance of Children below...Five, Board of Education Committee, Report.

1909 Royal Commission on the Poor Laws and Relief of Distress:
  Report, part 1, xxxvii [4499]
      part 2, xxxviii,
  Evidence xxxix (4625)
      xl (4684)
      xli (4835).

1910 PRO ED, *Teaching of Infant Care and Management*, Board of Education Circular 758.

School Readers

Bilton's Reading Books, 1869.
School Managers' Series, 1871–2.
Chambers National Reading Books, 1873.
Marshall's Universal Readers, 1875–7.
Pitman's New Era Geography Reader: 'Our Imperial Heritage' [*c.* 1910].

Theses

Dina Mira Copelman, 'Women in the Classroom Struggle: Elementary Schoolteachers in London, 1870–1914', PhD dissertation, Princeton University, 1985.

Anna Davin, 'Work and School for the Children of London's Labouring Poor in the late nineteenth century and early twentieth century', Birkbeck College, University of London, 1991.

Mary J. Hickman, 'A Study of the Incorporation of the Irish in Britain' with special reference to Catholic state education; involving a comparison of the attitudes of pupils and teachers in selected Catholic schools in London and Liverpool', PhD thesis, Institute of Education, University of London, 1989.

Deborah E.B. Weiner, 'The Institution of Popular Education: Architectural Form and Social Policy in the London Board Schools, 1870–1904', PhD dissertation, Princeton University, 1985.

Oral Material: Tape-recorded Memoirs and Transcripts

Where recordings were made by me, tapes and transcripts are in my possession and copies are deposited with the Sound and Video Archive of the London History Workshop Centre, now held at the Museum of London. For other material, catalogue numbers identify the collection and the individual. Thus Essex 284 points to individual 284 in the Essex Oral History Archive. (This holds the rich material from a major oral history project co-ordinated by Paul Thompson and Thea Thompson in the early 1970s, and I am grateful for the permission to use it.) SVA 9:59 indicates individual 59 in Collection 9 (i.e. tapes from the People's Autobiography of Hackney group which met at Centerprise Community Centre in Hackney in the 1970s, of which I was a member) of the London History Workshop Sound and Video Archive. Recordings made by Raphael Samuel are held by him: my thanks for their use. Where no location is given, tapes are in my possession.

Mrs A., born Waterloo 1903; recorded by Anna Davin, July 1978; SVA 1.

Mag Ayling, born New Cross, 1913; member of class at Goldsmith College, 1981–3; recorded in class, 15 June 1983.

Margaret A., born Pentonville, 1896; Essex 284.

Mrs Bartle, born Poplar, 1882; recorded by Anna Davin, July 1973.

Gladys B., born Hackney, 1904; recorded by R. Samuel, 1974.
Florence C., born Hackney, 1902; interviewed by members of Hackney People's Autobiography Group, 23 Oct. 1972. SVA 9:68; tape missing; my notes extant.
Bessie C., born Bermondsey, 1893; Essex 261.
Charles C., born Bromley-by-Bow, 1891; recorded by R. Samuel, c. 1974.
Wallie Easey (b. 1907), my notes of our conversation, 19 Dec. 1978.
William E., born Wapping, 1897; Essex 368.
Mrs F., born Portobello Rd, 1891; Essex 389.
Florence H., born Bethnal Green, 1892; recorded by R. Samuel, 1974.
Edith H., born Paddington, 1894; Essex 53.
Eliza H., born Poplar, 1900; recorded by R. Samuel, c. 1974. (See also Richman, *Fly a Flag for Poplar*, pp. 50–3.)
Mary H., born Canning Town, 1895; Essex 126.
Miss H., born Kensington, 1902; Essex 403.
Phyllis H., born King's Cross, 1908. I have used my notes of taped discussions of the SE1 People's History Group (SVA 1), to which Phyllis H. also belonged.
Amelia K., born Poplar, 1878; Essex 125.
Mrs K., born Battersea, 1897; Essex 197.
Albert M., born Hoxton, 1894; recorded by Anna Davin, February 1975; SVA 9. See also Elsie M.; and list of unpublished memoirs below.
Elsie M., born Hoxton, 1905; recorded by Anna Davin, Feb. 1975; SVA 9:71. See also Albert M. above; and list of unpublished memoirs.
Mrs M., born Hoxton, 1896; tape played at Hackney People's Autobiography meeting 4 April, 1974 (whereabouts of tape not known; I have notes taken then).
Miss N., born Shadwell, 1895; Essex 331.
Mr N., born Minories, 1899, grew up in Wapping; Essex 417.
Mary P., born Hackney, 1903; recorded by Anna Davin, December 1973; SVA 9:59.
Dick O., born Hackney [late 1890s]; SVA 9:64.
Mr C.G. Perkins, born Plumstead, 1899, recorded 1981 (following his letter to *Daily Mirror*, 19 June) by Rosemary Skinner: I have no copy of tape or transcript but took notes when she played tape in Goldsmith College class.
Walter ('Danny') P., born Spitalfields, 1903, notes of our conversation, 9 June 1975.
Celia R., born Waterloo, 1899, member of SE1 People's History Group, 1981; notes from our discussions.
Ada S., born Spitalfields, 1884, recorded by R. Samuel, c. 1974.
Frank S., born Hoxton, 1884; grew up in Battersea; Essex 225.
Grace Smith, born Kentish Town, 1905; from many conversations I have one set of notes, 29 Dec. 1975.
Rose U., born Bow, 1897; Essex 92.
Ethel V., born Whitechapel, 1895; recorded by R. Samuel, c. 1974.
Jack Welch, born Hoxton, 1903, recorded by Anna Davin winter 1974–5; SVA 9:58 (c.f. also Marie Welch, 9:57).
Marie Welch, born Kelly, Hoxton, 1904, recorded by Anna Davin winter 1974–5; SVA 9:57.
Mrs W., born Finsbury, 1896; Essex 342.
Jane W., born Limehouse, 1896; Essex 298.

Memoirs (Published and Unpublished)

George Acorn, *One of the Multitude*, 1911.
Ruth Adler, *A Family of Shopkeepers*, 1985.
John Allin and Arnold Wesker, *Say Goodbye: You May Never See them Again: Scenes from two East-End Backgrounds*, 1974.
Anon, *Narrow Waters: The First Volume of the Life and Thoughts of a Common Man*, 1935.
Eileen Baillie, *The Shabby Paradise: the Autobiography of a Decade*, 1959.
Thomas Patrick Barclay, *Memoirs and Medleys, the Autobiography of a Bottlewasher*, Leicester, 1934.
Ron Barnes, *Coronation Cups and Jam Jars: a Portrait of an East End Family through Three Generations*, 1976.
John Bellamy (b. 1884), 'Looking Back', *Profile* (Hackney Library Services), March and April 1969; and see *East London History Bulletin* 27, 28, Dec. 1973 and March 1974.

Eric Bligh, *Tooting Corner*, 1946.

Minnie Brittain (née Cowley, Richmond, 1907): untitled typescript lent to me in 1978 by Annette Kuhn (to whom my thanks). Copy in my possession.

Thomas Burke, *Son of London*, 1946.

Charles Chaplin, *My Autobiography*, (1964) 1966.

Ellen Chase, *Tenant Friends in Old Deptford*, 1929.

Richard Church (b. 1893), *Over the Bridge: An Essay in Autobiography*, 1955.

Margaret Cohen and Marion and Hymie Fagan (eds), *Childhood Memories: recorded by some Socialist men and women in their later years*, 1984.

Jack Common, *Kiddar's Luck*, (1951) 1974.

Liz Stanley (ed.), *The Diaries of Hannah Cullwick, Victorian Maidservant*, 1984.

Jack Cummins, *The Landlord Cometh*, Brighton, 1981.

Kathleen Dayus, *Where There's Life*, 1985.

Cecile De Banke, *Hand over Hand*, 1957.

George Elson, *The Last of the Climbing Boys: an autobiography*, 1900.

Edward Ezard, *Battersea Boy*, 1978.

Grace Foakes, *Between High Walls: a London Childhood*, 1972.

Winifred Foley, *A Child in the Forest*, 1974.

Helen Forrester, *Tuppence to Cross the Mersey*, (1974) 1981.

Rose Gamble, *Chelsea Child*, 1979.

Thomas Gautrey, *Lux Mihi Laus: School Board Memories*, 1937.

Samuel Gompers, *Seventy Years of Life and Labour*, New York, 1925.

Clara Grant, *Farthing Bundles*, 1931.

——*From 'Me' to 'We'*, [c. 1940].

Edith Hall, *Canary Girls and Stockpots*, Workers' Educational Association (Luton Branch), Luton, 1977.

Mary Vivian Hughes, *A London Child of the 1870s*, (1934) Oxford, 1977.

——*A London Girl of the 1880s*, (1936) Oxford, 1978.

Agnes Hunt, *Reminiscences*, Shrewsbury, 1935.

T.A. Jackson, *Solo Trumpet*, 1953.

Joe Jacobs, *Out of the Ghetto: My Youth in the East End; Communism and Fascism, 1913–39*, 1978.

Albert Stanley Jasper, *A Hoxton Childhood*, (1969) 1974.

Louise Jermy, *The Memories of a Working Woman*, Norwich, 1934.

Jewish Women in London Group, *Generations of Memories: Voices of Jewish Women*, 1989.

Allen Jobson, *The Creeping Hours of Time*, 1977.

Alice Lewis (born Fulham, 1898), untitled memories transcribed and edited by Heather Jimenez; lent to me by Sally Alexander (to whom my thanks).

Alice Linton, *Not Expecting Miracles*, 1982.

Elsie Mack (born Hoxton, 1905), 'Memories of London in the eyes of a child at the beginning of the century': brief manuscript memoir sent to Hackney People's Autobiography Group, c. 1973. Copy in my possession.

Greville Matheson Macdonald, *Reminiscences of a Specialist*, 1932.

Leah Manning, *A Life for Education*, 1970.

Ethel Mannin, *Confessions and Impressions* (1930), 1936.

Naomi Mitchison, *All Change Here: Girlhood and Marriage*, 1975.

'Mother Kate' (Katherine Anne Egerton Warburton), *Old Soho Days and Other Memories*, Oxford, 1906.

Arthur Newton, *Years of Change: Autobiography of a Hackney Shoemaker*, 1974.

William Nn [Norman] (born Poplar, 1896): typescript memoir sent to Raphael Samuel c. 1974 (copy in my possession).

Thomas Okey, *A Basketful of Memories*, 1930.

Francis Downes Ommanney, *The House in the Park*, 1944.

Ethel Page, 'No Green Pastures', *East London Papers* 9:1 and 9:2, summer and winter 1966.

Peckham People's History Group, *The Times of our Lives: Growing up in the Southwark area, 1900–1945*, 1983.

Victor S. Pritchett, *A Cab at the Door*, 1968.

Marcus Eli Ravage, *An American in the Making: the Life Story of an Immigrant*, New York, (1917) 1971.

W. Pett Ridge, *A Story Teller: Forty Years in London*, 1923.

C.H. Rolph, *London Particulars: Memories of an Edwardian Boyhood*, (1980) 1982.

Frederick Rogers, *Labour, Life and Literature: Some Memories of Sixty Years*, 1916.

Raphael Samuel, *East End Underworld: Chapters in the Life of Arthur Harding*, 1981.

Walter Southgate, *That's The Way it Was: a Working-class Autobiography, 1890–1950*, 1982.

Dot Starn (born Clark, Hackney 1899): brief untitled memoir sent to Hackney People's Autobiography Group, 1972. Copy in my possession.

Tierl Thompson (ed.), *Dear Girl: the Diaries and Letters of two Working Women, 1897–1917* [Ruth Slate and Eva Slawson], 1987.

Ben Thomas, *Ben's Limehouse*, 1987.

Tottenham History Workshop, *How Things Were: Growing up in Tottenham, 1890–1920* [1981].

H.S. Tremenheere (ed. E.L. and O.P. Edmonds), *I Was There: Memoirs*, 1965.

'Mother Kate' [Katherine Anne Egerton Warburton], *Old Soho Days and other Memories*, 1906.

Jack Welch (born Hoxton, 1903), untitled memoir transcribed and edited in 1974–5 by Dolores Hayden, from recordings made 1973–4 by myself and other members of Hackney People's Autobiography Group; in my possession. My thanks to Dolores Hayden.

Marie Welch (born Kelly, Hoxton, 1904): untitled memoir transcribed and edited in 1974–5 by Dolores Hayden, from recordings made 1973–4 by myself and other members of Hackney People's Autobiography Group; in my possession. My thanks to Dolores Hayden.

Edna Wheway, *Edna's Story: Memories of Life in a Children's Home and in Service, in Dorset and London*, Dorset, 1984.

Antonia White (ed. Susan Chitty), *As Once in May: the Early Autobiography of Antonia White and Other Writings*, 1983.

Frederick Willis, *101 Jubilee Road: a Book of London Yesterdays*, 1948.

——*London General*, 1955.

Kathleen Woodward, *Jipping Street* (1928), intro. Carolyn Steedman, 1983.

Muriel Wragge, *The London I Loved: Reminiscences of Fifty Years' Social Work in the District of Hoxton*, 1960.

Books

Nettie Adler, *Wage-Earning Children in England*, 1902.

Margaret Alden, *Child Life and Labour: Social Service Handbook 6*, (1908) 1913.

Michael Anderson, *Family Structure in Nineteenth-Century Lancashire*, Cambridge, 1971.

Anon ('Pearl Fisher'), *The Harvest of the City* [1884].

Anon ('A late Holiday Mother'), *My Cottage: a Story of Dr Barnardo's Village Home for Orphan and Destitute Girls, c. 1885.*

Anon ('One of the Crowd'), *Toilers in London*, 1887 (articles reprinted from *Daily Telegraph*).

Anon ('Riverside Visitor': possibly Thomas Wright), *The Pinch of Poverty: Sufferings and Heroism of the London Poor*, 1892.

Anon [possibly James Greenwood], *Children and the Labour Question* (articles reprinted from the *Daily News*), 1899.

Anon, *On Marriage—Address to Mothers*, SPCK, 1890.

Anon [Hubert Bland?], *After Bread, Education: a Plan for the State Feeding of School Children* (Fabian Tract 129), 1905.

John Thomas Arlidge, *The Hygiene, Diseases and Mortality of Occupations*, 1892.

Frances Armstrong, *Her Own Way, or, Kitty's Promise* [no date: 1890?].

Matthew Arnold, ed. F.S. Marvin, *Reports on Elementary Schools, 1852–1882*, 1908.

Mabel Kathleen Ashby, *Joseph Ashby of Tysoe, 1859–1919: a Study of English Village Life*, (Cambridge, 1961) 1974.

Katharine Axon, *Tenants of Johnson's Court*, 1890.

Nancy Ball, *Educating the People: a Documentary History of Elementary Schooling in England, 1840–1870*, 1983.

Theodore Cardwell Barker and Richard Michael Robbins, *A History of London Transport: Passenger Travel and the Development of the Metropolis*, 2 vols, 1963.

Thomas James Barnardo, *A City Waif: How I Fished for and Caught Her*, 1885.

——*The True Story of a Young Thief*, 1885.

Earl Barnes, *Studies in Education, 1896–7, 1898–1908*, 2 vols, 1897, 1908.

Barnett, Henrietta, *Canon Barnett, His Life, Work and Friends*, 2 vols, 1918.

M.L. Barry, *Hard Realities*, 1884.

George Christopher Trout Bartley, *The Schools for the People: containing the History, Development, and Present Working of each description of English School for the Industrial and Poorer Classes*, 1871.

G.P. Bate, *Report on the Sanitary Condition of Bethnal Green*, 1896.

Bedford Institute, *Spitalfields Nippers* (photographs by Horace B. Warner, *c.* 1900–1912), 1975.

George K. Behlmer, *Child Abuse and Moral Reform in England, 1870–1908*, Stanford, California, 1982.

Mary Eleanor Benson, *Streets and Lanes of the City*, 1891.

Chaim Bermant, *London's East End: Point of Arrival*, 1975.

G. Phillips Bevan, *The Industrial Classes and Industrial Statistics*, 1877.

Miss Bibby, Miss Colles, Miss Petty and Dr Sykes, *The Pudding Lady: a New Departure in Social Work*, 1912.

Charles Birchenough, *History of Elementary Education in England and Wales from 1800 to the Present Day*, 1914.

Clementina Black (ed.), *Sweated Industry and the Minimum Wage*, 1907.

——(ed.), *Married Women's Work, being the Report of an Enquiry Undertaken by the Women's Industrial Council*, (1915) 1983.

——and Adèle Meyer (eds), *Makers of Our Clothes: a Case for Trade Boards: Being the Results of a Year's Investigation into the Work of Women in the Tailoring, Dressmaking and Underclothing Trades*, 1909.

Charles Booth (ed.), *Life and Labour of the People in London*, Seventeen vols 1889–1903 (vol. 1, 1889; vol. 2, 1891; 10 vol. edn 1892–7; 17 vol. edn 1903).

1st Series: *Poverty*

2nd Series: *Industries*

3rd Series: *Religious Influences*

——*Old Age Pensions and the Aged Poor: a Proposal*, (1899) 1906.

William Booth, *In Darkest England and the Way Out*, 1890.

Bernard Bosanquet (ed.), *Aspects of the Social Problem*, 1895.

Helen Bosanquet (née Dendy), *Rich and Poor*, 1896.

——*The Standard of Life and other Studies*, 1898.

——*Social Work in London, 1869–1912*, 1914.

Arthur Lyon Bowley and Alexander Robert Burnett Hurst, *Livelihood and Poverty*, 1915.

Reginald Brabazon [later Lord Meath], (ed.), *Some National and Board School Reforms*, 1887.

Jacqueline Susan Bratton, *The Impact of Victorian Children's Fiction*, 1981.

Reginald Arthur Bray, *The Town Child*, 1907.

——*Boy Labour and Apprenticeship*, 1911.

Samuel Eddey Bray, *School Organisation*, (1905) 1912.

John Wesley Bready, *Doctor Barnardo, Physician, Pioneer, Prophet: Child Life Yesterday and Today*, 1930.

'Brenda' [Mrs G. Castle Smith], *Froggy's Little Brother*, 1875.

British Weekly Commissioners, ed. the author of Out of Work [Margaret Harkness], *Toilers in London, or Inquiries concerning Female Labour in the Metropolis*, 1889.

Fenner Brockway, *Bermondsey Story, the life of Alfred Salter*, 1949.

Barbara Brookes, *Abortion in England, 1900–1967*, 1988.

George Lewis Bruce, *Report to his Constituents on Eighteen Months' Work at the London School Board*, 1893.

Maurice Bruce, *The Coming of the Welfare State*, (1961) 1968.

Mildred Emily Bulkley, *The Feeding of School Children*, 1914.

Evelyn Bunting (ed.), *The School for Mothers*, 1907.

Frances Hodgson Burnett, *The Little Princess*, 1902.

John Burnett, *A History of the Cost of Living*, 1969.

——(ed.), *Useful Toil: Autobiographies of Working People from the 1820s to the 1920s*, 1974.

——*A Social History of Housing, 1815–1970*, Newton Abbot, 1978.

——*Destiny Obscure: Autobiographies of Childhood, Education and Family from the 1820s to the 1920s*, (1982) 1984.

Samuel Butler, *The Way of All Flesh*, 1903.

Christina Violet Butler, *Domestic Service: an Enquiry by the Women's Industrial Council*, 1916.

Mary Carpenter, *Ragged Schools: their principles and modes of operation, by a worker*, 1850.

——*Reformatory Schools for the Children of the Perishing and Dangerous Classes, and for Juvenile Offenders*, 1851.

Mary Chamberlain, *Old Wives' Tales: their History, Remedies and Spells*, 1981.

——*Growing Up in Lambeth*, 1989.

William Chance, *Children under the Poor Law*, 1897.
——(ed.), *Report of the Proceedings of the Third International Congress for the Welfare and Protection of Children*, 1902.
Valerie Chancellor, *History for their Masters: Opinion in the English History Textbook, 1800–1914*, Bath, 1970.
Doris Nield Chew, *Ada Nield Chew: The Life and Writings of a Working Woman*, 1982.
Childhood Society, *Report on the Scientific Study of the Mental and Physical Conditions of Childhood*, 1895.
Christine Collette, *For Labour and for Women: the Women's Labour League, 1906–18*, Manchester, 1989.
Vera K.A. Conway, *Peckham Park Schools* [1988].
Peter Coveney, *The Image of Childhood: the Individual and Society: a Study of the Theme in English Literature*, Harmondsworth, (*Poor Monkey*, 1957) 1967.
Samuel Rutherford Crockett, *Cleg Kelly, Arab of the City*, 1896.
Geoffrey Crossick, *An Artisan Elite in Victorian Society: Kentish London, 1840–1880*, 1978.
——(ed.), *The Lower Middle Class in Britain*, 1977.
Hugh Cunningham, *Children of the Poor: Representations of Childhood since the Seventeenth Century*, Oxford, 1991.
Sir Henry Harding Samuel Cunynghame, *Street Trading by Boys and Girls*, 1902.
James Currie, *The Principles and Practice of Common-School Education*, 1883.
Leonore Davidoff and Catherine Hall, *Family Fortunes: Men and Women of the English Middle Class, 1780–1850*, 1987.
Margaret Llewelyn Davies (ed.), *Maternity: Letters from Working Women*, (1915) 1978.
——(ed.), *Life as we have Known it, by Co-operative Working Women*, (1931) 1977.
J.E.G. De Montmorency, *National Education and National Life*, 1906.
John Denvir, *The Irish in Britain, from the Earliest Times to the Fall of Parnell*, 1892.
Charles Dickens, *Oliver Twist*, (1837–8) Penguin 1966.
——*Bleak House* (1852–3), Penguin 1971.
——*Hard Times* (1854), Penguin 1969.
——*Our Mutual Friend* (1864–5), Penguin 1977.
Anne Digby, *Pauper Palaces*, 1978.
——and Peter Searby, *Children, School and Society in Nineteenth-Century England*, 1981.
Robert Dolling, *Ten Years in a Portsmouth Slum*, 1896.
A.P. Donagrodzki (ed.), *Social Control in Nineteenth-Century Britain*, 1977.
Norman Douglass, *London Street Games*, 1916.
Kirsten Drotner, *English Children and their Magazines, 1751–1945*, 1989.
Olive Jocelyn Dunlop, *English Apprenticeship and Child Labour: a History, with a supplementary section on the modern problem of juvenile labour by O.J. Dunlop and Richard D. Denman*, 1912.
Henry Dyer, *Education and National Life*, 1912.
Carol Dyhouse, *Girls Growing Up in Late Victorian and Edwardian England*, 1981.
Harold James Dyos, *Victorian Suburb: a Study of the Growth of Camberwell*, Leicester, 1961.
——and Michael Wolff (eds), *The Victorian City: Images and Realities*, 2 vols, 1973.
Economic Club [Edith S. Collet and Miss Robertson], *Family Budgets: being the Income and Expenses of Twenty-eight British Households, 1891–1894*, 1896.
George Ewart Evans, *From Mouths of Men*, 1976.
Edith Farmilow, *Chapel Street Children*, 1900.
David Feldman and Gareth Stedman Jones (eds), *Metropolis London: Histories and Representations since 1800*, 1989.
Richard Findlater, *Lilian Baylis, the Lady of the Old Vic*, 1975.
William J. Fishman, *East End Jewish Radicals, 1875–1914*, 1975.
——*East End 1888: a Year in a London Borough among the Labouring Poor*, 1988.
Sheila Fletcher, *Women First: the Female Tradition in English Physical Education, 1880–1980*, 1984.
John Foster, *Class Struggle and the Industrial Revolution: Early Industrial Capitalism in three English Towns*, 1974.
Thor Fredur, *Sketches from Shady Places*, 1879.
Richard Free, *On the Wall: Joan and I in the East End*, 1907.
Flora Lucy Freeman, *Polly: a Study of Girl Life*, Oxford and London, 1904.
——*Religious and Social Work amongst Girls*, 1901.
Edmund and Ruth Frow, *A Survey of the Half-Time System in Education*, Manchester, 1970.
Peter Fryer, *Staying Power: the History of Black People in Britain*, 1984.

Alfonzo Gardiner, *Games, Songs and Recitations for the Kindergarten, the School and Entertainment*, Leeds, 1903.

Phil Gardner, *The Lost Elementary Schools of Victorian England: the People's Education*, 1984.

Mark Gertler (ed. Noel Carrington), *Selected Letters*, 1965.

Bob Gilding, *The Journeymen Coopers of East London*, Oxford, 1971.

John Gillis, *Youth and History: Tradition and Change in European Age Relations, 1770–Present*, New York, (1974) 1981.

Mark Girouard, *Sweetness and Light: the 'Queen Anne' Movement, 1860–1900*, Oxford, 1977.

George Gissing, *Thyrza, a Tale*, 1887.

——*The Nether World*, 1889.

——*Odd Women*, 1893.

John Gittings and Jo Manton, *The Second Mrs Hardy*, Oxford, 1981.

Charles J. Glasson, *Motherhood*, 1901.

Alice Bertha Gomme, *The Traditional Games of England, Scotland and Ireland*, 2 vols, 1894–9.

Linda Gordon, *Heroes of their Own Lives: the Politics and History of Family Violence*, New York, 1988.

John Gorst, *The Children of the Nation: How their Health and Vigour should be Promoted by the State*, 1906.

Robert Q. Gray, *The Labour Aristocracy in Victorian Edinburgh*, Oxford, 1976.

James Greenwood, *The True History of a Little Ragamuffin*, [1866].

——*The Seven Curses of London*, (1869) 1981.

——*In Strange Company: being the Experiences of a Roving Correspondent*, 1873.

——*Low Life Deeps: an Account of the Strange Fish to be Found There*, 1876.

——*The Prisoner in the Dock: my Four Years' Daily Experiences in the London Police Courts*, 1902.

Vivian Grey [Elliott E. Mills] and Edward Sydney Tylee, *Boy and Girl—Should they be Educated Together? A Study of the Principle and Methods of Co-education*, Oxford, 1906.

Hackney Workers' Educational Association, *The Threepenny Doctor: Doctor Jelley of Hackney*, 1974.

Catherine Hall, *White, Male and Middle Class: Explorations in Feminism and History*, 1992.

Tamara Kern Hareven (ed.), *Transitions: the Family and the Life Course in Historical Perspective*, New York and London, 1978.

Margaret Elise Harkness (writing as John Law), *Captain Lobe, a Story of the Salvation Army*, 1889.

——*Out of Work*, (1888) 1990.

——(ed. anonymously), *Toilers in London: Reports for the British Weekly*, 1889.

Mary H. Hart (preface by J. L. Davies), *The Children of the Street: Mary Carpenter's Work in Relation to Our Own*, 1880.

Thomas Edmund Harvey, *A London Boy's Saturday*, Birmingham, 1906.

George Haw, *No Room to Live*, 1898.

——*From Workhouse to Westminster: the Life of Will Crooks, MP*, 1907.

Kathleen Heasman, *Evangelicals in Action: an Appraisal of their Social Work in the Victorian Era*, 1962.

H. Llewellyn Heath, *The Infant, the Parent and the State*, 1907.

Charles E. Hecht (ed.), *Rearing an Imperial Race: Proceedings of National Food Reform Association Guildhall Conference on Diet, Cookery and Hygiene in Schools*, 1913.

Louis Heren, *Growing Up Poor in London*, 1973.

Octavia Hill, *Letters to my Fellow Workers, 1872–1893*, privately bound copy, no date.

J. Deane Hilton, *Marie Hilton, her Life and Work*, 1897.

Frank Hird, *The Cry of the Children: an Exposure of the Industries in which British Children are Iniquitously Employed*, 1898.

A.L. Hodson, *Letters from a Settlement*, 1909.

Colin Holmes, *Anti-Semitism in British Society, 1876–1939*, 1979.

Edmond Holmes, *What is and What Might Be: a Study of Education in General and Elementary Education in Particular*, (1911) 1917.

Pamela Horn, *The Rise and Fall of the Victorian Servant*, Gloucester, (1975) 1986.

——*Children's Work and Welfare, 1780–1880s*, 1994.

Mary A. Hubbard, *A Few Words to School and Schoolroom Girls*, 1884.

Anne Humpherys, *Travels into the Poor Man's Country: the Work of Henry Mayhew*, Firle (Sussex), 1977.

Stephen Humphries, *Hooligans or Rebels? An Oral History of Working-Class Childood and Youth, 1889–1939*, Oxford, 1981.

——and Pamela Gordon, *Out of Sight: the Experience of Disability, 1900–1950*, Plymouth, 1992.

J.S. Hurt, *Elementary Schooling and the Working Classes, 1860–1918*, 1979.
Bill Jay, *Victorian Candid Camera: Paul Martin, 1864–1944*, Newton Abbot, 1973.
Arthur William Jephson, *My Work in London*, 1910.
Harriet M. Johnson, *Children and Public Houses*, Liverpool, 1897.
Paul Johnson, *Saving and Spending: the Working-class Economy in Britain, 1870–1939*, Oxford, 1985.
Alan W. Jones, *Lyulph Stanley, a Study in Educational Politics*, Waterloo, Ontario, 1979.
Gareth Stedman Jones, *Outcast London: a Study in the Relationship between Classes in Victorian Society*, Oxford, 1971.
——*Languages of Class: Studies in English Working-Class History, 1832–1982*, Cambridge, 1983.
Emilia Kanthack, *The Preservation of Infant Life: Lectures to Health Visitors*, 1907.
Anne Cecil Kerr, *Memoir of a Sister of Charity: Lady Ethelreda Howard*, 1928.
——*Edith Fielding, Sister of Charity*, 1933.
Grace Thyrza Kimmins, *Polly of Parker's Rents*, 1899.
——*The Guild of Play Book of Festival and Dance*, 1907.
F.J. Kirk (Rev.), *Reminiscences of an Oblate of St Charles*, 1905.
Seth Koven and Sonya Michel (eds), *Mothers of a New World: Maternalist Politics and the Origins of New States*, London and New York, 1993.
Lynne Hollen Lees, *Exiles of Erin: Irish Immigrants in Victorian London*, Manchester, 1979.
David Levine, *Reproducing Families: the Political Economy of English Population History*, Cambridge, 1987.
Jane Lewis, *The Politics of Motherhood: Child and Maternal Welfare in England, 1900–1939*, 1980.
Peter Linebaugh, *The London Hanged: Crime and Civil Society in the Eighteenth Century*, 1991.
T. Livius, *Father Furniss and his Work for Children*, London and Leamington, 1896.
M.E. Loane, *Simple Sanitation*, 1905.
——*The Queen's Poor: Life as They Find It in Town and Country*, 1905.
——*Simple Introductory Lessons in Midwifery*, 1906.
——*The Next Street But One*, 1907.
——*From their Point of View*, 1908.
——*An Englishman's Castle*, 1909.
——*The Common Growth*, 1911.
Jack London, *People of the Abyss*, (1903) 1907.
George Alfred Norman Lowndes, *The Silent Social Revolution: an Account of the Expansion of Public Education in England and Wales, 1895–1935*, (1937) 1950.
Kenneth Lunn (ed.), *Hosts, Immigrants and Minorities: Historical Responses to Newcomers in British Society, 1870–1914*, Folkestone, 1980.
Philip McCann (ed.), *Popular Education and Socialization in the Nineteenth Century*, 1977.
George F. McCleary, *Infantile Mortality and Infant Milk Depots*, 1905.
James McCulloch, *Open Church for the Unchurched*, New York, 1905.
J. Ramsay MacDonald (ed.), *Women in the Printing Trades*, 1904.
Greville Matheson Macdonald, *Board School Laryngitis*, 1889.
John M. MacKenzie, *Propaganda and Empire: the Manipulation of British Public Opinion, 1880–1960*, Manchester, 1984.
Angus McLaren, *Birth Control in Nineteenth-Century England*, 1978.
Hugh McLeod, *Class and Religion in the Late Victorian City*, 1974.
Margaret McMillan, *The Child and the State*, Manchester, 1911.
Charles Frederick Gurney Masterman (ed.), *The Heart of the Empire: Discussions of Problems of Modern City Life in England*, (1901), Brighton (ed. Bentley B. Gilbert), 1973.
Somerset Maugham, *Liza of Lambeth*, 1897.
——*Of Human Bondage* (1915), Penguin 1963.
Jonathan May, *Madame Bergman-Osterberg: Pioneer of Physical Education and Games for Girls and Women*, 1969.
Augustus Mayhew, *Paved with Gold, or the Romance and Reality of London Streets*, 1858.
Henry Mayhew, *London Labour and the London Poor*, Four vols, 1861–2.
——John L. Bradley (ed.), *Selections from London Labour and the London Poor*, Oxford, 1965.
Edith L. Maynard, *Baby—Useful Hints for Busy Mothers*, 1906.
Andrew Mearns, *The Bitter Cry of Outcast London. An Enquiry into the Condition of the Abject Poor*, 1883.
Standish Meacham, *A Life Apart: the English Working Class, 1890–1914*, 1977.
Nick Merriman (ed.), *The Peopling of London: Fifteen Thousand Years of Settlement from Overseas,*

1993.

Hannah More, *Coelebs in Search of a Wife, comprehending Observations on Domestic Habits and Manners, Religion and Morals*, (1809) 1830.

Charles Morley, *Studies in Board Schools*, 1897.

Malcolm A. Morris (ed.), *The Book of Health*, 1883.

Arthur Morrison, *Tales of Mean Streets*, 1895.

Frank Mort, *Dangerous Sexualities: Medico-Moral Politics in England since 1830*, 1987.

Honnor Morten, *From a Nurse's Notebook*, 1899.

Richard Mudie-Smith (ed.), *Sweated Industries: being a Handbook of the 'Daily News' Exhibition*, 1906.

Frank Musgrove, *Youth and the Social Order*, (1964) 1968.

David Nasaw, *Children of the City: How our Grandparents Grew Up*, New York, 1985.

George Newman, *Infant Mortality: a Social Problem*, 1906.

——*The Health of the State*, 1907.

Arthur Newsholme, *Elementary Hygiene*, 1893.

——*Elements of Vital Statistics*, 1899.

William Oscar Emil Oesterley, *Walks in Jewry*, 1901.

Thomas Oliver (ed.), *Dangerous Trades: the Historical, Social and Legal Aspects of Industrial Occupations as affecting Health*, 1902.

Gilda O'Neill, *Pull No More Bines: An Oral History of London Women Hop Pickers*, 1990.

Joy Parr, *Labouring Children: British Immigrant Apprentices to Canada, 1869–1924*, London and Montreal, 1980.

Alexander Paterson, *Across the Bridges, or Life by the South London Riverside*, 1911.

Joseph Payne, *Why are the Results of our Primary Instruction so Unsatisfactory?*, 1872.

Dorothy Constance (Mrs C.S.) Peel, *Life's Enchanted Cup: an Autobiography. 1872–1933*, 1933.

People's Autobiography of Hackney, *The Island: the Life and Death of an East London Community*, 1979.

Douglas Pepler, *The Care Committee, the Child and the Parent*, 1912.

Leslie Phillips, *Pathology and Treatment of Abortion*, 1887.

Hugh B. Philpott, *London at School: the Story of the School Board, 1870–1904*, 1904.

Godfrey Holden Pike, *Children Reclaimed for Life: the Story of Dr Barnardo's Work in London*, 1875.

Ivy Pinchbeck and and Margaret Hewitt, *Children in English Society: vol.1, From Tudor Times to the Eighteenth Century*, 1969.

Ernest Pomeroy (The Honourable), *The Education Tyranny: the Education System Examined and Exposed, together with Practical Aids for Persecuted Parents*, 1910.

Charles Porter, *School Hygiene and the Laws of Health*, 1913.

Maggie Potts and Rebecca Fido, *'A Fit Person to be Removed': Personal Accounts of Life in a Mental Deficiency Institution*, Plymouth, 1991.

Charles Poulsen, *Victoria Park: a Study in the History of East London*, 1976.

Eric Law Pritchard, *Infant Education*, 1907.

John Pudney, *Crossing London's River*, 1972.

Edwin Pugh, *City of the World*, 1912.

Jill Quadagno, *Aging in Early Industrial Society: Work, Family and Social Policy in Nineteenth-Century England*, New York and London, 1982.

Mary Quinlan, *In the Devil's Alley*, 1907.

Percy Redfern, *The Story of the CWS: the Jubilee History of the Co-operative Wholesale Society Limited, 1863–1913*, 1913.

John Reeves, *Recollections of a School Attendance Officer*, [c. 1915].

Magdalen Stuart (Mrs Pember) Reeves, *Round About a Pound a Week*, (1913) 1979.

Margery Spring Rice, *Working Class Wives: their Health and Conditions*, (1939) 1981.

Ruth Richardson, *Death, Dissection and the Destitute*, 1988.

Geoff Richman, *Fly a Flag for Poplar*, [c. 1975].

W. Pett Ridge, *Mord Em'ly*, 1898.

Robert Roberts, *The Classic Slum: Salford Life in the First Quarter of the Century* (Manchester, 1971), Harmondsworth, 1973.

Adam Henry Robson, *The Education of Children Engaged in Industry, 1833–1876*, 1931.

Janet Roebuck, *Urban Development in Nineteenth-century London: Lambeth, Battersea and Wandsworth, 1838–1888*, 1979.

Roy Rosenzweig, *Eight Hours for What we Will: Workers and Leisure in an Industrial City, 1870–1920*, Cambridge and New York, 1983.

Ellen Ross, *Love and Toil: Motherhood in Outcast London*, New York and Oxford, 1993.
Richard Rowe, *Picked Up in the Streets, or Struggles for Life among the London Poor*, 1880.
Benjamin Seebohm Rowntree, *Poverty: a Study of Town Life*, 1901.
——*The Human Needs of Labour*, 1918.
David Rubinstein, *School Attendance in London, 1870–1914: a Social History*, Hull, 1969.
Mildred De Montjoie Rudolf, *The First Forty Years: a Chronicle of the Church of England Waifs and Strays Society, 1881–1920*, 1922.
Charles Russell and H.S. Lewis, *The Jew in London: a Study of Racial Character and Present-Day Conditions*, 1900.
Rowland Ryder, *Edith Cavell*, 1975.
David Salmon and Winifred Hindshaw, *Infant Schools, their History and Theory*, 1904.
Joseph Salter, *The Asiatic in England: Sketches of Sixteen Years' Work among Orientals*, 1873.
Raphael Samuel (ed.), *Patriotism: the Making and Unmaking of National Identity, vol. 2 Minorities and Outsiders*, 1989.
George E. Sargent, *The Story of a Street Arab*, 1882.
Ruby J. Saywell, *Mary Carpenter of Bristol*, Bristol, 1964.
Mary Scharlieb, *The Mother's Guide to the Health and Care of her Children*, 1905.
Malcolm Seaborne, *The English School: its Architecture and Organization, vol. 1, 1370–1870*, 1971.
G.R. Searle, *The Quest for National Efficiency*, 1971.
Richard Joseph Wheeler Selleck, *The New Education: the English Background, 1870–1914*, 1968.
Lord Shaftesbury (Anthony A. Cooper), *Speeches of the Earl of Shaftesbury upon Subjects having relation chiefly to the Claims and Interests of the Labouring Class*, (London, 1868) Shannon, 1971.
Evelyn Sharp, *The Making of a Schoolgirl*, (1897) New York and Oxford, 1989.
Robert Harborough Sherard, *The Child Slaves of Britain*, 1905.
Arthur Sherwell, *Life in West London, a Study and a Contrast*, 1897.
Harold Silver and Pamela Silver, *The Education of the Poor: the History of a National School, 1824–1974*, 1974.
Brian Simon, *Studies in the History of Education, vol. 2: Education and the Labour Movement, 1870–1920*, (1965) 1974.
C.H. Simpkinson, *A London Parish: Thirteen Years in St Paul's, Lorrimore Square, Walworth*, 1894.
George Robert Sims, *How the Poor Live*, 1883.
——(ed.), *Living London*, three vols, 1901–3.
Frank Smith, *History of English Elementary Education, 1760–1902*, 1931.
Hubert Llewellyn Smith (ed.), *New Survey of London Life and Labour*, vol.1, *Forty Years of Change*, 1931.
Reggie D. Smith (ed.), *The Writings of Anna Wickham, Free Woman and Poet*, 1984.
E.M. Sneyd-Kynnersley, *HMI: Some Passages in the Life of One of H.M. Inspectors of Schools*, 1908.
Thomas Alfred Spalding, assisted by T.S.A. Canney, *The Work of the London School Board*, 1900.
John Alfred Spender, *The State and Pensions in Old Age*, 1892.
Lucio Sponza, *Italian Immigrants in Nineteenth-century Britain: Realities and Images*, Leicester, 1988.
John Springhall, *Coming of Age: Adolescence in Britain, 1860–1960*, Dublin, 1986.
Jo Stanley and Bronwen Griffiths, *For Love and Shillings: Wandsworth Women's Working Lives*, 1990.
Maude A. Stanley, *Work About the Five Dials*, 1878.
——*Clubs for Working Girls*, 1890.
Carolyn Steedman, *The Tidy House: Little Girls Writing*, 1982.
——*Childhood, Culture and Class: Margaret McMillan, 1860–1931*, Cambridge, 1991.
Robert Louis Stevenson, *Virginibus Puerisque*, (1881) 1946.
Hesba Stretton [Sara Smith], *Little Meg's Children*, 1868.
Melanie Tebbutt, *Making Ends Meet: Pawnbroking and Working-class Credit*, Leicester, 1983.
Dorothy Tennant [later Stanley], *London Street Arabs*, 1890.
Edward Thomas, *The Childhood of Edward Thomas*, 1938.
Lilian Gilchrist Thompson, *Sidney Gilchrist Thomas. An Invention and its Consequences*, 1940.
Paul Thompson, *The Edwardians: the Remaking of British Society*, (1975) 1977.
Thea Thompson, *Edwardian Childhoods*, 1980.
Louise A. Tilly and Joan W. Scott, *Women, Work, and Family*, New York, 1978.
Flora Tristan, *Promenades dans Londres*, (Paris, 1840) 1982.
Jules Vallès, *La Rue à Londres*, (Paris, 1884) 1957.
Rev. Langton George Vere, *Father Cuthbert's Curiosity Case*, Catholic Truth Society, 1897.

David Vincent, *Bread, Knowledge and Freedom: a Study of Nineteenth-Century Working-Class Autobiography*, 1981.

Gillian Wagner, *Children of Empire*, 1982.

Judith R. Walkowitz *Prostitution and Victorian Society: Women, Class and the State*, Cambridge, 1980.

Francis Warner, *Report on the Scientific Study of the Mental and Physical Conditions of Childhood*, 1895.

Jeffrey Weeks, *Sex, Politics and Society*, 1981.

John Matthias Weylland, *These Fifty Years, being the Jubilee Volume of the London City Mission*, 1884.

Nanette Whitbread, *The Evolution of the Nursery-Infant School: a History of Infant and Nursery Education in Britain, 1800–1970* (1972), 1975.

Jerry White, *Rothschild Buildings: Life in an East End Tenement Block, 1887–1920*, 1980

——*The Worst Street in North London: Campbell Bunk, Islington, Between the Wars*, 1986.

Frances Widdowson, *Going Up into the Next Class: Women and Elementary Teacher Training, 1840–1914*, (1980) 1983.

Joseph Cotton Wigram (Bishop of Rochester), *Elementary Arithmetic, designed for the information of...Masters and Mistresses of National Schools*, 1832.

Montagu Stephen Williams, *Round London: Down East and Up West*, 1892.

T. Marchant Williams, *The Overpressure of Poverty and Drink, and the School Board for London*, 1884.

Francesca M. Wilson, *Rebel Daughter of a Country House: the Life of Eglantyne Jebb, Founder of the Save the Children Fund*, 1967.

Anthony S. Wohl, *Endangered Lives: Public Health in Victorian Britain*, 1983.

Women's Industrial Council, *Home Industries of Women in London: Report of an Enquiry into Thirty-five Trades*, 1897.

——*Home Industries of Women in London, 1906: Interim Report of an Enquiry*, 1908.

John Woodeson, *Mark Gertler: Portrait of a Painter, 1891–1939*, 1972.

Thomas Wright [writing as A Journeyman Engineer], *Some Habits and Customs of the Working Classes*, 1867.

——*The Great Unwashed* (1868), 1970.

Margaret A. Wroe, *Public Infants Schools*, Manchester, 1903.

Ailsa Yoxall, *A History of the Teaching of Domestic Economy*, Bath, 1965.

Israel Zangwill, *Children of the Ghetto*, 1892.

Articles

Nettie Adler, 'Juvenile Wage-Earners', *Progress*, July 1906.

Sally Alexander, 'Becoming a Woman in London in the 1920s and 1930s', in David Feldman and Gareth Stedman Jones (eds), *Metropolis London: Histories and Representations since 1800*, 1989.

T. Poynter Allen, 'Inquiry into the Present State of Education in Battersea', *Journal of the Society of Arts* (supplement), 12 Aug. 1870.

Anon ['Riverside Visitor'], 'School Board Work', *Good Words*, Edinburgh, 1872.

Anon ['Riverside Visitor'], 'Education and Boots', *Frasers Magazine* 22 (new series), Nov. 1880.

Count E. Armfelt, 'Oriental London', in G.R. Sims (ed.), *Living London* 1, 1901–2.

W.A. Armstrong, 'A Note on the Household Structure of mid nineteenth-century York in Comparative Perspective', in Peter Laslett and Richard Wall (eds), *Household and Family in Past Time*, Cambridge, 1972.

Paul Atkinson, 'Fitness, Feminism and Schooling', in Sara Delamont and Lorna Duffin, *The Nineteenth Century Woman; Her Cultural and Physical World*, 1978.

Stanley B. Atkinson, 'Law and Infant Life', in Theophilus Kelynack (ed.), *Infancy*, 1910.

Victor Bailey and Sheila Blackburn, 'The Punishment of Incest Law, 1908: a Case Study of Law Creation', *Criminal Law Review*, 1979.

Earl Barnes, 'Children's Ideals', *Pedagogical Seminary* 7, Worcester, Mass., 1900.

Edward Berdoe, 'Slum Mothers and Death Clubs: a Vindication', *Nineteenth Century* 29, April 1891.

Harry Blacker, 'Memoirs of the Mittel East', *Listener*, 16 March 1972.

Helen Bosanquet (née Dendy), 'Physical Deterioration and the Poverty Line', *Contemporary Review* 85, Jan. 1904.

Reginald Brabazon, 'Public Playgrounds', in his *Some National and Board School Reforms*, 1887.

Reginald Arthur Bray, 'The Children of the Town', in C.F.G. Masterman (ed.), *The Heart of the Empire* (1901), 1973.

Reginald Arthur Bray, 'The Ordinary Day School', Thomas A. Spalding (ed.), *The London School Board*, 1900.

James Crichton Browne, 'Education and the Nervous System', in Malcolm A. Morris (ed.), *The Book of Health*, 1883.

Fanny Calder, 'Cookery in Elementary Schools', in Reginald Brabazon, *Some National and Board School Reforms*, 1887.

W.G. Carson, 'The Conventionalization of Early Factory Crime', *International Journal for the Sociology of Law* 7, 1979.

Dominick Cavallo, 'The Politics of Latency: Kindergarten Pedagogy 1830–1960', in Barbara Finkelstein (ed.), *Regulated Children/Liberated Children: Education in a Psychological Perspective*, New York, 1979.

E.A.G. Clark, 'The Early Ragged Schools and the Foundation of the Ragged School Movement', *Journal of Educational Administration and History* 1, 1969.

——'The Last of the Voluntaryists: the Ragged School Union in the School Board Era', *History of Education* 11:1, 1982.

H. Acraman Coate, 'Some Phases of Poor Life', *Eastward Ho* 3, June 1885.

Clara Collet, 'Women's Work', in Charles Booth, *Life and Labour*, Poverty series 4.

Sean Creighton, 'Battersea and New Unionism', *South London Record* 4, 1989.

Geoffrey Crossick, 'The Emergence of the Lower Middle Class', in Crossick (ed.) *The Lower Middle Class in Britain*, 1977.

H. Cunynghame, 'Technical Education', *Eastward Ho*, Jan. 1887.

Leonore Davidoff, 'The Separation of Home and Work? Landladies and Lodgers in Nineteenth and Twentieth-century England', in Sandra Burman (ed.), *Fit Work for Women*, 1979.

Anna Davin, 'Imperialism and Motherhood', *History Workshop Journal* 5, 1978.

——'"Mind that you do as you are told": Reading Books for Board School Girls, 1870–1902', *Feminist Review* 3, 1979.

——'When is a Child not a Child?', in Lynn Jamieson and Helen Corr (eds), *Politics of Everyday Life*, 1990.

Helen Dendy [later Bosanquet], 'Children of Working London', in Bernard Bosanquet (ed.), *Aspects of the Social Problem*, 1895.

Carol Dyhouse, 'Working-class Mothers and Infant Mortality in England, 1895–1914', *Journal of Social History* 13, 1979.

Harold James Dyos, 'The Slums of Victorian London' [1967], in Dyos, *Exploring the Urban Past*, 1982.

David Feldman, 'The Importance of Being English: Jewish Immigration and the Decay of Liberal England', in D. Feldman and Gareth Stedman Jones (eds), *Metropolis London: Histories and Representations since 1800*, 1989.

——'Jews in London, 1880–1914', in Raphael Samuel (ed.), *Patriotism: the Making and Unmaking of National Identity, vol. 2, Minorities and Outsiders*, 1989.

Judith Fido, 'Charity Organization Society', in A.P. Donagrodzki (ed.), *Social Control in Nineteenth-Century Britain*, 1977.

George P. Field, 'The Ear and Hearing', in Malcolm A. Morris (ed.), *The Book of Health*, 1883.

John Field, 'Private Schools in Portsmouth and Southampton, 1850–70', *Journal of Educational and Administrative History* 10, summer 1978.

Peter Gordon, 'The Writings of Edmund Holmes: a Reassessment and Bibliography', *History of Education* 12:1, 1983.

Deborah Gorham, 'The "Maiden Tribute of Modern Babylon" Re-examined: Child Prostitution and the Idea of Childhood in Late Victorian England', *Victorian Studies* 21:3, spring 1978.

John Gorst, 'School Children as Wage Earners', *Nineteenth Century* 46, July 1899.

Rider Haggard, 'How Will Co-Education Influence the Future of our Race?', *Rural England* vol. 2, 1902.

P.E.H. Hair, 'Children in Society, 1850–1980', in Theo Barker and Michael Drake (eds), *Population and Society*, 1982.

F.W. Head, 'The Church and the People', in Masterman (ed.), *The Heart of the Empire*, (1901) 1973.

May Elizabeth Headdon, 'Industrial Training for Girls', in Reginald Brabazon (ed.), *Some*

National and Board School Reforms, 1887.

W.C.R. Hicks, 'The Education of the Half-Timer', *Economic History* 4, 1939.

Eric John Hobsbawm, 'The Labour Aristocracy in Nineteenth-century Britain', in Hobsbawm (ed.), *Labouring Men*, 1964.

——'The Formation of British Working-Class Culture', in *Worlds of Labour*, 1984.

——'The Making of the Working Class, 1870–1914', [1979] in Hobsbawm (ed.), *Worlds of Labour*, 1984.

——'Debating the Labour Aristocracy', [1979] in Hobsbawm (ed.), *Worlds of Labour*, 1984.

——'The Aristocracy of Labour Reconsidered', [1979] in Hobsbawm (ed.), *Worlds of Labour*, 1984.

——'Artisans and Labour Aristocrats?', in Hobsbawm (ed.), *Worlds of Labour*, 1984.

——'The Nineteenth-century Labour Market', [1964] in *Worlds of Labour*, 1984.

Edith Hogg, 'Schoolchildren as Wage Earners', *The Nineteenth Century* 42, Aug. 1897.

W.G. Howgrave, 'Report on Public Nurseries in London', *Charity Organization Society Reporter*, 9 Oct. 1872.

J.S. Hurt, 'Drill, Discipline and the Elementary School Ethos', in Philip McCann (ed.), *Popular Education and Socialization in the Nineteenth Century*, 1977.

Seán Hutton, 'The Irish in London', in Nick Merriman (ed.), *The Peopling of London: Fifteen Thousand Years of Settlement from Overseas*, 1993.

Henry Iselin, 'The Childhood of the Poor', *Macmillan's Magazine*, April 1907.

Gareth Stedman Jones, 'Working-class Culture and Working-class Politics in London, 1870–1900: notes on the remaking of a working class', [1974] in *Languages of Class*, 1983.

Frank Kelsall, 'The Board Schools: School Building 1870–1914', in Ron Ringshall, Margaret Miles and Frank Kelsall, *The Urban School: Buildings for Education in London, 1870–1980*, 1983.

Howard Angus Kennedy, 'Board School London', in G.R. Sims (ed.), *Living London* 1, 1901–2.

L.W. Kline, 'Truancy as Related to the Migratory Instinct', *Pedagogical Seminary* 5, Worcester (Massachusetts), 1898.

Seth Koven, 'Borderlands: Women, Voluntary Action, and Child Welfare in Britain, 1840–1914', in Koven and Sonya Michel (eds), *Mothers of a New World: Maternalist Politics and the Origins of New States*, London and New York, 1993.

Marion Kozak, 'Nursery at Wesley House', *National Childcare Campaign Newsletter*, Nov./Dec. 1985.

Ruth Lamb, 'How to Wash and Dress the Baby', *Girl's Own Paper* 2, pp.474–6. 23 April 1881; pp.611–13, 25 June 1881.

——'How to Nurse the Baby', *Girl's Own Paper* 2, pp.699–700, 30 July 1881.

Marghanita Laski, 'Domestic Life', in Simon Nowell-Smith (ed.), *Edwardian England*, 1974.

F.W. Lawrence, 'The Housing Problem', in C.F.G. Masterman (ed.), *The Heart of the Empire*, (1901) 1973.

Alan Lee, 'Aspects of the Working-class Response to the Jews in Britain', in Kenneth Lunn, *Hosts, Immigrants and Minorities: Historical Responses to Newcomers in British Society, 1870–1914*, Folkestone, 1980.

H.S. Lewis, 'Another View of the Question', in Charles Russell and Lewis, *The Jew in London: a Study of Racial Character and Present-Day Conditions*, 1900.

Jane Lewis, 'Parents, Children, School Fees and the School Board', *History of Education* 11:4, Newton Abbot, 1982.

——'Gender, the Family and Women's Agency in the Building of "Welfare States": the British Case', *Social History* 19:1, 1994.

R. Burr Litchfield, 'The Family and the Mill: Cotton Mill Work Patterns and Fertility in Mid-Victorian Stockport', in A.S. Wohl (ed.), *The Victorian Family*, 1978.

Mrs E. Lord, 'Domestic Economy', in Thomas A. Spalding (ed.), *The London School Board*, 1900.

Frances Low, 'Street Games', *Strand Magazine* 2, Nov. 1891.

John MacKenzie, 'Geography and Imperialism: British Provincial Geographical Societies', in Felix Driver and Gillian Rose (eds), *Nature and Science: Essays in the History of Geographical Knowledge*, 1992.

Thomas James Macnamara, 'Three Years of Progressivism at the London School Board', *Fortnightly Review*, Nov. 1900.

——'In Corpore Sano', *Contemporary Review* 87, Feb. 1905.

Henry Major, 'Educational Appliances', in Twelve British Workmen, *Modern Industries: reports* on *Industries and Manufactures as Represented in the Paris Exposition in 1867*, 1868.

Patricia Malcolmson, 'Laundresses and the Laundry Trade in Victorian England', *Victorian Studies* 24:4, summer 1981.

William E. Marsden, 'Residential Segregation and the Hierarchy of Elementary Schooling from Charles Booth's Surveys', *London Journal* 11, 1985.

——'Education and Urbanization in Nineteenth-century Britain', *Paedogogica Historica* 23:1, Gent, 1983.

——'Politicization, Pedagogy and the Educational Experience of English Children, 1850–1970', in Petter Aasen and Karin Ekberg (eds), *Historical Perspectives on Childhood*, Trondheim, 1990 (Norwegian Centre for Child Research, Report 17).

Anna Martin, 'The Mother and Social Reform', parts 1 and 2, *The Nineteenth Century and After* 73, May and June 1913.

——'Working Women and Drink', parts 1 and 2, *The Nineteenth Century and After* 78–9, Dec. 1915 and Jan. 1916.

C.F.G. Masterman, 'Realities at Home', in Masterman (ed.), *The Heart of the Empire*, (1901) 1973.

Margaret May, 'Innocence and Experience: the Evolution of the Concept of Juvenile Delinquency in the Mid-Nineteenth Century', *Victorian Studies* 17:1, 1973.

Theresa McBride, ' "As the Twig is Bent": the Victorian Nanny', in A.S. Wohl (ed.), *The Victorian Family*, 1978.

Keith McClelland, 'Some Thoughts on Masculinity and the "Representative Artisan" in Britain, 1850–80', *Gender and History* 1:2, 1989.

R.M. McLeod, 'Social Policy and the Floating Population: the Administration of the Canal Boats Act, 1877–99', *Past and Present* 35, 1966.

Charles Morley, 'An Eton for Nothing a Week', in his *Studies in Board Schools*, 1897.

George Newman, 'A Note on the London Death Rate for 1904', *Practioner*, 1905.

Arthur Newsholme and T.H.C. Stevenson, 'Decline in human fertility', *Journal of the Royal Statistical Society* 49:1, 1906.

Derek Oddy, 'Working-class Diet in late nineteenth-century Britain', *Economic History Review* 23:2, Aug. 1970.

Laura Oren, 'The Welfare of Women in Labouring Families: England, 1860–1950', in Mary Hartman and Lois Banner (eds), *Clio's Consciousness Raised*, New York, 1974.

Margaret Eleanor Pillow, 'Domestic Economy Teaching', *Special Reports*, PP 1897.

Edwin Pugh, 'Some London Street Amusements', in G.R. Sims (ed.), *Living London* 3, 1902–3.

Alice Ravenhill, 'Investigation into the Hours of Sleep among Children', *Child Study* 1, Jan. 1908.

Alastair Reid, 'Intelligent Artisans and Aristocrats of Labour: the Essays of Thomas Wright', in Jay Winter (ed.), *The Working Class in Modern British History: Essays in Honour of Henry Pelling*, Cambridge 1983.

Janet Roebuck and J. Slaughter, 'Ladies and Pensioners: Stereotypes and Public Policy affecting Old Women, 1880–1940', *Journal of Social History* 13, fall 1979.

Ellen Ross, 'Fierce Questions and Taunts: Married Life in Working-Class London, 1870–1914', *Feminist Studies* 8:2, fall 1982.

——'Not the Sort that would Sit on the Doorstep: Respectability in Pre-World War 1 London Neighbourhoods', *International Labour and Working-Class History* 27, Spring 1985.

Charles Russell, 'The Jewish Question in the East End', in Russell and H.S. Lewis, *The Jew in London: a Study of Racial Character and Present-Day Conditions*, 1900.

Raphael Samuel, 'Comers and Goers', in Harold James Dyos and Michael Wolff (eds), *The Victorian City: Images and Realities*, 2 vols, 1973.

——'An Irish Religion', in Samuel (ed.), *Patriotism: the Making and Unmaking of National Identity, vol. 2, Minorities and Outsiders*, 1989.

Joan Schwitzer, 'Building on Sound Foundations', *Hornsey Historical Society Bulletin* 20, 1979–80.

Harold Silver, 'Ideology and the Factory Child: Attitudes to Half-Time Education', in Philip McCann (ed.), *Popular Education and Socialization in the Nineteenth Century*, 1977.

Edith Simcox, 'Industrial Employment of Women', *Fraser's Magazine* 19, Feb. 1879.

Jack Simmons, 'The Power of the Railway', in Dyos and Wolff, *Victorian City* 1.

George Sims, 'Evicted London', in (ed.), *Living London* 1, 1901–2.

——'At the Front Door', in (ed.), *Living London* 1, 1901–2.

——'Sunday Morning East and West', in (ed.), *Living London* 1, 1901–2.

——'London "Up" ', in (ed.), *Living London* 3, 1902–3

Ning De Coninck-Smith, 'Copenhagen Children's Lives and the Impact of Institutions', *History Workshop Journal* 33, spring 1992.

Hubert Llewellyn Smith, 'The Influx of Population', in Booth, *Poverty* 3.

Samuel Smith, 'Industrial Training of Destitute Children', *Contemporary Review* 47, Jan. 1885.

Lyulph Stanley, 'National Education and the London School Board', *Fortnightly Review* (new series) 26, Oct. 1879.

Carolyn Steedman, 'The Mother Made Conscious: the Historical Development of a Primary School Pedagogy', *History Workshop Journal* 20, autumn 1985.

——'Prisonhouses', *Feminist Review* 20, 1985.

John Stewart, 'Ramsay MacDonald, the Labour Party and Child Welfare, 1900–1914', *Twentieth Century British History* 4:2, 1993.

Mary D. Sturge, 'The Claims of Childhood', *Journal of the Sanitary Institute* 20, 1899.

John F.J. Sykes, 'Hygiene and Sanitation in the Home and at School', in William Chance (ed.), *Proceedings of the Third International Conference for the Welfare and Protection of Children*, 1902.

Mary Tabor, 'Elementary Education', in Booth, *Life and Labour*, Poverty series 3.

Pat Thane, 'Women and the Poor Law in Victorian and Edwardian England', *History Workshop Journal* 6, 1978.

——'Women in the British Labour Party and the Construction of State Welfare, 1906–1939', in Seth Koven and Sonya Michel (eds), *Mothers of a New World: Maternalist Politics and the Origins of New States*, London and New York, 1993.

Edward Palmer Thompson, 'Mayhew and the Morning Chronicle', in Eileen Yeo and E.P. Thompson (eds), *The Unknown Mayhew*, 1971.

F.S. Toogood, 'The Role of the Crèche', in Theophilus Kelynack (ed.), *Infancy*, 1910.

Annemarie Turnbull, 'So extremely like Parliament: the Work of the Women Members of the London School Board, 1870–1904', in London Feminist History Group, *The Sexual Dynamics of History: Men's Power, Women's Resistance*, 1983.

Francis Warner, 'Report on the Physical and Mental Condition of 50,000 Children Seen in 106 Schools', *Journal of the Royal Statistical Society* 56, 1893.

Mary Waring, ' "To Make the Mind Strong, Rather than to Make it Full": Elementary School Science Teaching in London, 1870–1904', in Ivor Goodson (ed.), *Social Histories of the Secondary School Curriculum*, Lewes, 1985.

Jeffrey Weeks, 'Discourse, Desire and Sexual Deviance: Some Problems in the History of Homosexuality', in Kenneth Plummer (ed.), *The Making of the Modern Homosexual*, Totowa (New Jersey), 1981.

Arnold White, 'The Nomad Poor of London', *Contemporary Review* 47, May 1887.

Annie Whitehead, ' "I'm Hungry, Mum": the Politics of Domestic Budgeting', in Kate Young, Carol Wolkowitz and Roslyn McCullagh (eds), *Of Marriage and the Market*, 1981.

Anthony Wohl, 'Sex and the Single Room', in Wohl (ed.), *The Victorian Family, Structure and Stress*, 1978.

D.L. Woolmer, 'Caring for London's Children', in Sims (ed.). *Living London* 1, 1901–2.

Eileen Yeo, 'Mayhew as Social Investigator', in Yeo and E.P. Thompson (eds.), *The Unknown Mayhew*, New York, 1971.

Desmond Young, 'Charitable and Benevolent London', in Sims (ed.), *Living London* 3, 1902–3.

Index